# Textile Crafts

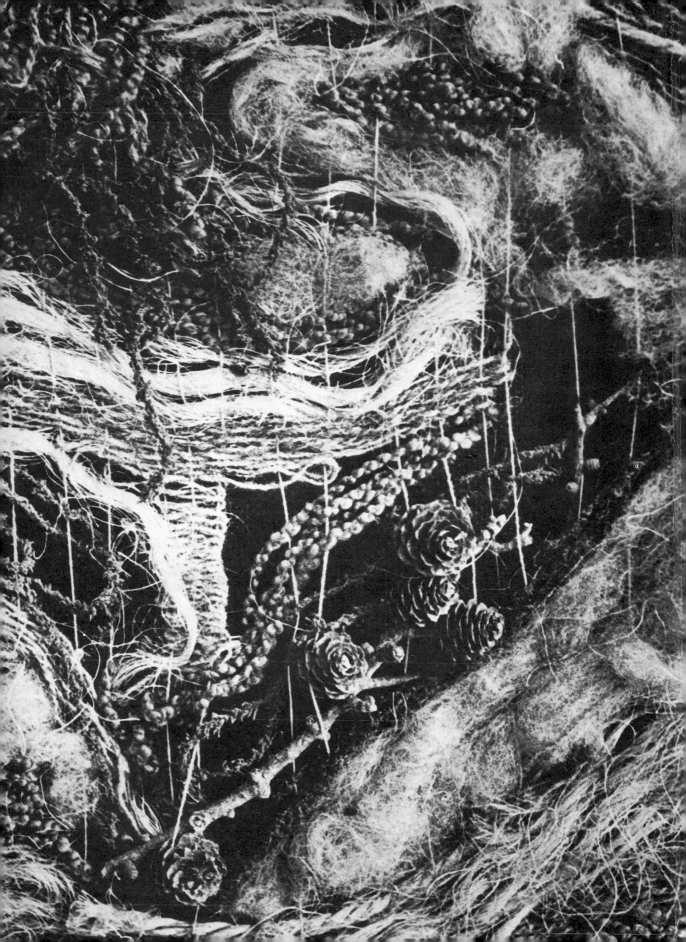

# Textile Crafts

Edited by
## Constance Howard

Pitman Publishing

Copyright © 1978 by The Herbert Press Ltd
Copyright under the Berne Convention

First published in Great Britain 1978 by Pitman Publishing Ltd
39 Parker Street, London WC2B 5PB

This book was designed and produced by
The Herbert Press Ltd
65 Belsize Lane, London NW3 5AU, England

House editor: Erica Hunningher
Designer: Judith Allan

Printed by Jolly & Barber Ltd, Rugby, Warwickshire, England

ISBN 0 273 01174 X

**1** *(frontispiece)* Detail from a student's first piece of work, constructed on card. Areas of texture interspersed with spaces were inspired by the twig with the small cones, around which they were designed. Cotton, wool, jute, hemp and fleece, with coloured fancy yarns, were among those used in the work. Other textile crafts and different techniques demonstrate the use of similar yarns in a variety of ways.
Photo: Frank McGonigal

# Contents

# Introduction

The wide variety of ways in which threads can be used for fabric structures and their embellishment prompted the idea of bringing together in one volume a selection of articles by textile artists, whose work, although different in concept, results from the manipulation of threads. Methods of fabric construction and related techniques of interlacing, twining, looping and knotting are included, and, since the success of any textile craft depends on the thoughtful use of yarns as well as techniques, the book opens with a chapter on fibres and spinning. Each article describes basic techniques as well as the artist's individual approach and suggests ways in which the subjects can be explored and developed.

Threads are universal and have been fashioned by twisting and spinning since pre-history. The interlacing of these to produce fabric is of ancient origin. Knotted examples have been discovered in Egyptian burial grounds and seen as garments carved on Assyrian bas-reliefs. Looped and twisted or interlinked techniques of constructing fabrics have also been found in fragments of cloth which possess great elasticity. Fabric made from spun threads superseded the use of skins for clothing; its manufacture today is still basically the method used by primitive craftsmen, although the materials have changed and, instead of the natural fibres of wool, linen, cotton or silk being spun, many threads are now man-made, synthetic and composed of such commodities as coal tar, seaweed, wood or glass. Rayon, nylon and acrylic fibres are products of the twentieth century industrial field and have become substitutes for those of animal or vegetable origin. Some fabrics are a combination of natural with synthetic threads, some are wholly synthetic and lack pliability. New ingredients are being used in thread manufacture, with tests carried out all the time to improve them. Their potential can be discovered by the artist only with experiment, the difference between natural and synthetic threads often leading to new ways in which interesting structures can be produced as their tensile strengths vary considerably.

The word thread comes from *thráwan* – to twist or to throw, and suggests that the single spun fibres were plied into different weights, loosely or tightly, twisted to the right or to the left. Slubs with smooth threads, wool with silk, bright with dull colours, delicate ones, heavy ones; a great variety was produced at an early date, the spinners becoming so skilled that a thread of gossamer fineness could be handspun. Many textures are manufactured today: smooth, hairy, slubbed, looped as in gimps, velvety as in chenille, plied with lurex to glitter. Threads are plied to make strings, cords and thick ropes for industrial uses; they are plied so that they may be stranded, as in some stranded cottons and wools for embroidery, they are strengthened for warps in weaving, or hardened for knotting as in macramé. For knitting and crochet they may be of one, two, three or four ply in weight, soft and malleable. With hand-spinning, a thread to suit a particular purpose can be made, from very fine to very coarse. With machine spinning and weaving and chemical dyeing, the manufacture of fabrics was revolutionized during the nineteenth century, but the discovery of synthetics has had strong repercussions in the textile trade; new ways in which to handle the man-made fibres have been invented and today knitted and pressed fabrics have become popular.

The textile crafts selected for this book have many points in common but are individual in their employment of threads. The weight and texture of the fibres determines to some extent the scale and quality of the finished work. The nylon warp is basic to the delicacy of the sprang illustrated on page 86, the cobwebby knitting on page 188 is worked with a slub yarn, while the small sampler of gold work on page 52 and the woven fabric on page 33 employ pure silk threads. The heavier the weight of a thread the more bulky the results (illus. 5) but with a combination of fine and coarse threads (as illus. 10) a purposely varied surface is obtained and, if the textures are different too, interesting experimental structures in fabric are possible (as illus. 14 and 22).

Some features are common to certain textiles and related to embroidery techniques and stitches. For example, in embroidery, knots – french knots, chinese knots and bullion knots – are made by twisting threads round a needle, securing them to the fabric by taking the threaded needle through the twists. Macramé uses the knot as an integral part of its structure. Crochet is the creating of fabric by vertical and lateral interlooping, while in knitting, web-like structures are made by looping one row of threads into the next, working back and forth with the knitting needles to build up the fabric. Loops are used in needle-made laces but are detached, worked one into another. Threads are looped over gauges to make fringes and tufting as in turkey work, while weaving loops are often worked into groups of pile, left uncut. The looped stitch is one of several used to secure the coils in needle-made baskets. A number of embroidery stitches such as double knot or palestrina knot, knotted cable chain and knotted buttonhole are really looped stitches, sometimes twisted as in twisted chain and some knotted buttonhole. Blanket stitch gives a simple loop which is the half hitch in macramé and similar to the looping of stitches in rows of crochet. Chain stitch is a feature of both embroidery and crochet.

Interlaced threads are the basis of weaving, from the simple over and under of single threads which produces tabby weave, to intricate pattern weaving such as damask. Tapestry weaving is built up on a warp that is concealed by the weft threads beaten down tightly. In embroidery, needleweaving is very similar to weaving with a shuttle or bobbin. The warp or weft is removed from a selected part of a firm fabric with threads counted easily; or a fabric may be woven specially for the purpose, omitting the weft in parts. The warp is interlaced with needleweaving in self-coloured or different colours of thread, to make close and open patterns (illus. 33). Different kinds of thread, such as dull with shiny textures, or fuzzy with smooth threads, give interesting surfaces. Groups of threads can be bound together to make bars by covering them with blanket stitch. In bobbin lace, simple twisting is similar to tabby weave, but by skilfully manipulating the bobbins on which the threads are wound very intricate patterns can be constructed. Running and backstitch can be interlaced, as in pekinese or threaded backstitch, to give decorative bands in embroidery.

The twisting of threads has been mentioned in making knots for embroidery, but sprang is essentially a twisted thread technique in which there are only warp threads, stretched and secured at both ends. The turning and twisting produces a pliable elastic-like fabric. Bobbin lace has threads fixed at one end with the free ends wound on to bobbins. Any number of such threads are twisted or plaited, being used either as warp or weft to make patterns. In embroidery drawn fabric techniques include the twisting of groups of warp or weft threads with a blunt-ended needle to make openwork patterns which are secured with embroidery threads taken through the twists. These can be built up into intricate borders of many twists if there is a sufficient depth of warp or weft to manipulate.

Interlinking of threads occurs in the construction of sprang and of lace, also in tapestry weaving when linking strips and colours together to close gaps (illus. 62).

Knotting, looping, interlacing, twisting or stitching to make fabric and pattern by manipulating the threads in a particular order or manner have similarities and differences which require knowledge of techniques as well as design. The balance of plain areas with pattern, the arrangement of open spaces with solid, the smooth with the knobbly or raised surfaces, the juxtaposition of colours and the proportions and relationships of these to one another, should be considered when designing and producing textiles or when embroidering fabric already made.

Holes are a feature of many textile designs. They are a part of the openwork textures in bobbin laces or those knitted and crocheted or woven on a loom. The planning of net-like areas or 'grounds' with more intricate or more solid pattern, the arrangements of small with larger holes, require skill and a sense of proportion. The weight of thread used often dictates the type and scale of work, since a knitted lace can have the fineness of a cobweb (illus. 114), a crocheted lace may be coarse (illus. 80), and a bobbin lace may be made with the thinnest of threads (illus. 135) or of a size to warrant the use of thick cords (illus. 10). Large wall hangings may contain very fine threads or very coarse ones according to the nature of the work; holes may be grouped with areas of more solid fabric, or the project may consist almost entirely of various sizes of holes (illus. 131). Loose tensions and mixed weights of thread produce interesting structures. Macramé can be fashioned with soft threads for garments or with firmer, harder types for hangings and articles for interior decoration. Holes are a part of this work with knotted, net-like fringings, very open areas mainly consisting of holes and closely worked areas which make firm fabrics. Sprang worked with fine threads may be manipulated to produce holes and open-work structures of great delicacy (illus. 39) or, with threads of a heavier weight, to make pliable stretch fabric (illus. 53). In tapestry weaving slits may be planned in the design where parts are woven as separate strips on one warp. The simplest means of making holes with embroidery techniques is with eyelets, using a stiletto to pierce the cloth. The edges are whipped or buttonholed with stitches of whatever length is required; in broderie anglaise, round holes and other shapes are whipped with stitches as small as possible or worked with narrow satin or close zig-zag stitches on the machine. Needleweaving can be fairly closely worked or very open, with large holes where bundles of threads are tightly wrapped or buttonholed together in groups to make spaces between them, or woven over threads in blocks leaving small spaces. Lace-like effects are also possible with pulled thread work where the aim is to stitch on a loosely woven fabric, pulling the threads together to make openwork patterns with holes of various sizes, but not to remove threads (illus. 32). The patterns can be worked horizontally, vertically or diagonally on the fabric. Cut work is planned to give a silhouette design with the background fabric cut away, the holes varied in shapes. Brides or bars can connect the edges of the holes for strength and for decoration, the results giving a lacy effect. Some coiled baskets are designed to leave open areas between the coiling elements.

Textiles cover a broad field and many ideas may be accomplished with threads as a basis. Three-dimensional structures can be woven, knitted, crocheted or made in macramé and sprang, baskets often being built for their interesting forms and textures, as well as for use, and sewn with embroidery stitches. Lace on a large scale is being made in orthodox and non-orthodox ways for wall hangings with thick threads and ropes, while embroidery is worked on three-dimensional fabric sculptures and soft forms, where it is incorporated as a part of the design. In fact the traditional ways of working with threads are being broken down and great freedom in their use has developed. Techniques are mixed; knitting and embroidery for example could decorate a hand-woven three-dimensional hanging with tassels worked in macramé; shells, feathers and beads may be woven into fabrics, sewn on to baskets and, with discrimination, used with embroidery. The coiled basket technique is used frequently as a part of woven structures in three dimensions, adding a contrast of texture to the cloth.

A reaction against mass production, and a desire for articles with a more personal quality, has led to a revival of crafts made by hand. Many people are working in textiles, as designers for industry or as artists producing 'one off' handmade articles. The use of mixed techniques and the experimental open-minded attitudes of textile artists has led to a resurrection of skills that at one time were given little consideration and are now some of the most exciting means of creating superb artefacts.

I would like to acknowledge and to thank everyone who has contributed to the finalising of *Textile Crafts*. I would like to give special mention to all the artists who wrote the articles as without these there would have been no book: Peter Collingwood, Eve de Negri, Zoë de Negri, Dorothea Nield, Helen Richards, Enid Russ and Margaret Seagroatt. Also my thanks to Mollie Picken who produced excellent drawings in a short time, to John Hunnex for many of the photographs and for most of the colour plates, to all the students and others who have lent work for inclusion in the photographs; and to those who have checked certain parts of the MS, among them Eileen Ellis and Rose Fielder.

Above all, I have had a great deal of support from Erica Hunningher who has improved and amended my contribution and from whom I have learnt much about the placing of words.

# Spinning
## Margaret Seagroatt

Ethel Mairet, writing thirty to forty years ago, urged the creative use of the then new synthetic fibres, seeing them as the start of a new tradition in textiles. She also argued that textile is the most interdependent of all crafts, and that the creative result of any textile is dependent on the thoughtful use of new raw materials as well as the traditional ones, one form of textile relating to others. Changes are always gradual and even today the textile crafts have still far to go in the exploitation of the qualities of strength, fineness, lustre and transparency of the synthetics in combination with the better-known characteristics of traditional fibres. Only a considered use of fibres, yarns, dyes and textile techniques combined with experiment can produce a truly aesthetically satisfying piece of work. Examples of creative uses of fibres and yarns, both dyed and in their natural state, spun commercially or handspun, are illustrated here and in subsequent chapters.

Fabrics are constructed from yarns and it is the nature of the fibres from which these yarns are spun and the character of the spinning which gives the final fabric its individuality. Whether it is a soft, warm woollen yarn for clothing, a coarse, thick yarn for rugs, a smooth, sleek thread for fine embroidery, a tightly spun yarn for lace or macramé or a variably twisted yarn for some sprang techniques, the character of that yarn is determined by the treatment of the fibres. In order to work successfully it is essential to know how the characteristics of each fibre affect its eventual use.

## Fibre classification

Textile fibres divide into two main groups, natural and synthetic, subdivided according to the following tables.

### Natural fibres

| wool | hair | | | | | silk |
|------|------|--------|------|----------|--------|-----------|
| sheep | camel | vicuna | cow | musquash | rabbit | silkworms |
| | llama | mohair | goat | squirrel | dog | spiders |
| | alpaca | cashmere | horse | beaver | | |

2 Woven hanging by Sue Lewis, 21 × 26cm (8 × 10in). The warp is of mercerized cotton painted with dye. Yarns spun and blended from especially dyed fleece are used freely with a cotton ground weft. Photo: John Hunnex

## Natural fibres

| | vegetable | | | | mineral |
|---|---|---|---|---|---|
| seed | stem | | leaf | | |
| cotton | linen | sunn | sisal | pineapple | asbestos |
| coir | hemp | kenaf | abaca | piassava | |
| kapok | jute | urena | N.Z. flax | raffia | |
| | ramie | nettle | | | |

## Synthetic fibres

### Regenerated

| Rayons | | | Proteins | |
|---|---|---|---|---|
| Viscose | Acetate | | Casein | Soya Bean |
| Cuprammonium | Alginate | | Ardil | |

### Man-made

| Polyamides | Polyesters | Polyvinyls | Polyolefines | Glass |
|---|---|---|---|---|
| Nylon | Terylene | Orlon | Courlene | |
| | Dacron | Acrilan | Polypropylene | |
| | | Courtelle | | |

**Wool**

All sheep are descended from three main types of wild sheep which still exist in remote places. The Argali, from Central Asia, has dense woolly fleece; the European Mouflon has a silky fleece, and most European breeds have been developed by cross-breeding from these two. The Bighorn from North West America has also had an influence on modern sheep breeds. British breeds are generally more woolly, while European sheep are silkier, culminating in the highly developed Merino.

British sheep, from which many of the world's present-day breeds originate, are of three main types, the characteristics of which are related to their habitat. These characteristics strongly affect their spinning properties. Down breeds or Shortwools inhabit warm dry areas with short grass; Mountain breeds live on exposed hills and uplands with little grass; Longwools thrive in bleak, wet districts with rich pastures.

The Down breeds have short, dense, fine wool, standing out from the body like the short grass of the chalky downs on which they feed. The staple length varies from 1.5 to 10cm ($\frac{1}{2}$ to 4in) and is crisp, white, crimped, non-lustrous, elastic and soft. The Southdown is the best known Down breed from which all the others are derived. They include the Shropshire, twice as large as the Southdown and related to the Welsh Mountain, the Suffolk, Hampshire, Dorset and Oxford Downs, the Dorset and Wiltshire Horns, the Herefordshire, Ryeland and the Devon Closewool. The Wiltshire Horn is unique in having no fleece, growing a coat like a dog and bred entirely for meat. The fleeces in this group are made into fine woollen fabrics and very light tweeds.

The Borders of England and Wales produce an intermediate type of sheep having a common origin in the Welsh Mountain or the Shropshire Down. These are the Kerry Hill, Clun Forest and Radnor, and they grow wool used in the Welsh woollen industry for hosiery, knitting yarns, flannels, blankets, felts and fine tweeds.

Mountain breeds have a coarse, medium-length staple used for heavy tweeds and carpet yarns. Scotch Blackface sheep have long, hairy outer coats which are composed mainly of kemp (hollow hair) which does not take dye. This protects the sheep from burrs and weather, and provides Harris tweed with its characteristically hairy surface with occasional white hairs. Herdwick, also used for tweeds and carpet yarns, is the hardiest Mountain breed, its Scandinavian origin fitting it to survive in the bleak, wet Lakeland hills and fells. Its softer fleece varies from white through brown to black. Other Mountain breeds include the Yorkshire Swaledale, the Derbyshire Gritstone and the northern Pennine Lonk. The Cheviot, originally from Spanish Merinos crossed with an indigenous breed, is an important breed with dense woolly fleece. This grows longer in the lowlands than on the hills and is used for Cheviot tweeds, hosiery, blankets and fancy worsteds. The Welsh Mountain has a finer fleece than most Mountain sheep, with a medium staple. It gives Welsh wool a characteristic softness combined with its hardwearing quality. It has a soft yet firm handle

3 Welsh mountain sheep on a hill farm showing the differences in quality of fleece within one breed. Photo: Frank McGonigal

suitable for the bedcovers, knitting wool and clothing fabrics produced in the Welsh mills. The hardy Exmoor Horn produces soft fine wool for West of England tweeds.

Longwools have a long, lustrous, curly or wavy fleece which gives it the smoothness and strength needed for worsted yarns. The most important breed, the Leicester, is found around the Midlands and is used for cross-breeding as well as wool. The Border Leicester, a cross between Leicester and Cheviot, lives on the Lancashire and Cumberland fells and is crossed with Swaledale, Blackface and Suffolk. Its fleece is wavy and silky. The largest British sheep, the Lincoln, whose long wavy fleece has reached a length of 80cm (32in), is used throughout the world for cross-breeding. Other Longwools include the Cotswold, whose white fleece is similar to the Leicester, and the Dartmoor and Devon Longwools. The Romney Marsh, whose isolated habitat led to the purity of its strain and whose fleece is exceptionally soft, has been exported to New Zealand and South America.

Miscellaneous breeds include the soft, fine-fleeced Shetland in shades of white to brown; the Jacob, a piebald Dorset sheep of Mediterranean origin; the fine-woolled, multiple-horned Manx Loghtan; and the half-wild St Kilda and Soay sheep. Some of these sheep are being preserved by members of the Rare Breeds Survival Trust.

The thirty-odd British sheep breeds, selectively bred for both meat and wool, have formed the basis of many breeds throughout the world, producing new breeds. These, like the New Zealand Corriedale and the US Territory breeds, are now typical of their environment.

The Merino is the most important of the other breeds. Introduced from Spain into Australia in 1790, it has been bred to produce a soft, dense, silky fleece on the many folds of skin which provide the maximum growing area. Bred mainly for wool, it flourishes on poor land and is crossed extensively with other breeds to alter their characteristics. It is widely used in the woollen industry for a great variety of materials. British Longwools have been crossed with Merino and the French Rambouillet to produce a strong, fine fibre. The wools from the sheep producing areas of South and West Australia, Victoria, New South Wales and Queensland all vary in quality and character. New Zealand's climate is similar to Great Britain's so is ideal for the sheep which derive from crossing Merino with British breeds. Merino is also bred in the Southern part of Africa, producing softer, finer, wool than that of the much coarser native Cape sheep. North African wools vary in coarseness according to the proportion of Merino interbred with local sheep. Many distinctive breeds in South America and the USA are a combination of a variety of British breeds and the Rambouillet. In North America the big Rocky Mountain sheep is indigenous to the North West and is descended from the Argali through the Bighorn.

The world has many other wool-producing areas. A great variety of sheep breeds are found in Asia, from the carpet wools of Baghdad and Bokhara to the large Marco Polo sheep from the high Pamirs and the fat-tailed, long-eared Indian sheep. Karakul wool from the Bokhara area is now being grown in Texas as well as in Southern Africa. China,

**4** The wool fibre, showing the overlapping scales. This structure is unique to wool and provides warmth as well as reflecting light. Artist: Mollie Picken

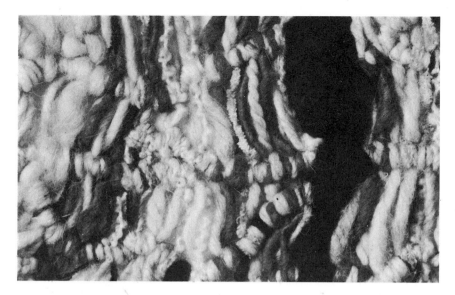

Turkey and the USSR, especially Siberia, have become increasingly interested in wool production.

THE WOOL FIBRE Composed of the protein keratin, the wool fibre consists of three concentric layers. The central medulla contains large, round cells, more marked in coarse fibres and kemp and absent or invisible in fine fibres like Merino. The cortex is filled with long, spindle-shaped cells which compose the bulk of the fibre. It contains pigment, and its cell structure provides strength and elasticity. Round the cortex lies the outer layer, or epidermis, which is composed of horny scales, the edges of which overlap from root to tip (illus. 4). Light reflects from the scales to give low lustre to finer wools with more scales and greater lustre to Longwools with fewer, but larger scales. The number of scales also affects entanglement, and therefore the spinning properties, and wools with fewer scales are less easy to dye. The scale formation, which is unique to this fibre and explains why 'there is no substitute for wool', also provides a good felting property. Felting, a wet process which compresses and entangles the scales, thickens and shrinks woven cloth, obscuring the weave. The wool fibre can be chemically modified to reduce its felting ability, and this reduces its propensity to shrink. Crimp, or wave, is another wool characteristic which is most apparent in Down breeds and Merino. The grease, which is exuded from the skin and stays on the fibre, may account for up to 20 per cent of the raw wool's weight. This is refined into lanolin for lipsticks and ointments.

Wool has three important properties: elasticity which causes it to regain its shape when stretched; resilience which makes it spring back when crushed; and water retention up to 30 per cent of its own weight without feeling wet, giving off heat in this state. These properties are important for clothing, carpets and for use in cold, damp climates. They are very difficult to imitate in a synthetic fibre.

### Other wools or hairs

These are different from wool in scale formation and most of them do not felt as well. They come mainly from the goat and camel families, and from rodents and similar animals.

Camel hair, from the two-humped Tibetan Camel, has special heat insulating properties combined with lightness. Its coarse outer coat is used for ropes, blankets and beltings, and its fine, short inner coat for coats and dressing gowns. The two coats separate easily and are brown in colour.

Peruvian Llama and Alpaca hair is somewhat similar to mohair and comes in shades of white through brown to black. It is used in the natural colour, being unbleachable, for linings and tropical suitings.

The Vicuna, also from Peru, is extremely wild, and only produces four ounces of fine inner hair every two years. It has great lustre, strength and beauty and is the finest and most expensive wool in the world, used for luxury coatings. It is now being cross-bred with alpaca to produce a paco-vicuna. This provides a cheaper but still luxurious fabric.

Mohair is the most important hair fibre which comes from the Turkish angora goat, now also produced in Africa and the USA. Used in fashion fabrics, knitwear, velvets, pile upholstery and linings, it has long, white, lustrous and resilient fibres which spin into a strong, smooth yarn which dyes well.

Cashmere comes from the Tibetan cashmere goat, also reared in China, India and Persia. Only four ounces of fine, soft undercoat are removed each year by combing, and special machinery is needed to separate it from the outer hair. This very expensive and beautiful fibre goes into fashion garments and luxury knitwear. Formerly it was made into Paisley and cashmere shawls.

Other hairs in use include cow and goat hair, mixed with wool for rug and upholstery yarns in Scandinavia, and, oddly, for gloves used for grooming greyhounds. Fur from musquash, squirrel, beaver and the common and angora rabbit are blended with wools to give a special quality to light tweeds. Dog hair from Old English Sheep Dogs, Samoyeds, Corgis and Poodles may be used successfully in handspun yarns, either alone or in combination with wool, and may be dyed easily too.

### Silk

Silk comes from the secretions extruded by the larva of the mulberry silkworm, *bombyx mori*, when it is spinning its cocoon. One of eighty types of moth which produce silk, *bombyx mori* alone lives on mulberry leaves. Wild silkworms feed on oak leaves, castor oil plants, etc., and produce Tussah and Eri silk, but *bombyx mori* can be more easily controlled. Once a mulberry plantation is established, rearing from specially selected eggs can begin as soon as the leaves appear. Stored through the winter in a cool place, the eggs are artificially warmed, sometimes in peasant communities by placing them next to the skin in small bags. Spread on trays in an incubator, the eggs hatch within thirty days into tiny, black, hairy caterpillars 3mm long. Chopped mulberry leaves sprinkled on perforated paper are placed over them, and they climb through the holes and start to eat. The sensitive, choosy creatures must have fresh, slightly wilted leaves, which, if too wilted, they refuse. Once started they literally eat until they burst. This happens four times in five weeks, by which time the silkworms are pale green, bloated with silk and 8cm (3in) long and ten thousand times heavier (illus. 6). They now seek a place to spin their cocoons. Bundles of twigs, straw or heather are provided and the silkworms climb up, already weaving their heads in a figure-of-eight motion which will eventually cover them with silk. As this happens the noise of eating gradually ceases and the rearing room assumes the quiet which is essential if the silk is to be extruded evenly. The liquid silk is contained in two glands which emerge in a tube in the head called the spinneret. On contact with air the liquid filaments harden and are bound together with serecin, a gum which comes from another gland. Within three days the silk covers the body, which shrinks and becomes a pupa, then a moth. The pupa is killed by heat to preserve the continuity of filament, though wild silkworms burst through the ends of the cocoons. Tussah silk is coloured pale brown in the process through the tannin in the oak leaves. Only about half the mile of silk on the cocoon is usable in filament form, the centre being thicker than the ends. The serecin is softened by placing the cocoons in hot water, stirring them with twigs and revolving brushes so that five or so filament ends are caught up at a time. They are then slightly twisted, reeled, then twisted again to form a yarn. The filaments are combined so as to make a uniform thread, and the waste filaments and short fibres from wild silk are carded and spun. The yarn or woven fabric is then boiled to remove the serecin.

6 The silk worm, fully grown and filled with liquid silk. It is now seeking a place to spin its cocoon. Artist: Mollie Picken

Silk is the longest and most lustrous of the natural fibres. It is also the finest, and the strongest in relation to its cross section. It will produce more cloth per kilo than any other natural fibre, and in addition has great beauty, both to the eye and touch, and even to the ear. It is produced in Japan, China, India, France, Switzerland and parts of the Soviet Union, though the best silk is Italian. In England the Lullingstone Silk Farm has produced limited quantities of yarn, mainly for royal occasions. Always associated with royalty, high rank and luxury it is still an important fashion fabric, though its use has been strongly challenged by synthetic fibres.

SPIDER SILK From time to time attempts have been made to produce a textile fibre from spider silk, defeated mainly by their cannibalism. The silk is uniform, strong and unaffected by humidity and temperature, so it has been used in optical instruments. There is a small picture woven from spider silk in Chester Cathedral, England.

### Seed fibres

COTTON The bush *gossypium*, which bears the cotton fibre, thrives in a sub-tropical climate. The yellow-white flowers drop and a seed pod, or boll, ripens for about fifty days. The cotton fibres which surround the

# Textile Crafts

seeds grow and compress within the boll, eventually bursting out (illus. 7). The bolls should be picked immediately they ripen, and ideally this is performed by hand several times in a season. Mechanical pickers, though quicker, pick up leaves, twigs and dirt as well as bolls. The fibres are separated from the seed by a toothed mechanism called a gin, and are compressed into bales, ready for carding and spinning. A second ginning removes the short fibres, or linters, still adhering and these are used as cellulose for rayon production. The seeds are crushed to make soap, the residue making cattle cake.

The fibre has three layers: the lumen, or cell contents at the centre; the inner wall, the main part of the fibre containing cellulose; and the outer cuticle, composed of deposits of wax and pure cellulose. The compression in the boll distorts the growing fibre, and when the cell contents dry and twist, the convolutions are fixed, which improves spinning properties. The cellulose is formed in minute threads, or fibrils, which make the fibre porous, readily absorbing moisture and becoming stronger as a result. This is one of the most important properties of cotton and accounts for the early development of an industry in Lancashire's moist climate. Fibres vary in length between 1.5 and 5cm ($\frac{1}{2}$ to 2in). Sea Island, from the West Indies, is the longest and finest; the silkiest comes from Egypt; medium staple is grown in the USA and USSR; short staple in India, China and USSR. The complex spinning machinery may only be able to spin one length of staple. Length and fineness vary in fibres on one seed, one boll, different bolls, plants or fields, so plants are developed for uniformity, while weather, pests (notably the boll weevil) and disease also affect spinning and dyeing properties. With the advent of humidity control many countries now manufacture cotton cloth, but Britain and the USA are still major producers.

Other seed fibres include tree cotton, a weaker version of cotton, used for wadding; kapok, similar but more buoyant, for stuffing upholstery and lifebelts; coir, from coconut husks, for brushes, matting, ropes and twines.

## Stem or bast fibres

LINEN The flax plant, *Linum usitatissimum*, produces linen, and grows in temperate and sub-tropical climates. The plant has blue flowers on a slender stem about 1 metre high, sown closely for fibre, less so for seed. The plants are pulled rather than cut to avoid weeds and reduce staining by soil. Laid to dry for a few days, they are then subjected to 'the long agony of flax', the series of operations the stems undergo before they become yarn. Rippling removes seeds and leaves by drawing through a comb, the crushed seed yielding linseed oil, the residue cattle cake. The fibres are held together by pectins, woody matter and cellular tissue, and these are softened by a fermentation process called retting, from an old Dutch word, *reten*, to rot. There are several types of retting. Dew retting, where the flax is spread on the ground, takes from

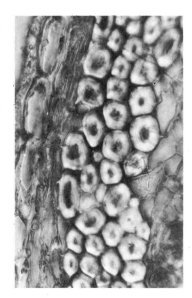

8 Section of a flax stem showing the fibre bundles between the bark and core. These cross-linked bundles help to give the flax fibre its strength.
Courtesy of the Lambeg Industrial Research Association

four to eight weeks. This slow process results in a poor quality, grey fibre, though it is useful in dry regions, such as parts of the USSR. Dam retting takes about ten days, weighted sheaves being immersed in prepared dams or ponds near the flax fields, particularly in Ireland. River retting has now been forbidden in Courtrai, Belgium, which produces the best flax, because the gasses given off by the process have caused pollution. Tank retting now produces the most uniform fibre by heating the water to 30°C, leaving the fibre for only three days. Double retting, drying between operations, produces the best fibre. Chemical retting in caustic or acid solutions takes only an hour or so, but produces a poor fibre.

After drying, the next process is breaking, which snaps the woody ·core on fluted rollers without damaging the fibres. Scutching or swingling removes the snapped core and some bark on a scutching board with a hinged handle. The waste, called shive, is used for fuel, and the short fibres, or tow, are spun into coarse yarns. Hackling separates and combs the fibres, which are drawn through pins set successively closer, providing more tow. This is carded and twisted loosely into a sliver before dry spinning, the finer fibres moistened in warm water before spinning to loosen the gums and make a finer, smoother yarn.

Flax fibres have a complex structure, lying in bundles embedded in pectinous gums between the bark and woody core of the stem (illus. 8). Each fibre is composed of shorter fibres called ultimates, also cemented

**9** *Figure I*, coiled basketry by Linda Watson. Using heavy manilla rope and dark brown wool, coils were stitched with linen twine to create a life-sized figure. Photo: Helen Richards

by gums, the cross-connections within these fibres giving it strength. It lacks elasticity but is fine, long and lustrous, the lustre making it suitable for table linens in damask weaves. It conducts heat well, so cool, though expensive sheeting can be made from it. Ethel Mairet described it as having a 'cool, heavy suppleness'. It absorbs water well so it is useful for towels and glasscloths, and its strength is utilized in quality twines, rugwarp and loom cord. Dyestuffs do not penetrate well and special techniques ensure the maximum absorption of the good quality dyes used, i.e. vat dyes. Crease resistant treatments have improved it for clothing purposes, and it stands up well to repeated washing. It is an expensive fabric, with declining use, but where wet strength is needed, as in sail and tent cloth, shoemaker's thread, bookbinder's twine and fishing line, it is still used. Rough ropes and sackcloth are made from scutching tow; coarse linen from combing tow; bank notes, cigarette and high grade paper from waste flax. The USSR produces most of the poorer grades of flax, good flaxes coming from Ireland, Holland and France. Egyptian flax is extremely strong, but Russian, Persian, Silesian and Austrian flaxes are weak. The best still comes from Courtrai, a pale straw colour, very lustrous, which explains the origin of 'flaxen' hair.

HEMP *Cannabis sativa*, the hemp plant, grows to a height of between 1.5 and 6 metres (5 to 20ft). Male plants produce fibre, female plants both fibre and seeds, the latter yielding oil. It is harvested and processed in a similar way to flax, the Italians even having a similar phrase, 'quello del cento operazioni' – substance of a hundred operations, and a symbol of suffering. Related to Indian hemp and hashish, it gives off a stupefying smell which gives harvesters violent headaches. It is coarser than flax, though structurally similar, but dyes more easily. It is used for rugwarps, quality twines and ropes, cables, nets, tarpaulins, sailcloth and canvas because it is strong and resistant to salt water. The finer Italian fibres are carefully processed to make table linens. Half the world total comes from the USSR, with Italy, Yugoslavia and the USA being important producers.

JUTE The stem of the *Corchorus* plant, like flax and hemp, contains the fibres between the core and bark. The fibre bundles grow in concentric layers, with very short ultimates, making it the weakest of the three fibres. It grows to 2.5 to 5m (8 to 15ft), and is retted in pools or flood waters from rivers, the initial processing being performed on the spot in the water. Once stripped it is dried on poles, and sent to the mills in bundles, though it is softened with oil before spinning to mitigate its harshness. Yellow to brown in colour, it is easily dyed and made into sacks, ropes, twines and backing for linoleum. The tow is used for upholstery, stuffing, papermaking and roofing felts. Curling when treated with caustic soda, it may be blended with wool for cheap clothing material. It is gradually being superseded by stronger synthetics which do not rot, and vinyl floor coverings which need no backing.

RAMIE OR CHINA GRASS Ramie comes from the stingless nettle *Boehmeria*. It is 1 to 2m (4 to 6ft) high, and is soaked in water after harvesting. The fibres are removed by decorticating, a scraping process, still expensively done by hand, but gradually becoming mechanized. The fibre is strong, white and lustrous, inelastic, absorbent and dyes well. It is used for canvas and packing materials, nets, sewing threads, upholstery and clothing fabrics. It grows in warm countries including China, Japan, N. and S. America, USSR and parts of Europe.

Sunn, from India and Uganda; Kenaf, from Africa, India and Pakistan; Urena, from Africa and Brazil are all bast fibres which are processed and used like jute.

Three species of nettle produce a textile fibre, *Urtica dioica* the Common or Great Nettle; *Urtica urens*, the Small Nettle; and *Urtica pilulifera*, the Roman Nettle. The nettles are retted to free the bark, then boiled to release the fibres which are then combed and oiled. In Europe nettles are used in small quantities for making twine, rope, canvas sailcloth and clothing and furnishing fabrics. There are many other bast fibres in the world used only locally.

### Leaf fibres

Fibrous veins run through leaves and it is the veins which give the fibres. They are extracted from each plant in a similar manner; the pulpy matter is scraped from the fibres which are dried before processing for spinning.

SISAL The Central American plant, *Agave sisalana*, is also widely cultivated in East Africa, South America and the East Indies. The fleshy leaves form a rosette, growing to 1 to 2m (3 to 6ft), the flower stalk attaining a height of 6m (20ft). After decorticating and drying, the fibres are spun into yarn and used for rope, twine, matting, rugs and ladies' hats. The waste, or flume tow, is used for coarse sacking and also yields wax, sugar and alcohol. The white yarn is stiff, strong and inflexible, holding its shape well when tightly spun, though the fibres themselves are delicate in appearance. These two characteristics can be used to advantage in many forms of decorative textile construction. Sisal dyes easily, the colour enhanced by its natural lustre.

Other leaf fibres are: abaca or Manila hemp, *Musa textilis*, from the Philippines, makes cordage and a fine, crisp, silk-like material; New Zealand flax, *Phormium tenax*, produces ropes, twines and sacking, and, traditionally, Maori costume; the Pineapple group, *Bromeliacae*, from the East and West Indies, South America, Hawaii and India are used for ropes, twines, threads and coarse and fine fabrics; raffia and piassava, from palm leaves, go into hats, horticultural use, brushes and handicrafts, and are grown in Africa and South America.

### Mineral fibre: asbestos

This is a rock which has crystallized into fibrous form, closely packed and greenish-white, looking somewhat like wood. It is fire-resistant, and strong if not very durable, being used for theatre curtains, fire-proof clothing and for insulation.

### Regenerated fibres

Regenerated fibres are derived from natural substances, while the true synthetics, or man-made fibres, are made from the simple elements of petroleum, air and water.

The synthetics originated with those who watched the silkworm spin its thread and pondered whether an artificial textile fibre could be made. Only during the last 300 years did these thoughts crystallize into a reality which brought about the synthetic textile industry.

Natural fibres consist of thread-like molecules which lie along the fibre in linked bundles, the linkage and alignment governing their varying properties. These are controlled by the way they grow, and can only be altered slightly, unlike a synthetic fibre controlled by man.

Synthetic fibres are all made in a similar way. The fibre-forming substance is manufactured in bulk, the molecules lying at random. The substance is heated or dissolved, and extruded through the fine holes of a spinneret to harden into a filament. This stretches and aligns the molecules along the fibre, which is stretched again to increase its cohesion and strength.

VISCOSE RAYON Cotton linters or wood pulp is boiled in caustic soda, then washed and compressed into sheets. After storage in a humid atmosphere the sheets are steeped in caustic soda, then compressed, dried and shredded into crumbs to form alkali cellulose. After ageing for a few days, they are treated with carbon disulphide and become orange, changing into cellulose xanthate. This forms an orange viscous solution when it is dissolved again in dilute caustic soda.

The otherwise lustrous fibre can now be de-lustred, usually by adding titanium dioxide. Ripening and further filtering increases the viscosity, and the liquid is then extruded through the 3000 holes of the spinneret. It enters a mixture of sulphuric acid and sulphates which convert the xanthate back to cellulose, which, because it is insoluble, forms viscose filaments.

CUPRAMMONIUM RAYON The raw material, cotton linters, is dissolved in a solution of copper and ammonia. The filaments passing through the spinneret partially harden in hot water, stretching in the process. Further hardening takes place in an acid bath, then the very fine, strong filaments are wound, skeined, washed and dried.

ACETATE RAYON Other rayons resemble cotton or flax, remaining as pure cellulose after processing. The cotton linters used for acetate rayon is changed into cellulose acetate after treatment with heat and chemical action. The flakes formed are dissolved in acetone and water, and extruded into warm air which evaporates the acetone, hardening the slightly stretched filaments. This is called dry spinning and is simpler than other methods.

Rayon filaments may be cut and spun on existing machinery, and are used for a range of yarns which vary from fine, lustrous filaments to carpet yarns. Compared with natural cellulosic fibres they have a high but controllable lustre; supply, and therefore price, is not governed by weather or disease; there are no impurities, so scouring is not necessary; they are more uniform and flexible. Acetate is more difficult, but other rayons are dyed with cotton dyes.

ALGINATE RAYON Extracted from seaweed, this is used as a support yarn and scaffolding for lace, fine fabrics and unusual woven effects, dissolving in soapy water. It is flame-proof, so useful for theatre curtains.

PROTEIN FIBRES Other attempts, with varying success, have been made to regenerate proteins for fibres. These have included Casein, from milk, which is sold as Fibrolane; Ardil, from groundnuts; Vicara, from maize; and fibres from soya beans and hides.

## Man-made fibres

POLYAMIDES: NYLON The raw materials of this truly synthetic fibre are coal or petroleum, air and water. Converted chemically into a substance which becomes molten when heated, a ribbon of it falls on to a slowly moving wheel, cooled by water. The resulting ribbons of plastic are broken into chips, and after reheating, the molten plastic is extruded and hardens upon contact with air. The filaments are then stretched to become stronger and translucent. Colouring or delustring agents are added before extrusion. Nylon is thermoplastic, so can be permanently pleated, the fabric melting slightly in the process. In structure it is like a smooth tube, so it tends to repel moisture and dries very quickly. It is extremely strong, but soft, and ideal for hosiery. It can be blended with wool and cotton and may be spun into extremely fine filaments for shirts and underwear.

The discovery of nylon heralded a revolution in fabrics, freeing women from the major chores of darning and ironing. This quiet revolution dates from 14 May 1940, when the first nylon stockings were sold in the USA. It has permeated almost every area of use, from clothing and bedding to upholstery and carpets, as well as industry.

Other polyamides include Perlon, Nylon 6 and 66, in multifilament and monofilament form.

POLYESTERS After the discovery of nylon a great number of man-made fibres, including other forms of nylon, were developed, all slightly differing in properties and used for similar purposes. Polyester fibres, such as Terylene and Dacron, are produced by reacting ethylene glycol (anti-freeze) and terephthalic acid, making long chain molecules. The production method is by molten extrusion, and the resulting strength and warmer handle are particularly suitable for blending in suiting and carpet yarns, as they can be crimped to resemble wool.

POLYVINYLS The polyvynil fibres include Orlon, Acrilan and Courtelle, all similar acrylic fibres based on acrylonitrile. This is based on solvents like dimethyl formamide, and may be either wet or dry spun after extrusion. The fibres can be high bulked by heat-stretching and cooling, and are used for many types of clothing, knitting and furnishing fabrics, also in industry.

POLYOLEFINES These include Courlene and Polypropylene and are made from polymers or co-polymers of ethylene in both filament and monofilament form and heated, extruded and stretched like other man-made fibres. They also come in sheet form which is stretched and fibrillated, that is, vibrated and stretched until it splits laterally, when it can be twisted into ropes and cordage. They are hydrophobic, so can be used for insulation; but are difficult to dye, so are mainly used in industry and in carpet manufacture.

GLASS FIBRES Glass marbles are heated to a molten state at very high temperatures and drawn through the spinneret in the usual way as a continuous monofilament, and on revolving drums a short staple filament. Glass fibre is used in the production of curtain materials and is used industrially and for insulation; because of its low abrasion resistance, however, it is not used for clothing. The fine filaments break, irritating the skin, so the yarns should be handled carefully.

## Fibre to yarn

The information on fibres makes frequent mention of their spinning properties. The character of a yarn is closely related to the fibres from which it is spun, and their size determines the fineness or otherwise of the yarn. A sleek, fine worsted is very different from a soft, yet fine woollen yarn, and both are different from a coarse, hairy carpet yarn. Silk and cotton have their own characteristics of lustre and fineness, while the synthetics, though extensively used commercially have yet to have their individual qualities exploited in handspinning. Craftsmen using yarn could, with profit, experiment with simple forms of hand spinning to create individual yarns. It is economically sound as well as creatively useful for embroiderers, for instance, to be able to spin small quantities of yarn in exactly the colours and amounts they need. A garment crocheted in 'granny' squares is ordinary enough; using a yarn handspun from Jacob fleece, however, creates a random pattern counter to the rigidity of the squares, lifting it into another class.

## The hand spindle

The simplest way of learning to spin is to learn to ply on a hand spindle. This may be bought, or improvised from a stick pushed through a weight or whorl. A knitting needle, a piece of dowel, a butcher's wooden skewer pushed through half a potato, a slice of turnip, a lump of plasticine or clay makes a spindle of the right weight. If it is too light the spindle will not spin properly and the yarn will tend to break if it is too heavy. Make a slip loop in the end of a piece of yarn and pass it over the top of the spindle until it rests on the whorl, tightening the loop. Pass the yarn under and round the whorl, passing it up the other side to the top and securing it with a half-hitch. Tie on two yarns and set the spindle spinning with the right hand while holding the double yarn in the left, between the thumb and the first finger, letting it trail over the back of the hand to keep it out of the way. Spin a short length in one direction, then in the other. You will find that the resulting yarn varies because you are plying it either with or against the direction of the original ply, and giving it either an s or a z twist, according to whether it is going in the same direction as the central column of the letters (illus. 11[2]). Moving your hand up the spun yarn you will have made a length of yarn very quickly, varying the tightness of the spin at will. This control is an essential ingredient of spinning and will stand you in good stead at a later stage. When the length becomes unmanageable, wind it up on the left hand in a figure-of-eight, round the thumb and the little finger, keeping it at tension. Release the half-hitch and undo the yarn from the bottom of the spindle, when you can wind the plied yarn round the spindle on top of the whorl, again keeping it at tension. Wind near the whorl rather than along the length of the spindle. When enough yarn has been wound, repeat the process until the spindle is full. Even on such a simple implement experimental yarn can be produced. Try plying with yarns spun or plied in different directions; extremes of thickness (illus. 12[11]); different colours; different lustres. One yarn can be held back while another spins round it or vice versa (illus. 12[12]); all these providing the basic techniques of spinning fancy yarns. When you have achieved a degree of confidence and competence you are ready for spinning wool.

### Fleece

Fleece is purchased as ready sorted matchings, or from a wool stapler as a whole fleece. With luck it may be possible to collect enough for experimental purposes from the hedgerows. Wool is the easiest fibre for the beginner to use because of its construction, and a medium staple, like Welsh Mountain, is most suitable for first attempts. I prefer to spin in the natural grease, which cleans and softens the hands, though if the fleece is to be dyed it must first be scoured by several immersions in soapy water, taking care not to entangle the fibres, and drying in a net bag after the final rinse. The fleece will have been folded sides to middle, rolled up and tied with the twisted tail end. Unroll it and remove obvious accretions, such as dirt from the tail end, thorns, burrs, insects, etc. Sort the fleece into qualities, the best being found on the flanks, the poorest on the extremities and the neck where it gets rubbed. It takes seven years to make an expert wool sorter in the trade, so do not be dismayed if you find it difficult. You may be able to sort three or four qualities, which would be adequate for your purpose.

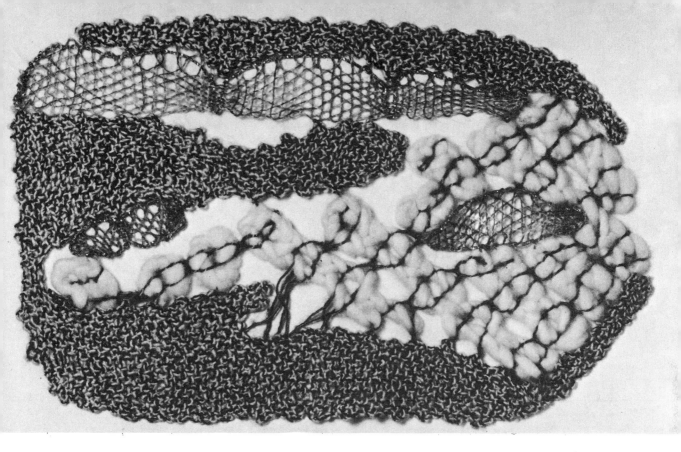

## Teasing

The fleece divides into separate locks, short and square in the Down breeds, longer and pointed in the others. Take one in the left hand, and with a slightly downward movement which takes advantage of the root-to-tip scale structure, draw the fibre sideways between the bent forefinger and the thumb so that it separates. The fibres will cling together, shedding the dirt and floating in an airy mass from the fingers, but not actually falling to the ground. When a small quantity accumulates, take it lightly between the finger tips, drawing it out and placing it together again several times, until the fibres lie parallel. They must be handled very gently or they will become matted.

## Carding

It is possible to spin straight from the teased fleece by spreading it out, keeping the fibres parallel, then lightly rolling between the palms to form a cylinder. A better yarn, however, is achieved by carding. Wool cards are made from rectangular pieces of wood covered with pairs of bent steel wires set in leather, each card having a handle. The fleece is drawn through the teeth between the two cards. Rest them on the knees, placing them back-to-back so that the handles project at opposite sides. The upper card, handle on the left, rests on the lower one with its handle on the right. Spread small pieces of teased fleece lightly on to the hooks on the surface of the upper card, then grasp the handles with both hands, thumbs underneath, forefinger resting on the back. Without changing the position of the hands, bring the lower card to

10 *Inlets*, lace by Janot Gross, 22 × 14cm (8¾ × 5½in). A photograph in a travel journal was developed into shapes and interpreted in weaving yarns, embroidery cottons and dishcloth yarn. Cloth stitch and half stitch provide some variety, but here texture of threads is more important.
Photo: John Hunnex

**11** The evolution of the spinning wheel:

[1] A hand spindle. This simple implement is capable of producing a variety of yarns, both plain and fancy. Its use preceded the spinning wheel and it is still used in many parts of the world.

[2] S- and Z-twisted yarn. The twist takes the same direction as the central column of the letters.

[3] Carding: the fleece is separated by the bent teeth of the card until the fibres lie parallel.

[4] The carded fibre is rolled between the cards, forming a rolag which traps a cylinder of air.

[5] Worsted spinning: the fleece is drawn out between the fingers in a triangular form which ensures that the fibres are kept smooth and parallel.

[6] Skeining: figure-of-eight ties are made in the skeined yarn. This makes sure that it does not tangle when immersed in water.

[7] The new rolag is joined to the end of the rolag being spun, bringing the two ends together and blending the fibres.

[8] The flax is bound to the distaff by a criss-cross tie which keeps the flax together while individual fibres are drawn away for spinning.

Artist: Mollie Picken

the top and lightly stroke the fleece on the left-hand card, rocking it slightly upwards (illus. 11[3]). Repeat this several times until the fleece is evenly spread over the surface, leaving it finally on the left-hand card. Now turn the right-hand card round to face the other card, with the handles in the same direction, and draw the card steadily upwards so that the fleece is transferred to the left-hand card. The small fringe protruding assists this process, and at no time does the hand grip change. Repeat in reverse, transferring the fleece from one card to the other until it is evenly spread, but carding lightly enough to keep the fleece on the surface. If the cards drag, or make an undue noise, you are digging the fleece in too far, or have used too much. After the last transfer, with the fronts still together, brush down again sharply so that the fleece is removed from the card. If it sticks at this stage, remove it carefully by hand, for it will be held only lightly by the wires. The way the wires are bent assists the carding and stripping processes.

## Rolags

Good cards have slightly curved backs, which facilitate the making of a rolag, or roll, which is the basis of woollen spun as opposed to worsted spun yarn. Lay the carded fleece on the back of one of the cards, and, taking it by the small protruding fringe, with the edge of the other card lightly roll it up between the backs of the cards until the fibres lie horizontally round a hollow cylinder (illus. 11[4]).

## Woollen spinning

As when plying, secure some woollen yarn to a spindle, and keep the rolag in the left hand, between the thumb and first finger, again hanging it over the back of the hand. Spin the spindle and when the yarn tightens against the fingers bring the rolag to it so that a few strands catch in the now tightly spun yarn. Continue spinning the spindle and hold the yarn about two centimetres or an inch from the rolag until it tightens once more. Release your hold on the rolag and open your finger and thumb, moving them back a little along it. Grasp the rolag again, drawing it out at the same time, when the spin already in the yarn travels up the fleece, making the new yarn. Initially it may be thick and resistant to drafting, so release more of the rolag while still drawing it out, when the fibres begin to slide and the yarn becomes thinner. It is important to open and close the finger and thumb rather than dragging them up the rolag, or the open character of the yarn will not be kept. A woollen yarn will be warm because the yarn takes the form of the rolag, which is an air space surrounded by fibres protruding at right angles to its length.

These initial stages are difficult to control with two hands and it helps if another person spins the spindle, otherwise it can be stopped between stages until a degree of skill is achieved. The experience of plying helps to give confidence in co-ordinating hand and spindle.

## Combing

This process is used for preparing long, lustrous fibres for worsted

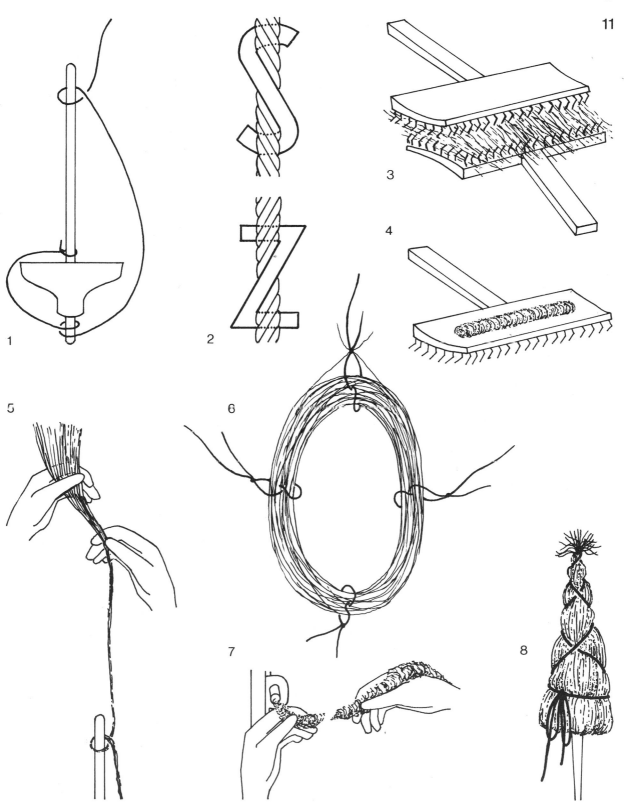

1

2

3

4

5

6

7

8

**12** [1] A simple spindle with a clay whorl.

[2] A grooved wooden spindle mounted horizontally.

[3] The spindle attached to a wheel by a driving band.

[4] The spinning wheel: the spindle, flyer and bobbin attached to the wheel by a continuous driving band: (A) Distaff to hold flax; (B) Bobbin, spindle and flyer; (C) Continuous driving band; (D) Wheel, driven by the axle crank, attached to the treadle; (E) Orifice through which the spinning thread passes; (F) Tension screw which tightens the driving band; (G) Treadle, worked by the foot.

[5] Bobbin, spindle and flyer (detail of 4B): (a) Bobbin, round which the spun yarn is wound; (b) Flyer, which winds the yarn round the bobbin; (c) Bobbin pulley, holding the driving band; (d) Flyer pulley, also holding the driving band which passes round the wheel and both pulleys; (e) Spindle axle, usually of leather, holding the spindle shaft; (f) Orifice, through which the spun thread passes on its way to the flyer hooks and moves along as the bobbin fills; (g) Supports.

[6] Axle crank, joined to the treadle by a leather strap or by a length of wood called a footman.

Fancy yarns:

[7] A slub yarn is made by letting the fibre go through the orifice at times without drawing it out so much. The sizes and intervals of the slubs can be controlled.

[8] Tufts of yarn or fibre can be inserted between the plied yarns.

[9] At intervals one yarn winds round the other at the same place, making a knot. Different colours and textures may be alternated to make different knots, which can also be of different sizes.

[10] A snarl yarn is made by retarding a tightly twisted yarn and suddenly jerking it forward while plying the two yarns.

[11] A fine yarn is twisted round a soft thick one to form a spiral.

[12] One yarn is retarded while the other spirals round it.

Artist: Mollie Picken

spinning, where a strong, smooth yarn is required rather than a warm, bouncy one. The fleece is not carded, but held by a lock and drawn through steel teeth. A comb may be improvised from a nylon hair-styling brush, a steel comb or even a wool card, clamped to a table. The lock is combed first from one end, then the other, the parallel fibres becoming a worsted top. The short remaining fibres, or noils, are carded and spun.

### Worsted spinning

The top is held in the left hand and drawn between the fingers to form a triangle as a few fibres are incorporated in the yarn (illus. 11[5]). The fingers are always held close to the spindle, and the drafting movement is necessarily confined. The long fibres in the yarn lie parallel and the lustre and fineness is preserved by the spinning method.

### Skeining

The spun yarn must be skeined for scouring and dyeing, and it is wound into a hank on the hands, a chairback or a skeiner. Knot the two ends together, leaving enough yarn to secure loosely through the skein in a figure-of-eight, tying in a cotton thread with it, and leaving a long end hanging. It is important to tie loosely, especially for dyeing, for dyestuff cannot penetrate through a tightly tied skein (illus. 11[6]). Secure three more cotton figure-of-eight ties, then lay the skein in soapy water. Soap is better than detergent, which removes too much grease and makes the wool harsh. Repeat the process until the yarn is clean, then give a final rinse in warm water. Never rub or agitate violently or the wool will felt, but rinse and wring gently and hang to dry in an airy place. The yarn is stretched by its own weight, giving a natural curl, but weighting the skein gives a straighter yarn. The yarn is now set and ready for weaving.

## The spinning wheel

Once the process of spindle spinning is mastered you are ready to learn to spin on a wheel. All yarn was once spindle spun, but a quicker method was needed as populations grew. The first step was to support the spindle horizontally, attaching it by a driving band to a wheel which was turned by hand (illus. 12[3]). Though these wheels still exist, the spinning is quite slow, for, like the hand spindle, it is a discontinuous process, the yarn being wound on in a separate operation. In 1533 the Saxony wheel was invented by Johann Jurgen, enabling the yarn to be wound on to the bobbin while the spinning proceeded. This was by means of a flyer and treadle, which Leonardo da Vinci had designed earlier, though it was never actually made.

### Treadling

Once again there are problems of confidence. To alleviate these, learn to treadle first. Sit on a chair, placing your right foot on the treadle

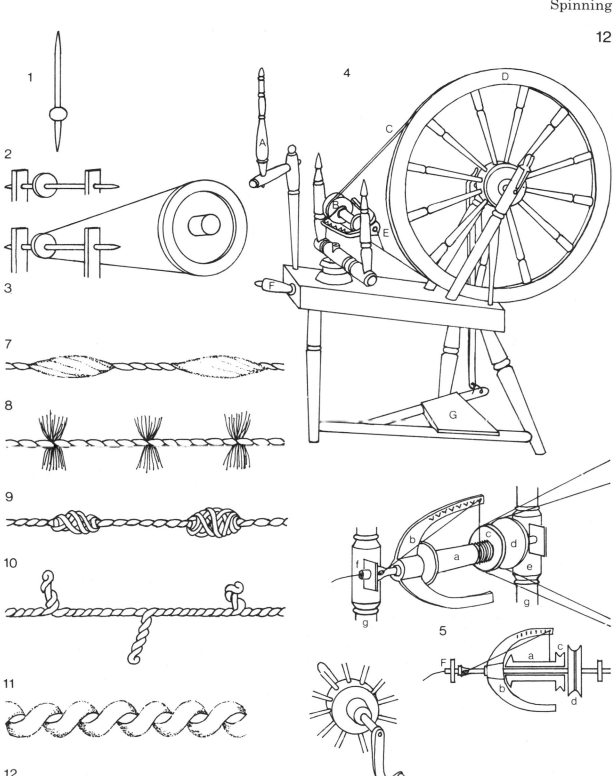

**13** Weft-faced silk fabric by Mary Restieaux, 107cm (42in) wide. The weft was dip-dyed at regular intervals with acid dyes in hanks slightly wider than the width of the warp, resulting in a shaded effect which shifts from side to side. Woven in two alternating vertical blocks of colour subtly blended and contrasted, the piece illustrates how an apparently random effect may be used to create a well controlled result.
Photo: David Cripps

(illus. 12[4]). Turn the wheel by hand, and the foot will follow, moving up and down with the treadle as the wheel turns. The wheel is in a state of equilibrium when the treadle and axle crank are at their highest, needing foot pressure to keep the wheel turning in the right direction, otherwise it will tend to slip back. Once you can control the treadling in either direction you are ready for plying.

## Plying
Tie a piece of yarn tightly round the bobbin and bring it over the guide hooks on the flyer, and through the orifice, using a threading hook, hairpin or bent piece of wire (illus. 12[4]). When the yarn is through the orifice tie it to two spools or balls of yarn running from separate containers or from a spool rack. Begin to treadle, letting the yarns run in freely, twisting and winding on to the bobbin. Experiment is possible in several ways. Try holding the yarn back while treadling, which you will find is perfectly possible. The yarns will twist more, but you are controlling them. Twist may also be controlled by the use of either of the grooves of the whorl, the smaller one producing a tighter twist at the same speed. Tension on the driving band, adjusted by the screw, also affects twist. Experiment, too, with fancy yarns in the same way as on the spindle. This is much easier on the wheel, as both hands are free to hold back one or the other yarn, to wind them over one another, to insert tufts at intervals, etc. (illus. 12[7 to 12]). Other fancy yarns can be made with thick and thin yarns, and yarns with contrasting colours and textures, as before.

## Woollen spinning
Spinning on the wheel is at once easier and more difficult than on the spindle. The rolag tends to disappear into the orifice in an alarming way, but both hands are free to operate, and the yarn is much quicker to produce. The experiments in plying and spindle spinning should have given confidence in handling the material, and by now there should be no difficulty in treadling slowly enough.

Holding the rolag over the right hand between the finger and thumb, begin to treadle slowly, holding back the yarn emerging from the orifice until you feel it tighten (illus. 12[5]). Hold the end of the rolag near the twisting yarn, and then release the twist so that the fibres from the rolag run up the yarn and entangle with it. Spin in the same way as on the spindle, holding back the yarn to form a twist, then letting the twist run up the rolag. The spun yarn should be released to wind on to the bobbin as soon as there is enough twist on it. As experience is gained, the length to which the rolag can be drawn out increases to an arm's length and the whole process becomes rhythmic.

## Worsted spinning
This is also easier on the wheel, partly because both hands are free, the fibres are long and the rhythm of the wheel helps to maintain a regular and even rate of drafting. The fibres are drawn out between the left hand and the right, spreading them over the forefinger of the left hand

and feeding into the orifice with the right, working close to it. Again, the spinning is a rhythmic process.

## Skeining

When the bobbin is full move the driving band across to the spindle whorl. This will free the bobbin and the yarn may be skeined straight from it. It is advisable to remove the yarn from the orifice and the flyer hooks as it is apt to catch.

## Fancy yarns

Further experiments in fancy yarns are possible, using combinations of the techniques described in spindle spinning and plying, using your own spun yarn. You will have already made a slub yarn inadvertantly in your early efforts. The fleece is spun alternately thick and thin (illus. 12[7]), and you may experiment with different colour blends of fleece as well as plying a very fine yarn with the slub for greater strength. Yarns of different thicknesses and twist may spiral round one another; snarl yarns can be produced by plying a hard and soft yarn, letting the hard yarn jerk forward sharply while retarding the soft yarn (illus. 12[7 to 12]). Fancy yarns can be made in many ways. I once wished to use a multifilament, very fine white nylon yarn with a black cotton slub yarn as a warp for a hanging, knowing that one would rub and break and the other would be too weak and snap. I twisted them very slightly together and completed the weaving with only three breaks in the yarn, the ends of the fine nylon filaments strengthening the slub as they rubbed and twisted round it. The ability to spin and ply unusual yarns specifically for a purpose gives any textile a personal quality which is entirely individual to its maker.

## Spinning cotton

The fibres are prepared traditionally by beating with a bow, especially if it is a short fibre. Yarn can be spun on a spindle supported in a bowl to reduce the weight on the yarn; in India it is a small, light metal one. The spinning method is similar to woollen spinning, but with a short draft, slightly untwisting between the finger and thumb as it is drawn out. This spins a fine, even yarn on the wheel as well.

## Spinning flax

This requires a specialized method which utilizes the distaff found on some wheels. The bundle of dressed flax is combed with a steel comb until it is smooth, leaving some short fibred tow. Try spinning a few of the combed fibres on a spindle by the worsted method, wetting the finger and thumb to smooth the spun yarn.

The long fibres will tend to tangle and must be specially prepared. Separate a small amount from the main bundle and tie one end either to your waist or to something firm standing on a table. Taking a few strands at a time, spread them out from the tied end in a wide fan, moving first from right to left, then in the opposite direction, resting the flax in a cloth in your lap or on the table. The thin film of fibres

14 *Dickon's Bonfire* by Maggie Riegler, 38 × 28.5 × 2.5cm (15 × 11¼ × 1in). This small hanging was woven on a frame. The cotton warp is wrapped mainly in lustrous synthetic yarns contrasting with the ground woven in wool, mohair and synthetic yarns in a plain weave interspersed with Soumak bands, some areas being brushed. The interest lies in the tactile contrasts of the wrapping combined with surface textures and unusual juxtapositions of colour.
Photo: Brian Blow

should be flattened with the palm of the other hand, alternate hands being used for the spreading. You will end up with a layered fan of crossed fibres, when you may cut the holding string. Remove the distaff and, unless it has a lantern cone, cover it with a cone of crushed tissue paper, then cover with more tissue and secure top and bottom. Place the cone on the fan of fibres and carefully roll them round it, then replace the distaff on the holder. A 2m (2yd) length of fine ribbon is secured round the top, and lightly criss-crossed round the cone of fibres (illus. 11[8]). It will now be possible, by drawing down a few fibres at a time, to spin the flax on the spinning wheel, damping and smoothing it as it is spun and keeping a pot of water near the fingers. The resulting yarn should be smooth, strong and fine.

### Spinning silk

As explained on page 17 the silk suitable for spinning is silk waste, or *strusa*. This usually appears as a ragged mass of stiff, whitish fibres which have to be de-gummed by boiling in soapy water. When rinsed and dried the fibre is soft and lustrous and can be combed, cutting it into lengths of 8 to 16cm (3 to 6in). It is then spun in a similar way to worsted, handling it gently as befits its delicate nature.

## Dyeing

There are several methods of adding colour to fibre, yarns and fabrics, and suitable dyes are available for different purposes.

### Natural dyes

Natural dyes are available from different parts of many plants, most of which may be found growing wild; yellows from birch bark, bracken, broom, golden rod; heather, onion skins, lichens and privet; greens from bracken, broom, reeds and privet; browns from oak, onion skins and walnuts; black from dock and elder; blues from indigo, blackberries, sloes and other berries; reds from lichens, madder, blackberries and other fruits; purples from elderberries, damsons and potentilla.

MORDANTS The dyestuffs are used with mordants, usually alum, tin, iron and chrome. These create a chemical affinity between fibre and dyestuff to make a fast colour. Mordants can also produce different colours when used with the same dyestuffs. Natural dyes are suitable for use with wool and cotton, which may be in yarn or fibre form, or as woven material. Mordant by adding 85 to 100g (3 to 4oz) of alum, or 14g ($\frac{1}{2}$oz) of tin, iron or chrome, plus a pinch of cream of tartar to each 500g (1lb) of material, covering with water and simmering from forty-five minutes to one hour with 500g of dyestuff tied in muslin. Sometimes the fabric is mordanted before dyeing. Leave the dyed material in the dyebath to take up more dyestuff if an even colour is not required, otherwise stir gently while dyeing, then rinse. Fleece should be loose in the dyebath, yarn should be skeined (see page 30).

**Synthetic dyes**

These are divided into several types; direct dyes (ICI Chlorozol and Durazol) for cottons and viscose rayons; acid dyes (ICI Comassie and Lissamine) for wool, silk and nylon; reactive dyes (Dylons) for cotton, linen, silk, wool and viscose rayon; vat dyes are very fast, but expensive and difficult to use. The other synthetics are difficult to dye by hand and need specialized equipment.

DIRECT DYES Use one tablespoon of salt for each 500g (1lb) of material. Mix one teaspoon of dye in warm water and add a little to enough water to cover the material. Bring to the boil and simmer for twenty to thirty minutes, then rinse thoroughly in cold water. If more colour is required, while dyeing lift the material out of the dyebath, stirring the dye solution in before immersing it again. Dyestuffs in the same range can be mixed, and a rough guide to the final colour is to drop some of the solution on to white blotting paper, or into a glass jar of water.

ACID DYES The same method of dyeing is used, adding three tablespoons of Glauber's Salts (sodium sulphate) and one tablespoon of 30 per cent dilute sulphuric acid instead of the salt, being extremely careful to add the acid to the water, not the reverse, and to rinse off any splashes, which can burn the skin and clothing.

REACTIVE DYES Cold water Dylon and multipurpose Dylon dyes are available in small quantities from multiple stores and hardware shops. The first are used for resist techniques, and would be useful, for instance, when colour elements are to be added to fabric before embroidering it (illus. 16), or when small pieces of material are required in a specific colour. Dissolve one tin or 10g ($2\frac{1}{2}$ level teaspoons) in warm water and add to 4.5 litres (8 pints) of cold water together with solutions of 4 tablespoons of salt and 1 tablespoon of soda dissolved in hot water. Dye up to 250g ($\frac{1}{2}$lb) material for thirty minutes, stirring constantly for the first ten minutes, then at intervals. Rinse thoroughly in running water, then wash in very hot, even boiling, detergent, rinsing again before drying. The multipurpose dyes use the same quantities of dye, material and water with three teaspoons of salt. The dye is dissolved in boiling water and added to the dyebath, then the material is entered. Add the salt over a period of twenty minutes, bring to a simmer and keep just under boiling point. Wash in hot detergent before drying. Timing and quantities are important, so is the hot detergent wash, which completes the chemical change brought about in the fibre. It is also important to scour very thoroughly before dyeing.

Different effects can be achieved by using dyes in unorthodox ways; tieing and dyeing fabric or yarn to produce resist patterns; cramming materials in the dyebath; dripping in strong solutions of colour or sprinklings of raw dye while dyeing; dyeing and overdyeing parts of skeins and fabric; dipping slowly in strong, boiling dye, then adding more water. All these produce both random and planned effects, but require a good knowledge of dyeing techniques.

# Embroidery
## Constance Howard

Embroidery has many facets. For creative expression fabrics and threads offer all that is required in the way of colour and texture, with malleability, to make very simple or very complex design statements. The aim here is to stimulate ideas for individual interpretation. By experimenting with fabrics and threads some knowledge of their behaviour may be discovered. The descriptions of basic stitches, their variations, ways in which they might be used, together with the manipulation of fabrics in relation to or combined with threads, provide a foundation on which to design for embroidery.

Embroidery can range in scale from a square of 5cm (2in) to a hanging 15m (50ft) in length, or even more, to suit a small country cottage or a large public building. It may embellish something useful such as a garment, dress accessory or household article; it may be for decoration only, such as an embroidered wall hanging, or have symbolic significance in an ecclesiastical setting. It may enhance a three-dimensional soft 'sculpture' or a fabric stretched tightly over a framework.

**15** *Landscape* by Christine Garwood, 152 × 121cm (60 × 48in). Applied patterned fabrics on unbleached calico are padded with terylene wadding and foam rubber. The padding is inserted on the front of the panel, under the applied tree forms and hillocks. The sky is stitched with zig-zag patterns in parts to give a ridged effect. Some of the foreground shapes and the tree trunks are padded to a depth of 13cm (5in). Photo: John Hunnex

## History

Hand embroidery has existed since the beginning of history, probably developing from the use of natural fibres to keep skins together, gradually becoming an embellishment of hand-woven fabrics. It began, as did other skills, in the east and was introduced to the west by travellers, by invasions of marauding armies, and through the trade routes which stretched across the northern hemisphere from China.

In Great Britain there are records of embroidery dating from Anglo Saxon times. England became famous throughout Europe during the period 1250 to 1350 for ecclesiastical embroidery, known as 'Opus Anglicanum', with its superb design and technical achievements. During the fifteenth century embroidery in England declined, with the deaths of many of the skilled workers in the Black Death of 1349, but in the sixteenth century England again became famous for domestic embroidery, particularly in the reign of Elizabeth I when costume and household articles were sumptuously decorated with stitchery, the richness of which has not been seen since. In the seventeenth century furnishings were lavishly embroidered, while the embellishment of costume declined, but this became popular again during the eighteenth century. Towards the end of the century with the Industrial Revolution, much of the hand embroidery declined, an embroidery machine was invented in Switzerland, the forerunner of machine embroidery in the nineteenth century, but embroidery of any importance deteriorated until it became a 'hobby', with Berlin wool work the favourite pastime.

In Europe where there was a so-called 'peasant' community, indigenous embroidery, full of vitality and with its own characteristics developed, in contrast to the sophisticated styles worked for the court by professional embroiderers; these two styles of embroidery, existing at the same time, continued until the twentieth century. In England there were no such divisions and during the nineteenth century there was little of importance being worked, although its revival towards the end of the century was boosted by such artists as William Morris.

The first so-called 'free' or 'art' embroidery on the domestic sewing machine, with the presser foot removed, was worked on the treadle machine in 1889 in the USA,* but this technique was not introduced into English schools of art until the late 1920s. During the 1930s there was a revival in all kinds of embroidery, partly due to the teaching of Rebecca Crompton; but this was curtailed by the second world war. During the 1950s a revival in many crafts took place, embroidery among them.

Today both hand- and machine-embroidery are popular, but the two techniques have definite qualities. There are hand techniques that can never be superseded by the machine and those which are better accomplished on the machine. Together they can complement each other. The sewing machine has removed some of the labour from hand stitching, for example a zig-zag stitch can be worked on the machine to neaten the raw edges of material rather than the tedious working of herringbone, buttonhole or oversewing stitch.

## Fabrics and threads

The nature of embroidery is such that it involves most aspects associated with the visual arts, but employs fabrics and threads to express ideas, rather than paint, inks or clay, although today all of these might be incorporated with embroidery. An individual approach depends on knowledge of how the materials behave. Experiment with different fabrics and yarns, invent stitches, combine two or more to make new composite stitches, mix techniques. Some results will be successful, some may not, but if small samples only are made, the knowledge that certain ideas come out well and some do not, will save hours of frustration when a large piece of work is attempted.

### Fabrics
It is possible to have fabrics made, by hand, to specification, such as those woven with areas left open in the warp for needleweaving or drawn thread work, or those loosely woven with close textures in which areas of pulled stitches can be worked to give lace-like patterns. Knitted and crocheted fabrics can also be made with coarse and fine

*Christine Risley *Machine Embroidery*.

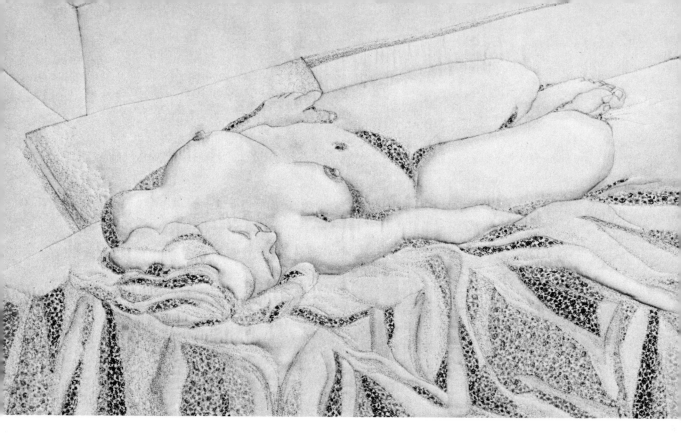

textures combined, embroidery being worked 'flat' on the finer surfaces.

There are many fabrics on the market today, opaque, sheer, rough, smooth, shiny and dull. Most of them are a mixture of natural and synthetic fibres or are wholly synthetic, very few being made entirely of natural fibres. Fabrics of natural fibres are always worth getting when available as they are pliable and their textures are pleasant to 'feel'. The wholly synthetic fabrics are often non-pliable, therefore to gather them or puff them up intentionally is a good idea as it is difficult to remove accidental wrinkles. The mixtures, such as polyester and cotton, terylene lawn, dacron and nylon organza, are easier to manipulate, some having the 'feel' and draping potential of natural fabrics.

If a fabric fascinates by its colour or texture, try it out before attempting to use it in an important piece of embroidery. By making small samples the qualities of fabrics can be discovered and their particular attributes can then be exploited. Try working loosely, then tightly with fabrics that look attractive; crush them, try to stretch them, pull them about and see what happens. If they look mauled or ragged and cannot be flattened, avoid them for surface stitchery but use them perhaps for gathered or folded effects, smocking and ideas where fabrics can be deliberately wrinkled.

For backgrounds, choose fabrics from which creases can be removed, which are pliable and do not retain needle marks. Most smooth, evenly woven fabrics such as pure woollens, some of the mixture woollens, fine linens, silks and cottons are good for backgrounds on which to embroider with surface stitches. If they are very

16 *Life Landscape* by Christine Garwood, 86 × 61cm (34 × 24in). A combination of techniques – applied padded areas, freehand painting and machine stitchery – are used to interpret this panel. Unbleached calico (muslin) is padded with terylene wadding and covered with semi-transparent organdie to give translucency. Applied sections of patterned fabric of small orange and reddish flowers on a pale yellow ground, using both the right and the wrong sides, create the effect of deep folds. A weak solution of water-based dye, painted directly on to the fabric, emphasizes the shadows. Zig-zag and satin stitches, worked on the machine, add definition.
Photo: John Hunnex

fine they are more easily worked if backed with thinner fabric such as fine calico (muslin) or cotton lawn tacked in place before the embroidery is started.

Organza of silk or nylon is fairly transparent, sometimes crystal in weave; it has a glisten, is stiff and puffs up well. Rayon is often lustrous and can be mistaken for pure silk, while rayon satin is easier to use than nylon satin, which is difficult to press. All these fabrics fray considerably when handled. This attribute should be embodied in the design where small areas of fabric frayed at the edges to make fringes can be used in appliqué.

The texture of a fabric is important in relation to the technique used. Fine machine stitching on a heavy slub of fabric would be a waste of time, but the sewing down of rug wool by hand or machine would be effective. Terry towelling stitched flat in parts by machine gives a contrast between the looped pile and the flattened pile. This technique can be used with velvet where parts of the pile are flattened with machine stitching. Velvet and other fabrics with a nap, corduroy and face cloth and some fur fabrics can be cut into shapes which are arranged with the nap going in different directions to reflect different tones. This quality in the fabrics should be used in design. Shiny fabrics such as silks and satins and plastics (vinyl) reflect light and make good contrasts with dull surfaces and if padded, small areas of brilliant colour on dark backgrounds look jewel-like. Shot silks and some shot cottons, found in furnishing departments, rely on light for effect as the warp and weft are of different colours, one of which shows more definitely according to the way in which the fabric is placed. Designs in which shapes cut in these fabrics are turned at different angles can be subtle as each shape changes slightly in colour according to the position from which it is seen.

Some fabrics are two sided, such as denim, one side being dark the other light, some have one shiny and one dull surface. Ideas for design can be developed from these qualities.

Very loosely woven fabrics, such as hessian (burlap) and linen scrim (theatrical gauze), are unsuitable for surface embroidery as the stitches pull through to the back and the surface is too pliable for firm work; but tie bunches of threads together and wrap threads irregularly and an interesting textured surface is made. Indeed, scrim is ideal for regular pulled work and for drawn thread work and it is also good for free experiments in needleweaving where new threads are worked into the fabric. Scrim is made of linen and withstands wear and light. Hessian is made of jute which is coarser and which tends to disintegrate; therefore it is suitable for trying out samples but is not recommended for permanent work.

Knitted fabrics stitch well and can be stuffed, but backing is necessary if they are to be worked flat. Felt is pressed, has no quality, no grain, but comes in brilliant and subtle colours, does not fray and can be manipulated easily. It is difficult to stitch as it tends to stretch but can be built up in layers: every scrap can be used and although it is uninteresting in texture it combines well with other fabrics.

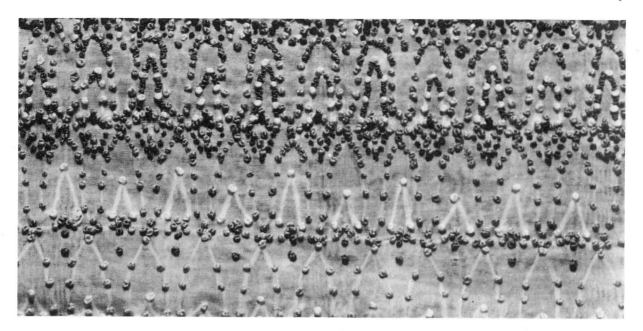

Patterned fabrics such as checks and stripes can be folded to eliminate both colour and pattern, large spots on fabric can be embroidered into, small spots can be a basis of built up stitch patterns. There is no reason why patterned fabrics should not be embroidered over if they help an idea (see illus. 16).

Transparent fabrics such as chiffon, voile, organdie, muslin, net and lace can be overlaid to produce different shapes and colours. The order in placing colours one over another can give different effects. These fabrics can be placed over patterned fabrics too and different colour changes occur.

Leather, suede and plastics (vinyls) can be sewn; the more easily handled plastic has a cotton backing but clear plastic can be hand sewn or machined with a coarse stitch provided that it is not unpicked, as it will split.

Odds and ends, such as braids, ribbons, laces, zips, buttons, bells, beads, feathers and fur are useful to collect but beware of gimmicks; they come and go according to fashion, some are amusing, some extraneous to design and bits and pieces stuck on to and unrelated to an embroidery do not improve work. But it is worth collecting such things as screws, nuts and nails, mirror glass (uncut), pieces of perspex and stained glass, paper clips, leather washers and various rings. Anything that fosters ideas is worth saving.

It is worth acquiring fabrics whenever they are available but as a collection grows the systematic storing of them can become a problem. Placing different textures of related colours in plastic bags (the same with threads) is one way to find colours quickly. Some embroiderers keep textures apart, such as sheers, silks, cottons and heavily textured fabrics in separate containers. Whatever system is evolved, some fabrics such as pure silks and velvets should be rolled, right side outwards,

17 Detail of a sampler using french knots by Paula Matthews, 27 × 20cm (10½ × 8 in). French knots in dark to light greys in perlé cotton, with white ones in anchor soft cotton, are spaced to give a crowded to open effect. The top layer of fabric is white organdie; a bright blue cotton with yellow flowers shows through. The knots are massed closely together and worked through both layers of fabric, gradually becoming less dense towards the bottom. The white knots are worked on the organdie only so that the threads between each knot show through from the back as chalky lines.

Compare the effect created with french knots with the woven gimp in illustration 79.

Photo: John Hunnex

over card or newspaper tubes to avoid permanent creasing, velvets being interleaved with tissue paper to keep the pile from crushing.

**Threads**

Threads are spun with a left-hand or a right-hand twist and must be tried out to see what difference the twist makes to a stitch. The character of a stitch depends on the thread chosen, knotted stitches being lost, for example, if worked in very fine threads. The choice of threads, their weights, colours and textures, should relate to the background fabric and to the design: too fine a thread disappears, too stiff a thread tends to stand off the fabric. Thick soft cotton, worked in satin stitch with back stitch or running stitch, for example, looks well on a fine fabric such as muslin or voile as both are pliable.

There are many manufactured threads from which to choose but those that are hand spun may be varied from very fine to coarse (see illus. 12[7 to12]). Parts may be spun with untwisted wool or cotton; they may be smooth or nubbly, with slubs. Threads may be plied, several of different colours and/or textures being twisted together. Some synthetic threads such as lurex spin well with natural fibres.

The choice in weight of a thread makes a difference to the scale and chunkiness of a stitch so that the whole character of an embroidery is changed. Sewing cottons and silk buttonhole twist are useful for fine stitchery. A very fine thread couched with a thicker thread such as soft cotton is effective as a line stitch. Slub threads cannot be worked through fabric but can be worked over bars of other threads to produce interesting textures. Knots are best worked in non-stranded threads which do not loop, such as coton-à-broder, soft cotton or wool.

A contrast in stitch textures can be made by exploiting the difference in the surface qualities of threads. Try using soft cotton with perlé cotton. Combine different hairy textures such as mohair with angora wool. Threads spun with lurex in silver, gold or copper, as well as various metal and imitation metal threads and even gold-surfaced paper lightly twisted over thread, provide reflective qualities. Combined with natural threads such as wool they can be used to make contrasting textures of shiny and dull. Fine crewel wool or persian would contrast well with floss silk. The mercerized cottons such as stranded, perle and coton-à-broder, have a sheen in comparison with dull soft cotton. Some rayon and nylon knitting threads also have shiny surfaces. Chenille couched closely gives a velvety texture but cannot be pulled through fabric unless it has a very loose weave.

Threads other than those generally used for embroidery can be incorporated to provide variety. Nylon fishing line, which is transparent, and some plastic strings of a similar texture make stiff knots and loops. Builders' twine is strong and stiff and linen carpet threads are coarse and suitable for knotted stitches. Jute and sisal are coarse and hairy and could be combined with rug wools in a piece of work on a large scale.

Cottons for machine embroidery are obtainable in numbers 30 or 50. Perlé cotton number 5 or 8 can be wound on the bobbin, as can soft embroidery cotton, for cable stitch worked on the underside of the fabric. Dentelle, a fine tightly twisted DMC thread gives a more interesting texture than the ordinary machine threads, particularly when it is whipped.

Colour is one of the main attributes of embroidery and there is an enormous range of colours in most types of thread, from brilliant to dull, from pale to dark. It is important to have exactly the right colours for a design: the design should be tailored to suit available yarns or the yarn must be dyed to match the colours of the design. The natural threads such as the brown, black and cream sheep's wool, and the natural linen threads always blend well together. Undyed wool may be obtained from weaving establishments and some undyed silk is available. Variegated threads are obtainable in stranded and perlé cottons and also in machine embroidery cotton.

## Equipment, tools and materials for design and embroidery

An assortment of coloured, white and tissue papers is useful for design. Magazine advertisements in colour are a valuable source of textures which may be translated into stitches. Graph paper is useful for geometric and some counted thread patterns, and for enlarging designs, while tracing paper or a similar transparent paper is useful for the repetition of patterns and for overlaying one pattern on another by tracing each out to make new arrangements.

The usual sewing tools and equipment, including tailors' chalk, thimble and tape measure are necessary, together with a good electric sewing machine. A ring frame of not more than 20cm (8in) is necessary for machine embroidery and a rectangular or ring frame may be required for certain techniques and stitches in hand embroidery. Finely pointed, small, sharp scissors are important for snipping cloth, for unpicking and for cutting threads.

Needles are often a neglected item but are very important as with the right type and size, threads are pulled easily through fabrics, stitches being worked more competently. Chenille needles are short with large eyes, and are used for thicker threads, size 14 large and 26 small. Crewel needles are longer with medium eyes for medium weight threads, size 1 large and 11 small. Tapestry needles are blunt ended, short with long eyes, size 13 large, 26 small, used for darning and counted thread embroidery as the ends do not split the threads of the fabric. Bead needles are very long, fine, with oval eyes and in sizes 10 to 13. Sharps and betweens are for regular sewing, the betweens being shorter than sharps with small round eyes; sizes 7, 8 and 9 are useful for quilting.

## Design

Design is the interpretation of an idea in a medium or media for a

**18** Design:
[1 to 4] Placing the main area of pattern by making an imagined line where required.
[5 to 8] Tension: the main area of a design pulls towards a certain point or boundary, creating a focal point:
[5] Central: static.
[6] At the base: depressing.
[7] At the top: uplifting.
[8] At the side: creates tension and pull to that area.
[9 and 10] By connecting shapes with invisible lines outside the areas of pattern, those inside relate to one another.
[11] A circle with parts cut out and the shapes rearranged is the basis for a new design.
[12] Counterchange of light and dark: simple tonal shift.
[13] Interchange of light and dark, slightly more complicated shift of tones.
[14] Open and closed shapes.
[15 to 17] Overlapping shapes.
[18] A leaf forms a basis for a variety of designs (see illus. 38[2]).
[19] An ordinary metal chair can prompt many ideas for design (see illus. 38[6 and 7]).
Artist: Mollie Picken

particular purpose. This does not mean reproducing reality exactly as seen, nor working entirely from within one's own imagination. It is a combination of ideas from observation and memory, fused with a personal outlook. Sometimes something as insignificant as a doodle, made when answering the telephone, can spark off an idea for design. A visit to an exhibition or a museum can promote ideas; a passing remark can set off a completely new train of thought, often the beginning of new ideas. A magazine illustration whose colour or subject matter attracts, reflections in a puddle or the brilliant colours of a sunset, raindrops trickling down a windowpane, all of these are exciting to someone who is aware of their possibilities for design. A personal interest in a subject means that unconsciously this subject will be observed more closely than others. Buildings can attract by their verticality, the pattern of windows, even the divisions of these into panes, or the silhouettes against the skyline, the variety of roof tops, the domes and the chimneys, they are all features which may be exaggerated or simplified as abstract shapes for design.

Everyone has ideas and sometimes with too many the mind becomes jumbled. This means that some selection is necessary. To train the eye and the mind to 'see', select by concentrating on one aspect of an object or subject at a time. Spend a given time, such as a week, on essentially linear objects – railways, grids, scaffolding, hair, folds in curtains; another time look at shapes such as fields, buildings, clouds and silhouettes. Study surface textures, look for things of a particular colour, find repeating patterns; but do not try to see all these aspects at once or nothing will be seen properly nor will it be remembered. Keep a notebook of sketches and written observations, where things were seen and when, as at different times of the day light changes, affecting colour and tone. A familiar object or setting will become much more interesting seen from any of these points of view and by this means more awareness of the environment is built up as well as more knowledge of details.

Unrecorded information is quickly forgotten. Any means of recording visual images may be used. Keep a folio of cuttings and photographs. For recording ideas, drawing is invaluable. To draw there must be greater concentration than in looking at a photograph with one view only; several views can be seen in looking at an object or a subject. All of these may be drawn and will be retained as memories much longer as they have been carefully observed. Study one aspect at a time, such as shape or texture, and use drawing to record what is really seen, not what is known; the result will be adequate for one's own purpose and with practice there will be more understanding and coherence each time drawing is attempted.

**Planning**
Design is dependent on careful planning. Before starting to use an idea for design, the following points should be determined:
1 The purpose of the embroidery. If it is for an interior design, the setting in which it will be seen must be considered. If for the decoration

19 Sampler by Kay Macklam, 30cm (11¾in) square. A small panel worked on creamy woollen cloth with applied circles set solidly in a mass of bullion knots towards the bottom, almost appearing to float away at the top. The circles are padded, some worked over in a variety of grey crewel wools in stem stitch stripes. The bullion knots are worked in multi colours, mainly in crewel wools.
Photo: John Hunnex

of a garment, the occasions on which it will be worn and the personality of the wearer are both important; fabrics and threads should be washable.

2 If durability is important, the embroidery should integrate with the fabric; machine stitching does this well. Small stitches worked into the counted thread of the fabric and pulled work where the threads of the fabric are drawn together to make lacy patterns are both suitable as they tend to strengthen rather than weaken the grounds into which they are worked. A loose technique or mixed techniques are permissible for a wall hanging or an article that receives little wear.

3 The choice of fabric or fabrics and threads suitable for the execution of the design. An example could be the selection of these for a wall decoration, commissioned for a first grade school where the children are encouraged to feel the textures. This situation might suggest fur, feathers, plastics, beads and sequins with thick threads on which to work chunky stitches. A garment where elegance is required might be embroidered finely in self-coloured threads on an expensive, plain fabric.

Rough ideas could be tried before a conclusion is reached as to the means by which the design is executed. The purpose of the embroidery and the choice of materials will impose certain limitations but one or more techniques could be intermingled. If there are alternative ways of interpreting the design, the choice should be that of the embroiderer.

## Design methods

One source may spark off many ideas, some must be discarded, others tried out. Make several rough designs based on a few of these, as one may be visually better than another. A written analysis of the differences between the rough ideas and the reasons for a final choice could be valuable in developing discrimination in selection of a design if one is working without constructive criticism from an authority on the subject.

The idea for the design might be developed as a geometric pattern or as a free flowing pattern or as a combination of the two styles (look at some of the designs of Japanese textiles where free forms are superimposed over geometric patterns).

Having determined the points of departure, the exciting but often arduous task is to translate these into a two-dimensional form, where colour and texture play a large part. This entails simplification. Select shapes and lines that retain the essence of the idea but realize that they can be changed in scale, may be cut up and reassembled, true perspective may be ignored and accidental and unimportant details omitted.

Cut out paper shapes and move them around in planning the main parts of the design. Rearrangements can be made quickly and unwanted shapes can be discarded. Different tones of paper – black, grey and white – can represent colours and their tones. A collage in full colour may be made using scraps of coloured tissue paper or colour advertisements from magazines. Threads can be sewn through paper

20 *Clouds* by Constance Howard, approx. 150 × 60cm (60 × 24in). The background of viyella and pure silk is divided into three areas of colour, with shell patchwork shapes applied in velvet, silk and batiked cotton. Some of the plain areas are padded in the Trapunto method of quilting, repeating the shell shapes. The background is worked in diagonal rows of running stitches that change in colour over the different areas. One colour, the bright blue, gives continuity across the whole area.
Photo: John Hunnex

or glued down to it, lines can be drawn in, to add to the main shapes, until there is enough detail from which to start the embroidery. Sufficient latitude must be allowed to alter or add to this as part of the excitement in the working out of an idea is its development as the embroidery grows.

If drawing or painting is enjoyed, the idea can be worked out in outline, without colour, or in flat areas of colour and then translated into stitches on fabric.

To obtain a better idea of the distribution of colours and textures to be employed, a small-scale collage in the actual fabric is useful, but it is advisable to avoid patterned fabrics unless they are of a suitable size in relation to the final embroidery.

A large piece of work should be designed to scale, for example of 1cm to 10cm (or 1in to 1ft). It can then be enlarged by photographic means to the final size, it can be squared up or redrawn or parts may be thrown on to a screen with an enlarger and worked out in sections.

Whatever method is used to work out the main elements of the design, small samples of stitches and their variations should be made in different kinds of thread on the background fabric or fabrics.

Sometimes it is interesting to work without any preliminary design, building up the embroidery as one feels inclined. The result may be a masterpiece or a disaster.

## Design elements

Embroidery is essentially two-dimensional although it may decorate a three-dimensional form such as a soft sculpture and, apart from a few technical details, the same principles apply to any two-dimensional surfaces in pattern distribution. Design consists of many opposing qualities, such as space versus pattern, dark versus light and large versus small (see illus. 18).

SIZE AND SHAPE The spot is a usual beginning, the smallest mark being a speck, hardly visible, which could be made with a minute seeding or running stitch in a fine thread. This spot may be of any size, isolated or one of a number within a defined area. If the area is large, the minute spot looks relatively smaller and almost disappears. A spot which almost touches the edges of a surrounding area, appears even bigger, a 7cm (3in) solidly stitched circle on a piece of fabric 10cm (4in) square would look huge in comparison to a french knot on the same size of fabric. A spot may be irregular in shape such as a smudge, or regular as a square or a circle. A series of nine exactly similar shapes placed at regular intervals to make three equal rows sounds boring, but worked in one colour, eight solidly, one in outline immediately there is a point of interest. Each spot could be worked in satin stitch or cretan stitch, again eight in one colour, one in another colour, or the stitches could be placed at angles to catch the light. A range of colours from pale to dark could be used, there are numerous permutations. Squares have more definition as they may be placed at differing angles. Worked in a shiny thread in one colour, solidly in stem or chain stitch, in rows

parallel to one of the edges, an arrangement of these squares could give strong tonal variations. Squares placed equally in parallel rows on a large scale could be interpreted in appliqué of contrasting textures such as velvet on wool with one or two squares stitched in thick threads, again in one colour only. These suggestions show that the simplest pattern of repetitive shapes can become fascinating. According to its interpretation, the respacing of these shapes, of equal or unequal sizes, gives infinite change.

The arrangement of larger with smaller spots within a given area is more difficult. They can be crowded or scattered, radiating and diminishing in size from a given point. There is always a personal choice, their distribution, size and shape should, however, be related to the problem and its scale. The proportion of pattern to background and the number of shapes within a particular area of fabric depends on the sizes of both.

Shapes are made by enclosing lines or by many lines laid side by side to make solid areas. A shape may be formal, geometric, regular or irregular. Contrast of shapes in a design gives liveliness but these should have some parts common to each – a curve or an angle or the repetition of a shape in another size – to give cohesion. This contrast such as large with small, jagged with smooth or open with closed shapes, gives vitality and interest to a design. The expression of an idea is influenced by the kinds of shapes chosen, by their distribution, by colour and to some extent by texture. Shapes other than circles have direction. Try out a random arrangement of shapes with a strong directional bias, such as wooden pegs, then try a collection of these shooting upwards in a concentrated group. Cut a shape in paper and distort it by stretching it, recutting and inserting pieces of paper to widen it or to give it more height, but retaining some of the original contour. Use both the distorted and the original shapes together in one design. Make another design using only the original shapes in order to decide which is more interesting. The grouping of shapes and the spaces between these are of equal importance.

THE LINE The line has many attributes. It can be straight, curved, or a combination of straight and curved lines, it can be wavy or slow and undulating or sharp, zig-zagging into jagged points. It can be intermittent as in running stitches, variable in weight as in back and running stitch. A line can be placed parallel with other lines, or crossed over them at an angle as in a simple grid structure consisting of lines crossing at right angles. A couched line may be sewn across a shape horizontally, vertically or diagonally.

The general direction of lines in a design can create mood, horizontal lines giving a calmer feeling than vertical or diagonal ones. A design composed entirely of curved shapes and lines appears 'soft' in comparison with one in which the shapes and lines are straight when the effect is rigid and harsh. A balance between curved and straight shapes and lines gives movement without the bias towards too soft or too hard an effect. Diagonal directional lines create tension in

21 *Country Landscape* by Julia Sorrell, approx. 25 × 20cm (10 × 8in). This sampler shows various techniques of gold work. Several kinds of gold thread, pure silks and stranded cottons are used for the embroidery. Japanese gold outlines some of the shapes, is also couched in coloured silks or maltese silk in successive rows in the stripes of the fields. Some gold passing is used, also couched down. The *or nué* technique occurs where coloured silks worked solidly make patterns and partially obscure the gold threads. Rough and smooth purl are used, some to couch down silk threads, others over padding for leaves. The stems of the hedge are in pearl purl.

Embroidery in metal threads, with their lustre and rich appearance, has a quality unobtainable in other types of work. Real gold threads provide the best results but synthetic ones are available as second best. Japanese gold thread, the most important, does not tarnish and is made in different sizes. Purls are finely coiled wires in lengths that may be cut into small beads and threaded. They are pliable so may be sewn over padding. Smooth purl, check purl, rough purl and pearl purl are made in one size, some in two. Plate in flat strips may be bent easily into crinkles. Passing is a gold thread widely used and very pliable.

Gold embroidery must be worked in a frame, preferably rectangular and adjustable, as most threads are couched down and the embroidery cannot be stretched afterwards. Maltese silk or other strong thread is used for couching with stitches 6mm ($\frac{1}{4}$in) apart. Linen is mounted first of all in the frame, then, keeping it loose, the background is sewn to it. Both fabrics are then made taut in the frame, ready for working. Padding of felt or waxed string is applied to the stretched fabrics afterwards to keep the threads on the surface of the embroidery and prevent them from sagging.

Photo: John Hunnex

opposition to the horizontal or vertical tendency in a design.

Threads are lines and a combination of fine and coarse, broken and continuous lines can make good texture. Machine embroidery is linear and continuous linear patterns are more suitable than broken ones.

TENSION The placing of one or more shapes within a boundary creates tension, towards the bottom they can appear to be falling out of the picture but can give weight; at the top they can appear to float or seem happier; in the centre they are static while towards one side the eye is drawn to that part containing most interest (illus. 18[5 to 8]).

RHYTHM Rhythm helps to co-ordinate a design, by repetition of shapes or colours in some order. As a preliminary, decide upon the placing of the pattern within the overall shape, drawing in guide lines on the roughs to indicate the main direction of this pattern, horizontally, towards one side or diagonally. These lines give a point of departure whereby the important shapes or lines are positioned, making it easier to add subsidiary ones to the design.

EMPHASIS AND SPACE Space gives emphasis to the pattern. A small, embroidered area of good colour and texture well placed on the fabric can be more telling alone than if surrounded with other patterns, but small shapes sparsely scattered look meagre on the background which dominates them. Tissue paper shapes overlapped create new shapes and also a feeling of depth, which may be achieved by overlapping transparent fabrics. Tone is more important than colour in giving spatial effects, dark or light tones receding or advancing according to their relative sizes and positions. An embroidery may be well executed but appear uninteresting, lacking vitality because no part has particular importance. Dominance of a part of a design or composition gives a focal point which is necessary if work is to have impact. This may be accomplished by several means, colour being one of the most noticeable. It may be brilliant or delicate, harsh or dark and muted. If a particular scheme is analysed, the successful one may be found to be mainly in one kind of colour, either warm or cool with dark, medium and light tones well organized, avoiding a spotty effect. Texture of surface can dominate by the contrast or flat stitches with raised stitches, by the use of shiny with dull or smooth with hairy threads, which affect the stitches worked in them. Again one kind of surface or stitch must be in greater evidence if to dominate as the point of interest. A design in one colour may be composed of many lines with fewer, small, solidly embroidered shapes, concentrated to give a dense area of pattern in contrast with the filigree effect of the lines worked in finer threads. The emphasis here is in the concentration of shapes which, had they been scattered, the lines would have been of more importance, particularly if coarser in texture.

COLOUR The colours and textures of fabrics and threads often promote ideas. Personal preference is a guide in choosing colours and one's own judgment, although intuitive, may be better than relying on colour theory; reactions to a particular colour scheme can be very different and hard-and-fast rules do not work. The best way to find out about colours and their reactions under different circumstances is to experiment with them.

Colour is never seen in isolation and all colours are affected by those next to them. A blue background with a red pattern, for example, looks different from the same ground with a yellow pattern; with red and yellow mingled it changes again.

There are a great number of different reds, blues and yellows: the pure hues, pure hues mixed with black or white which darkens or lightens them and hues mixed with grey which dulls them, also hues mixed with a little of the complementary or opposite colours, making each duller. Any two colours that mix as pigments and make black or grey are complementary. In large areas they look brilliant, while analagous colours, adjacent to one another, appear brighter if used together in small quantities. Warm colours are the yellows, oranges and reds; cold ones the greens, blues and blue-violet, but any one of these may be changed by mixing pigment. A red may become more blue such as a crimson which is colder than vermilion, while a blue may be made warmer and with red becomes more violet than a green-blue. A warm blue background with a carmine pattern appears purplish from a distance, with a yellow pattern it appears greener, but a cold blue such as blue-green with an orange-red pattern looks quite different and if shapes are small in scale the two colours will appear duller as they are complementary. This mixing of colours by the eye is called optical mixing and occurs with colours of equal value or intensity.

Threads are ideal for experiments in which two or more separate colours are embroidered such as small spots, french knots, bullion knots, seeding or link chain, touching one another almost to obscure the fabric on which they are worked so that from a distance they merge as one colour. The original colour combination may change and a shape containing blue and yellow stitches may include a few red ones, gradually eliminating the blue ones, until the blue have been displaced entirely by red stitches.

The subtle merging of colours by the use of tints (a hue mixed with white) or shades (a hue mixed with black) is worth exploration. Narrow stripes in two colours of equal value merge as one colour and on a wider stripe in two colours, one colour can be embroidered looking different on each. Try out colour changes with skeins of thread on different colours of fabric to see how they react; also try one skein of thread on different backgrounds before starting an embroidery, as sometimes surprising changes occur. Try working different stitches to experiment with colour and texture.

If an idea is worked out on paper in colour and it is decided that one colour must be changed, the whole scheme may be upset. By rearranging tones in a design the balance can be disturbed. Try a few roughs of the finished idea, changing the positions of the main areas of dark and light. If a dark tone is moved from the bottom edge to the top of the

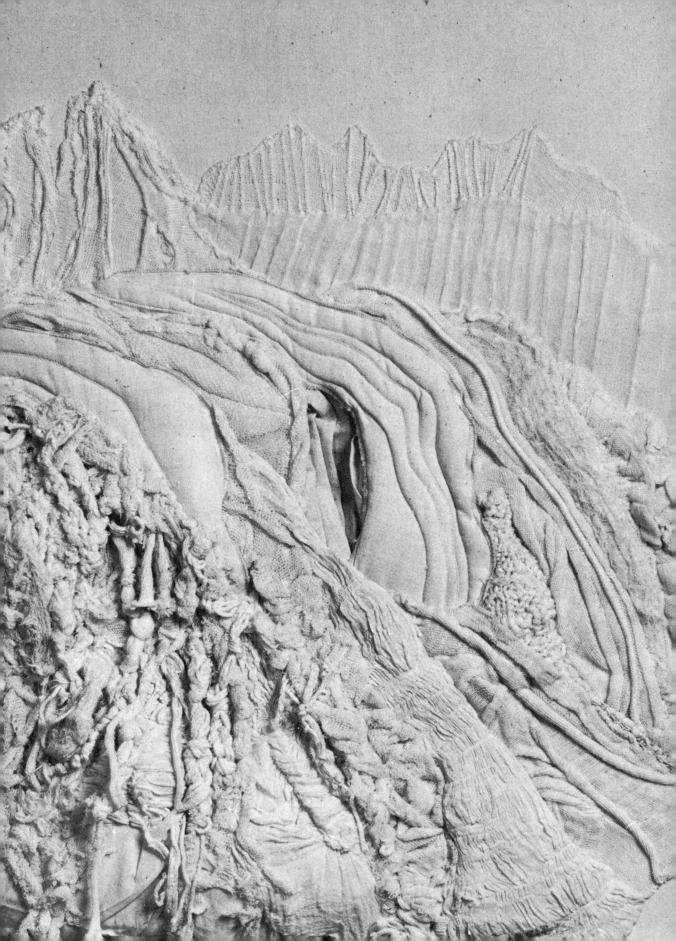

area, the light one taking its place, an unhappy heavy effect could result. Try a small embroidery on a white background and exactly the same one on a black background, using the same colours with some space between the stitches. Each will give a different weighting to the colours chosen.

TEXTURE In embroidery, texture can be exploited fully, one of the most interesting qualities of stitches and threads being the variety of surfaces obtainable with them.

The contrast of raised stitches such as knots, loops and those worked over bars, with flat, smooth ones, such as satin stitch, basket or fishbone stitches can make a simple pattern most exciting. Stitches darned into nets or open weave fabrics change the original surfaces, while lacy areas of pulled work with solid stitching in stem or chain create opposing textures. Circles of eyelets with circles of mirror glass give contrast with the small holes and the glint of the mirrors, while tufted areas with flatter areas in canvas work give variation of surface. These combinations of textures together with the contrast in those of the threads such as wool with perlé cotton, mohair with silk, knobbly with smooth threads will give endless varieties of interesting surfaces.

Added to these are the many kinds of woven fabrics with their smooth or rough surfaces, which may be combined with fine, lace-like or chunky knitted or crocheted ones. Leather, plastics, fur and feathers are only a few of the many other textured goods available to the embroiderer.

It is necessary to have a good idea of what one hopes to accomplish, to avoid the pitfall of employing textures in too great a profusion. It is better to start with very few; the more intricate the design to be worked, the more restraint should be kept in using colours and stitches; extra textures may be added where required as the embroidery progresses.

## Stitches

To learn a stitch is not difficult but to use it in an expressive manner, such as might be done by making meaningful marks with a pencil on paper, or with a brush on canvas, is often a matter of experience. By trying out small samples, different effects may be seen and discarded or used according to their suitability for the idea. The choice of thread, its colour, weight and texture, the scale of stitch related to weight and the angle at which the needle is inserted into the fabric, all produce different results. Most stitches have a common source and belong to one of three groups, straight, looped or knotted. A few of each kind are described below, with suggestions for experiment. The descriptions and diagrams of some of the variations produced by these stitches should be sufficient for any stitch to be tackled in a similar way. If a basic stitch is known, invent others by putting stitches together, by twisting threads in different ways, by changing the angle of the needle

22 Panel, detail, Jane Livingstone 60cm (24in) square. A variety of textured cream and whitish materials, some fine, some coarse, create a landscape with depth. Knitted areas, twisted and knotted fabrics and plaited fabrics, are combined with quilting, ruching, gathering and folding. Cording, tucking and uneven padded areas with superimposed rouleaux add to the depth of the panel. By limiting the colour, the textures have been fully exploited without becoming over complicated.
Photo: John Hunnex

when it enters the fabric. If stitches are just copied without a realization of what can be done with them, embroidery can be dull. Tension of stitch depends on practice and a frame could be helpful if there is an inclination to work too tightly or very unevenly.

## Straight stitches

RUNNING STITCH This is a versatile and effective means of creating lines or all over textures. The stitch can be long, short, regular or irregular in size and spacing. Small stitches, for example, in a thickish thread such as soft cotton, with equal size of stitch and space give a bead-like effect (illus. 20).

Rows of parallel running stitches worked regularly, in one type of thread with stitches under each other look quite different from those worked at random, especially if the threads chosen are varied. Rows of running in a thick thread alternating with a fine one such as perlé number 3 with one strand of stranded cotton or number 16 coton-à-broder, or with tapestry wool and cotton, on a smooth, medium weight background fabric, make good textures. The number of fine to coarse rows of stitches, with regular or irregular spacing and length of stitch give infinite variety.

Curves which make undulating lines, may be worked to give an appearance of depth, by adjusting stitches from long to short; concentric circles worked with long stitches diminishing to the centre, in one colour or in graded colours give a similar effect.

On transparent fabrics both sides of the stitches are seen, changing in colour according to the colour of fabric on which they are worked. Variations by threading and whipping in medium to heavy threads such as perlé numbers 3 or 5, or soft cotton can create braid-like stitches and ridges of wavy lines which are effective worked in close rows. Try similar and different kinds of thread and colour together. Bands of running stitches crossing one another in two strong colours appear to change where they cross and intermingle. Running stitches on the background round blind appliqué shapes are used effectively by Jean Ray Laury. A design may be left as a silhouette on a fabric, the background being covered with running stitches in a similar or different colour worked leaving the background plain. In threads of a contrasting colour and also of weight, the effect could be exciting, red on blue appearing purple, yellow on red, orange. Running stitch worked in two movements to make a stab stitch is used in quilting. Darning is also a running stitch and can be worked on the counted thread of fabric to give patterns. Holbein stitch is a double running stitch, worked on the counted thread of the material. Stitches of equal length and spacing are worked to follow a line, the spaces being filled in on a return journey, to make a continuous line.

BACK STITCH This gives a continuous line in comparison with running. It can be whipped or threaded, more intricately to produce pekinese stitch. A combination of back and running stitch is effective: both stitches are of equal length, the complete stitch consisting of a back

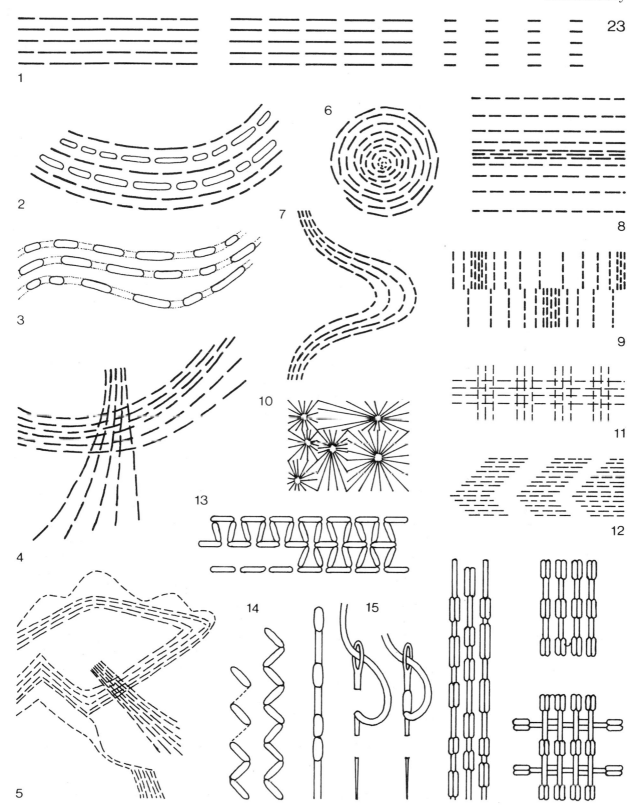

23

1

2

6

8

3

7

9

4

10

11

13

12

5

14

15

**24** Stem stitch:

[1] One stem stitch.

[2] Two stems.

[3 and 4] Twisted chain made through two stem stitches, not through the fabric.

[5] Random stem stitch in a fine thread.

[6] Stem stitch in level rows.

[7] Stem and outline stitches combined.

[8] Raised stem band freely worked.

Herringbone stitch:

[9] Closed herringbone in two colours and two weights of thread.

[10] Closed herringbone in a curve.

[11] Laced herringbone.

[12] Thin herringbone tied with a thick thread.

[13] Herringbone worked over a template.

Herringbone pile:

[14] To make a square of raised pile, draw a square on the cross containing a straight square. Work closed herringbone (double back stitch) as small and closely as possible for the first row round the square. Each subsequent row is worked over the previous row, round and round the square, getting shorter until the four small squares are filled up to the centre. Cut through all the layers of herringbone and a raised dome of gradated pile will spring up, leaving four quarters for the beginning of four more squares. If these are not required, cut them out.

[15] The diagram shows about the third to fourth row of closed herringbone; the dots correspond to subsequent rows, until the rows of stitches meet. They are cut through to make the pile. (It is impossible in a black-and-white drawing to show the first row of herringbone under other layers of stitching.) The straight lines show the gradated pile, the narrowest closed herringbone gives the lowest pile, the widest herringbone the highest.

Artist: Mollie Picken

*Described by Jacqueline Enthoven in *The Stitches of Creative Embroidery*.

stitch and a running stitch alternating.* Back stitch is attractive worked in a firm, thickish thread such as soft cotton, perlé number 3 or in linen thread as the stitch stands up from the background. Closely worked parallel rows with the back and running stitches exactly below each other produce a surface of flat and raised ridges; worked with stitches alternating a pleasant, bumpy texture results. Variety is achieved by changing the lengths of the stitches and by working two back stitches instead of one to give a more prominent raised look. This stitch can be used in a similar way to running stitch and with the back and running stitches carefully planned an interesting texture may be made by crossing rows at right angles.

A fine, filigree effect is achieved, as in black work, by working small geometric patterns on the counted thread of a material in back stitch. Another use of back stitch is called speckling or seeding and consists of small detached back stitches worked at random to give a textured surface. By using different colours and mixing threads, by spacing stitches from very close to scattered, gradations of tone as well as of texture are accomplished.

STEM STITCH AND OUTLINE STITCH In stem the working thread is to the right of the needle, in outline to the left. On transparent fabrics this stitch is useful as the under side can be a straight back stitch which may be whipped or threaded independently. By working so that the thread is alternately to the right or the left of the needle another stitch called cable stem or alternate stem results, looking well worked in a heavy thread as a border. Other variations are to work twisted chain through the overlapping stem stitches, or in portuguese knotted stem to work two back stitches over these. Both give slightly rougher lines and are effective in single rows or worked closely together. Stem may also be whipped to give a tight, raised line, in one or two colours. With a fine thread such as sewing cotton or one strand of stranded cotton, long stem stitches from 2 to 5cm (1 to 2in) worked in very close lines, alternating the overlapping to give an irregular surface, make a fine texture. By working in rows so that overlapping is regular, a striped or checked kind of surface results. Running stitch with stem stitch in alternate rows gives a good texture. Stem stitch worked over bars becomes raised stem band or portuguese border according to the way in which the stem stitch is arranged, but stem worked vertically over bars spaced irregularly in uneven lengths of horizontal rows of running stitches, can create an all-over raised texture. Worked in adjacent rows in a spiral, strong light and shade results from the different directions in which the stitches lie; worked in close parallel rows of alternating stem and outline stitch a similar effect is seen.

HERRINGBONE STITCH This is a broad stitch; it is very versatile (illus. 24[9 to 15]) its scale depending on the size and purpose of the embroidery. It can be worked in an even band, regularly spaced, or may be uneven and irregularly spaced. Rows of regular herringbone, each one threaded into the previous row, give a good all-over filling with slight

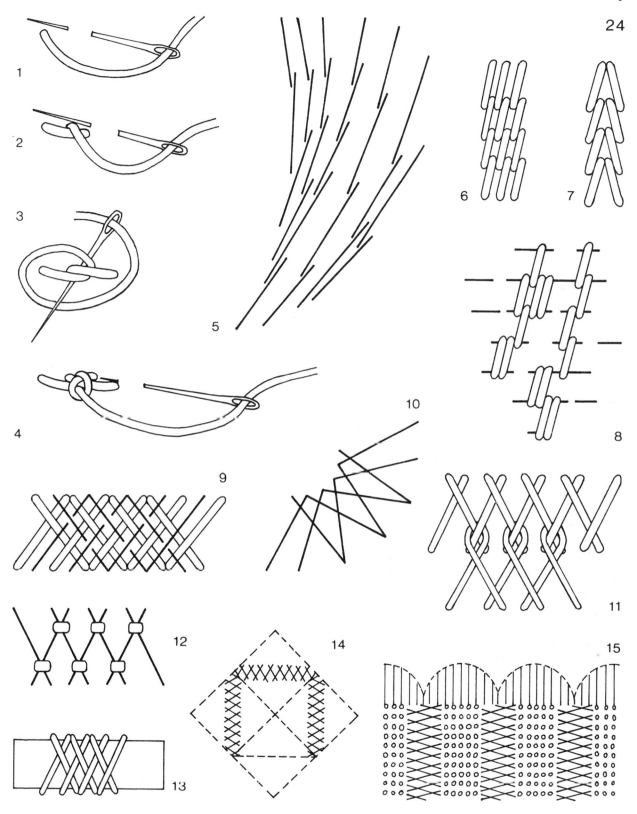

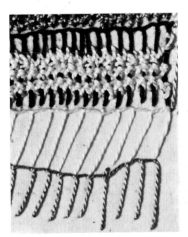

ridges. Worked so that one row fits into the next gives a denser effect. Rows of herringbone overlapped, in two colours, can give a three-dimensional effect as of shadows. Fine threads are effective tied down at the crosses with thick threads. The stitch is effective on net or transparent fabric as those stitches seen through from the back have a looped appearance on the front of the work. In shadow embroidery, closed herringbone is worked on the wrong side of the fabric, on the right side giving back stitches round the shapes in full colour, the crossed threads on the reverse side giving a faint colour with a slightly padded look. Raw edges of applied fabrics may be attached to a background with herringbone stitches, giving a softer appearance than by stitching with zig-zag stitch on the machine.

Herringbone is a good stitch for curves and circles as on one edge the spaces between stitches may be diminished or even overlapped, while on the greater curve they may be spaced apart, as necessary.

Herringbone was used on Victorian Berlin wool work to make a gradated pile surface on canvas (illus. 24[14, 15] Any suitable fabric may be used as the stitches do not need a counted thread background. It gives a stitch with increasing pile on each side of a flat, narrow channel which may be measured with a cardboard gauge. Work a very close row of herringbone, the width of the channel required, which may be minimal, with the stitches touching or overlapping one another on the wrong side of the fabric, looking like stem stitch. Work successive rows closely, each over the previous one, until sufficient are done. Cut through the middle of all the rows (a few at a time if there are many) with a pair of very sharp, fine pointed scissors. The longest pile is made by the widest stitch. If raised pile is required in the centre of a shape, two stripes or groups of herringbone must be worked to meet in the middle. It is inevitable that some of the extra herringbone pile will have to be removed when the stitches have been cut. For example, take an area $1.25 \times 2.5\text{cm} (\frac{1}{2} \times 1\text{in})$. Work herringbone vertically on either edge, overlapping until all stitches meet in the centre of the shape. They have also to extend above $0.5\text{cm} (\frac{1}{4}\text{in})$ outside the area. When the rows of herringbone are cut through, the central area will contain the longest pile, the edges being low. Those parts extending outside the original shape give half stripes and must be pulled out, unless more stripes of pile are required. If each row of herringbone is of a different tone or colour, the result can be striking.

## Looped stitches

BUTTONHOLE STITCH As a simple loop, this is known as blanket stitch, and was much favoured in the 1920s to sew down applied shapes of fabric. This stitch has many variations; it may be worked regularly or irregularly, knotted, twisted or interlocked. Interesting mesh-like textures are obtained by working successive rows, one into the next, with varieties of the stitch such as occasional knotting or twisting (illus. 26). It makes a good, solid band, or can be worked in mosaic-like patterns in one colour in different directions to give tonal changes. It is a good stitch for circles and curved lines as the stitch can be

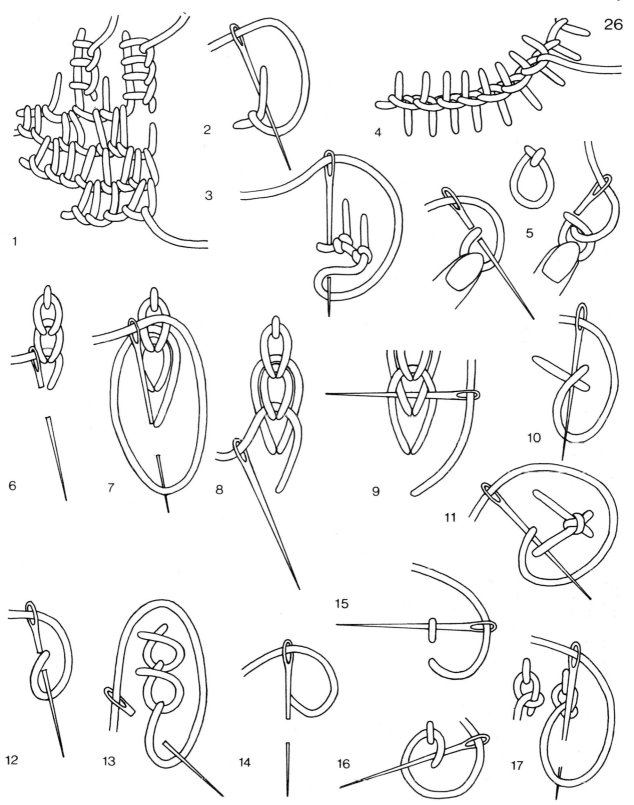

26

1

2

3

4

5

6

7

8

9

10

11

12

13

14

15

16

17

**27** Looped and knotted stitches:

[1] Cretan stitch.

[2] Cretan stitch worked diagonally.

[3] Cretan stitch showing the change in the crossover made by taking up different amounts of fabric in the needle at the top and bottom. By this means great versatility may be given to the stitch.

[4 and 5] Chinese knot, similar to a french knot except that it has a straight tail which may be elongated as required as [5].

[6] French knot: the thread is twisted clockwise twice round the needle rather than once to make a larger knot.

[7] The needle shown entering the fabric below the french knot, coming out again for the next knot. The finished knots show their bead-like quality.

[8, 9, 10 and 11] Palestrina or double knot stitch: the loops are taken over a diagonal bar.

[12 and 13] Variation of the double knot stitch (first made by Jacqueline Enthoven): a loop is made on the left-hand bar and another one on the right-hand bar to make a raised stitch.

[14] Continuing the double knot stitch to make the next stitch.

[15] A variation of double knot stitch in which the thread is taken through the right-hand bar and down through the left-hand one, over and through the right loop again, making a buttonhole stitch. This produces a raised effect and in thick thread a very lumpy result.

[16 and 17] To work the bullion knot: bring the needle out at (b) and back to (a) according to the length of stitch required. Bring it through again, just leaving the eye showing. Wind sufficient twists on the needle (clockwise), then pull both needle and thread through the twists, smoothing them carefully. Insert the needle in (a) again, tightening the thread to make an evenly twisted coil.

[18] Bullion knots.

[19] The coil taken back and the needle inserted for the next stitch.

Artist: Mollie Picken

worked closely or openly and tapered to fit decreasing or increasing shapes.

CHAIN STITCH This has so many variations that several must be mentioned. Worked spirally as in stem stitch, or in stripes with the direction of stitches reversed in each row, the tones change. Chain stitch worked with a tambour hook rather like a fine, steel crochet hook in a tambour frame to keep the fabric taut is used for attaching beads. The Cornely machine is used for chain stitch in the trade today.

Twisted chain which gives a knotted line can be combined successfully with other stitches to make composite ones. Twisted chain stitch worked in close rows gives a rough, knobbly texture. The kind of thread and the angle at which the needle enters the fabric influences the character of this stitch; for example a free loop is made by taking a very small amount of fabric up in the needle, as for twisted chain in movement, bringing the needle right through, then making a small crossing stitch to tie down the loop on the right side but keeping the thumb on the side of the loop to prevent it being pulled to the back. Knotted cable chain gives a thick knotted line in a heavy thread and may be combined with other stitches to give braid-like effects. Broad and heavy chain may be combined and worked together to give another braid. Square chain, double chain, raised chain band and crested chain may all be varied and give broad bands, braid-like or lacy and open according to the ways in which they are worked.

CRETAN STITCH This is one of the most versatile and exciting stitches with which to experiment. It can look quite different according to spacing and the thread in which it is worked. Its appearance changes according to the angle at which the needle is inserted. In very fine thread it appears lacy; in a coarser thread it can be closely knit to make solid spots. Rows may be interlocked or a row in one colour stitched over another row. The crossover may be changed to give diagonal lines for design (illus. 27[3]). A circle can be spaced to produce a spiral or other arrangement by changing the position of the cross-over which depends on the amount of fabric taken up by the needle.

## Knotted stitches

FRENCH KNOT The thread may be twisted round the needle once or twice; knots may be worked one on top of another or scattered to make different surface textures. These knots can look like beads, or when closely packed a rough texture results (see illus. 17). The stitch is ideal for colour exercises using a pointillist technique.

CHINESE KNOT These are smaller than the french knots (see illus. 27). The stitch can have a tail and has one twist which looks slightly looped. It can be worked in close regular rows.

DOUBLE KNOT STITCH This is a looped stitch (illus. 27). Worked very closely together it gives the appearance of beads. It may be varied and

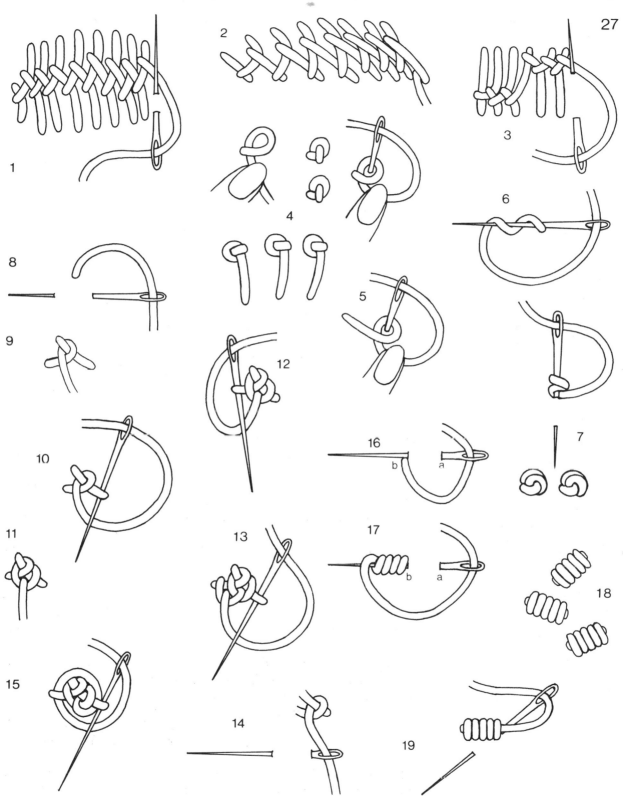

**28** Couching:

[1] Four strands couched together or a skein bunched up, then the four strands opened up to two.

[2] Thick thread couching thin thread.

[3] Thick thread couching thick.

[4] Thin thread couching thick.

[5] Two threads couched at random in a coil.

[6] Burden stitch over three threads.

[7] Burden stitch over six threads producing a basket weave effect.

[8] Three ways of couching down thread: very closely, with buttonhole and with fly stitch.

[9 and 10] Roumanian couching.

[11] Thread looped and couched.

[12 and 13] Hungarian couching.

Artist: Mollie Picken

is a basis of other stitches. It may be worked singly, combined with buttonhole stitches or others to produce interesting textures and braid-like lines.

BULLION KNOT This flat coiled knot, made by twisting thread round the needle, can be worked in long or short lengths.

## Couching

Many colour changes and patterns may be made by couching, a method by which one or several threads are laid on a background and secured by stitches worked over them (see illus. 28). Most couching is more quickly worked on a frame which keeps the fabric taut and leaves both hands free.

The tying down thread may be similar to those being couched down or it may be lighter or heavier. Take a coarse thread such as rug wool or a bunch of finer threads and sew them to a background with soft cotton, using a horizontal oversewing stitch placed at regular intervals. The tying down stitch may be evenly or unevenly spaced with some stitches close together, some far apart. Different colours of thread may be used to make patterns in groups of oversewing stitches. This method gives a line, but many lines together give solid stitching where the pattern and colour can be made quite elaborate. Bands of stitching with thick, pulled up threads between flat areas give a strong, bumpy line. Some Indian embroidery contains whole skeins of cotton threads, bunched up and sewn down with groups of stitches in self-colour to give weight and contrast to the other patterns in fine silk threads. Several colours may be put together with other, unrelated colours, or with alternating colours that match these threads, to sew them down.

As well as straight stitches other stitches such as buttonhole, fly stitch or herringbone may be used to secure threads. Threads may be sewn on the machine with zig-zag stitches or stitched with straight stitching if thick, as in rug wools, to give a braid-like effect.

In roumanian and bokhara couching, a continuous thread is used for the laid threads and for those stitches tying them down. Both methods are useful in stitching over large shapes but each is different in texture. In roumanian couching (illus. 28[9 and 10]), long slanting stitches secure the laid threads, hardly showing, but a variation is to space these threads slightly apart and to work over them with long slanting stitches at regular intervals. The crossing threads will give horizontal stripes where they make double thicknesses and attractive patterns may be made by changing the spacing and the lengths of the slanting stitches. In bokhara couching the tying down thread is worked with small, visible slanting or straight stitches, these making patterns over the laid threads. In both cases the positions of the tying down threads may be indicated on the background fabric if specific patterns are required.

Burden stitch (illus. 28[6 and 7]) is another interesting couching stitch where good colour changes are possible. Threads of similar or

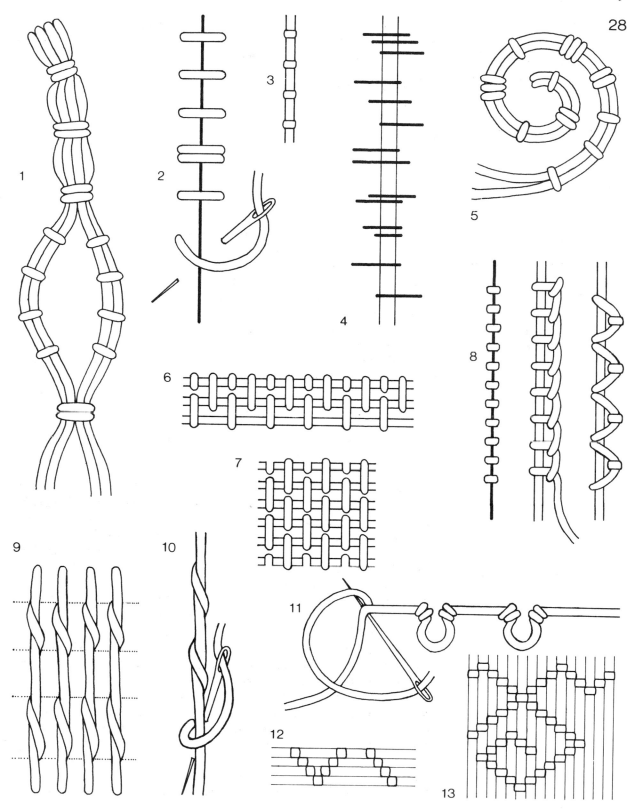

different colours are taken across a shape and are sewn down at right angles with longer stitches than in ordinary couching, spaced so that in the following rows the couching stitches alternate to make a kind of basket pattern. This stitch is found in gold embroidery but is one with which to experiment as it has possibilities for exploiting colour in surface work. By respacing and working over two threads or even three or more, open or close fillings are made.

What is known as laid work is another form of couching, where a complete shape, often large, is covered with long threads laid side by side to obscure the background. These threads are kept in place with small stitches, often in a similar thread, to make diaper and other patterns across the surface of the laid threads, the direction in which they are laid giving effective changes of light and shade. A frame is essential for this work.

## Embroidery techniques

Embroidery can be formal or free in concept or a combination of the two styles, according to the inclination of the embroiderer and the ultimate purpose of the work. Techniques may be mixed, as may threads and fabrics, provided they suit the scale of the work and its concept.

Surface stitchery, some types of counted thread work in which stitchery is worked to correspond with the weave of the fabric, and cut work are described below. Suggestions are given on suitable threads and fabrics, on aspects of design to stress or avoid and on stitches particular to certain techniques. A list of books which give detailed accounts of procedure in designing and in carrying out the ideas for particular types of work is given in the bibliography.

### Surface stitchery

Working designs entirely in threads has been popular at different times in history as a means of creating a wide variety of textures and the number of techniques, fabrics and threads available today provides the contemporary embroiderer with such a vast range of possibilities for working rich surface textures that it becomes difficult to make decisions and to eliminate unnecessary elements. Too much planning can result in a stodgy piece of work: the ideal at which to aim is a balance between the basic planning of an idea and the use of ideas which occur as the work evolves. As work proceeds, think of what is being expressed by the stitch, chosen for a line or a shape. Would another stitch have been more emphatic? Is the thread of the right weight or is it too heavy or too light? Are the colours looking well together? Should the surface be rougher or smoother in parts?

Surface embroidery can be rich in texture working very few stitches. If too many are used, with too many different colours, confusion results. Do not use different stitches for their own sake but make each one meaningful. Exploit one stitch by working it in different direc-

tions, such as spirally, horizontally and vertically, sometimes closely packed, sometimes spaced apart. Take one stitch and try to change its appearance by altering its proportion or by putting the needle into the fabric at different angles. Raised stem band, worked on bars can be quite changed visually by spacing the preliminary stitches differently at the beginning. Twisted chain and some other stitches are varied in appearance according to the way in which the needle enters the fabric. A balance between solid stitching and open areas, between smooth and rough stitches, between flat and raised, is effective.

Stitches can be used singly as spots or combined to make areas of contrasting textures. A line stitch with a spot or a wide stitch, a continuous line with a broken line, together give contrast, added to which is the colour of the background fabric and of the threads. The direction in which a stitch is placed in relationship to another gives contrast of tone. It may be vertical, horizontal or diagonal; blocks of satin stitch worked in this way, in one colour of thread, will look darker or lighter according to their positions. Spirals of chain or stem vary as their direction changes in the light and as this phenomenon is particularly applicable to embroidery, make use of it.

Different textures and weights of thread can be used for surface fillings. If some threads are shiny and some dull, some handspun and knobbly and some smooth and fine, greater contrast results. Different

**29** *Waterlilies* by Jane Iles, 73 × 109cm (29 × 43in). On a background of pale cream satin over a backing fabric, this panel includes areas of knitting, shallow padding and solid stitching. Dyes have been applied with a spray diffuser to produce a watery effect, particularly in the central area which represents the lily pond. The doll's face in the pond is thinly padded, with the features worked in back stitch; other stitches include straight stitch, chain and variations of chain, and feather stitch. The faint images of the lilies are achieved by placing white card between the satin and the backing fabric.
Photo: John Hunnex

colours and tones, for example, from dark purplish-red to pale blue-green, add further possibilities for contrast and variety.

When starting to use stitches consider the compatibility of fabric and thread. Too coarse a thread on fine fabric can pucker it. Too fine a thread disappears on a heavily textured fabric. On a sheer fabric both the backs and the fronts of the stitches are seen, so should be chosen with care and exploited. A design may be made in which both the threads behind the fabric and those in front of it are used (illus. 17).

If the embroidery is for a garment or functional item, surface work will be limited to stitches securely fastened to the background fabric but if the piece is for a framed wall hanging or it embellishes a three-dimensional soft 'sculpture', a very free approach is possible. Long threads may be thrown loosely across the surface, contrasted perhaps with tightly worked stem stitch and french knots, or similar stitches, sometimes completely obscuring the background fabric. Threads may be left hanging on the front of the work like fringing, unevenly distributed, contrasted with carefully worked areas such as smooth satin stitch.

**Machine embroidery**
The machine can be used for varied effects in surface stitchery as well as for much of the laborious hand sewing in many of the techniques where fabrics are manipulated. Satin stitch, whip stitch and couching are more quickly worked on the machine, although the results are different from hand stitching. A combination of hand and machine embroidery can be effective.

An embroidery worked entirely with surface stitchery on the machine is successful in small rich patterns. On a large scale it can appear thin as it is essentially a line technique. If this embroidery has not been attempted previously, keep the presser foot on the machine and work straight line patterns in different kinds of thread, on a firm, smooth fabric. Number 50 machine embroidery cotton gives a fine line, number 30 a thicker one. The stitch tensions are slightly changed for the thicker threads, the bobbin screw being loosened while the top tension with the machine cotton may be slightly tightened.

Cable stitch is worked, with a thick thread such as perlé cotton number 5 or 8, or soft cotton wound on the bobbin, with the right side of the embroidery face downwards when quite thick lines are possible. Massed together they make good texture and a mixture of thick and thin lines can produce a good pattern.

Instructions are given with the machines on using automatic patterns and zig-zag stitches. Try these using different threads and sizes of stitch, work backwards and forwards, with the lines as continuous as possible. For couching, thick threads can be sewn with straight stitching or with the zig-zag stitch in thread as invisible as possible.

When confidence has been acquired, remove the presser foot, lower the feed and work as freely as possible. Most fabrics are put in frames for this stitching as they must be taut. Whipping, pulled fabric stitching, lace-like patterns and other effects are possible with practice,

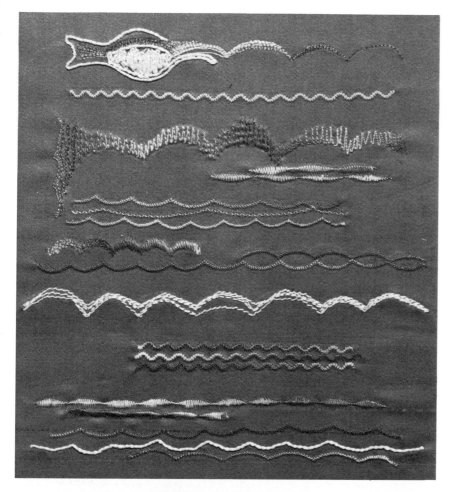

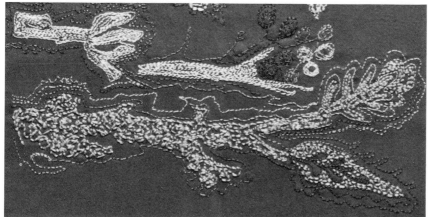

30 and 31 Machine samples by K. Norris, worked on the domestic sewing machine on bright blue cotton satin. Machine cotton and fine perlé cotton in pale fawn, dark cream, yellow and tan are used for the stitching.

30 (*from top to bottom*): Straight stitching with cable stitching; a very fine automatic pattern; free stitching with the feed dog dropped and the presser foot removed; various automatic patterns, including shallow scallops; freely worked scallops using zig-zag stitch to give almost a satin stitch; fine lines of scallops using automatic patterns; larger scallops in straight stitching worked freely; very fine scalloped and other automatic patterns; and finally three lines of shallow scallops with the centre line in cable stitch using a silk thread sewn down closely (here the fabric is worked with the right side facing the bed of the machine and the bobbin wound with thick thread).

31 Motifs showing machine stitching: free stitching with fine outlines and (*below*) free outlines enclosing what is known as 'mossing', worked with the right side of the fabric face downwards on the machine and held in a frame to keep the work taut; the loops are obtained by loosening the bobbin tension and tightening the top tension.

Photos: John Hunnex

once control of the machine is gained, but until its possibilities are known, make textures, change threads and tensions and read all instructions carefully, then experiment, as design can be more easily attempted once the limitations of what can be done are understood.

## Pulled work

This is a type of counted thread embroidery in which threads of fabric are pulled together with stitches to make lacy patterns, the looser the weave of the fabric, the more open the result. Linen is excellent for pulled work, but any loosely woven fabric with a well defined warp and weft may be used.

Most pulled work is more easily executed on a frame, especially if an even tension is required, but some free stitchery is more successful if the fabric is not too taut.

The aim in the design is to obtain a varied texture of very lacy areas with large holes, smaller holes and more solid parts with surface stitching of satin and various buttonholes, the choice of other stitches depending on the fabric on which they are to be worked. Design on the counted thread should include simple shapes. Roughs can indicate the size of holes with dark parts scribbled in, also the possible direction in which the stitches are to be worked. Eyelets of different sizes and blocks of threads wrapped together tightly, satin stitches and others are fairly easy to show on paper; other areas can be referred to worked samples to see their visual effects.

Usually it is suggested that the working thread should be of a similar weight to that of the fabric, non stranded and strong such as perlé number 8, coton-à-broder or linen thread. If the fabric threads are strong enough some of these may be used, the intention being to make the working ones as invisible and as near in colour to the fabric as possible for a lace-like effect. Work with a coarse thread, such as soft cotton, perlé number 3 or coton-à-broder number 6, or a strong, coarse weaving cotton on a fine fabric of uneven weave, inventing ways of making holes. Try self-coloured threads then black or white threads on a coloured fabric, then colours on other colours. The lacy effect may be destroyed but something different and as interesting may result from these experiments. If the fabric is very loose, slub cottons and chenille, even narrow braids and ribbons can be used for pulled work of an unorthodox nature.

## Drawn thread work

This technique entails the withdrawal of threads from the fabric, either of the warp or the weft and sometimes of both, to give square holes. The remaining threads are reworked with embroidery threads.

As for pulled work, any loosely woven fabric from which threads can be withdrawn easily may be used: linen scrim is a good choice; hessian is suitable for practice pieces but for a lasting piece of work it is better to have a stronger fabric. For fine work, voile is loosely woven and is ideal for delicate embroidery. As threads are removed from the fabric it becomes weakened until reworked, so a frame must be used if any degree of firmness is to be kept.

This technique can be used to create a wide variety of effects. Bands of warp or weft threads may be tied in bunches, wrapped, worked over with stitches such as raised chain and raised stem band, re-woven with free needleweaving or worked in geometric patterns to make solid areas of stitching. Threads may be knotted together, overcast in groups to give firm lines enclosing cell-like structures with uneven spaces between them. Threads may be withdrawn to make very large or small spaces, behind which may be placed other fabrics or embroidery of a different kind. Several layers of drawn fabric placed one behind another in a box-like structure, the very large holes in the foremost layer, the last one mainly in solid stitching, would make a fascinating three-dimensional project.

A strong thread is necessary when pulling the fabric together but for wrapping and needleweaving a mixture of different kinds of threads, such as wools, cottons and synthetics is suitable. Needleweaving with fine to coarse threads, including slubs, angora and chenille gives varied textures, these giving bumpy, fuzzy or velvety surfaces.

**32** (*Opposite page*) Small sample of pulled thread work by Constance Howard, worked on pale grey even weave linen in two thicknesses of white linen thread. Four-sided stitch, eyelets, wave stitch, back and satin stitches are used for the patterns. Bunches of threads are pulled together tightly to give ridges and a variety of patterns. Photo: John Hunnex

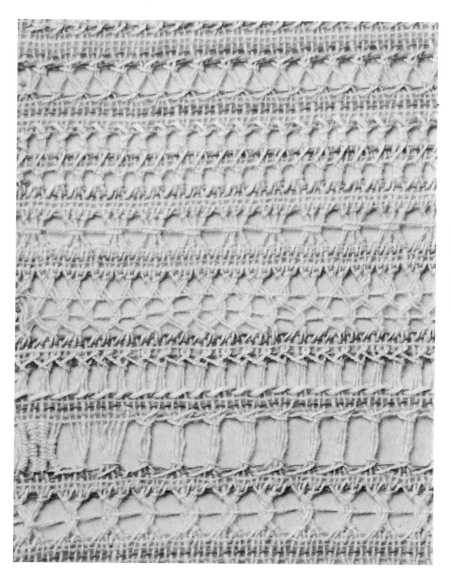

**33** Drawn thread sampler: weft threads in groups have been withdrawn from a coarsely woven cream furnishing fabric, with fine lines of fawn woven into it. From the top downwards, cream perlé cotton and cream anchor soft cotton are worked in hem stitching to give a chevron effect. Three rows of hem stitching come below, then groups of threads, twisted with a needle and kept in place with perlé cotton loops. Herringbone and overcast stitches make the band below, then hem stitch worked to give open rectangles of bunches of thread, with twisted threads below.

Note the similarity in texture of this piece and the woven sample, illustration 75.
Photo: John Hunnex

Embroidery in self-coloured thread but in different weights can be used to work lace-like structures in buttonhole, between wrapped groups of threads, sometimes fine, sometimes coarse.

Drawn thread patterns may be worked out roughly on paper after exploring the possibilities of tying, wrapping and generally playing with ways and means on samplers. Black or coloured paper is better than white paper for making rough designs as the spaces can be indicated more easily if left dark; wrapped lines, small areas of drawn threads and parts of the fabric left unworked can be scribbled in with white chalk or a light felt-tipped pen, or brushed in with white paint. The balance of the dark with the light parts is more easily seen in this way.

### Canvas work

There are more books on canvas work, often erroneously called 'needlepoint', than on any other kind of embroidery. Originally it was embroidery worked on coarse linen in tent stitch and other stitches.

Single thread canvas, which has 4 to 6 threads to the centimetre (11 to 14 per inch) is more versatile than the double; all types of stitch may be worked on it using a blunt ended needle; counted thread stitches used for canvas embroidery are mixed with free stitching; surface stitches, such as french knot and bullions, loops and raised stitches may also be worked on canvas; parts of the canvas may be left un-worked. For wall decorations any kinds of stitch are permissible, but a balance between the flat and the more knobbly ones is advisable, with a contrast between areas worked conventionally, those worked freely and canvas left unstitched, A completely flat surface, using tent or cross stitch worked properly on the wrong side of the embroidery, that is with longer stitches on the back than on the front, is strong and suitable for upholstery as the stitches integrate with the fabric. On fine canvas a mixture of threads such as perlé, soft cotton, real silk if obtainable, and woollen threads could be used, together with raffine gold fingering and some of the synthetic threads. Some stitches consist of two combined and could be worked in a dull and a shiny thread, or in a grey with a brilliant colour. Rice stitch, double stitch and scottish stitch would look well worked in two different colours or textures of thread. Crewel wools or persian which are fine are suitable for canvas embroidery as by working with two or three threads in one needle, the stitch may be altered in weight, two different colours or three may be worked at one time to give a mottled effect, or two threads of similar weight but of different textures such as perlé number 3 or 5 and crewel wool could produce an interesting surface. Tapestry wool is coarser than crewel wool and again suitable for some stitches but it is not as versatile as finer threads. Persian wool strands may be used as crewel wool.

Rug canvas can be put together with embroidery canvas to obtain coarse and fine textures. Large scale embroideries may be worked on rug canvas almost as tapestries, with flat stitches and pile combined, using various types of rug wools, raffine, cords and rags, as well as

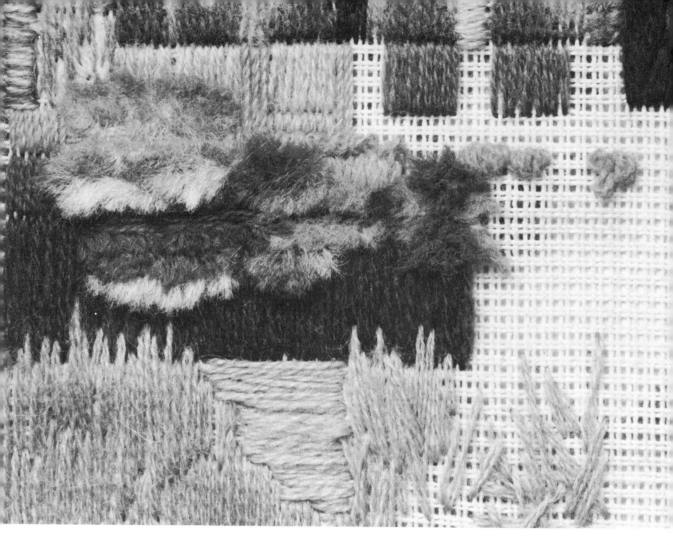

strips of leather and plastic. Small experimental pieces of work are useful, combining unlikely materials to see the effects. A large scale embroidery of this kind, in which many different kinds of textured threads and other fabrics are used, might be better worked in few stitches, as the result could be too 'exciting' and spotty with variety of stitch, colour and texture.

The use of a frame for canvas work depends on the worker's skill in handling the canvas to prevent it stretching.

Canvas work depends on colour, texture and mass for impact. Mass rather than line should be aimed at in design, with contrast of tone. Colour can be fully exploited too in this embroidery, as can tone, resulting from the direction in which the stitch is worked. The scale of the work also has to be considered as a large piece of stitched canvas can become very heavy.

**34** Canvas work (detail) by Becky Mullins, 11.5 × 13cm (4½ × 5in). Double thread canvas is used for the background; free and counted thread patterns are mingled. Satin stitch, turkey knot for the pile, cross stitch with long straight stitches used freely give depth and show the variety of effects that can be achieved with this simple technique. Bare canvas is purposely left unworked to make another texture. Brilliant cerise and pinky oranges for the pile, against mid brown and dull red, create a strong focal point.
Photo: John Hunnex

## Black work
The black work produced in England during the sixteenth century consisted of small geometric patterns built up with silk on the counted thread of finely woven linen. Holbein stitch was used, or double run-

**35** Black work sampler, 9 × 20cm (3½ × 8in), with patterns worked in even linen in stranded cotton. The interest is obtained by working from open patterns to closed ones in small back stitches.
Photo: John Hunnex

ning for fine outline patterns, and the small fillings within the shapes which were mainly floral, gave a delicate, filigree effect. Heavy outlines in braid or knotted stitches in black enclosed the patterns. Sometimes red or green silk was used instead of black, with gold thread introduced into the richer embroideries. As it developed many more stitches were introduced.

The technique if played around with has many possibilities. Today an effect of tone is aimed at, the outlines of shapes are often omitted, giving a freer effect; but within the shapes the smaller patterns are still geometric and repetitive. The more delicate ones are often simpler and open, with the darker areas of tone worked in closer more concentrated pattern to give density.

The repetitive patterns are best worked out on graph paper. One pattern worked in different sizes can be an interesting exercise, or a pattern within a pattern, until the closeness of the stitches gives a very dense tone. Another way in which to obtain tone is to work with one strand of stranded cotton, then two and then with three, repeating the same pattern but becoming denser.

The design may consist of any shapes without sharp points, a number of adjacent shapes making an abstract area of patterns and tones being more usual now, than the filling in of floral devices. Gold thread or lurex thread enriches some of the designs and examples in which a number of colours have been introduced into one piece of work can be tried out. They tend to lose the filigree quality of the delicate patterns, also the richness of tone, but an example worked in monotone from dark to light could be interesting.

If a coarse fabric on which the threads can be counted is available, the scale of the work could be changed so that coton-à-broder or perlé, soft cotton and wool could be substituted for the fine threads on the smaller scale. Black work, white work and gold work may be combined successfully, some areas being worked formally, some freely.

## Darning

This consists of two types, pattern darning and irregular darning, both of which require a loosely woven fabric with well defined warp and weft. The weight of working thread is usually about equal to that of the fabric as the aim is to give the darning an appearance of being a part of the fabric. Today thicker and thinner threads used on one piece of work given an interesting, textured surface which can be planned. A blunt ended needle is used for the darning. Patterns are made by taking up one or more fabric threads at defined points, the stitches increasing and decreasing in length according to the design, worked in close, parallel rows (illus. 23[12]).

Damask darning is worked vertically and horizontally with stitches of equal length. Work one way first of all, then the other. Both sides are alike and if two colours are used, of equal tone value, the result can give the look of shot silk.

Double darning consists of close rows of equal lengths of stitch, worked in two movements, the first a row of equal running stitches and spaces, the second filling in the spaces, exactly in the same holes as the previous stitches. Two near tones of colour can produce interesting effects. The stitches can be worked to correspond, exactly below one another in each row, or can be worked to give diagonal rows by moving one thread along on each row. Experiment with the technique to make further variations.

A pleasant filling pattern called Japanese darning consists of parallel rows of stitches of equal length spaced alternately, the distance between the rows depending on the scaled pattern. These stitches are linked together with diagonal stitches; again, two colours could be used (illus. 23[13]).

In irregular darning stitches can follow shapes; they can be made irregular in length and are a means of filling a background or pattern quite quickly. A mixture of shiny with dull threads creates a good texture and on an openly woven fabric some slub threads will go through the fabric to give a knobbly effect.

DARNED NET* The charm of this technique is in seeing the back and front of a stitch through the net. Hexagonal net is usual for this work; it is woven so that working horizontally a different effect from working vertically is produced with the same stitch. Most ordinary stitches such as running, back stitch, satin, herringbone, feather, etc. may be used to make intricate patterns but solid fillings are worked in darning or linen stitches.

The fabric must be taut to work well: the design is drawn in indelible ink on dark, stiff paper and tacked or basted to the back of the fabric to keep the net firm and flat. The design may be moved for repetition of pattern. Sometimes designs are worked entirely in outline, the more continuous the better as all thread ends must be darned carefully through to the back when the work is complete.

Use a blunt ended needle and non-stranded threads. One strand is suitable as is sewing cotton; fine linen threads are better still if obtainable, those called lace-linen threads being ideal. The thickness of thread may be varied if wished, as it is when fine darned patterns are worked in thin threads but the shapes are outlined in heavier ones to give emphasis.

An effect of darned net is obtainable with machine embroidery worked in outline, with rows of stitching close together to give solid areas. Fine and coarse threads may be used, but a variety of stitches is not possible.

Darning on square net is not so usual today but the results can be quite fascinating. The making of square net is of very ancient origin and, from the utilitarian purpose of making nets for fishing, developed into an attractive form of embroidery. Square mesh darning was also worked on a kind of filet net canvas and a finer version called lacis. Today the square net curtaining available in furnishing departments can be used. Embroidery on square net is also possible on the machine, using satin stitch. This requires some practice and is better attempted once skill in controlling the machine has been acquired.

*A comprehensive account of this kind of work is found in *The Encyclopaedia of Needlework* by Thérèse de Dillmont, a DMC publication.

### Cut work

In this type of embroidery areas of fabric are cut away to make spaces, with the raw edges of the fabric secured with stitches.

Broderie Anglaise with small cut out shapes edged with whipstitch or fine buttonhole is one form of cut work. In Richelieu embroidery the pattern remains in the fabric; the background is cut away but shapes are connected with brides or bars with picots added. In Renaissance work the bars are used without picots. Venetian embroidery imitated Venetian lace but is worked on fabric and has thickly padded outlines, with shapes connected by plain bars. Particular types of cut work are practised in other countries: Hardanger work in Norway and Hedebo work in Denmark, for example.

Today cut work is less popular but it can be an interesting means of decorating costume and household articles. The satin stitch edgings and bars can be worked on the machine, thus eliminating the laborious covering of the edges of the pattern with hand stitched satin or buttonhole stitch. A firm, closely woven fabric is best for this work. All the shapes are outlined in hand running, or straight stitch by machine, then are worked over in buttonhole or whipstitch, the knots being on the edges to be cut, or satin by hand or by close zig-zag, or satin stitch by machine. The shapes between the pattern are cut away after the hand embroidery is finished, but for machine embroidery, if bars and lacy fillings are to be worked, these shapes must be cut away before working across the spaces, otherwise the stitching will go into the material. In machine embroidery, two layers of fabric may have the pattern stitched round with close zig-zag or satin stitch, then parts of one layer are cut away, within the design, leaving the background in double material, or the background is cut away leaving the design in double material.

Design for cut work should aim at a balance between the solid fabric left and the areas cut away, to give a kind of coarse filigree effect without the addition of bars which complicate the work. Symmetrical patterns may be made by folding tissue paper and cutting holes of different shapes and sizes, none too large; more advanced designs can be drawn out on tracing paper, the areas to be eliminated can be blocked in with paint or other media and by holding the design up to the light it can be seen whether any shapes are completely detached from others so that the work could fall apart.

### Fabric manipulation

Designing with fabric may be sufficiently interesting by itself, but if the objective is to use threads, even more exciting ideas are possible as the stitches worked by hand or machine add depth and texture to folds, pleats and tucks. Gathering such as smocking, ruching, puckering and draping, gives dimension to fabrics which are further enriched with stitches. Interest is created between these areas and those left flat and unadorned. A background fabric is necessary for most manipulated

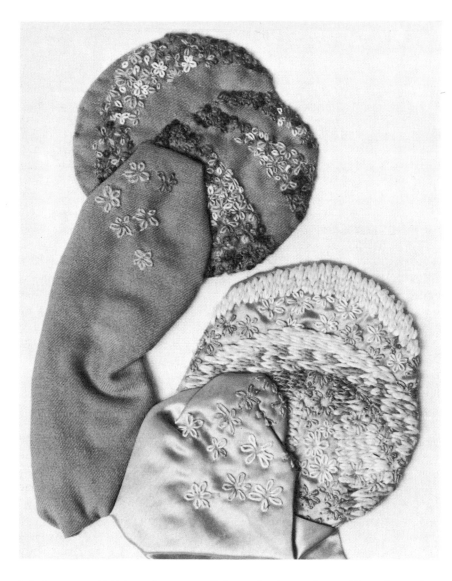

**36** Fabric manipulation with surface stitchery by Julia Coster-Longman, 25 × 20cm (10 × 8in). Experiments with fabrics to make sock-like shapes, folded and twisted to make shadows. Pink satin and bluish pink darker wool are applied to a white rayon linen background. Chain, chequer chain, link chain stitches and some knots are worked in stranded cottons and crewel wools in pinks, yellows, orange, turquoise and other colours, into small flower shapes. Photo: John Hunnex

fabrics, even if it is not seen, as it is easier to apply smaller pieces to a flat background after they have been gathered or draped than to work with large pieces which are difficult to control.

## Draping

This is best attempted with a fabric that does not crease easily, is not stiff, but has some body in it and is of a medium weight. Dress velvet, corduroy, some woollens and some mixture fabrics are suitable. Fine knitted fabrics drape well, some of the light angora woollens are ideal, but some of the synthetics are too bulky and would not drape at all. Crush pieces of fabric in the hand to see what happens. If they crease avoid them, if they are too springy they will not keep the folds well.

Cut the fabric on the bias with sufficient extra to make deep and/or shallow folds within the shape to be filled, the surplus being removed when the draping is satisfactory. Mould and pull the fabrics loosely to make curves, pin in place when necessary and play around with several fabrics to get the feel of them. The first attempts can be a mess as there is usually a tendency to try to fold one piece of fabric in several ways. It is better to let the folds follow one another naturally in a rhythmical sequence, curved or straight or merging one to another than to force the fabric against its obvious pull. This draping is better tried out than described, but as a contrast to flat fabrics both can add vitality to shapes. With practice draping becomes easier and also the final results can be envisaged. Stitchery can be worked within the folds, the folds themselves may be flattened in parts, with stitching to enhance them and to keep them in place. Small, almost invisible stitches in self coloured thread can be sewn through the draped areas to the background, instead of using embroidery.

**Gathering**
Random gathering gives a bumpy surface with stitches going in lines in various directions. Gathering can be very regulated as in conventional smocking, where the rows of running stitches are parallel with the stitches evenly spaced. Large circles gathered unevenly, then pulled tightly with the thread, create puffed up shapes which could be padded, then stitched or flattened as loose shapes on the surface of the fabric. Allow a good amount of extra material for experiment and try out different directions of running before deciding what is required, whether lines are to be placed close together, worked with small stitches to produce a tight bumpy surface, or whether the lines are to be further apart, with large stitches, to produce an undulating texture.

When applied to a background, gathered fabrics can be manipulated further as the folds can be moved around with a needle, some being bunched up, some flattened before they are secured. Fairly fine fabrics, neither too soft nor too stiff, gather easily. Thin calico, fine cotton, voile and muslin create soft, close folds. Felt gives a heavier undulating surface which may be further emphasized by some padding if desired. Gathering threads may be stitched into fabric, drawn up tightly and wound round pins to enable the tension to be altered as required. For uneven smocking the gathering may be even, in parallel rows, as for regular smocking, but small back stitches catch the folds together irregularly, sometimes with groups of stitches close together, sometimes far apart. When the gathering threads are removed, an uneven honeycomb-like surface should result, with large and small hollows. Another way is to make folds as the work proceeds, sewing two or even three together at intervals, with back stitches. A narrow striped fabric is an aid to this type of smocking as it avoids a too random approach if folds are made in the stripes. Shallow folds combined with deep folds, caught freely in this way, make a good background for stitches which can be looped or knotted to make textures that lurk in them, perhaps in strongly contrasting colours, so that sometimes they are seen, sometimes they are almost hidden, according to the point of view. Large fabric shapes may be gathered into smaller areas of background shapes

to create puffy folded effects which appear to be padded. The folds are kept in place with very small stitches; the large shapes must fit exactly into the smaller ones, for example a large circle may be gathered to fit into a smaller circle, when it is slip stitched into place. Embroidery between the folds which should not be deep can be most attractive, but must be suitable to the idea of the whole work. A circle composed of a strip of fabric tightly gathered at the centre, opening out to flat at the outer edge, with rows of gathers gradually diminishing to none, is a basis for different interpretations in embroidery.

## Tucks

These are made by folding fabrics in parallel lines, to give loose pleats which are kept in place by stitching on the double fabric, leaving the folds free, with areas of single fabric between these. 'Pin tucks' are narrow, 3mm ($\frac{1}{8}$in) in width, and are more easily stitched on the machine with the pin tucking device. Tucks can be much wider or gradated

**37** Detail from a panel mounted on a wooden frame, 27 × 24cm (10$\frac{1}{2}$ × 9$\frac{1}{2}$in), by Margaret Hobbs. Ruched butter muslin is stitched with cording to pull up the gathers. Behind the muslin, white cotton painted with dye, gives a merging pink and green area and painted black spots.
Photo: John Hunnex

from narrow to wide, according to the design and scale of the embroidery. Groups of tucks alternating with plain fabric, gradated tucks with gradated amounts of single fabric between each, could be effective, particularly if self-coloured embroidery is worked on the plain areas. Stripes of horizontal tucks placed between stripes of embroidered fabric look attractive in selected stitches in self-coloured threads or in a contrasting texture to that of the fabric.

A complete piece of embroidery needs careful planning to avoid fussiness, unless the tucks and plain areas are on a very large scale. Small areas of tucks with embroidery contrast well with larger, plain areas of fabric, particularly if carried out in a monochromatic colour scheme. Wide, horizontal tucks sewn in a contrasting colour of thread, in running stitches are a simple means of decorating costume. Striped and checked fabrics may be folded to eliminate one or more colours, folded at regular intervals the pattern and colour changes. These folds are most successful if sewn down with stitches, either horizontally across the folds, or vertically down the folds, with one of the colours of the fabric. For example a black-and-white checked gingham could be folded to give horizontal stripes of grey and white or grey and black. Horizontally across these folds a wide stitch such as tied herringbone could be worked, in white on the grey, or in grey or white on the black, each row being tied with an alternate colour. Folded on the bias, more complicated patterns may be made which make a good basis for more intricate stitches. Wide tucks can be cut into with parts folded back to give broken effects or triangular points; between these embroidery could be worked as small, varied patterns. In a brilliant, contrasting colour quite fascinating work could be evolved, with elaborately tucked areas contrasted with plain areas, both of which could be embroidered with couched lines. Rows of fine tucks with machine embroidered patterns between each tuck give a good texture and interesting pattern at the same time, and for dress decoration arrangements of tucks alternating with embroidered areas have many possibilities.

Fabric should be chosen according to the effect required. Crisp hard tucks require fabric that presses into firm lines; a soft, almost draped effect would best be achieved in a knitted fabric or a very fine woollen. If knitted fabrics are selected, parts to be embroidered should be backed with fine cotton or an iron-on fabric – otherwise they stretch too easily making good tension of embroidery difficult.

Puckering can be intentional or accidental if stitches are pulled too tightly to make slight creases in the fabric. Fine silk or cotton cut just off grain, sewn loosely on a background can be puckered as stitches are worked, as the fabric can be pushed into slight bubbles and secured with detached stitches such as french knots, crosses and link chain. If a pattern is being worked which incorporates puckering, the fabric would be pushed up when required, but this should appear deliberate. Tucks can be corded to give ridges, if in coloured threads with transparent fabrics, delicate, pastel effects being achieved. Embroidery can be worked on fabric before tucking it so that when folded the tucks are enriched.

## Quilting

Throughout history quilted articles have been made for warmth and in many cases for decoration. The main types of quilting are English, Italian and Trapunto, each giving a different effect. So-called shadow quilting using felt shapes between sheer fabrics is a technique which gives padded effects to an embroidery.

In English quilting (wadded quilting) three layers of fabric are used as this type is for warmth. The under layers should be firm or may be of the same fabric as the top layer; the middle layer consists of padding of sheep's wool, domette, terylene or dacron wadding. The three layers are basted together, the top one slightly looser than the under one, to allow more padding to come uppermost. Areas of closely stitched parts contrasting with the unstitched puffed up areas create the interest in this quilting. English quilting can be worked on the machine with ordinary straight stitching but if tightly padded the pressure of the foot must be lessened.

In Italian quilting or corded quilting, cords are used instead of padding. This type has no warmth and is used for decoration only. Narrow channels of double lines make the patterns; adjacent channels make a solid pattern or any pattern consisting of thin, ribbon-like double lines of stitching may be built up. Two layers of fabric are basted together then stitched, the channels being threaded from the back with quilting wool or with coloured cords or wools if using transparent fabrics. Italian quilting with straight channels is worked easily on the machine with a twin needle, but corners cannot be turned without lifting the presser foot.

Trapunto quilting (stuffed quilting) is also decorative, with small patterns raised on a flat background. Two materials are basted together, a more pliable one on the top, that is seen, an under, firmer one which is usually hidden. The shapes to be padded are stitched round, the padding of animal wool or kapok is pushed through small slits made in the under fabric, which are sewn up after the shapes are stuffed.

In shadow quilting, very brightly coloured felts are trapped between layers of transparent fabric, or, starting from the centre of the design or from one edge of a piece of work, shapes are stitched almost all round and stuffed; then the sewing is completed; the next shape or shapes are stitched and stuffed as the work proceeds, until all are stuffed. This eliminates slitting the fabric, so that the back and front are alike and can be hung to be visible from both sides. If terylene wadding is used for padding, under white organdie it gleams, making good clouds. Finely chopped, brightly coloured rags can be used as stuffing too, between any colours of transparent fabric; the back may be of a different one from the front. Felt shapes can be built up in layers to obtain depth. The felt shapes of the design are basted to the back fabric, the front is then basted to the back and running stitches are taken through the two fabrics and round the edge of the shapes to secure them. With white transparent fabrics over the bright felts the effect is delicate; with black organdie or coloured chiffons exciting

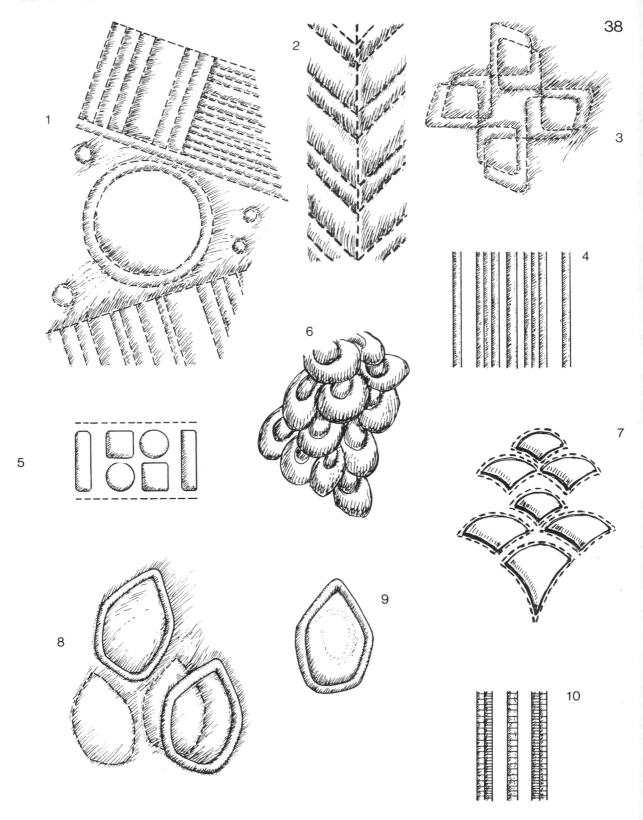

colour effects are achieved.

The stitches used for quilting are back stitch, chain stitch and running, the subtler effects being obtained with running stitches as they give a softer appearance than back or chain stitch. Running through three layers of fabric in English quilting produces smaller stitches on the back of the work than on the front. If both sides of the quilting are to be alike, stab stitch worked with the embroidery in a frame gives more equal surfaces but it is done with two movements, using both hands, one under and one above the work.

For decoration any surface stitches may be added after the fabrics have been quilted. In shadow quilting double back stitch, Indian shadow stitch and french knots are effective worked behind the top fabric or through both fabrics.

## Appliqué

This is a technique of applying one fabric to another to make a design. Patterned and plain fabrics may be mixed, different textures may be placed together. The shapes for the appliqué are applied to a background, with straight weaves (grain) of each corresponding, if a smooth, unwrinkled result is required. The edges of the shapes may be left raw, stitched by hand with herringbone, or other stitches, or by machine with zig-zag stitch or satin depending on the effect wanted. They may be turned under and hemmed or slip-stitched, this being termed blind appliqué, a technique used in applied patchwork. Running stitch worked round the outside of these shapes is effective but any type of stitch may be worked into the background or on the shapes. As some fabrics fray badly, simple shapes, avoiding acute angles and narrow points should be used as the basis for design of this work. Rich effects are obtained by the addition of surface stitches to both applied pieces and to the background.

## Reverse appliqué

This is a method in which two or three layers of fabric are placed one over the other and each layer is cut away to reveal the one below. Others can be placed again on top of these, up to four or five layers being put together. Design is best worked out in coloured tissue papers, one for each layer of fabric, the topmost one having most fabric cut away. Exciting examples of this kind of appliqué are seen in the traditional molas worn by the Indian women of the San Blas islands, where all cut away edges are turned under and hemmed carefully. Machine satin stitch or close zig-zag stitch may be substituted today. Colours are bright and primary on the old garments and a variation using the machine, with primary colours of fabric and thread could be to stitch round the cut shapes with different colours, such as bright blue on red, pink on green. Delicate colours of fabric and thread could be explored; for example, the bottom layer of fabric could be transparent, with several layers of opaque but light weight fabrics on top. Designs in which each area cut away allows more light to penetrate, down to the transparent fabric, could be used effectively.

38 Quilting:

[1 and 2] English (wadded) quilting with areas of close stitching contrasted with unstitched, puffed up areas.

[3] English quilting, the design based on the metal chair in illus. 18 [19].

[4] Italian (corded) quilting.

[5] Trapunto (stuffed) quilting, machine stitched.

[6] Trapunto quilting reminiscent of forms seen in the section of a flax stem (illus. 8).

[7] Shadow quilting. Running stitches through two layers of white organdie and other sheer fabric, are stitched round brightly coloured felt shapes (similar to the applied and stuffed shapes in illustration 20) to keep them in position after basting them to the under layer. The thickness of the felt gives a slightly raised look, and the overlay of organdie subdues the colours.

[8] Italian and English quilting combined in a design based on illustration 18 [18].

[9] Italian and Trapunto quilting combined.

[10] Shadow quilting: coloured threads pulled through narrow channels stitched through dark organdie.

Artist: Mollie Picken

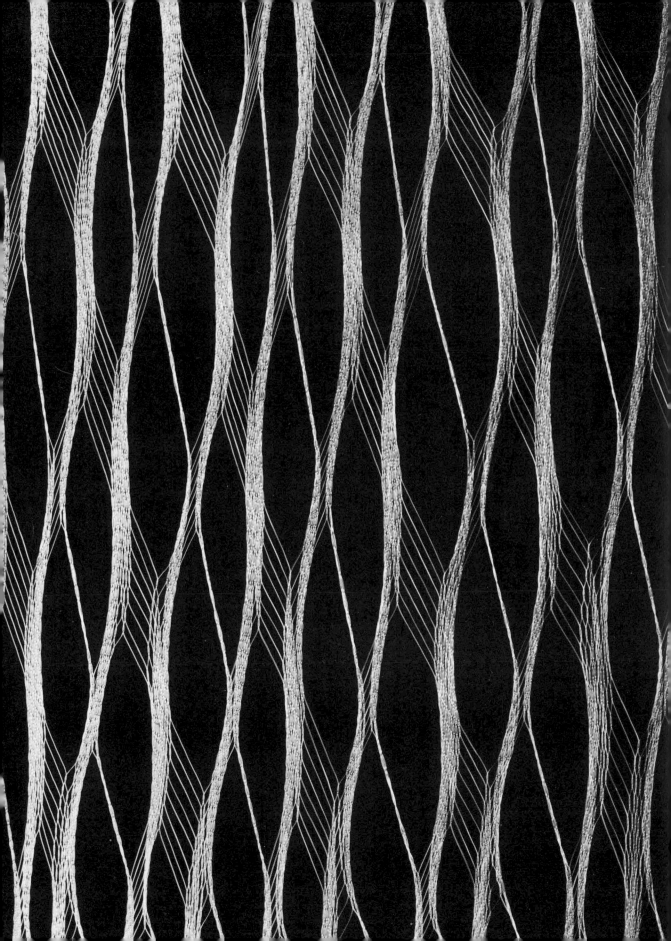

# Sprang
## Peter Collingwood

If three short lengths of yarn are hung from a nail on the wall, they can easily be worked together, just as hair is plaited or braided, to form a three-strand plait. If the three pieces of yarn are very long, the work will have to be interrupted frequently so that the thread crossings that annoyingly begin to build up lower down can be combed out.

If the lengths of yarn are also fixed at their lower ends by another nail, so that they are held tightly between these two points, the position will be different. As the hands cross two threads near the top, the contrary crossing of these two threads below cannot be combed out; it is as it were trapped by the lower fixing point. So as crossing follows crossing, a plait grows not only from the top nail downwards, but inevitably another plait begins to grow from the lower nail upwards, the two being perfect mirror images of each other.

This illustrates the essence of the textile technique known as sprang – the simultaneous production of two fabrics (the two plaits) by manipulating the parallel threads of a warp fixed at both ends. This operation is a rearrangement of the warp threads, no new threads are added.

Using more than three threads, the operation is of course more complicated. The threads are manipulated row by row at the top of the warp. Both these thread crossings and those that appear below are forced to the two ends of the warp with a flat stick, so that two equally compacted fabrics are made; one grows from the top of the warp downwards, the other from the lower end upwards. Any technical variation, design or mistake made in the upper fabric is faithfully mirror-imaged in the lower one.

Eventually these two fabrics reach so far towards the middle of the warp that only a short length of unworked threads is left between them. At this meeting point, some form of fastening has to be introduced to prevent the contrary crossings of the two fabrics from undoing. The resulting fabric is a fringeless rectangle with four selvages. Alternatively the work can stop short of this point and the unworked threads can be cut, the result being two identically shaped fabrics each with three selvages and one fringed edge.

The manipulation of the threads can take many forms but basically there are only three thread structures: *interlinking, interlacing* and *intertwining* (illus. 44[1,2 and 3]). It is interesting that all of these structures can also be produced in other, non-sprang, ways, for example by working on a set of hanging threads fixed only at one end. So the discovery of any of these structures in some ancient textile is by itself no sure indication that sprang was the process used.

39 Detail of a hanging by Noemi Speiser: omitting rows of interlinking in selected places on a nylon warp.
Photo: Hinz

**40** Coptic cap showing vertical panels of hole designs and treble twists; also tapering at the top by using 2/2, 4/4 and 8/8 interlinking. Museum Narodave, Warsaw

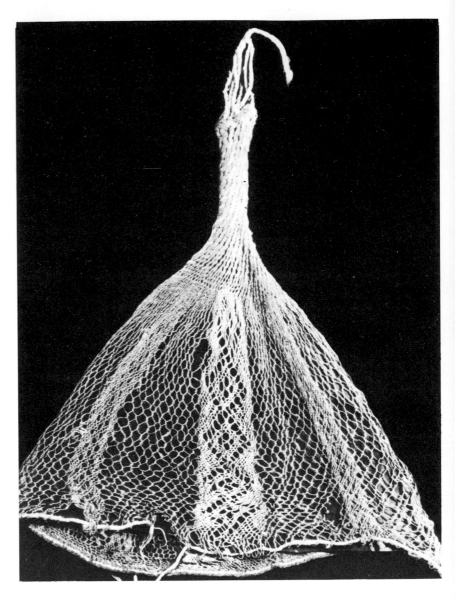

Though in the past there have been a confusing number of words used to describe this technique, sprang, a word of Scandinavian origin which has no connection with our verb, to spring, is now employed internationally. The word first occurs in written records of the middle ages, but probably it then had a less restricted meaning. Other words still in use in Europe are *Egyptisch Vlechtwerk* (Holland), *Stäbchenflechterei* (Germany), *Pinnbandsflätning* (Sweden), *Pleteni na ramu* (Czechoslovakia), and *Siatkowa* (Poland).

## History and uses

The earliest European piece of sprang comes from one of the Danish bog burials at Borum Eshöj, dated to about 1400 BC. It is a woman's hairnet made of wool and the advanced technique suggests the method had been long in use. It was the discovery of this piece in 1871 and the slightly later discovery of bags and caps in the Coptic graves in Egypt (AD 400 to 700), which first brought sprang to the notice of experts. In fact they were initially very puzzled by the method and made various incorrect suggestions as to its manufacture. But once sprang was established as a technique with its own special characteristics, it was realized that its distribution had once been almost world-wide, although it only lingered on as a living craft in a few isolated places. Apart from many important Danish pieces, there were other European finds in Norway (including a possible sprang frame in the Oseberg ship burial of AD 850), Spain, Switzerland and England (a legging from Viking times found at York). Peru as would be expected yielded many fine examples from 500 BC onwards as also did the much later civilization in S.E. United States from AD 1200.

All sprang fabrics have one feature in common, great stretchability in all directions, and this has dictated their uses both past and present. These include most types of body covering, such as caps, hairnets, hoods, scarves, shirts, dresses, belts, mittens, gloves, leg coverings and other articles such as carrying bags and hammocks. Before the invention of knitting, sprang was the quickest way of making a stretch fabric; the ease with which knitting can be shaped during making probably led to knitting almost completely eclipsing sprang except for some specialized uses.

These included the military sashes, a different colour for each country, worn by most European army officers from 1700 to 1850. They were made of silk and the many points of similarity between them suggest a common, as yet unknown, place of manufacture. Almost up to the present day, for many women in east European villages a sprang headdress of some type was an essential item of clothing. There is literary evidence that suggests the use of sprang as a decorative border, sewn to the edge of a woven cloth, which can be traced back to about 1400.

Today sprang is still used traditionally in Columbia and Guatemala

41 Part of a hood in blue wool from Paracas, Peru, about 600–500 BC; interlinking with holes.
Courtesy of the Textile Museum, Washington DC

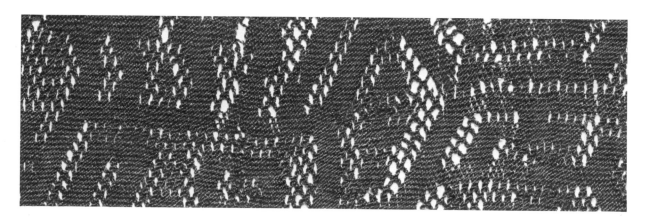

**42** Woollen cap designed by M. Matoušková, 1965, Central Office of Popular Art, Czechoslovakia. Courtesy ULUV, Prague

for making bags and hammocks and in Pakistan for making cotton belts. In Czechoslovakia there is a strong movement to revive sprang for modern fashion wear and some excellently designed caps, hoods and even full-length dresses have been made. Elsewhere its present day use is mainly as a purely decorative textile, for which it is well suited with its many possible textures, its stretchability and its ability to become three dimensional. It is probably the last of the half-forgotten off-loom techniques to be revived, because it has very definite rules that have to be assimilated before any freedom in design is possible. But these rules exercise a benign influence on the design, generally limiting it to simple geometric shapes.

## Equipment

All that is needed is some device to hold the threads in a stretched condition but which can also adjust to the gradual shortening of the warp that is an inevitable part of the process. Many expedients have been tried, but a four-sided frame is the most frequently used piece of apparatus. It can be quite large, standing on the ground, with the warps stretched between two cross cords (illus. 43 and 44[4]) or a smaller frame used on the lap, with the warp stretched between two rods (illus. 44[5]), or an even smaller one suitable only for sampling or for making very small items (illus. 44[6]). Obviously the size of the frame limits the size of the resulting fabric.

## Yarns

A sprang fabric can theoretically be made out of almost any type of thickness of yarn; traditionally wool, cotton, silk, linen and other bast fibres have been used. Ideally the thread should be smooth, elastic and with little twist, but when beginning, something easy to see and handle, such as heavy rug wool, is advisable.

It can only be found by experiment how many threads of a certain yarn, worked in a certain technique, will produce a fabric so many centimetres or inches wide. This is because no width-controlling device (like the reed in weaving) is used; however closely or openly the threads are laid when warping, they will find their own width after a few rows have been worked.

A warp of about forty threads will be sufficient for learning the basic technique.

## Warping

First a cord is tied across the centre of the frame; this is the *safety cord* (illus. 44[8]). Start by attaching the warp yarn (in the form of a ball, not a skein) to the lower cord at the left-hand side. Then carry the ball

up the frame, passing behind the safety cord and then over the top cord.
Then bring it down the frame, passing in front of the safety cord and
under the lower cord (see illus. 44[7]). Looking at the frame from the side
(illus. 44[8]), there are two crosses made in the warp, one above the safety
cord, one below.

Continue in this manner, working across towards the right, until
enough threads have been warped and end by tying the yarn to the
lower cord. This ensures that an even number of threads are warped.

44 The three thread structures
used in sprang:
[1] Interlinking.
[2] Interlacing.
[3] Intertwining.

Three types of sprang frame:
[4] Four-sided frame, standing
on the ground, with the warps
stretched between two cross
cords;
[5] Smaller frame used on the lap,
with the warp stretched between
two rods;
[6] Even smaller frame for making
very small items.

A warp of twelve threads:
[7] seen from the front; (A) and (C)
are warping cords, (B) is the safety
cord.
[8] from the side, showing the two
crosses made, one above the safety
cord and one below.
Artist: Mollie Picken

While warping aim to lay the threads with as even a tension as possible. But tension can be adjusted after warping, any looseness being worked to one or other side and the initial or final knot retied. As already mentioned, the exact spacing of the threads on the cords is not necessary. A striped warp can be made, the knots joining different colours lying at the lower or upper cord.

When warping is complete, slip a flat stick, or *sword*, into the opening in the warp occupied by the safety cord. Push the sword up and down, forcing the warp crosses to both ends of the warp. This manoeuvre will also show up any mistake. which should now be corrected. Leave the sword at the lower end of the warp.

## Interlinked spring

Of the three thread structures, interlinking is the one most used and with the most variations.

### Basic technique

The simplest form of interlinking is described to introduce the basic technique of sprang. Because one thread interlinks with one thread, it is called 1/1 interlinking. The work is done by repeating two rows over and over again; these are called the plait and overplait row, names derived from an early Dutch book on the subject.

PLAIT ROW: BEGINNING THE ROW Put the fingers of the left hand into the opening in which both the safety cord and the sword are lying. This opening divides the warp into a front layer consisting of the odd-numbered threads and a back layer consisting of the even-numbered threads. The left thumb lies across the front layer, which is therefore in the grip of the left hand. Slide the left hand up near the top of the warp.

Now with the index finger and thumb of the right hand, pick up the first two threads from the back layer, the two lying at the extreme right in this layer. Take these into the right hand. Then from the front layer threads, held in the left hand, release the first thread, the extreme right-hand one. With the right index finger make it come to lie behind that finger (see illus. 45[1]). This is the first interlinking of the plait row and this type is not repeated until the next plait row is worked.

PLAIT ROW: CONTINUATION OF THE ROW With the thumb and index finger of the right hand pick up the next back layer thread (not two threads, as in the above interlinking) and take it into the right hand to join the two already there. Then release the next front layer thread from the left hand and guide it to the back of the right index finger. Now three threads are in the right hand and two behind it.

Repeat this across the warp, always picking up one back layer thread and releasing one front layer thread.

As the work proceeds it will be seen that the left hand holds fewer and fewer threads, the right hand more and more, and that what were

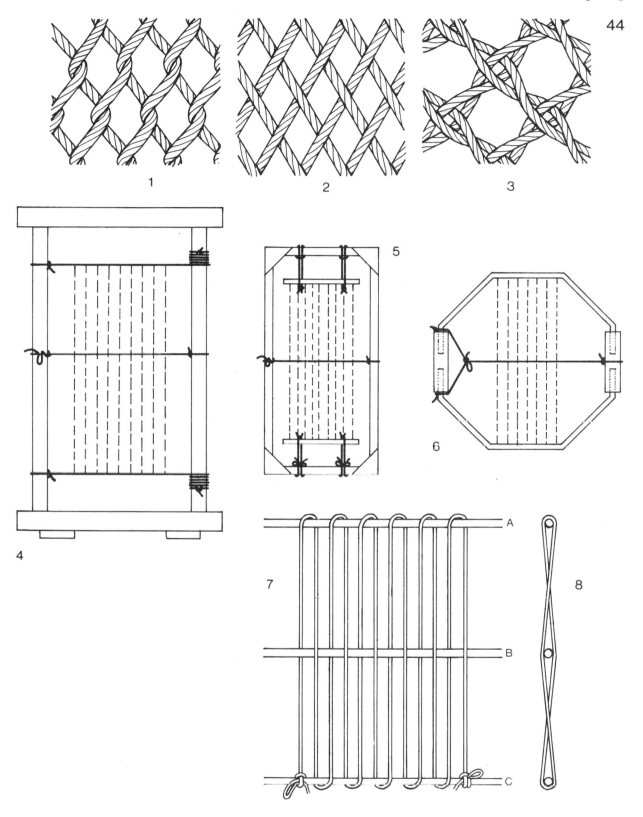

back layer threads at the start become front layer threads (lying in the right hand) and what were front layer threads become back layer threads (lying behind the right hand).

PLAIT ROW: ENDING THE ROW Eventually only three threads will be left, two being in the left hand and one behind it. With the right hand, pick up the single back layer thread in the usual way, then release the two front layer threads and let them join the others behind the right hand.

The left hand is now free of threads and can untie the safety cord at the left side and insert it in the new opening or shed occupied by the right hand. Once this is done and the cord retied at the left, the interlinkings of the first row are safely preserved. Remove the sword from the initial shed, put it into the new shed and push it up and down, driving the interlinkings firmly and evenly to both ends of the warp.

When the sword is pushed to the top of the warp there are two front layer threads lying together at the extreme right, and two back layer threads lying together at the extreme left; elsewhere front and back layer threads alternate regularly (see illus. 45[2]). This reflects the different types of interlinking in the row just completed.

OVERPLAIT ROW This row is much simpler as only one type of interlinking is used throughout; nothing special is done at the start and end of the row.

Put the left hand into the shed occupied by the safety cord as before. With the right thumb and index pick up the first back layer thread and take it into the right hand. Then release the first front layer thread from the left hand. Make sure this *is* the first one, i.e., the right-hand one of the two front layer threads lying together. If the two have become twisted, trace them upwards to establish which is which.

The row is continued thus, always picking up one back layer thread and releasing one front layer thread. At the end, be careful that the two back layer threads lying together are picked up in the correct order.

As at the end of the plait row, the safety cord is now withdrawn from the previous shed and inserted into the new shed, and the sword used to push the new set of interlinkings equally to both ends of the warp.

At the end of the overplait row, it will be found that the threads are back in the sequence they lay in when warped. The plait row shifted them sideways and the overplait row returns them to their original position. This zig-zag movement builds up the diamond shaped mesh which is characteristic of interlinking; it also explains the shortening of the warp as the work proceeds.

To continue with the sprang, keep on repeating plait and overplait rows alternately. The presence or absence of two front layer threads lying together at the right always indicates which type of row has just been completed, and therefore which type should next be done. But if by mistake two rows of the same type are done one after the other, it will be found that warp threads are only twisted around each other; there is not the typical zig-zag movement.

After a few rows it will become apparent that the interlinkings in the upper fabric are the mirror image of those in the lower (see illus. 00). In the upper the threads cross right over left, in the lower left over right.

If the hands are pulled apart when working, opening the fabric out, the threads involved in the next interlinking are made more visible. This makes it possible to work with very fine threads. As each back layer thread is picked up, notice that it passes under two front layer threads. If it is not doing this, some mistake is being made. The only exception to this rule is the very first back layer thread in a plait row and the very last back layer thread in an overplait row.

## Abbreviations

There is a way of abbreviating the instructions for some of the sprang techniques, rather as knitting instructions are written out. The letter B, stands for 'the next back layer thread', the letter F, for 'the next front layer thread' and B/F means 'pick up the next back layer thread and drop the next front layer thread'. Brackets around a symbol means it is to be repeated as often as necessary. No brackets means it has to be done once only. A number outside the bracket means it has to be repeated that number of times.

So the two rows described above can be abbreviated thus:

B/2F $\leftarrow$ (B/F) $\leftarrow$ 2B/F    Plait row
$\leftarrow$ (B/F) $\leftarrow$    Overplait row

As the arrows show, the instructions are read from right to left, i.e., in the direction the row is worked.

The direction of the stroke, /, indicates the direction of twist where the two threads interlink (illus. 45[3]). So the techniques outlined above can be called 1/1 interlinking, or, using the convention applied to spun yarns, Z-twist interlinking. Of course, threads can be interlinked in the other direction to give 1\1 interlinking or S-twist interlinking. These descriptions apply to the interlinkings done by the hands at the top of the warp; naturally at the lower end, the twist is in the opposite direction. So if the hands are making Z-twist interlinking, the fabric forming at the lower end of the warp will be in S-twist, and vice versa.

There are other ways of working, such as using a stick to hold the new interlinkings or working at the bottom of the warp instead of at the top, but the way described above is the commonest method.

## Further details of working

1 When learning it is a good idea to put a short length of yarn in each shed at the lower end of the warp as it is made. If a mistake is discovered, the work can be undone back to one of these pieces of yarn, which provides a baseline for the next attempt. If not needed, they can be pulled out.

2 Mistakes can be corrected either by undoing back to a straight line as described above, or the work can be allowed to undo partially so that there is a triangular opening of unworked threads leading up to

the mistake. When this is corrected, the triangle is reworked either row by row or by interlinking on a diagonal.

3 Some workers prefer to have two safety cords. One is in the shed, the other hanging from the frame. At the end of a row, the latter cord is drawn into the new shed; only then is the former cord withdrawn. This is doubly safe as at all times there is a cord in position.

Two cords are essential if a wide warp is being worked as the interlinkings have to be done in stages. The left hand holds as many threads as it can manage and they are interlinked in the usual manner. The free cord is then drawn into this new shed and the left hand, moving to the left, takes a new group of threads. When these are interlinked, the cord is drawn into this part of the shed. So the work proceeds, section by section, until the whole width has been worked and the cord lies in the new shed right across the warp.

4 Difficulty is often experienced in keeping the upper and lower fabrics equally beaten up and compacted, resulting in the meeting line being off-centre. To overcome this, small additional sticks or rods are used. After each row, two sticks are put into the new shed and one is pushed up and one down. No sword is used. After five rows, for example, ten sticks will be in the warp, five near the top, five near the bottom. At this stage, the two sticks first inserted, i.e., the highest and the lowest, are slid out and all the others moved to keep the growing fabrics tightly compacted. The two sticks removed go into the next shed formed. Then the highest and lowest sticks are again slid out and the others moved up and down.

This method is often confined to the lower end of the warp (see illus. 43). Only one stick is put into each shed and it is pushed downwards.

5 As the two fabrics approach the centre of the warp, the lack of space makes each row progressively more difficult. Eventually the left hand will not fit into the shed and a single finger has to be substituted. The sword is removed to make more room. The work of the right hand can be helped with a knitting needle. But however they are performed, the last few rows are awkward and slow. The safety cord is left in the final shed.

These difficulties can be avoided if the final rows are worked by interlinking on a diagonal.

**Ending with one fabric**
However the final rows are done, some form of fastening is introduced at the meeting line to prevent the contrary twists of the upper and lower fabrics from undoing.

CHAINING The method most used traditionally is chaining. Using either a crochet or latchet hook, the threads at the centre are chained into each other. The great advantage of this method is that the fastening is as elastic and stretchable as the surrounding fabric. There are many possible variations.

1 Only the threads lying in front of the safety cord are chained, working from right to left. At the left selvage, the fabric is turned over

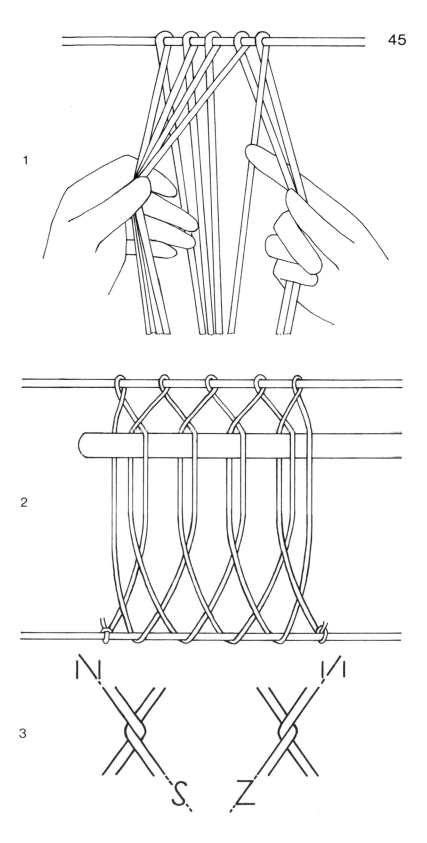

**45** [1] The position of the hands after the first interlinking of a plait row.
[2] Position of the threads at the top of the warp after the plait row.
[3] S- and Z-twist interlinking.
Artist: Mollie Picken

and the chaining continued using the threads lying behind the safety cord. The final loop has to be tied to the fabric to prevent the whole chain from undoing. Then the safety cord can be pulled out. This method produces a narrow ridge back and front, and can be varied by using two threads as the unit in chaining, by giving each loop a twist before the next thread is pulled through, by working two rows of chaining and so on.

2 The chaining can be done so that both the threads lying in front of the safety cord and those behind are worked together. The cord is gradually withdrawn, releasing pairs of threads, a back and a front, which are the units used in chaining. This type gives a large ridge but only on the front of the fabric (illus. 47 and 50[1]). Again the final loop has to be tied.

LEAVING THREADS OR RODS IN THE FINAL SHEDS If the final use of the fabric does not demand a stretchable meeting line, then threads can be laid in the final shed or sheds (see illus. 51). Their ends must be knotted or darned in to keep them in place. If the fabric is to be mounted in a frame, a stiff rod can be left in the final shed and its two ends attached to the frame.

### Ending with two fabrics

If, rather than one fabric, two are wanted, the work stops well short of the centre of the warp and the unworked threads are cut. To prevent their twists undoing, the cut warp ends can be knotted, plaited or whipped, but more usually before cutting a line of chaining, using separate threads, is worked at the fell of the upper and lower fabric (illus. 46).

46 White cotton cap from Poland, mid nineteenth century, showing hole designs and the use of 2/2 4/4 interlinking.
Courtesy National Ethnographic Museum, Warsaw

TREATING END LOOPS OF WARP When either one or two fabrics have been finished off as described above, they can be slid off the cords or rods between which the warp was laid. The end loops will not undo, but the edge can be made firmer by chaining them into each other and the final loop tied; or a fine cord can be run through the loops.

### Shaping

The typical product of the sprang process is either one or two rectangles of fabric. But the fabric can be shaped either during or after production.

SHAPING DURING PRODUCTION Extra warp threads can be added after the work has proceeded for some way by stretching two new cords across the frame and laying extra warp threads between them. These new threads can be added either at one or both sides to make side panels which increase the width suddenly or they can be interspersed among the existing warp to make a gradual widening. Once the new threads are in place, the next row of interlinking will include both these and the original threads.

Other ways of varying the width depend on varying the actual

**47** Double twist interlinking used selectively to give a block of horizontal stripes on a background of diagonal stripes. The meeting line is chained, making a ridge on the front of the fabric, as in illus. 50[1]. Photo: John Hunnex

thread structure being used, without increasing or decreasing the number of warp threads. Thus if holes are introduced or the structure changed from double to single interlinking, the fabric becomes wider. If interlinking is done using two threads as the unit instead of one, i.e., 2/2 interlinking, and then this is followed by 4/4 interlinking and even 8/8 interlinking, the fabric will become narrower. This is how the Coptic caps were brought to a point (illus. 40) and it can also be seen towards the bottom of illustration 46.

SHAPING AFTER PRODUCTION The simplest way of shaping a sprang fabric is to fold it along the meeting line, seam up the two sides and so form a bag; a cord running through the end loops of warp makes a draw string (see illus. 50[3]). If a single hole has been made at the centre and the seaming done only part way, a simple upper garment is made with neck and arm openings (illus. 50[3]). If the selvages are sewn to each other to make a tube, then one end pushed into itself to make a double thickness tube, the sort of cap shown in illustration 41 is being developed. If strings in the warp end loops of a very wide fabric are pulled tight, thus gathering the fabric at its two ends, another sort of cap is made (illus. 50[3]).

There are many possibilities; and as long as the work is carefully planned before beginning, most shapes can be achieved, even something complicated like a pair of gloves.

48 Large piece of interlinked sprang by Jules and Kaethe Kliot, before it was stretched between the pavement and the third floor of the Transamerica building, San Francisco, as part of the Fiber Allusions Show in 1974.

## Variations in the interlinked structure

So far only the simplest interlinking has been described which gives a close diamond shaped mesh. This can be made more interesting by using two or more colours in the warp. If the warp is made with two colours alternately (an A B A B sequence), it will show narrow cross stripes when interlinked. If it is made with an A A B B sequence, it will show diagonal lines. If it is made with an A A A B B B sequence, it will show small triangles. These and other sequences can be combined in the same warp, either as stripes or in areas (illus. 47).

A few of the many variations are described below, but the point should be made that as with most basically simple textile techniques the variations are endless and more are being discovered, or re-discovered, all the time.

### Hole designs

Every group of people that has made sprang fabrics in the past has used holes as a method of patterning (see illus. 40 and 46). This could be because at its simplest a hole is the result of failing to interlink two threads which should have been interlinked. So it is not difficult to progress from this common mistake to the controlled placing of holes which will make an openwork pattern against the normal interlinked meshwork. The few essential rules are best learnt by working a diamond shape of holes, which is shown in abbreviated form thus:

**49** One of a pair of woollen gloves made by Peter Collingwood in four hours, Christmas Day 1972. Photo: John Hunnex

A DIAMOND OF HOLES

| | | | | | |
|---|---|---|---|---|---|
| B/2F ← | (B/F) ← | 2B/F . B/2F ← | (B/F) ← | 2B/F | Row 1 |
| | ← | (B/F) | ← | | 2 |
| B/2F ← | (B/F) ← | 2B/F . 2B/2F . B/2F ← | (B/F) ← | 2B/F | 3 |
| | ← | (B/F) | ← | | 4 |
| B/2F ← | (B/F) ← | 2B/F . (2B/2F) × 2 . B/2F ← | (B/F) ← | 2B/F | 5 |
| | ← | (B/F) | ← | | 6 |
| B/2F ← | (B/F) ← | 2B/F . 2B/2F . B/2F ← | (B/F) ← | 2B/F | 7 |
| | ← | (B/F) | ← | | 8 |
| B/2F ← | (B/F) ← | 2B/F . B/2F ← | (B/F) ← | 2B/F | 9 |
| | ← | (B/F) | ← | | 10 |
| B/2F | ← | (B/F) | ← | 2B/F | 11 |

New holes are always started and existing holes are always closed in a plait row, so the first row above is such a row. At the centre of the warp, pick up one back layer thread and drop off *two* front layer threads, then immediately pick up *two* back layer threads and drop off one front layer thread. These two interlinkings start the first hole, which appears between them. The row finishes normally.

The second row is a simple overplait row, as are all even-numbered rows in this technique. It is only the plait rows which influence the pattern.

In row 3, a plait row, the normal interlinking is continued until there are five threads between the last interlinking and the hole; three of these will be *in* the left hand, two *behind* it, exactly as shown in illustration 50[2]. This is the moment to carry out the interlinkings indicated, i.e., pick up one back layer thread and drop two front layer threads, then pick up two back layer threads and drop two front layer threads, then pick up two back layer threads and drop one front layer thread. The effect of these three interlinkings is both to close the first hole and to start two new holes, correctly placed, below it. Row 4 is an overplait row which simply lengthens the holes. In row 5 the normal interlinking is stopped at exactly the same place, i.e., five threads away from the right-hand of the two holes. The four interlinkings which follow close these two holes and start three correctly placed holes below them.

By now the pattern of interlinkings will be clear. At the right-hand side of the area of holes, there is always a B/2F interlinking, at the left-hand side there is always a 2B/F; between these two there is an increasing number of 2B/2F interlinkings. It will be found that there is always one less of the latter than holes that are being made in that row.

The triangular area of holes which is now being made could obviously become wider and wider, but following the instructions above, after an overplait row, the area begins to decrease in width to form a diamond.

In row 7, normal interlinking is continued until there is only *one* thread between the last interlinking and the most right-hand hole; this one thread is *in* the left hand. This is the moment to carry out the interlinkings shown. Row 8 is a normal overplait row. In row 9, normal interlinking is stopped exactly as in row 7. Row 11, a plait row, will close the final hole.

So when making an increasing shape, the interlinkings making the holes are begun when five threads away from the nearest hole, but when making a decreasing shape, they are begun when only one thread away. These are the two rules for moving from normal interlinking to an area of holes, i.e., what is happening at the right-hand edge of the diamond.

There are two further rules when moving from an area of holes to normal interlinking, i.e., what is happening at the left-hand edge of the diamond. For an increasing shape, make as many 2B/2F interlinkings as there are holes in the row above; for a decreasing shape, make one less 2B/2F interlinking than there are holes in the row above.

These rules allow any design to be worked, especially if the boundary lines between the two areas always run on diagonals. A vertical boundary can be achieved by applying the increasing and decreasing rules alternately for succeeding plait rows.

There are many variations with hole designs. For instance, a hole does not need to be closed two rows after it has been started, but can continue for as long as desired. Due to the elasticity of the surrounding fabric, such a hole will gape wider and wider until it is finally closed.

Holes can be spaced differently so that two, three, six or eight threads lie between them, not four as in the above description. This can produce a much more circular outline to the holes. Often traditional fabrics use the open texture produced by holes for the background and the close 1/1 interlinking for the image. Several of the early sprang instruction books written around 1920 treat holes as the only way of patterning and have various systems for drafting such designs on squared paper.

Long holes or slits are essential to the design of some sprang garments, for example, for a neck opening or for separating the fingers in the gloves. Whereas in weaving a piece of fabric with four slits would be slow to make, as five separate wefts would be needed, in sprang it could be as quickly made as a piece with no slits. This useful property should be remembered when designing.

To make holes right across a fabric, the following four rows are repeated.

| | | |
|---|---|---|
| ——— ← (2B/2F) ——— ← | Row 1 |
| ——— ← (B/F) ——— ← | Row 2 |
| B/F ← (2B/2F) ——— ←B/F | Row 3 |
| ——— ← (B/F) ——— ← | Row 4 |

## Interlinking with a double twist

The interlinkings considered so far are of the simplest type, the two threads engaging with each other with the minimum amount of twist that will hold them together (see illus. 52[2]). Several techniques are based on the idea of increasing this twist to give double twist interlinking. This has an immediate effect on the overall course taken by a warp thread (see illus. 52[3]). In normal single twist interlinking, each warp thread runs roughly parallel to the selvage, making only short deflections to right and left to link with the threads on either side. So if the warp were striped, the colours would run straight from one end of the fabric to the other as in a woven cloth. But using a double twist, each warp thread takes a diagonal course and consequently any warp stripes either of colour or of different materials will also move diagonally. This can give interesting diamond shaped areas where two such stripes cross.

The double twist is naturally slower than the single. After each interlinking is made, the two threads have to be given one more twist before they take their position in or behind the right hand. It will be found that the back layer thread picked up goes behind the right hand and the front layer thread dropped off goes into the right hand, i.e., the opposite of what normally happens. At the first and last interlinkings of a plait row, do not give a double twist to the extreme outside thread, otherwise these threads will be in the wrong position for working the next row.

Double twists do not have to be used right across a warp, but can be used only in selected places to alter the colour sequence in a warp (see illus. 47).

Double or treble or quadruple twists can be used simply as a way of

50 [1] Chaining the meeting line, using both back and front layer threads together.
[2] Hole designs: position of the threads when a new hole should be started.
[3] Making a bag, a garment and a cap from a finished piece of sprang. Artist: Mollie Picken

increasing the distance between the interlinkings in successive rows and so of making a more open fabric. This was done in both early Danish and Coptic fabrics. A treble twist has been used between the vertical panels showing hole designs in illustration 40.

## S-twist interlinking

So far, all interlinkings made with the hands have been in Z-twist, the only S-twist being that which forms of itself at the lower end of the warp. Many techniques depend on the hands making both types, either whole rows of S- and Z-twist or changing from one twist to the other within a row. Whereas with Z-twist, it is the right hand which does most of the work, in S-twist it is the left.

End a normal Z-twist overplait row, then start as follows:

PLAIT ROW: BEGINNING THE ROW With the left hand in its normal position in the shed, slip the left thumb under the two right-hand front layer threads, then with the thumb and index finger pick up the most right-hand back layer thread. Draw this to the left under the two front layer threads, which are now allowed to drop from the left hand. Then place the back layer thread in the right hand, the front layer threads going behind this hand.

PLAIT ROW: CONTINUATION OF THE ROW Slip the left thumb under the next front layer thread and pick up the next back layer thread and give it to the right hand, the front layer thread going as before behind this hand.

PLAIT ROW: ENDING THE ROW At the end of the row, three threads remain, one front layer thread and two back layer threads. Slip the left thumb under the front layer one and pick up the two back layer threads in the same way as just described.

At the end of the plait row, there will be two back layer threads lying together at the right selvage, and two front layer threads lying together at the left selvage, i.e., the opposite of the state at the end of a Z-twist plait row.

OVERPLAIT ROW As with Z-twist, this is the simpler row, one back layer thread being picked up and one front layer being dropped off, as described above, right across the warp. But notice that the first back layer thread is lying hidden behind the right selvage and that the last front layer thread is floating in front of the left selvage. These odd positions are due to the change from Z- to S-twist. Once the latter is established by the first two rows, threads will lie in their normal positions.

The work continues by alternating plait and overplait rows. These two rows can be abbreviated thus:

| | | | | | |
|---|---|---|---|---|---|
| F\2B | ← | (F\B) | ← | 2F\B | Plait row |
| | ← | (F\B) | ← | | Overplait row |

**50**

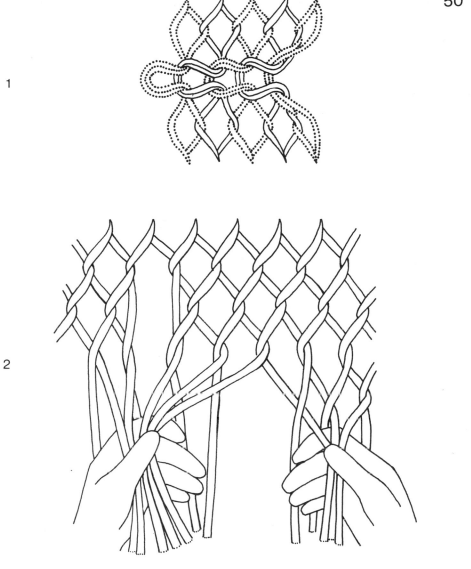

1

2

3

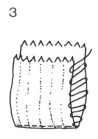

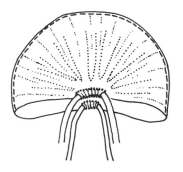

The angle of the strokes shows that all the interlinkings are in the S direction.

### Z- and S-twist interlinking

The change from one twist to the other can only be made after an overplait row. This implies that a stripe of either type must contain an even number of rows.

Whereas a fabric made entirely with Z-twist or entirely with S-twist has a strong tendency to curl up on itself, an effect that subsequent pressing cannot completely overcome, a fabric made with alternating stripes of Z- and S-twist lies almost flat with just a little waviness at the edges. The ability to combat this curling effect by the calculated combination of S- and Z-twist is one of the more difficult aspects of sprang.

If the work is examined carefully at the junction between two stripes of opposite twist, it will be seen that there is an interruption in the normal diamond mesh. Threads, instead of interlinking with each other, are simply crossing each other. This is inevitable and is made use of in the production of interlaced sprang.

Obviously stripes of the two types of twist can be made by working, say, four rows in Z-twist, then turning the frame upsidedown and working another four rows in Z-twist, then returning the frame to its original position and working another four rows in Z-twist and so on. There is nothing against this method except that it does not teach the hands to make S-twist, which is necessary for the next step.

AREAS OF S- AND Z-TWIST INTERLINKING Here both S- and Z-twist interlinking are used in every row and are so arranged that areas of the two types are built up. If these areas have angled boundaries (triangles, diamonds or diagonal stripes), there is an interesting three-dimensional effect. Where one area abuts on another there is a marked difference of surface level (see illus. 51).

The interlinkings involved in making a diamond in S-twist on a background of Z-twist are given in abbreviated form:

| | | | | | |
|---|---|---|---|---|---|
| B/2F | ← (B/F) | ← (B\F) | ← (B/F) | ← 2B/F | Row 1 |
| | ← (B/F) | ← B\B . F\F | ← (B/F) | ← | 2 |
| B/2F | ← (B/F) | ← B\B . F\B . F\F | ← (B/F) | ← 2B/F | 3 |
| | ← (B/F) | ← B\B . (F\B)×2 . F\F | ← (B/F) | ← | 4 |
| B/2F | ← (B/F) | ← B\B . (F\B)×3 . F\F | ← (B/F) | ← 2B/F | 5 |
| | ← (B/F) | ← B/B . (F\B)×4 . F/F | ← (B/F) | ← | 6 |
| B/2F | ← (B/F) | ← B/B . (F\B)×3 . F/F | ← (B/F) | ← 2B/F | 7 |
| | ← (B/F) | ← B/B . (F\B)×2 . F/F | ← (B/F) | ← | 8 |
| B/2F | ← (B/F) | ← B/B . F\B . F/F | ← (B/F) | ← 2B/F | 9 |
| | ← (B/F) | ← B/B . F/F | ← (B/F) | ← | 10 |

These instructions include two hitherto unused types of interlinking, one between two front layer threads and one between two back layer threads. This is a difficult though rewarding technique and it is beyond

51 Areas of S- and Z-twist interlinking, showing the three-dimensional effect. The meeting line is
fastened by a laid in weft.
Photo: John Hunnex

the scope of this chapter to describe it in detail, but the following
points can be made:

1 It does not matter whether the pattern is started in a plait or
overplait row.

2 Both plait and overplait rows are pattern-making rows; compare
with hole designs where it is only in the plait row that the pattern is
made.

3 The moment to start the S-twist interlinkings which make up the
central diamond is when the right-hand of two back layer threads lying
together has been used in a normal Z-twist interlinking. These two
threads appear after the first row and act as a useful guide in all
subsequent rows.

4 If the technique is worked correctly there is no interruption to the
normal diamond shaped mesh. There should be no holes or crossed
threads. The only variation is in the direction of twist at the interlinkings.

VERTICAL STRIPES OF S- AND Z-TWIST INTERLINKING If rows 5 and 6 above
are repeated over and over again vertical stripes will appear. They
have no three-dimensional effect, but several of them are often used,
especially near a selvage, to overcome the curling effect mentioned
above.

**Lattice sprang**

As already mentioned, starting a plait row by picking up *two* back layer threads established the degree of lateral movement of the threads in this and the following rows. But a plait row can begin by picking up three or more back layer threads. The abbreviated instructions then become:

This increases the lateral movement of the threads, which are seen to cross each other in the form of a lattice between each row of interlinking. When the fabric is stretched sideways, this stripe of crossed thread makes a dense texture and the intervening interlinkings show as small holes.

**Other variations**

All the variations described so far depend on altering just one feature of the basic interlinking, e.g., the amount of twist, the direction of the twist, the number of threads involved in the twist. But there are other variations, such as the following.

1 The introduction of extra rows of interlinking which do not reach either selvage. This is seen in illustration 40 where the denser vertical panels have three rows of interlinking for every one row in the intervening parts.

2 The working of pairs of extra threads which twine through the interlinked structure, always moving on diagonals, a favourite technique of the Coptic workers in sprang.

3 The making of raised ridges.

4 Double interlinked sprang; the working of two differently coloured fabrics, one behind the other, and the interchanging of threads between them to make a reversible two-colour design.

**Interlaced sprang**

In interlaced sprang, each thread moves diagonally until it meets a selvage; it then changes direction and moves on the opposite diagonal until it reaches the other selvage and so on. As it moves on one diagonal it naturally meets all the threads moving on the opposite diagonal and it interlaces with them in some sequence, such as going over one, under one or over three, under three (see illus. 52[4]).

Because it does not involve the twisting of threads, interlaced sprang will always lie absolutely flat. It has not the great stretchability of interlinking but it has enough elasticity to make it a favourite method for belts, such as the Hopi wedding sash. It is often used in combination with interlinking to produce a fabric with more of the latter's stretchability but none of its tendency to curl.

In interlinked sprang, it was noticed that at the junction between a

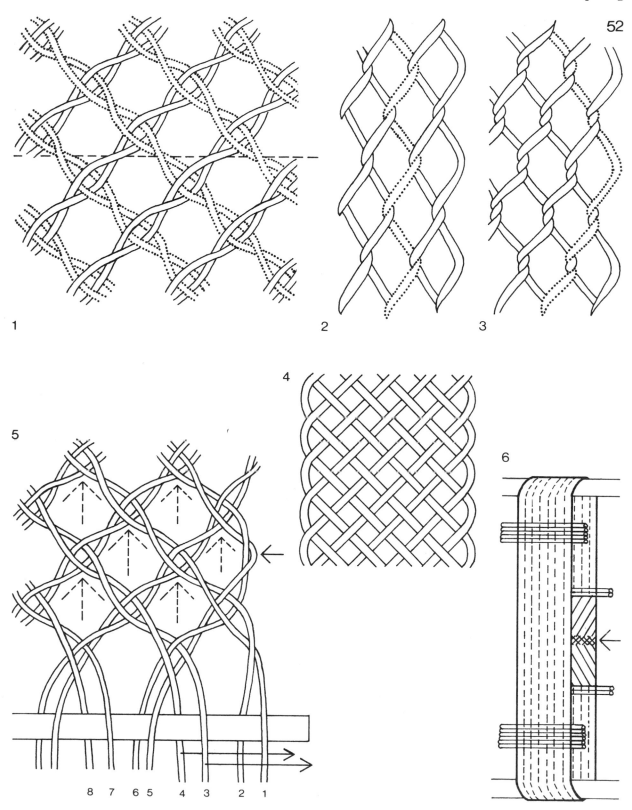

52

1

2

3

4

5

8 7 6 5 4 3 2 1

6

stripe of S- and Z-twist there appeared a row of crossed threads. The interlaced structures are all produced by alternating *single* rows of S- and Z-twist so that only crossed and interlaced threads result and no interlinking. So, although in the instructions the same symbols are used and the hands move in the same way as in interlinked sprang, no interlinking is actually produced.

Just as there are many interlacings possible in weaving, so there are many in interlaced sprang. A few are described below.

**Over one, under one interlaced sprang**
This is the simplest possible type of interlacing and corresponds to the plain weave of woven cloth.

The first row is a normal Z-twist plait row, thus:

$$\text{B/2F} \quad \longleftarrow \quad \text{(B/F)} \quad \longleftarrow \quad \text{2/BF} \quad \text{Row 1}$$

The second row can be done in several ways which all produce the same result:

a) Start with an S-twist of the first two front layer threads, carry on with S-twists of the next back layer with the next front layer threads and end the row with an S-twist of the two final back layer threads, thus:

$$\text{B\textbackslash B} \quad \longleftarrow \quad \text{(F\textbackslash B)} \quad \longleftarrow \quad \text{F\textbackslash F} \quad \text{Row 2}$$

b) Turn the frame over and do the following row in Z-twist:

$$\text{F/F} \quad \longleftarrow \quad \text{(B/F)} \quad \longleftarrow \quad \text{B/B} \quad \text{Row 2}$$

Return the frame to its original position.

These two rows are then repeated.

Due to the diagonal movement of all the threads it will be understood that any colour stripe in the warp will also move diagonally and build into diamond shapes.

**Over two, under two interlaced sprang**
Once the threads are made to pass over and under two or more threads, it will be found that each interlacing has two types, one in which the threads lie in horizontal ribs, or wales, and one in which they lie in vertical ribs. Of the two types the one with horizontal ribs is always the easier to do, as follows:

$$\text{F/F} \quad \longleftarrow \quad \text{(B/F)} \quad \longleftarrow \quad \text{B/B} \quad \text{Row 1}$$

This row in Z-twist begins by interlinking the first two back layer threads with each other and ends by interlinking the last two front layer threads; in between there are normal back with front interlinkings.

Again, the second row can be done in several ways:

a)    B\B ——————— ← ————— F\B ——————— ← ————— F\F    Row 2

A row of S-twist beginning with an interlinking of two front layer threads.

b) Turn the frame over and work exactly as for row 1, thus:

F/F ——————— ← ————— (B/F) ——————— ← ————— B/B    Row 2

Return the frame to its original position.

Rows 1 and 2 are repeated. Some looseness will be found at the selvages where threads unavoidably have to pass over or under three threads. Illustration 53 shows this technique used on a striped warp.

### Over three, under three interlaced sprang with horizontal ribs

F/F ——————— ← ————— (B/F) ——————— ← ————— B/B    Row 1

Reverse frame, then:

F/2F ——————— ← ————— (B/F)    ←    2B/B    Row 2

### Combining interlinked with interlaced sprang

There are many ways of combining interlinking and interlacing; one is described below, a structure used on scarves, often tie-dyed, worn by bedouin women in Tripolotania.

B/2F ——————— ← ————— (B/F) ——————— ← ————— 2B/F    Row 1
              ← ————— (B/F) —————    ←             Row 2
B\B ——————— ← ————— (F\B) ——————— ← ————— F\F    Row 3

These three rows are repeated.

Interlaced sprang can be combined with interlinking in areas, not row by row as described above; it can also be worked as a double fabric.

53 Over two, under two interlaced sprang with horizontal ribs, showing the movement of colours in a two-colour warp.
Photo: John Hunnex

## Intertwined sprang

Intertwined sprang has had little historical use but it has much to offer the modern explorer of sprang. Its structure, though very open, has far more stability than interlinking, showing no tendency to waist when on the frame or to curl up when off the frame.

As in interlaced sprang, all threads move on a diagonal course; but here they move in pairs, the threads of each pair twisting round each other, as in illustration 52[1]. Where one pair meets another, moving on the opposite diagonal, the threads pass through each other in one of two ways: either the top thread at the crossing point comes from the pair on the left (as shown at the top of illus. 52[1]), or the top thread comes from the pair on the right (bottom of illus. 52[1]). The former is called a left-over-right crossing, the latter a right-over-left crossing. It is the way the twining pairs of threads grip each other at these crossing points which gives the structure its stability.

**Left-over-right crossing**
Starting with a warp whose number of threads is divisible by four, the crossings are done row by row as described below. It is assumed that this is the first row being done on a warp or that it is following an interlinked overplait row. As the movements are quite different, the abbreviations used so far cannot be applied.

ROW 1 Insert the left hand into the shed as usual and concentrate the attention on the four threads about to be involved in the crossing, labelled 1 to 4 in illustration 52[5], where a stick replaces the left hand. The left-hand pair, 3 and 4, must pass through the right-hand pair, 1 and 2, in the way shown by the arrows, then each pair has to be given a twist.

Slip the right thumb and index between threads 1 and 2 and, picking up thread 4, draw it into the right hand. Then push thread 3 over 1 with the tip of the left thumb. These two movements produce the crossing, the next two will produce the twisting. Push thread 3 to the back with the right index finger, so now thread 4 is in the right hand and thread 3 behind it. As the index comes back to the front, pick up thread 2 on it and take it to join thread 4 in the right hand. At the same time drop off thread 1 from the left hand and make it lie behind the right fingers together with thread 3.

So now what were the two back layer threads, 2 and 4, are in the right hand and what were the two front layer threads, 1 and 3, are behind the right hand.

This set of movements is then repeated with the next four threads and so on all across the warp.

ROW 2 In order to establish the diagonal movement of the threads, this row begins by simply twisting the first two threads. So the first back layer thread is picked up and the first front layer thread is dropped off, exactly as at the start of an interlinked overplait row. All this does is to add twist to two already twisted threads and they will make a loop at the selvage, like the one arrowed in illustration 52[5]. After this the next four threads are treated exactly as described for row 1, and so on across the warp. The two threads left at the end of the row are given a twist just as the first two were.

Rows 1 and 2 are repeated.

**Right-over-left crossing**
The idea is the same here except that thread 4 has to pass behind 1 and 2, and thread 3 has to pass between 1 and 2. This is a more awkward movement for the fingers, hence the left-over-right crossing is the one normally used as the basic structure. The threads are twisted in pairs after the crossing just as before.

**54** (detail) and **55** Intertwined sprang: combining the two types of crossing on a warp of two colours. Photo: John Hunnex

The pushing of the twists to both ends of the warp is harder in intertwined sprang. Either the warp can be beaten up and down in sections with the sword, or a stick can be inserted into the mesh and used to force the twists in the right direction (see the dotted arrows in illus. 52[5]).

## Variations

1 COMBINING THE TWO TYPES OF CROSSING There is no need to make a row all of one type of crossing. The type can be changed as the row is being worked so that areas of the two types are gradually built up. On a one-colour warp these areas will show slightly due to the altered direction of the surface threads.

If a striped warp is being used, the coloured threads will move diagonally. If left-over-right crossings are being used, it is the threads moving downwards to the right which will show on the surface and those moving downwards to the left which will show on the back. Altering the type of crossing at any point will of course reverse this (see illus. 54 and 55).

2 REPEATING ONE ROW If after row 1 another row exactly similar is worked, the four threads involved in the first row crossings are crossed again in the second row. There is thus no diagonal movement of threads giving the typical diamond shaped openings, but instead narrow four-strand braids are built up with vertical slits between them. These braids will continue to lengthen as long as row 1 is repeated. The braid will stop immediately row 2 is worked. If the four threads involved in each crossing are of two different colours, these will spiral round each other.

3 MULTIPLE TWISTS A fabric with larger openings can be made by giving more than one twist to each pair of threads after they have passed through each other.

4 USING MORE THAN ONE PAIR OF THREADS AS THE UNIT Instead of passing one pair of threads through one pair, two or even three pairs are passed through each other then twisted in the normal way. This is a little more awkward to do, but gives a much heavier and thicker fabric.

5 EXTRA TWINING THREADS Extra pairs of threads can be made to twine their way through the intertwined structure. This can be done in several ways, allowing the extra threads to show only on the back or only on the front, or equally on both sides or not at all.

6 DOUBLE INTERTWINED SPRANG Two layers of intertwined sprang can be worked simultaneously and threads interchanged between the layers to make a design.

7 COMBINING WITH OTHER STRUCTURES Interesting one-colour fabrics can be made by combining areas of interlinking and intertwining.

## Circular warp sprang

All the techniques described so far come under the heading of flat warp sprang. In other words there is a flat sheet of warp threads, every thread of which is involved in some manipulation row by row. But there is another quite different type of warp which is arranged as a continuous tube or ring, as shown in illustration 52[6].

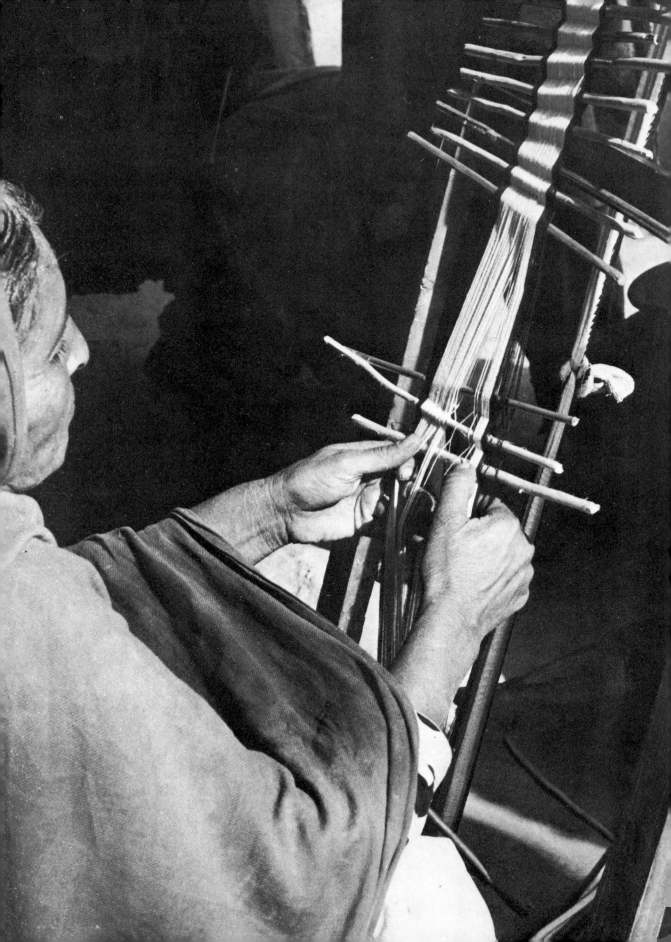

This tube of threads is generally stretched between two bars. These may either be part of a frame (see illus. 57), or the upper may be attached to some support and the lower may be tensioned by putting the foot on it. These two bars separate the warp into a distinct front and back half, and it is only on the threads of the front half that the sprang manoeuvres are carried out. So the front half is divided into back and front layer threads and the hands work these threads, row by row.

After each row, two sticks are inserted into the shed and one is pushed up and one down the warp; no sword is used. Soon there is little space left for the hands between the upper and lower sets of sticks so these are pushed over the top bar and under the bottom bar respectively and thus into the back half of the warp. Here the sticks are pulled out one by one, each leaving behind the twists it has carried from the front.

Thus the fabric begins to appear at the back and the meeting line between the two halves is actually the first part to be made (see arrow in illus. 52[6]). The meeting line in circular warp sprang is simply where the interlinkings of the S- and Z- twisted halves abut on to each other. There is of course no extra feature here such as chaining or laid-in wefts, as found in the meeting line in flat warp sprang.

As the fabric grows it gradually extends into the front half of the warp. The threads are usually cut before the two parts of the fabric meet in the front. So a long fabric with fringes at both ends is made, suitable for belts. If the two fabrics are allowed to meet in the front and are fastened at their meeting line by chaining, then a completely tubular fabric is made.

The warping for this method is usually done on four pegs arranged as a triangle with two pegs at the apex. Each time the thread is led round the triangle, it is taken round a different peg at the apex, thus making a cross in the warp. This establishes the order of the threads when the warp is stretched between the two bars and gives the initial shed for the work to begin.

A circular warp has been used wherever a long, usually narrow, stretch fabric has been wanted, for example, for the cotton belts from Pakistan, the Hopi wedding sash, woollen belts from many parts of Europe, the silk military sashes, baby slings from Guyana.

The techniques described for a flat warp can all be done on a circular warp, though some are made more difficult by the presence of the sticks. The most popular have been hole designs and double twist interlinking on a striped warp. Work has to be done with great accuracy as a mistake is only discovered when the sticks are being pulled out at the back and at this stage it is difficult to correct it.

If a piece of card is put into the back half of the warp before the sticks are pushed round, the sticks are prevented from meeting, thus two separate fabrics are made, each with two fringes. As neither of these fabrics has a meeting line, this shows how the absence of this normally characteristic feature in a fabric does not exclude sprang as the process used in its making.

**57** Circular warp sprang: making a cotton belt in Pakistan on a free-standing frame.
Photo: J. Powell

# Weaving
## Enid Russ

Woven fabric is made when a vertical set of threads called the warp, of which each individual thread is a warp end, is interlaced by a sequence of horizontal threads called the weft, known separately as weft picks. To understand this structure make a detailed examination of a sample of woven fabric by fraying it carefully, one thread at a time. Notice that the thread that is pulled out is permanently waved in the form in which it has passed under and over the other threads, and that these poke up or down on either side of it, changing position as each thread is withdrawn. This indicates that all threads are bent throughout the structure and are much longer than the cloth's woven length or width. Observe also that the construction depends on all ends and picks supporting each other. Therefore the spacing of the warp must be worked out in relation to the thickness of the weft yarn for which it is to make room, and to the pattern of intersection that is to be woven.

There are three distinct ways in which the spacing of the warp is controlled. Each is related to a type of loom, which imposes its tradition of weaving. The first is related to the practice of nomadic peoples, familiar with the use of cords, poles and pegs. Their warp was tied between two parallel poles, laid on the ground and pegged apart with the warp tight. It was of limited length and widely spaced. Weft was put in freely and rammed down to cover it. Twining and knotting enriched the fabric. This is the origin of the ancient tradition of tapestry, carpet and rug weaving and produces weft dominated structures. Nomands wove while the camp rested and rolled the work into a bundle when the tribe moved on. When the weaver could work in a settled situation the separate poles were put into an upright frame.

In the second method the whole warp is extended without spreading between rods. One rod is attached to a fixed point and the other to the weaver's body so that the warp can be slackened or tightened. The weft is pulled through hard so that it lies straight in the fabric, cramming the warp ends into a minimum and therefore consistent width. This is the principle of backstrap loom weaving which makes warp dominated fabric, usually in narrow widths.

In the third method the loom has parts which impose a mathematical spacing on the warp and allow the weaver to control the structure and character of fabric through subtle relationships between the spacing of warp and weft.

Tapestry weaving is discussed here in detail as one of the basic forms of woven structure using simple equipment. The principles of narrow loom weaving are outlined as an introduction to the modern loom and to the making of balanced weaves.

**58** Detail of sample weaving by Pam Price, 31cm (12in) wide. The warp is of 2/12s mercerized cotton at 14epi entered in sections of differing widths on pairs of shafts on an eight-shaft loom. The ground can only be woven in plain weave, but the various sections can be built up in a number of sequences so that wefts that pass between every end in the warp make different shapes (compare with illus. 59).
Courtesy of Liverpool Polytechnic

## Yarns for weaving

The choice and use of yarn should be intentional and controlled. An understanding of the making of yarns, so as to recognize the way they are likely to behave will help the weaver to make an interesting and practical choice (see Chapter 1, pages 25 to 36).

Almost all yarns are made by coaxing fibres into a longitudinal arrangement and twisting them so they are locked together. There are two important ways of doing this, associated properly with the handling of short wool fibres on the one hand, and long wool fibres on the other, but applicable in a broad sense to the spinning of any raw material under the heading of short or long fibres.

### Short fibre yarns

Material which comes in short fibres, such as the fine crimpy wool from sheep with close fleeces, cotton, waste silk and man-made fibres cut short in imitation of these, are prepared in a disorderly way. Because the fibres lie across the direction of the yarn they adhere easily, and twist into a springy open yarn. This characteristic is most strongly marked in wool. Cheviot and Harris yarns, Welsh woollen and all mule-spun yarns are examples.

Short fibre yarns spun as one-ply or singles thread can be used for weaving but few are strong enough to stand strain and are therefore unsuitable for warps. Most singles yarns are inclined to snarl but this springiness enables them to engage flexibly and snugly with each other. This characteristic of snarling can be seen in illustration 59, in which handspun yarns provide the main feature.

Wool singles are often lightly oiled to give strength and are then suitable for warps. Oiled wool must be used in this state – if the oil is washed out for dyeing it must be replaced for weaving and washed out of the fabric afterwards.

Singles of cotton or linen are weak yarns but when two or more are plied together they become much stronger. Their natural appearance may be brightened and strengthened by mercerization.

### Long fibre yarns

The long fibred materials include the silky fleece from long-haired sheep, mohair, flax and their man-made imitations. These are prepared carefully to preserve the lustre of the fibres and to prevent tangling. The fibres are arranged in line with the yarn they are to make. They are tightly twisted because of the closeness of the fibres and to prevent them slipping. These singles yarns are so over-twisted as to be unusable and must be doubled, or plied into a yarn of several strands before they can be used.

This way of spinning wool is called worsted spinning and makes smooth, hard and stable yarns. Worsted is a beautiful yarn but behaves in its own special way. It has a comparatively stiff quality and does not submit to bending about in the fabric very freely, tending to move in long curves. Examples of worsted spinning may be observed in rug and carpet yarns, made in that way so that the cut ends stand up, in knitting and embroidery wools because of the need for a smooth finish, as well as in fine worsted yarns designed for suitings and upholstery.

## Fancy yarns

Yarns which have been spun or doubled in various ways to make them decorative and irregular are available in all sizes. Look closely at the way they have been put together in order to understand their strength and structure, so gaining ideas for devising your own yarns. Many are dependent on thin threads to bind the parts in place and this indicates a yarn that is not as strong as it looks. Such yarns should not be used where strength is important.

Yarns of a variety of sizes or thicknesses can be made – any number of thinner yarns may be run together to make up a thick yarn. This gives an opportunity to blend colours and styles of yarn. Threads of different materials such as wool, rayon, cotton or linen twisted together, may not associate well. This can be interesting when the yarn is woven into the fabric and its parts move independently. Notice the difference between yarn made of parts twisted in the same direction and of the same ply and yarn made of assorted parts.

Other ways of making thick and stylish threads include crochet chains, French knitting and finger knotting.

## Yarn counts

The thickness of yarns is often described in numbers which are known as yarn counts. There are different counting systems for each natural fibre and several for wool. Each is associated with the district or country where the yarn is manufactured, or with the style of yarn.

The numbers indicate the length of yarn in relation to the weight. In general, the greater the length of yarn, the finer it is and the higher the

**59** Detail of sample weaving by Anne Briggs. The warp is home-spun wool at 16epi with 48 ends on shafts 5 to 8. Weft picks weave through alternate blocks in twill weave and pass under the intervening blocks. Roving, thick handspun or multi strand yarns are used for weft which, weaving into every end, frames the shapes as they are built alternatively.
Photo: John Hunnex

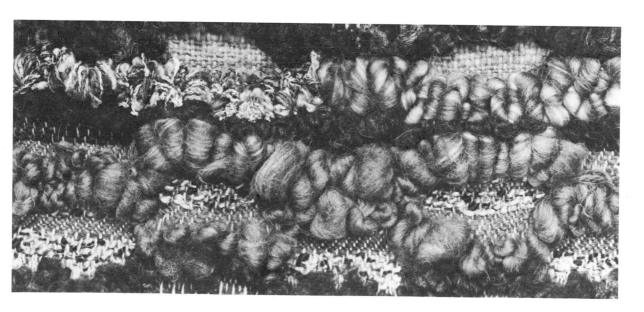

60 [1] The frame loom with the two
rods in position in the hooks. One
pair of ends is in place.
[2] and [3] show how these are attached.
[4] The side view of the frame loom
showing the rods (A) in cross-
section resting in the outward-
facing hooks.
[5] Weaving on the frame loom:
pairs of ends are in place with alternate ones lifted and weft yarn
passing beneath.
[6] The structure of tapestry weave
with a curve of weft before it is
beaten down. The horizontal cross-
section shows how the warp ends
are in a straight line with room
between for the free passage of
weft. The vertical cross-section
shows the warp straight, with the
weft picks touching each other on
either side. Compare this with illustration 64[9] showing the cross-
section of normal plain weave (this
is the same whether a vertical or
horizontal cross-section).

Fitting shapes together in tapestry. Always weave the shape
that is reducing in width upwards
first, and bring the next shape over
it:
[7] Two shapes woven alongside,
the reducing shape first.
[8] One shape woven horizontally,
the second built over it and following the shape. Make more weft allowance when the angle is sloped.
Artist: Mollie Picken

count number. A low number, therefore, indicates a thick thread and
higher numbers indicate yarns of increasing fineness. A single figure
means a singles or one-ply yarn. Two numbers separated by a stroke
show the number of strands plied together to make the yarn, as well as
the count. This low number usually precedes the count: 2/20s is a yarn
in which two strands of 20s cotton have been plied together.

Continuous filament yarns such as silk, rayon and synthetics are
described in deniers: low numbers mean fine yarns and the size of yarn
increases with the denier number.

An international system called the Tex system exists, based on
metric weights and measures, but the count system, based on fixed
weights, is still in general use.

### Dyed yarns
Vegetable and commercial dyes can enlarge and vitalize a limited
range of yarns (see pages 36 to 37). Dyeing can be used not only to give
a required colour but also to cover an unwanted or disagreeable one.
Hanks of yarn may be tightly bound in sections or may be festooned
over the dyepot so as to be partially submerged. An interesting use of
festoon-dyed yarns can be seen in the colour illustration on page 149.

## Tapestry weaving

In tapestry the warp ends are of a plain yarn stretched tightly across a
frame. They are equally and accurately placed. The natural elasticity
of yarn permits selected ends to be pulled forward with one hand while
weft yarn is passed between the raised and stationary ends with the
other. When released the raised ends spring back to their original taut
position; therefore the weft interlaces the warp threads, from the front
of one end to the back of the next, without strain, its thickness separating each consecutive warp end from the next. When the work is
removed from the frame it adopts the width dictated by the sum of the
warp thicknesses and the weft pushing between each warp.

Every row, or pick, of weft packs directly on to the top of the
previous one completely covering the warp, so that the structure of
tapestry can be visualized as a series of vertical rods, embedded in and
held together by the weft.

Whatever your intention to invent and experiment, it is best to begin
by perfecting the conventional technique so as to grasp the relationship between warp yarn thickness, or size, the spacing of warp
ends, the size of weft yarn, and the weft length allowance that produces
a stable, true and rich structure. All failures, errors and deviations
from this should be carefully observed and the reasons for them understood. Yesterday's aberration may be the germ of tomorrow's idea.

### The frame loom
Although elaborate looms have been developed for tapestry weaving, a
frame loom is all that is needed.

**61** The scaffolding loom is shown at the left in profile, describing one side of the construction. The vertical bar (A) has two couplers (B) attached, supporting the horizontal upper and lower bars (C) and (D). The ground support (E) and the optional extra bar (G) are held in place by finials (F). (G) carries a coupler (H) which holds the optional leash bar (K). The position of a leash is shown at (L).

To the right of the illustration the bars (K, C and D) are shown from the front of the loom with the warp (W) winding over bars (C) and (D) and leashes (L) in place. The strings (S) are shown attached to the vertical support, taken through the warp and pulled tight to tension it.

Artist: Mollie Picken

A wooden frame is illustrated on page 122. It consists of four pieces of wood $2 \times 4$cm ($\frac{3}{4} \times 1\frac{1}{2}$in), two of which are 60cm (24in) long and two 40cm (16in) long. The two short lengths are laid on top of the two longer pieces to make a rectangular frame. The four corners are screwed together using at least two screws at each corner. A large cup-hook, capable of retaining a rod 2cm ($\frac{3}{4}$in) in diameter, is screwed into the centre of each corner with the hook facing outwards.

Small portable frames are suitable for exploring and testing ideas. The maximum size on which the tension can be controlled is about $60 \times 40$cm ($24 \times 16$in). It is possible to use larger wooden frames, but the strain put on the frame by the warp is better dealt with in a stronger construction.

A free-standing tapestry frame can be made from standard scaffolding parts. The tube should be of steel as aluminium will bend under the strain of warping. The example illustrated opposite suggests using lengths of steel tube of 180cm (6ft) for the sides and for the upper and lower bars. This provides an area of approximately $160 \times 125$cm ($5 \times 4$ft) for weaving. The frame is easily dismantled so a selection of different lengths of steel tube would provide the weaver with the means of making frames to suit required sizes of work, or a very long frame on which small pieces could be made simultaneously side by side. The requirements are:

4 lengths of 180cm (6ft) standard steel tube for the sides and for the upper and lower bars

2 lengths of 90cm (3ft) standard steel tube for the feet

4 double couplers MK II to couple bars to uprights

2 pairs of fixed finials to fix feet to uprights.

Place the two short lengths of tube on the floor parallel to each other and 180cm (6ft) apart, or the length of your horizontal bars. Set a fixed finial in position halfway along each. Drop one upright steel tube into each, tightening the finial with a spanner. Screw a coupler to each upright at the height at which you wish to set the lower bar. Put the bar in position and tighten the coupler. Fix the upper bar in its appropriate position in the same way. The structure of the loom is shown in profile to the left of illustration 61.

### Choice of yarns for tapestry weaving

Sensitivity to the quality of yarns and materials and to their behaviour in construction will open many ways to original work.

For tapestry weaving the warp must be strong and smooth enough to permit the weft to push down into place. A yarn of several strands twisted together is therefore suitable and also has the elasticity necessary for keeping its tension. Cotton twine serves most purposes. Flax yarn is strong but does not stretch and is difficult to tension, but if one wants to make for instance, small exquisite pieces to use in garments, then wool or even silk might be used to give the right quality.

Wool is the most sympathetic material for the weft, responding well to the movements required of it in tapestry and pile weaves. When choosing materials for experimental work or for hangings, any yarn

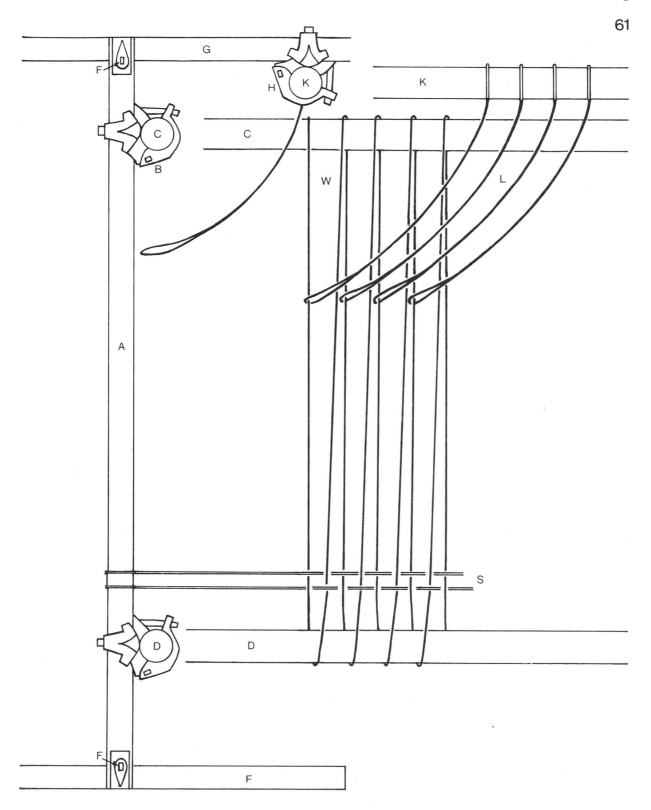

can be used as weft, provided it is thick enough to maintain the degree of weft spacing that has been decided upon. It can be chosen for its lustre or dullness, smooth or rough surface, stiffness or softness, or for any quality that the weaver recognizes as expressing his idea.

As well as multistrand yarns and constructed yarns (see page 121), all kinds of materials can be considered for the weft. Collect ribbons and coloured paper, especially cellophane and other scrunchable materials, to use in strips. Fabric of all kinds, plain or patterned, cut, or ripped to produce a shaggy edge, is eloquent when woven. String of all kinds, from parcel string to Christmas glitter, will have uses, especially if several are twisted together.

If it is intended to emphasize the structure of tapestry weaving choose hard yarns that hold their shape and are well-defined. Yarns described as string and twine, made of long-fibred materials like sisal, hemp and flax, all of which dye well, or polypropelene which does not, have the clarity of form to suit this purpose.

Ropes and cords can be made of soft fibres but their compact structure gives them hardness and definition. It is a simple matter to make cords from a number of threads of equal length knotted at each end. The length is twisted tightly and when doubled back on itself twists into a cord. Two people manage this best, holding and twisting each end, and then bringing them together high with a central weight pulling the halves tight, before they are released.

**Warping the frame loom**

On the small wooden frame warps can be tightened by hand. Cut the warp yarn twice the length from dowel to dowel plus at least 20cm (8in) for tying. Halve the length and hitch the centre over the far dowel and tie it with a snitch knot over the front dowel, after pulling the two ends away from yourself to tighten it as firmly as possible (see illus. 60). Each length thus provides two warp ends and they must be spaced accordingly. Once the required number of warp ends have been tied, weave in several picks of a hard thick yarn to equalize the spacing and to give an edge to weave against.

The scaffolding frame demands a different method for putting sufficient tension on the warps. Tie one end of a ball of warp yarn to the bottom bar of the frame. Then hand the ball up and over the top bar. Take it once round to give purchase and then pull it very tight. The ball is then passed down and under the bottom bar, keeping to the same side of the frame. A turn may be taken round the bottom bar before it is tightened again. Do this for as many warps as are needed plus two extra warps. These are used to guide the weaver in keeping a straight edge. When the warping is completed knot the end to the bottom bar.

To present the warp ready for weaving and to increase the tension, two weft strings are put in (see illus. 61). To enter the first string, the end of the ball of yarn is knotted to the lower edge of one side of the frame. The ball is carried between the warp ends, passing before each near warp and behind the next far warp alternately. After completing the passage pull the thread as tight as possible and knot to the opposite side of the frame. This first string keeps the warp ends in line and in order. The second weft string is entered in the same way but in the opposite order, completing two lines of weaving, equalizing the tension and establishing the setting of the warp ends. Several more picks of weaving should be added to further equalize the warp spacing.

## Tapestry weaving methods

Such a generous amount of weft is needed to make the dense structure of tapestry weaving that it is best controlled in short passages. Wind a small amount of weft around the thumb and little finger in a figure of eight and secure it with a half-hitch. This is called a dolly. Beginning at one edge pick up as many alternate warps as can be held easily, and pull them forward (this is shown in an exaggerated way in illus. 60[5]). If you begin at the left edge do this with the right hand and the left can then pass the dolly through leaving an arc of weft (see illus. 60[6]). Continue across the whole width so that the weft lies in a series of arcs. Then beat down the weft with a tapestry fork or with the fingers, observing that the weft is able to move right round the rigid warps, covering them and filling the spaces between without strain.

Because of this interrupted method of putting in the weft it is feasible to have a number of dollies taken up and woven in turn and left hanging on the front of the work as the weaving progresses. In fact, if a large area of one colour is to be woven it is better to use several dollies of the same colour, taking them to and fro in changing positions along the weaving edge in alternating directions, rather than continuing with one yarn for the whole width. It is easier to maintain the weft fullness in this way, and the turns add subtle detail to the appearance of the weave. Dollies of various colours or yarns can be used to build up areas of colour or surface side by side. The numerous ends can be left hanging, trapped by the tightly packed structure. To have a clear view of the work push them through to the far side, but for speed and efficiency of weaving all ends are best left on the near side of the work. This is suitable for work with a right and wrong side.

Since the beating of the weft is intermittent across the width of the work, any shape may be built up above the rest as long as it does not overtop an unwoven area, making it impossible to open the warps properly for weaving the piece below. Before a widening area can be filled in the surrounding areas must be built up (see illus. 60[7 and 8]).

It is most conducive to confident experimental work if the weaver relies on a minimum of aids for selecting warp ends and beating them down. The hands can easily select and control the work in a small frame loom but, if necessary an aid to the selection of warp ends in a large piece of work can be incorporated into the scaffolding frame. A stick can be passed under alternate warps and hung in position above working level. It is then easy to pick up groups of alternate warp ends from the top of the stick. Cord loops, known as leashes, can be tugged forward in small bunches to raise the other set of warps. Leashes are made from heddle twine. Knot the end of a length of twine round the extra bar at one side, in line with the first pair of warp ends. Pass it down to pick up the further warp end, carry it up and knot it round the bar again. Continue in this way, picking up each alternate end in a loop, or leash. These must be equal in length and should hang in an easy curve (see illus. 61), so that the weaver's hand can reach up and pull them down to raise the required warps.

### Design and structure of tapestry

Choice occurs at every stage in the making of a textile. Even the simple techniques of tapestry weaving suggest opportunities and the need for aesthetic judgment. In the past variations of the basic technique were developed in response to structural needs, as well as to the demands of pictorial expression. In Peruvian weaving, for example, there is a predominance of all-over geometric patterns with recurring slits. Since most of this weaving was used for garments it is likely that the slits not only had visual value but also that they changed the fabric into a structure more sympathetic to the wearer because the slit cloth responded to draping and movement.

So the study of traditional ways of dealing with details of drawing and design is valuable for its help in handling our own attempts at pictorial tapestry and because traditional pieces can provide an understanding of the structure on which such pictorial representation is based. This can be the genesis of ideas more concerned with the structure of tapestry than with what it can portray. The weaver is not concerned with the sort of pictorial representations that are made on paper or canvas. Many of the variations in technique, some of which are described below, cause distortions in the work which are characteristic of tapestry, where forms are described in surface movement as well as in line and colour. For example, the piling of weft in curves disturbs the straight line of the warp, the overlapping of weft at junctions of colour makes a vertical ridge, and the too close insertion of lines of tufts with insufficient space between raises a horizontal ridge. When a flat fabric is intended such distortions are regarded as errors to be avoided and corrected, but the creative weaver may wish to consider the form as well as the surface of the weaving and may therefore control and use such factors as a positive element of design.

The concept of tapestry as a rigid fabric and its restriction to flat rectangular shapes can be reconsidered and its potential explored as a more mobile fabric or as a sculptural medium.

### Variations of tapestry technique

The basic techniques show how shapes and colours can be built up alongside each other. If two such shapes woven in different yarns have vertical edges a division occurs between them. As the wefts turn away from each other they leave a slit. The following examples of the traditional ways of using slits or of avoiding or disguising them indicate the kind of sources that can provide structural motifs.

1 The slit may be emphasized by leaving a single warp end unwoven between the two areas and wrapping it separately in a thread of special colour or quality (illus. 62[6]). This is typical of Peruvian

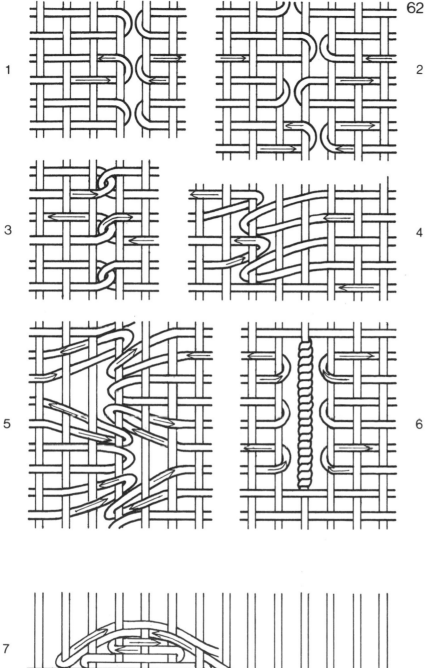

**62** Some vertical joins in tapestry with the weave spread out to make the path of the weft clearer. It is always advisable to bring wefts towards or away from each other (note the direction of arrows).

[1] Vertical slit with clearly defined edges.

[2] Weft turns alternately on each side of one warp end so that the join is flat but there is no slit. The edge is blurred.

[3] Linked vertical turns: each turn must be made correctly for a neat edge.

[4] Turns alternate round the same warp, giving a ridge.

[5] Several consecutive weft picks on one side turn on the same warp. The same is done with the same number on the other side. The groups of weft pack down and give a flat surface with a toothed edge.

[6] Vertical slit with an intervening warp, bound for emphasis.

Outlining shapes in tapestry:

[7] Outlining a shaped area with continuous weft is likely to cause distortion.

[8] A flatter outline is more suitable for outlining steep shapes. A weft pick starts from each side and zig-zags round the form to be outlined, meeting at the top.

Artist: Mollie Picken

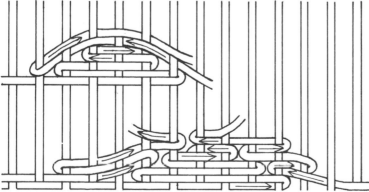

63 *Seascape* by Pam Richardson, 61 × 61cm (24 × 24in). This tapestry was woven in a variety of wools on a cotton lay line warp set at 6epi and approx 41cm (16in) wide. In spite of the shape of the woven area the same number of ends is woven evenly throughout. The imagery has been developed by using subtle changes in the angle of the weave, and the consequent deformation of the woven shape and surface has been wittily commented on by extending the image on to the formal wooden shape that encloses it.
Photo: John Hunnex

weaving. There are examples of fabrics which have been turned into a mesh-like structure by close repetition of the slit motif.

2  The division may be sewn together on the wrong side, using a curved needle. This method keeps the surface flat and creates a feature in which the shadow cast within the slit may be seen as reinforcing the drawing that it indicates.

3  To prevent a slit the two wefts may be crossed over each other before returning (illus. 62[3]). The turning must match the lie of the weft and be consistent, or clumsiness results.

4  Several consecutive wefts from each side of the division in turn may be taken round a central warp end (illus. 62[5]). These beat into a smooth and level fabric and produce a toothed edge to the colours.

5  Each weft may be taken round the same warp end in turn (see illus. 62[4]). This piles the warp into a ridge at the division but blurs the colour separation.

Because the smallest mark that can be made in tapestry weaving is a horizontal mark, and because these marks are most readily put together in lines of weft, the most easily expressed lines and shapes in a design will be those that follow the weft direction. A design with many vertical lines or dominant vertical shapes, therefore, is better managed if woven from the side, so that when taken off the loom it is turned and hung with the warp in a horizontal position and the weft vertical. The large medieval wall tapestries with their standing figures and flame-like foliage are almost always woven in this way. The making of a deliberate choice of direction according to the demands of the design can be seen in Coptic weaving.

Different colours used in sequences in the weft can make varieties of line and colour (illustrated in the fine cotton tapestry weaves by Pam Price on page 134 and in the colour illustration on page 150 where parts of the drawing are conveyed in this way):

1  A single pick makes a dotted line.

2  Two consecutive picks make a wavy line.

3  Alternating lines of colour extending and intersecting from two adjacent shapes make an area of blended colour.

4  Alternating picks of colour make vertical stripes.

5  By reversing the order of the two colours regularly the stripes may be changed into checks.

The forming of shapes is done not only by building them up in horizontal lines of weft as in illustration 63. A curved shape may be drawn in weft by piling lengthening turns of weft over each other or by carrying weft at an angle round an already formed shape (illus. 62[7]). Since this elongates the amount of weft space between warps it is difficult to maintain a flat surface. When tension is released the warps, in adjusting themselves will move out of the vertical position and surface distortion in the way of puckers and blisters may occur which enliven the surface. This is illustrated in the framed tapestry on page 131.

Outlines can be carried round shapes in the same way. If the shape is too steep for the weft to move comfortably in a single line, particularly if it is to go round a humped curve (illus. 62[8]), it is better to build round

# Textile Crafts

**64** Some decorative techniques in tapestry (with the weave spread out).

[1] A twining thread, caught round a warp end when the weft pick is made, catches random warp ends as weaving proceeds.

[2] Discarded warp ends are cut and used as weft to make a shaped edge.

[3] Soumac weft passing over three warp ends and back under one.

[4] Soumac weft passing over three warp ends and back under two.

[5] Soumac weft passing over two warp ends and back under one.

[6] A simple way of putting in fringe or tufts.

[7] Two simple knots for the fringe.

[8] Calculating epi from a thread wound closely round a ruler to a measured width (see page 140). In this example 21 threads represent the number of warp ends, and the spaces needed for the weft to pass through, in this width of fabric.

[9] A cross-section of plain weave. Alternate threads represent 9 warp ends.

[10] A cross-section of 2/2 twill weave. Two out of three thread spaces are 12 warp ends.

Artist: Mollie Picken

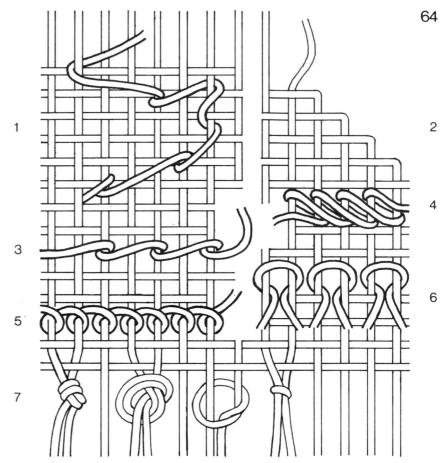

64

1
2
3
4
5
6
7

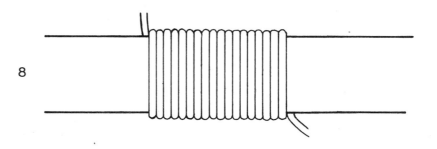

8

9

10

the sides of the shape in a zig-zag movement working separately from each side to the middle.

The overall shape of a tapestry may be established during the weaving process. To make a circular tapestry, for example, leave the warp exposed where it is not needed. The ends are then darned into the back so that they are concealed. Alternatively, as warp ends are no longer needed for weaving, they may be cut off the frame, turned at right angles and woven into the work (illus. 64[2]).

When the whole piece is removed from the loom an edge can be made by knotting or twining the warp ends before darning them in at the back.

Whatever the shape of a tapestry the method of hanging needs to be considered, not after it is completed but while it is being planned. The weaving of a few extra inches for a hem to hold a rod, or the retention of warp ends for loops at strategic intervals may be important factors in the design of the work.

Shaping can also be thought of not in the negative way, of taking away from a rectangular shape, but in a positive way as the narrowing or widening of form. The width of a piece of weaving is the sum of warp ends and intervening weft thicknesses, and therefore a change of width will accompany a change in the structure.

If weaving is begun with two or more ends taken together and woven as one, and these are later separated and woven singly, the weaving will become wider, and the fanning out of the weaving will emphasize this. Thus one might begin with seven three-fold ends, divide them later into fourteen alternately double and single ends, and finally use them as twenty one single ends. In the frame loom, ends can be slid along the rods to assist changes in the way they are weaving. It is also possible to widen the weaving by adding extra warp ends within the fabric. Similarly to make the work narrower warp ends can be discarded at intervals in the width of the weaving, or reduced in number by weaving two or more ends together as one. When the work is taken off the loom it will take on a curved form, the construction being similar to that which can be observed and studied in baskets.

Extra warp ends added between the original warp ends and coloured differently to make identification easier can be woven separately to make a second layer. When the warp is being thus modified during weaving it should be woven from the hitched end up, leaving the knots at the top. These can then be undone and retied as often as is necessary. In weaving areas or strips of a second layer it may be advisable to weave the background first so as not to confuse the warp ends. While untied the extra warp may then be passed between the ground warps, or through slits left in the ground weave so that it can be woven on the other side. Such an experiment must be considered in terms of form since both sides of the weaving become of equal importance.

Weft plays an equal part with warp in the structure of tapestry so changes in shape can also be contrived by changes in the thickness of weft. Indeed when design is deeply concerned with structure the size of yarn becomes of great significance. Even such details as those already

described in connection with definition of line and shape, can become important features if carried out in yarn thick enough to make the structure apparent. Notice in the photograph of Sue Edwards' construction (illus. 67) how such a detail has made a hinge – a significant motif from which an important structure could develop.

The Coptic weavers of the third to the seventh centuries AD in Egypt wove small, beautifully detailed tapestry bands and panels to enhance and to decorate their garments. Lines of drawing which were too fine to be expressed through the normal tapestry weave were put in directly with surface threads. One end of such a thread would be locked into the weaving, left hanging as the work progressed and then carried across the surface where a line was required and twined round a suitable warp. This adds surface tracery as well as definition of drawing to the weaving.

This technique is related to a special structure called Soumac weave associated with the weaving of carpets. In this method a weft pick, instead of passing directly through the shed is carried forwards over two or more warp ends and back under at least one less end. It thus progresses in a series of overlapping floats of weft (illus. 64[3]). Lines made like this must be alternated with plain tapestry weave or the structure will become slippery. The Soumac weave may be used for the whole surface or as a partial embellishment. In both cases the extra weft lies on top of the fabric and causes little distortion. Variations are shown in illustrations 64[4 and 5]. The direction in which the warp ends are picked up is important. It can make the angle of the floats consistent or alternated, both in one pick of work or in consecutive picks.

Many yarns show their full beauty as they hang free. Their cut ends, single or massed, also have a special quality. Short lengths of any yarn can be knotted into a tapestry as the weaving proceeds, singly or in rows separated by picks of weaving. Two simple knots are shown in illus. 64[7]. For an all-over pile the knots should be put in across the whole weft and the rows of knots separated by several rows of plain weaving if it is to lie flat. Any addition of cut yarn will be found to contribute a new quality not only to the surface appearance and the feel, but also to the weight and behaviour of the weaving.

The cut lengths are made by wrapping the yarn round doubled card of suitable width from which it may be cut in equal lengths. These may be introduced singly or in bunches. Folded yarns may be left as loops instead of cut ends. The type of knot used will help to determine the way in which the tufts hang and they may of course be cut to any length. Even the way in which the cut yarn untwists contributes to the character of the work. This can be studied in the variety of effects shown in the characterization of foliage in illustration 71.

### A balanced structure

Narrow loom weaving, in which only the warp is visible, developed among many different and widespread cultures and provided for a

**65** and **66** (*opposite*) Patterns in tapestry weave by Pam Price, in plain and mercerized cottons on plain cotton warp at 8epi, the patterning results from thoughtfully controlled weft colour sequences, which are given extra effect through the choice of matt or lustrous yarns. Strong colours are used. The scale of the components is controlled and suggests how details which appear as features in a design may be rearranged and repeated to become an all-over pattern or a ground weave for other features (see illus. 69).
Courtesy of Liverpool Polytechnic

**67** (*left*) Detail of weaving by Sue Edwards, warp 31cm (12in) wide. This is one of a series of experimental pieces which suggest ways of designing with the structure of weaving. It was made on a frame loom (see page 122). The warp is thick cotton rug warp yarn at 4epi. The weft is of the same yarn. The weave is tapestry weaving over two warp ends at a time. Occasional weft picks are pulled up on the wrong side and knotted so as to gather the work. A piece of sisal rope is bound with rug warp yarn and used as two consecutive picks of weft. This becomes a loop for hanging – a hinge – and a rib, giving form to the gathered material.
Photo: John Hunnex

variety of needs. The strong narrow strips made handles and harnesses, slings and sashes, and could be sewn side by side to make garments, cloths and hangings. The warp was often made between two distant pegs by a child running to and fro with a ball of yarn, and recording the order of warp ends. One end of the warp is attached to a fixed point such as a tree or a hook on a wall. The other extremity is tied to a stick retained across the weaver's lap by a sash round his back. As the weaver leans forward and backward the warp is made easy or taut. Ingenious arrangements of sticks and leashes are used to separate alternate warp ends so that the weaver can lift them to make a space through which he passes a shuttle, trailing weft.

The weft is pulled as tight as possible so that it lies absolutely straight. The warp ends relax to enclose the weft, crammed into their minimum width, and thus maintaining a controlled structure half the width of the total number of ends in the warp.

Elegant devices which can be seen in museums and studied in books on primitive weaving, deal with the problems posed by the length of warp, the build-up of warp in front of the weaver, and the management of the sticks and leashes.

When these parts were put into a frame they evolved into the loom with which we are now familiar, with parts to care for each requirement in the handling of the warp. The length of warp is wrapped round a beam at the back of the loom from which it can be unrolled. The cloth as it is woven winds on to a beam at the front of the loom. Arrangements for lifting selected warp ends to allow for the passage of the weft are hung in the frame above the loom. In floor standing looms these can be controlled by pedals. In addition the warp passes through a reed which spaces it according to the weaver's design. The warp and weft can thus be put together so that they play equal parts in the appearance and construction of the cloth.

If warp and weft play an equal part, a fabric is constructed which drapes either way and stretches diagonally. The variations of design in this type of weaving are infinite, but all may derive from an understanding of the simplest cloth construction, and of the functions of the parts of the loom.

## The loom

The loom provides:
1 A means of relaxing and tightening warp tension.
2 A means of separating the warp ends into a shed through which the weft can pass.
3 A means of controlling the spacing of the warp.

Looms differ greatly in size and construction, but most variations are concerned with more or less elaborate ways of separating the warp ends into a shed. Apart from this the working of one loom can be readily applied to the working of another.

The parts are set in a rectangular frame which may rest on a table or be set on the floor on its own supports.

1 At the back of the loom is a roller called the warp beam on which a warp of some length can be wound. It is held in position in one of two ways. A toothed wheel or ratchet with a pawl can hold the beam in a number of positions at a fixed tension. A friction brake consisting of several turns of rope round the beam with a weight at each end of the rope, the heavier on the outside, provides free tension, with the beam held in any position and able to move in response to the movements of the warp in weaving. The usefulness of a loom is greatly increased if it has two warp beams so that the work can be controlled at two different tensions.

2 About halfway along the loom there is a structure which supports the shed-opening mechanism. A number of rectangular frames or shafts are hung at right angles to the warp. Each carries many cords or wires each with an eye in the centre through which a single warp end passes in a prearranged order. These are called heddles. As the shafts are raised or lowered the warp ends that they carry follow and the shed opens. The arrangement of warp ends that are lifted can be varied according to the number of shafts available, and the sequence in which each one is threaded. The shafts are lifted in different ways. In table looms each shaft is usually hung by a cord or chain. The cord passes through the frame, ending in a knob which when pulled to raise the shaft can be locked in that position. Chains are attached to metal levers which can also be locked when the shaft is in a raised position.

Floor looms have pedals so that the lifting of the shafts can be controlled by the feet while the hands attend to the weaving. In the simplest type four shafts are paired and hung by cords over a pulley. They are attached below to their lam or bar swinging from the side of the loom. The lams are then attached to the six pedals according to the grouping in which the shafts are to be lifted. The most useful and well-balanced tie-up is as follows. The two middle pedals are attached to shafts 1 and 3 and 2 and 4 respectively so that alternate ends can be lifted by pedals 3 and 4; the four outside pedals are attached to shafts 1 and 2, 2 and 3, 3 and 4 and 4 and 1, so that any consecutive combination of pairs of ends can be lifted by depressing pedal 1, 2, 3 or 4.

These attachments are made either by cords or chains. The movement is balanced so that while the pedals depress some shafts, the rest rise. This makes a wide opening for the shuttle and an equal tension on all the warp. Looms with more elaborate means for controlling larger numbers of shafts are available for those wishing to do technically advanced weaving.

3 Between the frames and the front of the loom is the very important spacing equipment. A long narrow frame swings in either a hanging or standing position, being pivoted from the sides of the loom. It carries the reed which has bars set at given numbers per 10 centimetres (dm) or per inch. Reeds are known by this number. In the metric system a 10 reed may indicate either a reed with 10 dents or spaces to the centimetre or a reed with 10 dents to the dm. When the sizing is in inches a 10 reed has 10 dents to the inch. The warp ends pass through the reed spaces in order. The reed swinging in its frame is used to beat down the weft and the distribution of the warp is thus controlled at its moment of entry into the cloth structure. The reed should be made of rustless steel.

4 At the front of the loom is another roller called the cloth beam which can be locked in different positions with a ratchet and pawl. The front of the warp is knotted on to a stick attached to the cloth beam by cords or an apron of cloth. The fabric is wound on to this as it is woven.

### Choosing a loom

When choosing a loom, look for a good length behind the shafts so that an extent of warp is exposed. This allows the tension to even out and also leaves room for a good opening of the shed without strain. The reed should swing near enough to the shafts for a large part of the shed opening to be available to the weaver for putting in the weft. This should also be within comfortable reach of the weaver.

When deciding on the type of loom consider the sort of work likely to be woven on it. Choose a four-shaft loom with six pedals for weaving lengths of cloth in simple weaves. It is kindest to the warp and quick and efficient to use.

If you want to design and experiment, choose a table loom up to 61cm (24in) wide. Do not try to work any wider on a table loom as it is tiring and difficult to manage. Have at least eight shafts to the loom and have it fitted with two warp beams.

## Preparing to weave

To set up a loom in the expectation of making a particular fabric means that detailed preparation must be made. We must know which yarns to choose for the warp. We must decide what colours they are to be. They must be arranged in a reasoned order and spacing. We must know in what order they are to be lifted and how to set up the loom to achieve this, and we must know what yarns woven into the warp will combine with it to produce the fabric we have in mind.

This is a formidable requirement which can only be understood by long experience or by building on known traditions. Both these means are dismaying to the enthusiastic and creative weaver and may appear to hinder originality and innovation in design.

It is tempting to make a random choice of yarns, arranging and weaving them according to fancy, but this is likely to produce disappointing results. At best disordered relationships in yarn structure give no identifiable ideas to develop, and at worst the warp may prove unweavable.

### Planning a piece of work

Before starting a piece of work its exact purpose must be decided. If you want to make fabric by the metre for curtaining or upholstery, or if you want it to make up into garments, begin with a warp about 20 to 25cm (8 to 10in) wide on which to try out different ways of weaving it. From the samples made it will be possible to choose the most suitable design and modify it if necessary.

It is important to start with the correct warp yarn as this will be present in all the samples. Until experience is gained there will be a certain amount of guess-work in making this choice, but a selection between wool, cotton and other materials may be made according to the fabric in mind. Think carefully about the thickness or size of yarn that is chosen. A cloth is at least twice as thick as the yarn of which it is

**68** Hanging by Sue Lewis, 2 × 26cm (8 × 10in). The warp is of 2/12s mercerized cotton set at 16epi and woven on four shafts in a straight draft. The hanging re-creates the mood of sketches of the seashore through the colour and texture of yarns spun and blended from especially dyed fleece which is used freely with a cotton ground weft. Weaving is preceded by painting the warp with dye as part of the colouring of the piece.
Photo: John Hunnex

woven. Get into the habit of examining any fabric that is of interest in order to know what to expect of different kinds of yarn.

If you are beginning weaving and feel overawed by the thought of designing, make the warp for a small article such as a cushion cover, table mat or scarf so that you have a familiar shape in which to arrange your ideas. Use plain white yarn throughout in wool or cotton. This will provide the opportunity to play with weft yarns of different types and colours, in stripes of varying width, at the same time exercising judgment when arranging them in a restricted area.

If you wish to experiment freely use the warp as a notebook or sketchbook, without considering an end product. Set up a plain white warp in the material, such as wool or cotton, whose qualities you wish to explore. If the white of the warp becomes intrusive or boring it can be painted with cold dye – all over, in stripes or as single ends.

### The warp

The warp is a scaffolding or background on which the fabric will be built. It must be recognized that its colour and indeed all its qualities will be modified by the weft, and that the weft yarn is more suitable for adding the richer decorative effects. There are severe practical limitations to the types of yarn that can be used satisfactorily as warp. Since the warp yarns have to pass through the heddles and reed and also have to be stretched and relaxed frequently they should be chosen with at least some of the following features:

1 Strength: a closely-twisted structure made up of more than one strand. Strength is tested not only by trying to break the yarn in the hands. The strain which the warp will undergo is more a matter of friction. If the yarn frays when pulled between the thumbnails it is not likely to survive in the warp.

2 Smoothness: mercerized cottons and linens are more suitable than their untreated counterparts. Hairy yarns sometimes cause the greatest distress of all. As they lie close together in the loom the surface hairs entwine and the constant tearing which accompanies the movements of the shed can destroy the yarn altogether.

3 Consistency throughout the length of the yarn. It is possible to include fancy yarns of irregular structure with loops or other features in the warp, although they are more suitable for weft. They will handle more easily in the warp if they are used as single yarns at intervals among plain yarns.

### Warp calculations

Before beginning to make a warp you must know how many ends of warp will be needed to weave the width of fabric required. In order to work this out consider the structure of plain material in which the warp ends lie side by side, held apart by the thickness of a similar weft yarn pushing in between each one and its neighbour.

To calculate the number of warp ends using metric measurements, wrap a length of yarn round a ruler (illus. 64[8]), laying the turns closely to cover 1cm, and count them. Every other turn represents a warp end lying in the fabric. Half the number is therefore the number of warp ends in 1cm. Ten times this figure (or five times the original total) gives the number of warp ends required to make 1dm (10cm) of plain fabric. This is recorded as ends per dm or e/dm. This calculation determines the choice of reed size and how it is to be threaded.

To calculate the number of warp ends in inches, wrap the length of yarn round a ruler to cover $\frac{1}{4}$in. Half the number of turns gives the number of warp ends in $\frac{1}{4}$in and four times this figure (or twice the original total) gives the number of ends required to make 1 inch of plain fabric. This is recorded as the epi. If the warp yarn is very thick it may be necessary to cover $\frac{1}{2}$ inch to get an accurate estimate of the epi and the calculations will have to be adjusted.

Multiply the e/dm or epi by the width of the warp to find how many warp ends are needed. At least four warp ends at each side must be made double to make a strong selvage. The number should be not less than four, and is usually best calculated in multiples of four. The selvage can vary in width in relation to the total width of the weaving from 6mm or $\frac{1}{4}$in for a warp 20 to 25cm or 8 to 10in wide to 2 to 2.5cm or $\frac{3}{4}$ to 1in for a warp 1m or 36in wide. The extra ends to make the double selvage ends must be added to the total number of warp ends required. Thus if there is to be a selvage of four double ends at each edge, eight ends must be added to the total.

If the weaving is to be a particular width when finished the warp should be made a little wider to allow for the take-up or contraction of the fabric when it is removed from the loom. This cannot be predicted accurately unless samples have been woven and measured.

The warp for a finished piece of known length must have about 10cm (4in) added to the metre or yard for warp take-up and a further 5cm (2in) added to the metre or yard for the shrinkage which will occur particularly in the case of wool or cotton. Approximately 1 metre or 1 yard must be added to the total length required for the part that cannot be woven, and for knotting. The weaver will become familiar with the length needed in his own loom by experience.

It is advisable to weave carefully documented samples, measured before and after washing and pressing, so that take-up and shrinkage can be calculated accurately before starting a piece of work of any size. A warp for samples should be at least 3 metres or yards long, otherwise as much warp will be wasted as woven.

EXAMPLES OF WARP CALCULATIONS
Warp no.: 1
Purpose: samples
Finished length:
Finished width:
Warp length: 3 metres                           3 yards
Warp width: 25cm                                10in
e/dm: 80                                        epi: 20
selvage: 8 (2s) $\times$ 2
Yarn: 2/20s mercerized cotton
No. of ends: (25cm $\times$ 8) + (8 $\times$ 2) = 216    (10in $\times$ 20) + (8 $\times$ 2)
                                                   = 216

Warp no.: 2
Purpose: length of cotton fabric designed in
          warp no. 1
Finished length: 4 metres                       4 yards
Finished width: 95cm                            36in
Warp length: 4m + (11.5cm $\times$ 4)*          4yd + (4$\frac{1}{2}$in $\times$ 4)*
           + 1m waste = 5m 46cm               + 36in waste = 5$\frac{1}{2}$yd
Warp width: 95 + 5cm = 1m                       36 + 2in = 38in
Yarn: 2/20s mercerized cotton
e/dm: 80                                        epi: 20
selvage: 16 (2s) $\times$ 2
No. of ends: (100cm $\times$ 8) + (16 $\times$ 2) = 832   (38in $\times$ 20) + (16 $\times$ 2)
                                                   = 792

*Calculated from measured samples of 11.5cm take-up and shrinkage to the metre or 4$\frac{1}{2}$in take-up and shrinkage to the yard.

**69** [1] The layout of a warp on the warping board. As these boards vary in shape and arrangement no standard diagram can be given for obtaining the length of warp required. Note the positions of the two crosses and the ties. (A) is the back of the warp and (B) is the front.

[2] The warp has been chained and the back stick (C) inserted in the loop. String is tied on the other side of the back cross at (A).

[3] A detail of the next stage in handling the warp. The cross, its ties removed, is spread along the back stick (C) and is then used to select ends in order, so that the proper number can be placed in the spaces between the teeth (D) of the raddle (E).

[4] The arrangement of the front of the warp after the length of it has been wound on to the back beam. The ties have been removed and the two shed sticks (F) have been inserted, one on each side of the front cross and tied. They remain behind the four shafts (G). Each end passes through one heddle (H) and through its space in the reed (K).

Artist: Mollie Picken

## Making the warp

In tapestry weaving the warp yarns may be put on the loom individually. When making a warp of considerable length for a complex loom, however, it must meet the precise requirements of correct and equal length, with the right number of ends in the right order, and no possibility of their being disarranged.

To use a warping-board arrange the pegs on the board to give the required warp length, with at least two pegs for one end of the warp and three for the other. This is shown in illustration 69[1], where a board is shown on which any number of pegs can be inserted. The warp must be started where there are two pegs on which to make the back cross, as at 1 and 2. The warp can be carried to and fro across the board using other pegs until it is the right length and must finish where the front cross can be made on three pegs in a row, as at 3, 4 and 5.

Following illustration 69[1], make a non slip loop in the end of the yarn and put it on peg 1. This will be the back loop of the warp. Carry the yarn outside peg 2, and follow the planned course to the front peg 3, crossing between the two preceding pegs 4 and 5. Go round the front peg 3, cross back between the next two pegs 4 and 5, follow the course again, and cross back between the last two pegs 1 and 2 to be ready to go round and start again. There are now two ends on the board. The two crosses between pegs 1 and 2 and pegs 4 and 5 must be maintained as they are the means of keeping each end in order. As warping continues count the total number of ends put on and tie them in groups of twenty to avoid constant recounting. Keep the tension firm and even all the time. Finish with a non-slip loop round the last peg. Using a different and easily distinguished thread, tie loops round both crosses, and round each half of the warp on either side of them. This secures the crosses and makes them easy to identify and separate later. Tug each loop gently to check that no end is left out. This is a stage at which it is impossible to be too careful. When completely satisfied, slip the larger front loop off the pegs, put in the right hand and draw the next section of warp through. Continue looping the warp through itself as though crocheting, removing it from the board without disturbing it until the back loop is reached. Do not draw this through but leave it ready to start the next operation, which is to spread the warp out to its proper width so that it can take its place in the loom.

## Dressing the loom

SPREADING THE WARP The warp is spread out on a raddle, which has pegs at 1cm ($\frac{1}{2}$in) (or known) intervals and a movable cap. Its length should be a little more than the width of the loom.

Clamp the pegged part of the raddle to the edge of the table; measure and mark where the warp must be placed to be centred in the raddle. Pass the back-stick of the loom through the back loop of the warp as shown in illustration 69[2]. Knot cord to one end of the stick and pass it between the two halves of the warp on the other side of the cross. Tie it to the other end of the stick. Make sure the cross is flat and held securely. Remove the warp ties so the warp can be spread out on the stick.

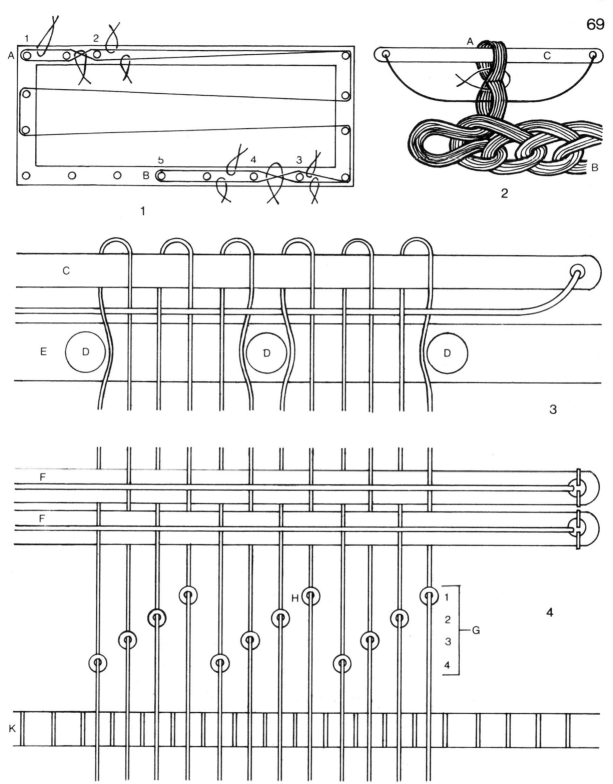

1

2

3

4

Rest the stick behind the raddle dropping the chain into the lap. Remembering how many double ends have been allowed for the selvage and counting them so, and keeping exactly to the order of warp ends in the cross, take the number of ends appropriate to the first raddle-space and drop them in the first marked space. Continue across the whole warp and check that it fills the correct width. Fit the raddle-cap in place and fix it securely. Keep as much of the warp as possible chained up. Every operation should be accomplished with a minimum of effort and disturbance. The distribution of warp ends on the back stick and on the raddle is shown in illustration 69[3].

Remove the raddle from the table and rest it in the loom behind the shafts with the warp chain hanging forwards, tying it securely in the loom. Use the pairs of cords attached to the back beam to tie the back stick in place, parallel and close to the back bar, placing them so as not to interfere with the position of the warp ends as they lie in line with their places in the raddle. Use snitch knots (illus. 60[2 and 3]).

BEAMING This is the process of winding the warp on to the warp beam, with every end in approximately the correct place and at an equal tension. If a warp is put on well it is a pleasure to weave.

The method of beaming described below can be carried out single-handed, with least wear and tear on the warp. It depends on the fact that many yarns have greater strength than a few, and that taut yarns are easier to manage than slack ones.

Begin by sliding the end of a strip of brown wrapping paper, wider than the warp, between the strings and the beam, so that it can wind on with the warp and support it. Then lock the ratchet of the warp beam. Move the heddles to either side, remove the reed and make the centre of the loom as open as possible.

Stand in front of the loom. Take the chain in both hands and undo enough to pass from the back beam through the loom to your hands as you stand well back. This should expose a fair length of straight warp which should not be too disarranged. However tangled or uneven it may seem, resist the temptation to comb it or pull parts of it tighter. Take the whole warp and shake and jerk it firmly. It was made of equal lengths, and if a good length is handled at once, it should soon equalize. If there are tangles, through threads sticking together, pull the whole warp tight with one hand and 'spring' sections of the warp with the other, so as to split the sticking groups without disturbing them. Do not use the fingers as a comb because of the likelihood of tearing the entwined yarns.

As soon as the warp looks even lay it down so that the chain hangs in front of the loom. Lean from the front if possible and without touching the warp turn the warp beam a few times watching that no ends snag round the raddle pegs. Lock the ratchet. Then bracing yourself against the front of the loom, grip the warp and pull hard and firm until it tightens on the beam. Continue in this way until the end of the warp is about 20cm (8in) in front of the heddles, inserting a stick between the warp and the brown paper at different positions on the beam, after every few turns of the beam. This system of putting the ordered warp on slack, pulling it very tight and then allowing it to slacken again means that the ends are all firm and equal round the beam but not so tight as to be stretched and strained. It is important to preserve the roundness and elasticity of the warp yarns. The inserting of brown paper and sticks not only makes this technique possible but also means that when warps with yarns of different size, or with spaces, are put on, these variations will be supported, and thinner yarns will not bed down between the thicker ones.

ENTERING THE HEDDLES (THREADING UP) When most of the warp is safely wound on, the rest of it can be introduced into the lifting and spacing parts.

Take the two warp sticks. These are flat with a hole at each end and are longer than the width of the warp. Slide them between the two layers of the warp, one on each side of the front cross. Tie a cord from end to end of each stick, over the warp. Ensure that the cross is safely secured. Hang the two sticks behind the heddles so that the cross is about level with the heddle eyes and close to them. Calculate the number of heddles needed for each shaft. Move half the excess heddles away to the right so that when the entering is finished there is not an excess of unused heddles weighing down the left of the shafts.

Cut through the end of the warp loop. It is a good idea to cut a few loops at a time from the right, enter them and then cut a few more so as to minimize the chance of the ends falling out of the cross. Sit or stand comfortably close to the heddles. In some large looms parts can be removed so that the weaver can sit inside.

Take a threading hook. Put it through the first heddle-eye on the first shaft and pull through the first two ends. Taking the proper number of double ends for the selvage at the start and again at the end, continue drawing each end in order through the first heddle-eye on the next shaft, according to the predetermined order. As entering proceeds the ends drawn through can be bunched and looped in half-bows to keep them from falling back. Check the entering all the time. Mistakes must be corrected immediately. If overlooked they can involve re-threading the whole warp.

ENTERING THE REED Put the reed, of correct size, into the reed-holder. Mark the part to be threaded so that the warp is centred. Undo the bunches of ends and using a flat reed-hook draw the appropriate number of ends through each reed space or dent (see illus. 69[4]). Use this opportunity to re-check the threading. Loop groups of ends in slip-knots again to prevent them slipping back.

TYING THE WARP TO THE FRONT BEAM Carefully remove the cords supporting the shed-sticks and draw the warp forwards so that it lies horizontally in the loom. See that the strong front stick is tied by pairs of cords in snitch knots to the cloth beam, or to a stick in the hem of an apron of cloth attached to the cloth beam. It must be parallel with the beam. Start in the centre. Take a group of ends about 15 to 20mm ($\frac{1}{2}$ to $\frac{3}{4}$in) wide and stroke the ends even. See that they are not caught by the shed-sticks. Take the bunch over the front stick, part it, bring the two parts up on each side of the bunch behind the stick and tie singly over the top, pulling tight. Working from the middle and alternately from side to side, tie the rest of the warp. Bunches should be narrow enough for there to be little deviation from the straightness of the ends, but not so small that they are pulled too tight.

Go back to the first bunch tied, draw the two ends up tight and tie a bow. When the whole width is tied, drag the back of the hand across the warp with the eyes shut, and sense any differences in tension. Correct these by tightening or slackening the appropriate bows. This can be a moment of great satisfaction: the warp so recently disarranged and vulnerable, is now set in order and under perfect control, ready for the shuttle.

## The weaving process

Lift the shafts that raise every other end across the warp and put a narrow warp stick into the shed. Beat it into place. Make the opposite shed and put a similar stick into it. This will firm the tension and spread the warp from the bunches. Put weft on to a stick shuttle. Open the first shed with the reed back against the heddles. The left hand lies on the reed. Put the shuttle into the shed with the right hand, aiming slightly towards the reed and close to it thus utilizing the major space in the shed and making it difficult to pick up unwanted ends. Draw the shuttle out quickly with the left hand, only as far as is needed to clear the warp. An artistic flourish will only release an unmanageable length of weft from the shuttle. The weft should pull sharply at the selvage at an angle of about 30 degrees. Use the free right hand first to grip it at the selvage, and then to stop the weft in the centre moving while the left hand draws it down to a sharp angle at the other selvage. The weft should make a slightly flattened triangle. The right hand brings the beater down to push the weft straight and into place. To make this triangular weft shape is important. It is neat and economical at the selvages but as the sloping centre part meets the beater it is rippled away to spread itself generously through the warp. The fabric must contract a little in width as it moves away from the reed but there must always be enough weft to permit it to stretch to meet the beater without strain.

If the loom is operated by pedals the weaving sequence can become much more rhythmic as the feet operate the shafts while the hands cope with shuttle and beater. If in addition a roller shuttle is used it should trail the right amount of weft and the hands need not stop to arrange it.

The sequence of weaving becomes:

1 Pedal as first hand takes beater back.
2 Second hand enters shuttle.

3 First hand catches and draws out shuttle.

4 Second hand beats once as shed closes.

It is important to beat as the shed closes and not to take the beater back until the shed has been reopened. This locks the weft in place in one movement. In this way the repetitive movements of weaving will be done with economy of time and effort on the part of the weaver and a minimum of wear and tear on the warp.

## Design: simple weaves

There are weaves for creating special structures and effects for which the shafts must be threaded and lifted in particular patterns. Most of these are developments of the simplest weaves. If these are studied and the way to use the shafts and heddles understood, it will be possible to progress to more complicated weaves, and to use them in original ways.

### The use of shafts

It is one thing to have a warp in the loom and instruction in how to weave. This is a straightforward skill which can be learnt and perfected with practice and observation. What cannot be told, and what must be decided for oneself, is in what sequences and groups to lift the shafts, and what yarns to use for weft. These two choices are closely interrelated.

Go back to the loom threaded in a straight sequence and number the shafts from the nearest, (one), to the furthest, (four). Before beginning to weave lift each shaft in turn, and then in each possible combination, and notice what happens:

a Lift every fourth end so that weft laid across will be very exposed.

b Lift three out of every four ends so that weft laid across will be almost hidden.

c Lift two adjacent ends leaving two ends down between each pair.

Each of these three possibilities can be lifted in four positions. For example, in (a) you can lift each shaft in turn to make four picks. Any such lifting of shafts in a progressive sequence makes a twill weave.

d Lift alternate ends across the warp, and lower them to lift their opposites.

This makes plain weave.

PLAIN WEAVE This is the simplest and commonest structure in weaving. Each weft pick passes over and then under every warp end. Because the threads are interlocked at every position in the weave it is potentially a firm structure. Nowhere is the weaving more than two threads thick. If the warp and weft are of similar size they will play an equal part in the appearance of the fabric so that if, for example, they are of different colours, these will be blended. The notes on the calculation of warp spacing are based on the construction of plain weave and if this is properly worked out and woven, there should be about as many picks as ends to the centimetre or inch.

**70** *Flambeaux* by Enid Russ, 43 × 64cm (17 × 25in). Two warps were made for this small hanging. The first warp is of 3/18s plain cotton, dyed blue and then festoon dyed in brown (the warp is looped over sticks suspended in a dye-bath so that colour only occurs in parts of the warp). It is entered at 24epi on shafts 3 and 4 of a four-shaft loom. The second warp of 2/6s plain cotton is half as long again as the first and also festoon dyed. It is entered as intervening stripes on shafts 1 and 2 at 12epi and is carried on a weighted stick at the back of the loom so that it can be pulled up independently of the rest of the warp. The weft is raffia. Its stiffness is necessary for controlling the structure of the loosened and manipulated extra warp as it twists and re-enters the weaving. Photo: John Hunnex

TWILL WEAVES These are weaves in which a pattern of intersection in one pick is moved along to begin one end later in the next pick, and so on. The weaves made in this way are dominated by diagonal lines. If two adjacent ends out of four are lifted in sequence this makes a 2/2 twill with the warp and weft showing equally on the surface of the cloth. In this fabric there are less intersections than in plain weave and so the calculation for warp spacing must be modified. Weft passes between every second warp end and therefore two out of three of the threads counted on a given space on a ruler are warp ends. The warp must be spaced closely enough for the weft to beat down to give about the same number of picks as ends to the centimetre or inch, and the diagonal line of the weave should be at an angle of 45 degrees. Illustration 76 shows how to adapt the method of calculating e/cm and epi for plain weave, to any other construction by analyzing the arrangement of weft intersection.

This balance is important when designing cloth. If the warp is too open the fabric will be stiff and unbalanced because there are too many weft yarns packed down on to the over-spaced warp, rather like the structure of tapestry. The fabric will not have good draping qualities.

## Design: developing simple weaves

Weaving is made up line by line. These lines are the first and most natural motifs with which to design. Experiment thoughtfully with changes in the colour and texture of weft yarns to make stripes. Consider the infinite variety with which they may be planned, both in width and arrangement, and it will become apparent that a personal statement can be made without deviating from the simplest weaves. Two picks make the smallest possible stripe, and even one pick makes a speckled line. There is no upper limit to the width of a stripe. Widths, colours and tones of stripe may be contrasted or complemented. Stripes may be made within stripes, and they may be increased and decreased in width to convey shading. This is a way of designing which can be managed better in weaving than in any other medium. Keep these apparently simple notions very much in mind and as your vocabulary of weaves increases you will find many personal ways of using them.

Simple plain and twill weave constructions can be developed to make elaborate and interesting fabrics. The methods, once understood, can also be used to transform complicated weaves.

### Simple weaves as ground weaves

Weaves such as plain and twill can be used as a background for both formal and free decoration. Yarns which would be too thick to take their place in the ground structure can be put in as surface weft in various ways. An example can be seen in the horizontal lines of fancy yarns in the illustration on page 118. Such methods can be used for yarns of any kind and the weight and character of the fabric will be

changed. The surface addition of very fine yarns modifies the colour, weight and texture of a fabric in a subtle way (see illus. 73).

To introduce extra weft while proceeding with a simple weave and before changing from one pick to the next, lower only one of the two shafts that are raised so that one shaft is raised and three shafts are down. The weft put through this shed will lie on top of the one just woven. This introduces a three-dimensional quality into the weaving which can be used to change, to enrich, or to define a new design. Thicker yarns can lie comfortably in this way, adding weight and a horizontal emphasis to the fabric (illus. 75).

Brocading is a method of introducing intermittent or isolated motifs. The ground must be woven continuously. Extra weft, entered with a single shaft lifted, can be put in as short lengths making lines or marks on the fabric. It can turn to and fro on the surface, and the ends can be pushed to the back or left on the surface (illus. 73). Surface weft can be prepared as small dollies (see page 127) and laid to and fro on the surface. One shaft will be lifted at a time and the shafts should be varied to keep the warp tension even. The shapes of motifs can be drawn lightly on the warp with a felt-tip pen before weaving. Brocading also adds weight to the fabric according to the spacing and solidity of the brocaded shapes.

Loops of yarn lying on the surface of the fabric, whether they are closely packed, sprinkled regularly or isolated, will change the quality and appearance of a fabric even more dramatically. Weft is put loosely into a shed and before it is beaten into place, it is picked up with a

**71** and **72** *Sefton Park* (detail) woven by Sue Lewis, 77 × 66cm (30 × 26in). This park scene (complete below in illus. 72), developed from colour sketches of the subject, is woven on a two-shaft rug loom. The warp is of 6/14s cotton lay line. Most of the weaving is in simple tapestry technique. The white background is woven in mercerized cotton, and the weft for the coloured ground is blended from strands of fine wool and rayon. The increasing use of soft yarns towards the top implies distance. Details are emphasized with loosely made Soumac weave, with cut and uncut tufts knotted in. The regular structure of the bridge is indicated by the use of alternate black and white weft picks.
Photo: John Hunnex

**73** *(above)* Detail of weaving by Enid Russ. The yarn is 2/28s botany wool, woven on a four-shaft loom, using a straight draft. The entering varies freely between one and two ends per dent in a 14 reed. The warp is partly dyed. These two factors are solely responsible for modifying the colours of the weft, as similar yarn and plain weave have been used throughout. The same yarn is also used to brocade small areas: the brocading yarn is pulled in a doubled loop repeatedly from the same side of a shape with one shaft lifted, enriching the surface with the doubled weft, and outlining the shape on one side with curls or loops.
Photo: John Hunnex

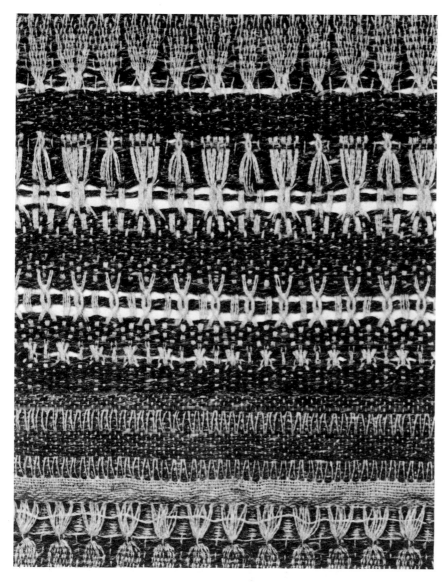

**75** Detail of sample weaving by Julia Turnbull, 42cm (16in) wide. The warp is of 2s blackface wool set at 20epi entered in a straight draft on eight shafts. The weft is of the same blackface wool, berber wool and a gimp wool. The stiffness of the worsted style warp expresses with clarity the twisted structures that the artist has manipulated, and contrasts with the dense passages of berber yarns and gimp.

Compare this woven piece with the drawn thread sampler (illus. 33).

Photo: John Hunnex

**74** *(opposite page) Figure 2* by Noel Chapman, 21 × 31cm (8 × 12in). The warp is 2/12s white mercerized cotton at 24epi and is woven in 3/1 twill on a four-shaft loom. The weft is made of two strands of mercerized cotton in yellow and blue and one strand of looped rayon space-dyed in navy and scarlet. This primary colour combination, broken by diagonal lines of white warp makes a steely ground effect which sets off the numeral most skilfully since its origin was on an old locomotive in York Railway Museum. To make the numeral, every other cotton weft is pulled up in loops over a 4mm (size 8) knitting needle between every four ends in a staggered pattern. This makes a good density of pile and a clear delineation of the number in a different colour from the ground weave.

Photo: John Hunnex

darning needle or stick to make rows of loops (see illus. 74). Weave several picks to lock the loops in position before withdrawing their support.

The weft may be pulled up to make isolated random loops or left to hang from the surface as wisps or threads. This way of using scraps of yarn or fibre can add delicate effects to the weaving, exposing qualities in the yarn which are hidden when it is trapped in the weaving. They can be related to warp and weft stripes which they may extend, cross, fill or change in many ways.

When the surface is not too compact, and if loosely twisted or looped yarns are used it may respond to brushing with a stiff, preferably wire, brush. This must be done in a sensitive way so as to tease fibres out of the cloth structure without tearing the fabric. The brushing should

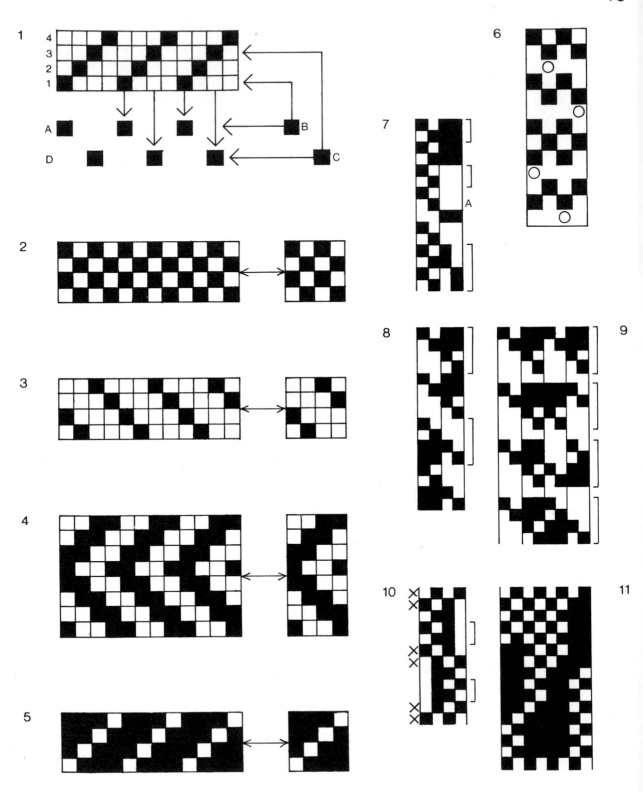

continue until there is a sleek surface in which the fibres are amalgamating with the fabric. This can merge colour in a subtle way and create a fabric of rich, soft handle, with a very special appearance. Experiments should be made in brushing fabrics that feature colour in stripes or checks, and restricted to parts of the design so that brushed and unbrushed surfaces complement each other.

## Spacing simple weaves

When the weft is about to be beaten down the beater may be withheld to leave the warp exposed in an unwoven horizontal strip. This idea can be repeated to make open stripes and light-weight fabric. Narrow unwoven stripes can be controlled by hand, but to control the width of deeper unwoven bands fold a piece of stiff paper to the required width and put it in as weft. It can be removed later to leave the space. In plain weave the picks on each side of the piece of paper will be in the same shed and likely to float together. Therefore make two strips of paper each half the width of the space required and weave them into consecutive sheds, removing them when the weaving is finished.

Spaces may also be left in the warp to make open vertical stripes. These can be combined with unwoven weft stripes to make a lacy fabric.

Unwoven bands can be made more decorative and less insecure achieving effects reminiscent of drawn-thread work (see illus. 75 and 77). Take short lengths of weft and use them to twist, twine or knot, or otherwise bind or bunch warp yarns in the course of weaving. They should not be pulled so tightly that the woven part is strained, nor should the beater be brought down so as to tear the warp – it must be able to spread back to its position in the reed when ordinary weaving is resumed.

# Recording and describing

A code in which the threading and weaving of a fabric can be recorded is as important to the weaver as musical notation is to the musician. Point paper in styles to suit any type of weaving is used. Handweavers are recommended to use good-sized squares divided into eights, but any squared paper will do. In the illustrations (76 and 78) marked squares are solid but any mark such as a stroke, dot or circle can be used; solid squares and circles differentiate between two warps.

## The draft

This makes a graphic record of the shape of the entering of the warp. Each shaft is represented by one horizontal line of squares. Ends are represented by the vertical lines of squares in the same block. The shaft on which each end is entered is marked.

## The lifting pattern

The horizontal lines in the draft are extended to the right and then

**76** Setting out weaving particulars.

[1] The draft records the arrangement in which the warp is entered in the heddles. Each of the four horizontal rows of squares represents one shaft. Each vertical row of squares represents one warp end and the marked squares show the shaft on which it is entered. Compare with (G) and (H) in illustration 69 [4]. The arrows are the lifting patterns. Each horizontal row represents one pick and the marked squares show which shafts are lifted. For example, (B) on column 1 is read along shaft 1 and the marked squares on that line are recorded in line with (B) at (A). (C) can be treated similarly in line with (D). It is in column 3 and is read along shaft 3.

The pattern of marked squares produced is the design which describes the pattern of intersection of the weave, black squares mean warp up.

[2] The design for plain weave.

[3] Weft-faced twill – 1/3

[4] 2/2 twill reversed.

[5] Warp-faced twill – 3/1.

[6] A suggested lifting pattern for brocading. The normal marking provides plain weave. The lifts marked with an O can be used for extra weft.

[7 to 11] Lifting patterns to use with drafts 78 [2 to 6]. Brackets show sections that can be repeated.

[7] Possible lifts for draft 78 [2]. A is the lift that can be used for inserting a rod to make loops.

[8] Lifting patterns for double weave, on four shafts (see 78 [3]).

[9] Lifting patterns for double weave on eight shafts (see 78 [4]).

[10] Lifting patterns for distorted weaves on four shafts (see 78 [5]).

[11] Lifting patterns for distorted weaves on eight shafts (see 78 [6]). Try a thick thread for weft when using lifts marked A.

Artist: Mollie Picken

**77** Ways of enriching warp and weft spacing: decorating unwoven warp.
[1] Manipulated leno weave.
Decorating spaced warp.
[1] Weft bouquets.
[3] Spanish lace.
[4] Looped weft.
Artist: Mollie Picken

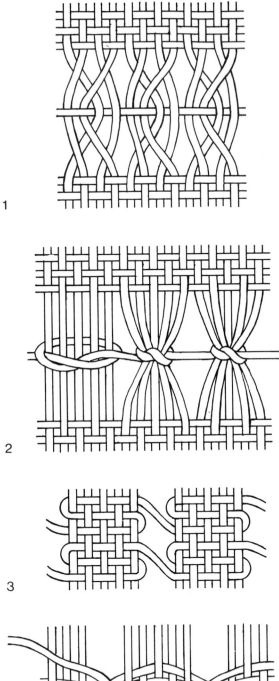

1

2

3

4

turned downwards in sequence at right angles. The top line of the draft relates to the right-hand vertical line. Each shaft is represented by a vertical line. Each pick is represented by a horizontal line of squares. The shafts that are lifted for each pick are marked.

### The design

This is the recording on squared paper of the pattern of warp and weft intersections as the fabric is woven. In straightforward structures the design may resemble the weaving, but if there is distortion or double cloth, the connection between design and weave is less easy to follow. Illustration 76[1] shows how to set out the draft and lifting pattern so that they can be read together to give the design. The arrows show how to relate the shafts lifted to the warp ends, so that the squares can be marked in the design. These marked squares indicate that the warp is lifted. This means that consecutive vertical marked squares indicate warp floats. Consecutive horizontal unmarked squares indicate weft floats.

## Extensions to plain weave

An imaginative use of shaft threading in plain weave may be applied to other weave constructions, transforming them as completely as the elementary structures.

### Distorted plain weave

Plain weave can be woven on a minimum of two shafts. Therefore if a loom has four shafts the warp can be threaded in sections, the first with ends alternating on shafts one and two, the second on shafts three and four, and continuing thus across the warp.

By lifting alternate shafts you can still weave plain fabric right across the width but if the shafts are lifted in any other order the weft in the alternate stripes behaves differently. It is a good idea to analyse what can happen to one pair of shafts, say one and two, while three and four continue with plain weave, and to investigate the warp in this way.

Four different movements are possible for one pair of shafts:
1 Both shafts can be down so that the weft lies on top.
2 Both shafts can be up so that the weft is carried beneath.
3 The odd-numbered shaft is up.
4 The even-numbered shaft is up.

Any of these positions can be maintained by one pair of shafts while several picks are woven with the other two shafts alternating and thus plain weave can be maintained on shafts one and two while the other pair move independently. It is established that the warp can be controlled separately in vertical divisions by different groups of shafts. The more shafts there are the more elaborate the weaves that can be put together (as suggested in illus. 78). There are endless permutations possible in this use of four shafts. The variations can be carried on continuously or as isolated features with both pairs of shafts reverting

**78** [1] The layout of a warp in the loom when two separate warps are used at once. Compare with illus. 69.

A marks the stick used with the ground warp.

B marks the sticks used with the extra or second warp.

The two back sticks and the two pairs of shed sticks keep the two warps separate until they come together through the heddles and reed.

Drafts for extended uses of plain weave.

[2] Suggestions for drafting plain fabric with an extra warp. Ground warp is shown as solid squares. Extra warp is shown as circles. Brackets underneath show that the extra warp ends go into the same dents in the reed as the ground warp. It is assumed that the ground is entered at 2 ends in each dent.

[3] Draft for double cloth using four shafts. The ends to be used for each cloth are indicated by different markings.

[4] Draft for double cloth using eight shafts.

[5 and 6] Drafts for distorted weave using four or eight shafts. An end on an even-numbered shaft is always followed by an end on an odd numbered shaft for plain weave to be maintained across the fabric.

Artist: Mollie Picken

to plain weave. Every structure should be related thoughtfully to yarns of different colour, size and texture. This type of draft provides opportunities for the weft to play a more positive part in the design, weaving in and out of the fabric and then emerging in floats with its colour and character undiluted.

### Extra warp on plain weave

The warp can be used to make vertical rather than horizontal emphasis. An extra warp can be introduced for this purpose. Two shafts, the two nearest the weaver, are used for a plain ground fabric. They are chosen because they will carry most ends and it is an advantage for them to have the maximum opening of the shed. Shafts three and four carry the ends which will make the extra warp. The ends entered on shaft three can be used in the fabric independently of those entered on shaft four.

The denting of this type of warp needs special consideration. If the extra warps are scattered intermittently across the fabric it will probably be best to have a ground weave of regular denting. The extra warps are then entered in the same dents as the ground warp end alongside, and do not add to the width of the warp. This is shown in the brackets under the draft in illustration 78[2] and in the work layout (illus. 78[1]).

This is a warping arrangement for which it would be very useful and exciting to have two warp beams in your loom, mentioned when the choice of a loom was discussed. This is shown in illustration 58 where a spaced extra warp of fancy yarns weaves loosely through a ground fabric. Two warp beams were used to control the differences in yarn and weave.

If the loom is so equipped, make the two parts of the warp separately. Make one warp for the ground weave that is to be threaded on the front two shafts, and wind on to the nearer warp beam. Then make a second warp of the extra ends that is to darn in and out of the length of the fabric and after careful raddling so that the extra ends are superimposed on the correct ground weave ends, wind them on to the further warp beam.

Hang the two warps close behind each other so that the ends can be taken from either warp for threading, and then draw them in the reed and tie up as usual (see illus. 78[1]).

The simplest use of this drafting and warping arrangement is to weave plain weave on the front two shafts while the two shafts carrying the extra warp remain in the up or down position together or separately, for a certain number of picks. This will make patterns of warp floats on the surface of the fabric. As these are not being intersected in the cloth as much as the ground weave they are likely to become slack and so the beam on which they are wound can be tightened to compensate for this.

While the extra ends are in a lifted position an implement similar to those suggested for making loops can be laid beneath them and the extra warp beam eased so that loops can be made. The needle or rod

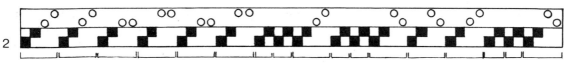

## 78

2

1

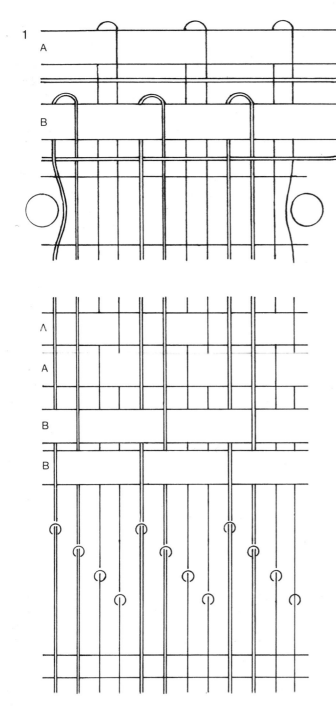

A

B

3

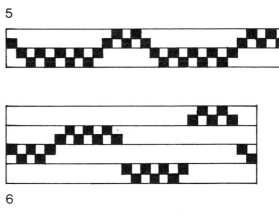

4

5

6

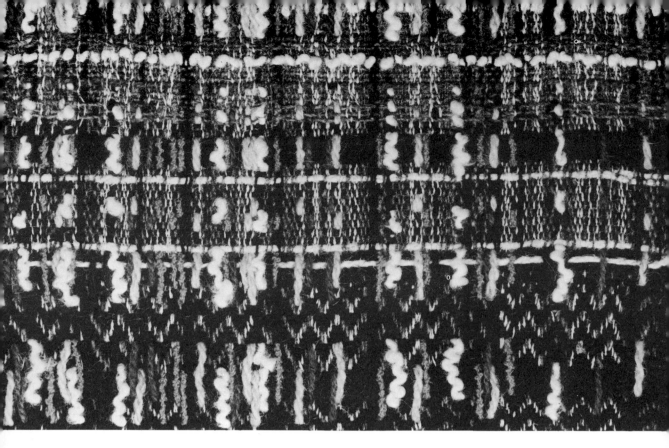

**79** Detail of sample weaving by Inese Aivars, 42cm (16in) wide. This sample shows design as an expression of the structure of fancy yarns. The ground warp is of a free mixture of natural wool singles entered on six shafts in a point draft at 16epi. The gimp and rug wools are beamed on a second warp beam and entered occasionally, and in addition to the ground warp in the reed. They occupy two shafts alternately. This extra warp darns in and out of the ground fabric. The lengths of floats are successfully calculated to display the form of the yarns. There is also an interesting relationship with the rare picks of similar yarn.
Photo: John Hunnex

must not be removed until the weaving is secure. This is a very simplified version of the making of velvet and pile fabrics. The lifted extra warp can also be used to hold down extra weft, or it can be laced and bound as described for unwoven warp (page 155).

This is an idea which can be explored whenever there are more shafts available to the weaver than are needed for a particular structure, and made much more flexible if there are two warp beams in the loom.

## Double cloth in plain weave

If plain cloth can be woven on two shafts, then two plain cloths can be woven on four shafts. If they are to be superimposed the threading for each cloth must be alternated. This is usually done in a straight draft with every other pair of ends serving the same fabric. If the structure of each is to be sound the equivalent ends from each layer must enter the same dent in the reed. Therefore the whole warp is entered twice as close as it would be if it were a single fabric (illus. 78[4]).

The best weaving sequence is to lift the shafts making the upper layer and weave two picks on the underneath one. Then leaving this down weave two picks on the upper layer and continue thus. By changing the cloths over at intervals the two layers become one interesting fabric with horizontal tubes. Padding can be inserted between the layers and if the two layers are made in separate warps, one of them can be tightened so that the other makes a loop or tuck. This simple structure opens many possibilities for bold manipulation.

160

## Cloth finishing

A piece of work taken from the loom is not a fabric. It is still only a piece of weaving, often awkward in structure because its component yarns are stiff from the tensions and pressures of the loom. It is necessary for the yarns to be relaxed, but this must be done not only without disturbing the structure, but so that the appearance of the weave and the handling of the cloth are enhanced.

The most effective finishing aid is water to which fibres respond in their own different ways. Care must be taken to use it appropriately. Check that dyes are fast before wetting coloured work, especially in warm water. Normally wash and rinse in hand-warm water at the same temperature. Iron on the wrong side over a thick pad, especially if surface features need to be raised, not flattened. If washing is unsuitable the weaving may be steamed. Experiment with samples, considering this as much a part of designing as all the previous processes.

Cotton shrinks in water because the yarns absorb it and swell, causing the construction to cramp and lock. Wash and rinse in warm water. If you iron cotton with a hot iron while it is still damp you will be able to stretch the fabric and restore it to its original size. Fine cottons can be given much more quality and firmness if they are lightly starched.

Linen responds to similar treatment. Because of its inelasticity and stiffness the yarns do not readily cohere as they are woven. This cohesion can be encouraged, and a smooth, polished, flexible fabric developed, by the process of beetling. Lay the damp fabric absolutely flat between sheets of stiff clean paper and hammer it methodically all over with a mallet. Keep looking at the effect so that you can stop as soon as you are pleased with the result. Press dry with a hot iron.

Wool if oiled must be scoured in a dilute solution of washing soda to sponify the oil which can then be rinsed out. Soda must not be used on unoiled wool and if it or other yarns are mixed in the weaving, the fabric had best be washed in soap flakes until the oil is removed, and then it must be thoroughly rinsed.

In water, wool fibres move and migrate from yarn to yarn, shrinking and felting the cloth. Rubbing and squeezing encourages this. The fabric should be treated during washing according to the effect desired. Warm wet wool is very plastic but as it dries it will set in shape. Washed woollen samples should be placed on a soft board, worked into shape, pinned out accurately and left to dry.

Large pieces, or woollen samples which are being shrunk, are dried on a roller, or any cylindrical wooden shape. It should have an end-to-end groove to take a rod so as to preserve a smooth circumference. Do not use metal pins or rods as these will rust. Grip the end of the cloth with the stick in its groove and roll it on absolutely smooth and true. Hold down the other end of the cloth with a flat stick tied on to the roller clear of the cloth. Any grooves, creases or distortions will remain in the cloth. The roller is stood on one end to drain, and reversed after twenty-four hours so that the cloth does not sag to one side. As it dries under its own pressure the fabric retains its quality.

# Crochet
## Eve de Negri

The image of crochet has changed. Now the emphasis is on the use of interesting textural contrasts, on innovation and pleasing design. Fixed rules have been swept aside making way for a more inspirational and creative style. A beautiful piece of crochet may exhibit but one or two of the simplest stitches.

In the past much attention was paid to technicalities and to the use of complicated stitches for their own sake. Technique is no longer the 'master'. Stitches are more likely to evolve from the needs of the inventive designer, through working directly with the materials. It is better to learn by doing, exploring and discovering as the crochet develops. Experimentation and personal discovery allow the inspiration to flow from the crochet itself, one row inspiring the next.

Crochet responds to unorthodox methods and to unplanned ideas. It may be added to at any time – an edge is an invitation to grow a shape for a few more rows or add a border. Crochet is fast and easy to accomplish; because it is an 'instant' craft something is being made as soon as the work is started.

80 Wall hanging by Eve de Negri, approx. 76cm (30in) long. In natural colours incorporating unspun fleece, this piece includes a wide variety of crochet stitches (double, treble, shell and various lengths of chain) to create solid and open areas. The more textured side of the stitch (the 'wrong' side in conventional crochet) is used in places to contribute to the rugged effect. Photo: John Hunnex

## Stitches

The basic stitches of crochet are chain stitch (ch st), slip stitch (ss), single crochet (sc), double crochet (dc), treble (tr), double treble (dtr) and triple treble (tr tr) (see illus. 81). Linked chain stitches form the beginning of most crochet, as the 'cast-on' step known as the foundation chain (fch).

There is a difference in the stitch names given to crochet stitches in the USA and the UK. It is most important to note the differences between the two and establish that it is known which is being used. Because the American names better reflect the symbols used instead of

| BRITISH STITCH | AMERICAN STITCH | STITCH HEIGHT IN CHAINS | NUMBER OF WRAPS OVER HOOK | NUMBER OF TURNING CHAINS EQUAL TO HEIGHT OF STITCH |
|---|---|---|---|---|
| Chain | Chain | 1 | none | none |
| Single | Slip | 1 | none | none |
| Double | Single | 1 | none | 1 |
| Half treble | Half double | 2 | 1 | 2 |
| Treble | Double | 3 | 1 | 3 |
| Double treble | Treble | 4 | 2 | 4 |
| Triple treble | Double treble | 5 | 3 | 5 |
| Double triple | Triple treble | 6 | 4 | 6 |

**81** Crochet stitches (US names) and their symbols:

[1] Chain stitch: all crochet builds on a base of chain stitches.

[2] Slip stitch (UK single crochet): a joining stitch which adds no height.

[3] Single crochet (UK double crochet): the shortest of the basic stitches.

[4] Half double crochet (UK half treble): taller than single crochet.

[5] Double crochet (UK treble crochet): twice as tall as single.

[6] Treble crochet (UK double treble): produces looser work.

[7] Double treble crochet (UK triple treble): one stitch taller than treble.

[8] Triple treble crochet (UK quadruple treble): the tallest of the stitches, it produces the loosest work.

[9] Shell: a group of three or more stitches worked into one stitch.

[10] Puff: a cluster stitch variation in a closed pattern.

[11] Cluster: two or more stitches gathered into a group.

Artist: Mollie Picken

words in many published patterns, these have been used throughout this chapter.

Chain stitch, slip stitch and single crochet are low stitches and have no wraps (without height); the other stitches obtain their respective height from the number of wraps which have to be worked off before the stitch is completed, each wrap (or wool round hook, wrh) giving extra height except in the case of half double crochet (half treble UK).

Chain stitch is the lowest stitch in crochet, so called because there are no wraps before the stitch is made. Chain stitches have many uses: to make increases to cover holes and slits, to suspend decorations and hangings, for fringes and for open areas (mesh patterns) and many other purposes. Chains may be single (as above), double or treble. Double and treble chains make thick ropes and are good for belts, necklets, girdles and so on. They can be used for the foundation chain if a strong edge is needed. When making double chain the new stitch is always worked off from the stitch at the left of the chain. Short lengths of chain are useful for making open areas. Chain loops are often joined to the main edge with slip stitches.

## Basic principles and experiments

The basic stitches should be learned and practised until they can be made effortlessly. With practice, rhythm and speed are improved, contributing to a better appearance of the finished crochet. The simplest way to start using the stitches is with a medium sized hook, such as an F or G (USA) 5 or 6 (UK). Holding it with the hook turned towards you, loop some yarn, such as a three or four ply sport-type yarn, over your fingers, make a slip knot (illus. 98[1]), and make a foundation chain. Turn the row and try to work some basic stitches into the foundation chain.

Work freely – anything that can be managed with a hook and yarn is acceptable at this stage. Let the rows grow in a creative way. Rather than waste time trying to get perfection, work on, and try to understand why the experiments are not 'perfect'.

Get to know the tools and materials by experimenting with the same stitch using different yarn. Then try the same stitch with a different hook, compare the samples and file the results for reference.

Collect and identify all the different yarns that are available. The range is enormous. Natural and synthetic, dyed and undyed, spun, partly-spun and unspun, novelty bouclé, mohair, cow-hair, string, raffia and many metallic and other fibres give interest to crochet (also, see Chapter 1). The collection could be labelled and filed for reference.

The texture of the yarn affects the appearance of the colour, too: shiny yarns look quite different from matt ones.

Colour is very important in crochet. It sets the mood and character of the project. Well used, colour can highlight important areas of a design. Notice colour in everyday life and in nature. Experiment with cut-out random shapes of different colours, laying them down in some

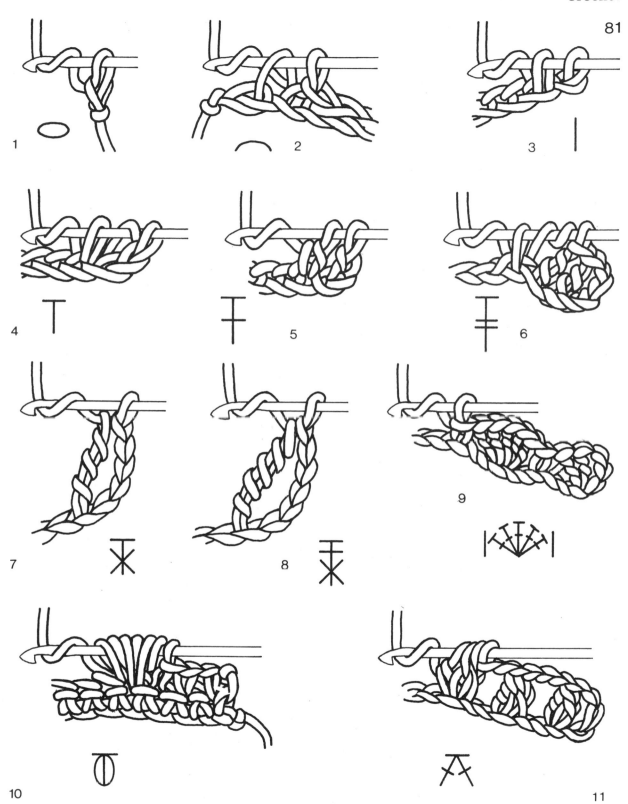

1

2

3

4

5

6

7

8

9

10

11

**82** An abstract design and subsequent meanderings, outlining simple shapes, that could relate to a cellular structure or to the flax fibres shown in illustration 8. It is also reminiscent of a section through an agate. The use of different but related colours and textures of yarns, of various hook sizes and of a variety of stitches (single, half double and double) all contribute to the energy of the piece.
Photo: John Hunnex

sequence or plan that could be interpreted in crochet. Watch the distribution and balance of colour. Make experiments using the same design with different colour schemes. Compare the effects and try to analyse them.

Collect samples of yarns and fabrics. Try sorting them into groups of hot and cold colours, and into groups of possible colour combinations. Observe those which appear harmonious and those which seem discordant. Look for colours which give the effect of brightness and heat and those which suggest peacefulness, coolness or sombreness. Underline the effect you wish to create by the use of subtly suggestive and/or related colours. If you need a colour not obtainable, dye the threads with commercial dyes, intermixing these dyes like paints to get the colour or shade required.

Some colour schemes are sophisticated or fashionable, others have a feeling of simplicity: strong primary colours have a bright, naive look. Contrasting colours may be bold and jazzy or soft and muted. Black and white is striking; shades of only one colour can be effective. The range of shades is enormous. There are even various shades of black: blue-black, greeny-black, reddish black, warm or cold blacks. There are many variations of beige, cream, natural, white, off white and grey. Neutrals and 'no-colour' schemes are effective when different textures of yarn are used and textural stitches are made. Threads of different textures and colours can be used together as one thread to make tweedy effects.

Avoid colour contrasts for their own sake. Too many within one area can be disturbing and can obliterate the design. The use of unconsidered colour does not make a piece interesting – better to leave it simple if you are unsure and try more experiments.

### Sample squares and tension
Start by making some sample squares about 12cm (5in) square. Should it be necessary to calculate the number of rows and stitches to a centimetre or inch for a particular project, measure between the boundaries of 10cm (4in). Cut a window of 10cm or 4in from a piece of card and place it over the pressed sample when calculating.

Tension is controlled by the way the yarn is held, which should be neither too tight nor too loose. Some people crochet tighter or looser than others. Check your own tension and adjust it if necessary by changing the size of the hook. If the tension is tight, use a size larger hook, if the tension is too loose, use a size smaller hook.

### Stitch entry
There are different stitch entries, used to make different stitches. Normal entry is when (a) the hook is inserted into beneath the two horizontal bars of each stitch, or (b) hook inserted into the space between two stitches. With the entry (a) the stitches formed lie on top of the stitch below; with (b) the new stitches lie beside the stitch below. Practice making normal stitch entries and noticing the different effects of (a) and (b) before trying the further variations below.

Row down entries are made by inserting the hook into the corresponding stitch one, two or several rows below the stitch being the 'next stitch'. The yarn is pulled up and forms a textural effect on the surface which is interesting in two colours.

Around the post or stem entry is made by inserting the hook around, behind or in front of the vertical bars or post (stem) of the stitch to be worked. This gives another textural stitch.

Entry into only the back loop or front loop of a stitch causes one loop to stand out, forming a ridged effect or horizontal rib. When used in a narrow band, ridged crochet gives the appearance of ribbing in knitting and takes the place of ribbing in a piece of crochet fabric.

### Stitch height (illus. 81)

Stitch height is determined by the number of wraps of yarn put around the hook for a stitch, each wrap being part of the working of the stitch. When starting a new row or round, the yarn must be brought up to the height for the stitch which is going to be used. This is known as compensation. To do this, it is necessary to end the preceding row with a turning chain. These turning chains are needed to keep the edges straight along the sides of the crochet. Without the correct turning chains the side edges would begin to slant inwards or outwards. The turning chain sometimes stands for the first stitch, but not always. Extra chains are therefore added to the turning chain to stand for the first stitch of the next row. This is done in cases where the stitch next to be used will be higher than half double crochet. The number of turning chains equal to the height of the stitch is shown in the table on page 163. The last chain stands for the first stitch in the new row (in double crochet, for example, the third chain is the first stitch of the new row).

By varying the height of the stitches interesting and unusual effects can be introduced with only basic techniques. Undulating edges begin to form and when emphasized with stripes or other stitches the result is satisfying. A straight row of stitches may be turned into a curve simply by the addition of some stitches of different heights being placed at strategic spots.

Vary the effectiveness of this method of adding interest by choosing a different stitch entry. Petals and flaps, for example, may be worked off the horizontal ridges produced by entry into one loop using stitch heights which range from low through high, back to low for each petal or flap. Petals may be spaced or overlapped, deep or shallow, curved or pointed.

### Direction

The element of direction is important in the design of crochet. By working the rows in different directions, variation and often textural interest are added. By a change of direction solid areas are given a feeling of movement in stationary masses of colour or simple stitch patterns.

Crochet is usually worked to-and-fro horizontally across the rows but any piece of crochet may be turned so that the entries are made

**83** Crochet dress by Eve de Negri. The idea started with the central circular motif worked round and round until the desired shape was obtained. From this beginning the garment grew as it was not preconceived. A variety of stitches, including filet crochet, double, treble and clusters, provide decoration. The frill around the bodice is made by working several stitches into the same hole and is crocheted in angora wool. The sleeves and skirt 'grow out' from the bodice and are shaped as they are worked. Bands of holes and shell clusters introduce varied textures into the skirt and emphasize its subtle colour. Refer to illustration 117 [6] which shows a garment with a similar basic structure. Photo: John Hunnex

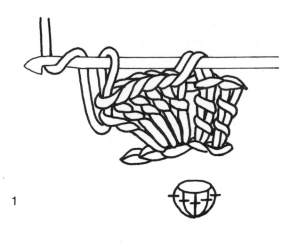

84

1

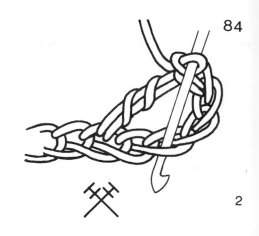

2

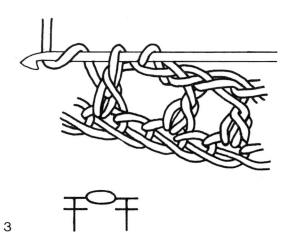

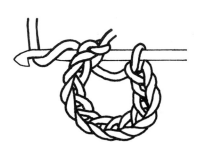

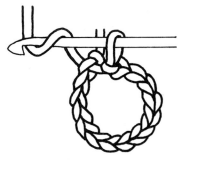

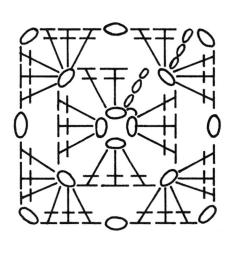

3

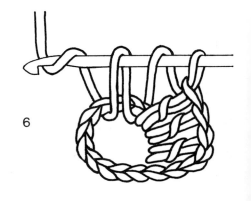

4

5

6

7

along a side edge, into the surface, around an inserted motif or in fact any way the worker pleases. Striking directional effects are achieved by outlining a motif in various colours, emphasizing the outline shape and creating a new edge which could branch off in another direction, as finger extensions (see page 175), for example. When spaces are filled in between motifs another direction is worked.

Crocheting short rows (rows which are turned before completion and worked over a second or more time) create directional interest. Contrast colour could be used to add further point to this method.

Patchwork effects made by working off in all directions in a random manner give interesting directional effects. A variety of stitches and yarns should be used, as well as different textures and colours. This makes an excellent sampler for various experiments.

Tubular crochet is directional: round and round. By changing the stitches from groups of low ones to groups of high ones and back again, at random spots in the rows, an interesting undulating directional effect can be made. Because there is no return row, patterns are easy to crochet into the tube. Bobbles and stripes look effective. Beads and other decorations may be an amusing addition. Tubular shapes can be worked off rings and frames. First cover the ring with tape or by closely crocheting over it. Work the stitches into this covering. Tubular shapes may also be supported along their length by rings and wires.

Stripes and chequered patterns are an easy way of adding direction as well as colour interest to crochet. The yarns are worked in two or more colours, each colour is twisted with the new colour as it is changed, and 'floated' along behind the work or enclosed by crocheting the stitches over it. Colour changes within a row or round are best made by working the first part of the stitch in the old colour and the last part of it with the new colour, dropping the former colour and continuing with the new one. Blocks of colour are alternated to form the chequered pattern.

Stripes may be single low stripes, all worked from the same side, breaking off the yarn at the end of a row and rejoining to the first stitch of the new row every time. Stripes made with textured stitches or textured yarns are very attractive. Stripes made with ridged crochet stand out from the background colour. Stripes worked round and round look better when one set of colour stripes is worked on one side of the piece, and then the tube is turned inside out and the next set of colours is crocheted.

## Increases and decreases (shaping)

Increasing and decreasing form the basis of creative crochet. The shaping of geometric shapes, free shapes and motifs for decoration or for structure is made by increases or decreases or both.

Decreasing by skipping a stitch or stitches is easy but it leaves a gap. Working two stitches (or more) together as one is the simplest way to

**84** Crochet stitches and their symbols:

[1] Popcorn or raised bobble stitch: this stitch gathers a shell into a fat cluster.

[2] Crossed double crochet (UK crossed treble): a stitch with a twist in an alternating pattern.

[3] Filet mesh, an openwork pattern with many design variations, formed by working 1 or 2 dc, 1 or 2 ch, 1 or 2 dc, along row. Blocks of dc may be worked into the chain spaces to form patterns.

[4 to 6] To make a round: join any number of ch with ss to form a ring into which any other stitches may be worked for a circular motif.

[7] Making an Afghan square: corners 3dc, 1ch, 3dc. This illustrates the use and value of the symbols. Once these are understood, the method is simple to follow. Instead of writing out instructions, even the most complicated stitches can be indicated in diagrammatic form, showing the curve of any increases or decreases. The diagram shows each row or round at a glance.

Artist: Mollie Picken

**85** Free form design using single, double and treble crochet and short lengths of crochet chains joined with slip stitch. Areas of double and treble crochet clusters are worked into the holes to give greater density.
Photo: John Hunnex

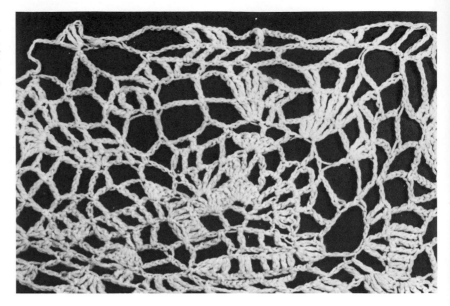

decrease, but it also tends to leave holes where the decreases have been made, and those may not be desirable. This may be overcome by starting to work the first part of say a double crochet stitch, leaving it on the hook unfinished, then working the next stitch, and with the final movement pulling the loop through both the finished and unfinished stitches. In this way the decrease space is blocked in and no hole appears.

When a decrease is needed but no extra height is intended, the stitches before the increase should be slip stitched over to the point of the decrease. This is sometimes done on edges, as for stepped-edges, or armholes, or for slits and apertures such as buttonholes and pockets or purely decorative apertures. Alternatively, stepped-edge decreases can be made by working across the row to the point where the decrease starts; then turning back and working across the row to the next point within the beginning of the decrease and again turning back. This is repeated as often as it is needed to decrease at the edges. Usually, a row without decreases is interspersed between decrease rows, unless a rapid decrease is intended.

Increases are made by making two or more stitches out of one stitch. There are various ways of doing this.

V-stitches are increases of one stitch: one double crochet, one chain, one double crochet into the same stitch. This in itself is a decorative stitch and is often used in borders or even as an overall fabric. However, compensating decreases are necessary in the instances where the stitch is used purely as decoration. This involves skipping a stitch for the decrease. In this case the hole which is left is added decoration. Two V-stitch increases are used to make corners on a straight piece of crochet or to turn a circular motif into a square.

The principle of corner increasing is that V-stitch (or other forms of) increase are continually made into the marked stitches for the corner.

86 The chequered pattern, in which contrasting blocks of colour are systematically arranged, adds direction as well as colour interest. More complicated colour patterns can be made by first plotting them on graph paper.
Photo: John Hunnex

87 (below) Different stitch sizes in one piece of work. An area of tighter stitches, made by changing to a smaller hook, can be used for shaping as well as for adding textural interest. Shiny, narrow woven tapes are used that give a geometric quality to this crochet.
Photo: John Hunnex

Sometimes corners have two V-stitches with one or two chains placed between them. Traditional Afghan corners are usually worked with three stitches instead of two, or with two sets of three stitches with one or two chains between them at each corner (illus. 84[7]).

Increases are used to cover slits and other openings. A cast-on or foundation chain of the correct number of stitches is introduced over the aperture. This closes, for instance, a buttonhole which has been skipped or slip-stitched over to make the opening. In the suitable return row the hole is closed over.

Large increases are made on edges by working a foundation chain of the number of stitches to be used, and, not forgetting the extra turning chains, the row is crocheted as usual. Additions such as this may have any number of stitches and may be added at any convenient edge. They may even be started from the surface of the crochet. An example of such an increase extension is that of fingers or miniature half ovals (illus. 90[3]). An extension chain of the number of stitches for the length is added at marked places along the row, or at random. Over these increases the fingers are worked.

## Circular shapes

Circles may spiral or they may be made with every row-ending defined. The basic method for making a circle as a spiral is as follows. Start a foundation chain of five or six chains. Join with slip stitch. Using single or double crochet, work twelve stitches into the ring. Mark the last stitch with a small safety pin or other marker. Continue increasing in every stitch, doubling the number, move the marker up at the end of every round. Continue increasing in the next two or three rounds, unless the circle starts to ruffle, then stop increasing for a while and introduce some even rounds. When making circles it is important to learn to judge the best amount of increase to add, and

**88** A circular motif worked into an asymmetrical shape by adding extra rows at the base. The shape is completed by outlining. A narrow woven braid with great pliability is used for this piece of work.
Photo: John Hunnex

when to modify it. To some extent this depends on the size of the hook, the yarn thickness and the height of the stitch.

Circles with defined endings to the rounds are made as follows. Start as for the spiralling circle. Double the number of stitches into the circle up to twelve stitches. Join with a slip stitch. Depending on the height of the stitch you are using, make the suitable chain to bring the yarn up to the right height for the next round. In the next three rounds increase with a V-stitch into every stitch, as before (unless the circle starts to ruffle), at the end of every round, join ss and start next round with chain to stand for first stitch.

Cupped shapes start to form when the basic circle is insufficiently increased. The circle edges turn up and 'walls' form, making the cup-shape. When making cupped shapes, if rapid or gradual increases are made, the cup edges will fan out again and make yet another shape.

Ruffled edges are made by very rapid increasing of several stitches into every stitch in the round or row. Hat brims are started like this, the increases either being controlled or allowed to form a ruffly brim.

Asymmetric discs are started as circles, but the height of the stitch is changed as well as short rows being introduced. Turns may be made at random or they may be planned. The asymmetry may be completely on one side only or be a little on one edge and more on another. The edge may be undulating all round with a bias to one part (illus. 88).

Large or small arcs or shell shapes are made by changing the stitch height from low on the inside edge (curve) to high on the outer edge (curve). The shape is started from a short foundation chain, the first stitch being the lowest, the next stitch a little higher, the next higher, until the last is a very high stitch. On the return row, the process is reversed.

Half circles start from a small ring of foundation chain, only half of which is covered in the next row, and the work is turned at the end of each row, rather than worked round and round. The principle of increasing over outer curves is seen here, for increases must be introduced over the upper curve to keep the half circle flat. These shapes are good for starting a design.

**Squares and hexagons**

Points are introduced into a circular shape to turn it into a square, pentagon, hexagon or other angular form. To change a circle into a square, first count the number of stitches on the last round worked (this may be after few or many rounds). Divide the stitches by four for the corners and mark each corner stitch with a marker. On the next and subsequent rounds work a corner increase (or more if desirable). The square will form from the circle. By dividing the stitches between the number of points required and marking them and increasing in each marked stitch, pentagons and other shapes are easily made in the same way.

**Oval shapes**

These are made from a length of foundation chain, unjoined at the ends. This should be approximately the length equal to the inner line of the oval shape (an oval shape may be drawn and the crochet matched to it). Allowing for turning chains, start to crochet into the foundation chain using single or double crochet. Work into each stitch until the one before the end. Into this stitch work a V-stitch increase. Work next stitch, work a V-stitch into the underneath of the f.ch. and continue working along the underneath of the f.ch., back to the beginning again, working the increases as before to make the beginning of the curve for that end. (It may be necessary to work two increases into the stitches for the curved ends if double crochet is being used or if the yarn is thick.) Mats could be made this way if a large hook were used with raffia or thickish string or hemp.

Half ovals are made in a similar way, but only one curved end is made and the other end left flat. Work back and forth over the stitches along the upper and lower edges of the chain and increase only at one end, leaving the other end straight and untouched.

Fingers are miniature half ovals worked off a base row or edge of crochet fabric. Curves are made over the tips of each finger, with an increase at either side of a central stitch; at the base of the finger where it joins the main part of the work, a decrease is made within the angle. (Note that while increases are made over curves, decreases are made within angles or inside curves).) Fingers are usually in contrasts or outlined in different colours. If continually outlined, the spaces within the fingers gradually become filled in and the edges of the fingers may be slip stitched together. An interesting border or insertion is made in this way, or fingers may just sprawl out at random within a piece of crochet.

## Conical shapes

These are made from rings of tubular crochet. Insufficient increases form slanting 'walls' which gradually narrow down to a tip, forming the cone.

## Triangular shapes

Triangles are made either by starting from the base and decreasing or starting from the apex and increasing.

Starting from the base, make a foundation chain the width required for the size of the triangle, plus turning chains. Just before the last stitch, decrease two stitches together at the end of every row, or every alternate row depending on the shape the triangle is to be.

Starting from the apex, start with three ch.sts. Increase into the second chain twice. Continue increasing in the second stitch one in every row. Increases or decreases made at both ends of the row give another shape.

Diamonds are begun from the tip of a triangle increased to its width, then decreased back again to a point.

Star shapes are made with elongated diamond shapes added to a crocheted disc and joined with slip stitches.

Spool shapes are worked from the base of a triangle almost to the tip, but just before the tip, increases are started to bring back the width again.

Open triangles are formed by making a foundation chain long enough to form the inside opening of the triangle. Work around this, forming the shape by introducing three increases at points marked for the corners. By working on the outer edges, increasing each time, the corners will form and the inside will remain open. Open triangles are effective when formed into a circle and joined together with long chains.

## Making use of motifs and shapes

The simplest and most interesting way to use motifs and shapes is to make them in 'batches' of different kinds. These may be laid out on a background sheet and arranged in different experimental ways until a satisfactory design is made. Do not be content with the first arrangement, make a note of it, and then try to improve the design or get more ideas by shifting the shapes about. The shapes should be pinned and attached flat on the paper with slip stitches or chain links, or they may be taken up one by one to join. Linear effects and borders can be tried out with strips of paper or tapes laid down with the shapes. Interpret these experimental strips in chains or rows of crochet. Batches of motifs and shapes may also be used for making garments and functional items such as cushion covers.

Giant sized motifs are useful starting points for large hangings and shawls (illus. 89). The hooks and threads used for traditional Irish crochet motifs were extremely fine and the crochet resembled fine lace. When reinterpreted in modern crochet on very large hooks with thin threads, the results can be very striking. Such giant motifs can be used in random or 'controlled random' designs, starting from a giant central motif and working outwards through the use of additions of more motifs and by outlining. Giant motifs can be put together with extended stitches and chains for openwork effects.

### Experiments with shapes
1 Make a f.ch. of about 25 sts. Turn and work back with a row of stitches of various heights. Repeat this row several times using different stitches. Make a series of chain loops, each loop having 8 to 10 chains. Catch each loop to the main piece with ss, attaching here and there at fairly regular intervals. Outline the whole piece with these loops. Make another shape and join to the first at one corner. Outline round the whole piece, making a new larger shape. Outline again, using stitches of different heights. Now continue on this experimental piece in any way you choose.
2 Make a f.ch. large enough to form an open ring when joined with a ss. Into this ring put some long trebles (tr. with the yarn pulled up about twice the usual amount) or use double or triple treble, winding the yarn several times over the hook and working off loops in pairs.

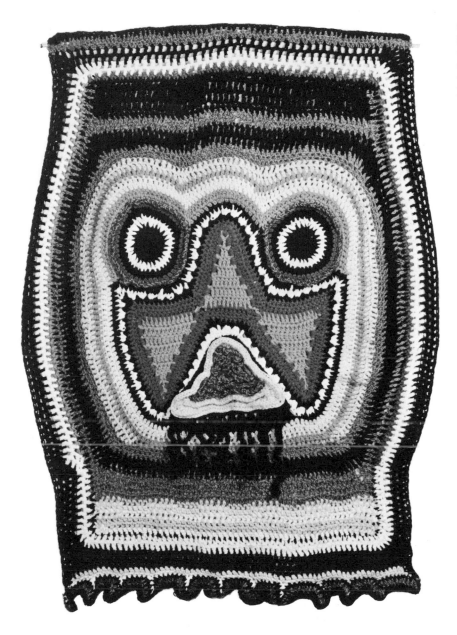

**89** Mexican hanging, approx. 1.5 × 2.5m (5 × 8ft). Motifs can be used to form pictorial designs, heavily outlined with bold colours. Raised work and ruffling give emphasis. Photo: John Hunnex

Intersperse these long stitches with chains of two or three stitches to give an openwork appearance. Make a round of large chain loops joined with ss as in the previous experiment. Work groups of stitches making 5 or 6 long trebles into some of the stitches with chains between them.

## Textural stitches

Yarn texture is an obvious way to introduce texture into the work.

**90** Making use of motifs.
[1] Hanging made up of practice shapes: hexagon, pentagon, octagon, triangles, diamond and circles and squares. Outline all the motifs with contrast edging of single crochet before joining together. A border and fringe complete the piece.
[2] Building up shapes from ovals, triangles, oblongs.
[3] Fingers are worked off edges by chain extensions which are outlined several times, increasing over curves at finger tips and decreasing at the angles between.
[4] Fake 'Argyll' waistcoat using odds and ends. Make fourteen diamond shapes and four half diamonds. Join them together in single crochet in a different colour. The back, borders and shoulders are simply double crochet in the same colour.
Artist: Mollie Picken

Even thin gossamer threads give texture, as do shiny silky ones, and glittery metallics, synthetic straws and raffia, as well as coarse rough strings. Mixing different yarn textures so that areas are contrasted is an easy way to change the effect of a simple stitch pattern.

Every stitch has texture of some kind. More emphatic textural interest can be introduced into crochet with textural stitches. They add richness and depth, even dimension to the surface. The texture of the yarns used should not be so fancy or colourful that they detract from the stitch itself. Aran type crochet patterns, for example, made with bobbles, clusters and crossed stitches, and patterns worked into the surface or around the stems of stitches, look most effective in the typical natural and off-white shades of Aran yarn. The thickness of these yarns adds bulk and importance to the textural stitches. Together they create an effect of 'light and shade'.

Textural stitches such as open clusters (fans and shells) or closed clusters (popcorns, puffs and bobbles) may be used as all-over texture pattern or they may be used in certain areas only. A design may incorporate areas textured with pile or loop stitches while those surrounding them are left smooth and flat. Depth and contrasting shadows are brought to the piece in this way.

Single or double crochet stitches may be worked into a preformed or commercial mesh so that they stand out like pile or fringes. The crochet is started at one corner of the mesh and, following the rib of the meshwork upwards, across and downwards in an undulating row, the holes are gradually filled in (illus. 95). Shaded or toned effects look well used in this way or in stripes of contrasting colour rows. A slightly ruffled effect can be introduced if sufficient stitches are worked in each direction.

Experiment with textural stitches by making a mesh (illus. 84[3]) or buying curtain net and, with a small hook and yarn, work double crochet around the ribs of the mesh and across the horizontal bars and back down the vertical rib again. Repeat this across as a row, up, across and down, in rotation. About three stitches should fit an average open-grid mesh. Break off the yarn at the end of each row, work all rows from the same side. If sufficient rows are worked the fabric has an overall pile.

**Chain loop pile**
This is worked by first making a few rows of single crochet. Now work a row of single crochet into the back loop of alternate stitches across the row, placing a chain loop of ten chain stitches between each stitch. On the next row, work one double crochet into every stitch of the last row. Repeat these two rows as often as required. Chains of a longer length may be used, for a longer pile, or shorter chains for a tufty pile.

**Rya-type pile**
This is made with pre-cut lengths of yarn. The effect of the pile is furry, shaggy and warm. The pile is knotted into a mesh background of crochet, made with a large hook and double crochet stitches. Bundles

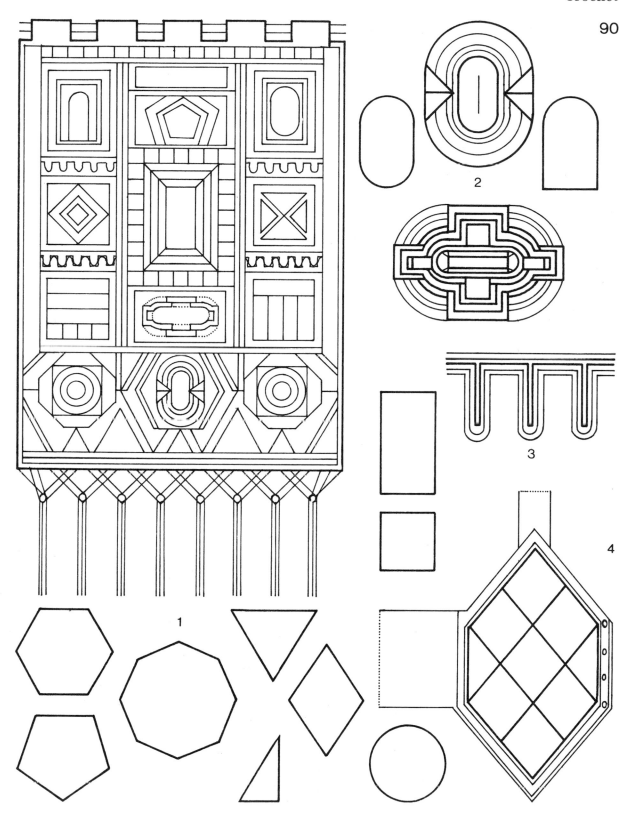

1

2

3

4

of yarn should not be worked into every space unless bulkiness is required. Make a sample of crochet pile by working one single crochet into every stitch of a crochet piece. Turn and insert the hook for the next stitch, yarn over two fingers, raising one a little to extend the length of yarn into a longer loop. Catch a thread and draw a loop through the stitch. Finish the stitch and continue. In the next row, work a single crochet into every stitch. Repeat these two rows. The loops should fall away from the worker. Thicker or thinner pile effects are made by spacing of loop stitches. Extra loops may be inserted between those suggested above.

### Fans and shells

These are known as open clusters because the stitches are not finally drawn together (see illus. 81[9] and 91). Silk and lustrous threads and ribbons look especially beautiful worked in this stitch (illus. 96). Worked with a single crochet between them, these stitches create a textured yet undulating effect. An all-over pattern of one colour may be made, or a two-colour alternating scheme, or even a mosaic-like

**91** Spaced shell stitch makes a loose or open fabric: work a chain stitch between shells and work each row in the same way, shell upon shell. Here chain loops have been added as edging.
Photo: John Hunnex

**92** Shell stitches worked into one another give a more closely worked effect, good texture and an interesting undulating edge.
Photo: John Hunnex

effect may be made using several colours in different formation. Fans and shells are made by working five or seven double crochet stitches into a single stitch. The odd number allows for a central stitch which can be pulled up slightly to emphasize the fan or shell shape. A single crochet stitch is placed between each shell group to emphasize the shape of the groups. In the following row, a shell is placed into the single and a single is placed into the centre stitch of the shell group. This is continued all over.

## Bobbles, puffs and popcorns

These are known as closed clusters (see illus. 81[10] and 84[1]): the stitches are worked almost to the final loop of the stitch, left on the hook until two, three, or five increased stitches are added and then the whole cluster is worked off with one loop.

## Crossed stitches

These are worked as groups of two or four with the stitches worked 'out of order'. For a two-stitch cross work the second stitch first, then

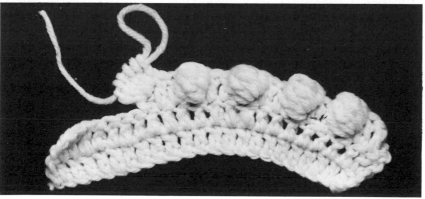

**93** Popcorns or bobbles, made by working several stitches into the same stitch, then drawing a single stitch through all the stitches at once.
Photo: John Hunnex

**94** Popcorns worked at right angles to the rest of the work, thus changing the direction. This stitch is useful as an edging for clothes.
Photo: John Hunnex

work the first stitch. For a four-stitch group: third, fourth, first, second. Insert the hook around the stitches and pull through the loops so that the stitches cross either to the front or to the back. The loops must be pulled up a little to give the extra length needed for crossing. These stitches look very interesting made with double-knit yarn.

### Pulled up stitches
Worked into rows down, pulled up stitches are textural, especially when worked with bulky yarns or in stripes of different colours, arranged so that the pulled up stitches of one colour are pulled over the stripes of another colour.

## Openwork stitches

Light filtering through the spaces of crochet fabric creates a most attractive aspect of this textile. Positive and negative shapes and spaces play their part in the composite design. Open shapes can be used with solid shapes to emphasize or repeat the positive elements, to complement or contrast them.

A design can be worked as almost nothing more than a 'collection of holes' joined together with the minimum of threads in the form of chains or long strands of yarn or elongated stitches. Openwork crochet may be sprayed with plastic resin or starch to stiffen it and to hold its shape.

As well as achieving spatial effects with basic crochet stitches, meshwork can be made with filet, arch (mesh) stitch or knot stitch. The mesh may be open and light, or heavy and strong, depending on the type of yarn used and the hook it is worked with.

### Filet mesh
This is made by the vertical posts of the stitches being equal in height to the width of the space between them which is closed over with chain stitches. This makes a grid-type mesh of exactly square form. Stitches between the posts of the double crochet stitches are skipped and the chains between the double crochet stitches are equal to the skipped stitches in number. In good filet mesh the stitches are well defined, the chains regular and close and the heads of the double crochet stitches are closed and firm. The double crochet stitches are worked into the top of the stitch below so that the stitches fall exactly on top of each other, keeping the box-like form.

The horizontal effect of filet is emphasized by making the usual filet row of double crochet and chains, but on the return row using single crochet with the chains instead. This gives a firmer mesh. Another variation is made by using trebles with one chain between them, alternated with a row of single crochet and chains. This is useful when uneven yarns have to be used.

As well as being spatial, filet mesh may also be pictorial with graphic patterns worked into the filet with solid stitches. Any motif, initials or

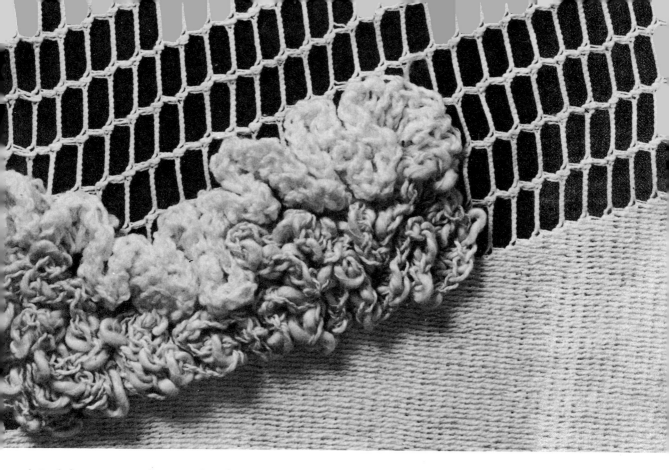

pictorial scene may be translated into pattern so long as there are angles and not curves. Designs are usually charted on graph paper, drawn by placing crosses into the spaces to represent the shape of the motif or picture. Blank spaces are left for the background. Pictorial effects are worked in the crochet by groups of double crochet stitches. One double crochet is placed into every chain stitch in the block to be filled in; the other spaces are left empty as usual in filet. The filling stitches must be worked over the entire chain, not into each single chain loop. Turning chains must be equal to the height of the double crochet plus the two chains for closing the space (when a space occurs on the edge).

Filet mesh makes an excellent background for relief stitches, as well as for weaving-in other yarns in striped or tartan effects, or threading through with ribbons, braids, leather thonging (lacing), or rag-strips.

Relief patterns can be worked with groups of double crochet stitches either scattered all over the mesh or made as alternating vertical panels of mesh and relief. The patterns may need working out first. Shell-groups or closed clusters can be used for the relief patterns. Chain loops worked out from the stitch and back again can be made to form relief 'flowers' all over the mesh surface or as a border.

Zig-zag embroidery (Florentine embroidery) is imitated by crocheting zig-zagging rows in stripes of chain stitches with a fine hook into the crochet mesh. Make allowance in the calculations for the stretchiness of mesh fabric. Make the stretch 'work' as part of the design.

**95** Rows of ruffling worked over a filet net grid. Ruffling is achieved by working many stitches into one hole. Various types of yarn contribute to the ruffled texture. Photo: John Hunnex

## Net mesh

This is made with arch stitch patterns of three, five, or seven chain loops. A very openwork fabric results which stretches in both directions. The form is made up of an equal number of chain stitches placed on either side of one central stitch. The middle stitch is placed over the entire middle stitch of the chain loop (not into the stitch). A single crochet is used for this. An alternating pattern of mesh loops controlled by single crochet results.

## Adding tactile interest

The tactile interest and dimensional effects of crochet may be enhanced by incorporating almost any decorative item: beads, sequins, shells, seeds, stones, driftwood, broken jewelry, twigs and branches, corks, washers, springs, etc. However, beware of the trap of loading the crochet with found objects just because it seems a clever thing to do. Suggestion is often more effective. Whatever is used must relate to the overall piece. The decorations should not conflict with the crochet, nor with each other, neither should there be more found objects and miscellania than the crochet can support. Decorations should be worked in with the crochet rather than be sewn on afterwards. Thread beads and sequins on to working threads and carry them along with the crochet stitches, slipping down the bead or sequin at the allotted place next to the relative stitch. The bead must fall away from the worker. When large beads are used it is advisable to add one or two chain stitches over the bead before working the next stitch.

Shells with natural or drilled holes in them look effective with certain kinds of crochet, for example with metallic threads for jewelry. Large shells may need a 'cage' to support and enclose them. Make a backing in single crochet, which corresponds to the shape of the object to be inserted. Work a round or two beyond the base, lay in the object, then tighten the edge and work more rows, decreasing a little to make certain that the object is really held within the cage. Spot it at the back with a little white paste for extra adhesion. Mirrors and mica, stones and gems can be held in this way. Feathers can be joined in too; they must be trimmed at the ends and the ribs bound with matching thread and a loop formed, to suspend the feather or bunch of feathers from the crochet stitch.

Fabrics may be incorporated in the crochet. Pieces of plastic, suede and leather may be punched with holes along the edge and used as a starting point for the crochet (illus. 96). Fabrics which will not easily punch may be edged with buttonhole or blanket stitching, the loops used to start the crochet. Fragments of fur or fur strip could be used in the same way with insertions of crochet to join the pieces.

Leather may be cut into long laces and used as 'yarn'. Fur could be shredded and added in, as could bits of knitted fabric, and strips of rags and jersey. As well as forming the starting point for some tubular crochet (see page 171), wire rings, both large and small, may be in-

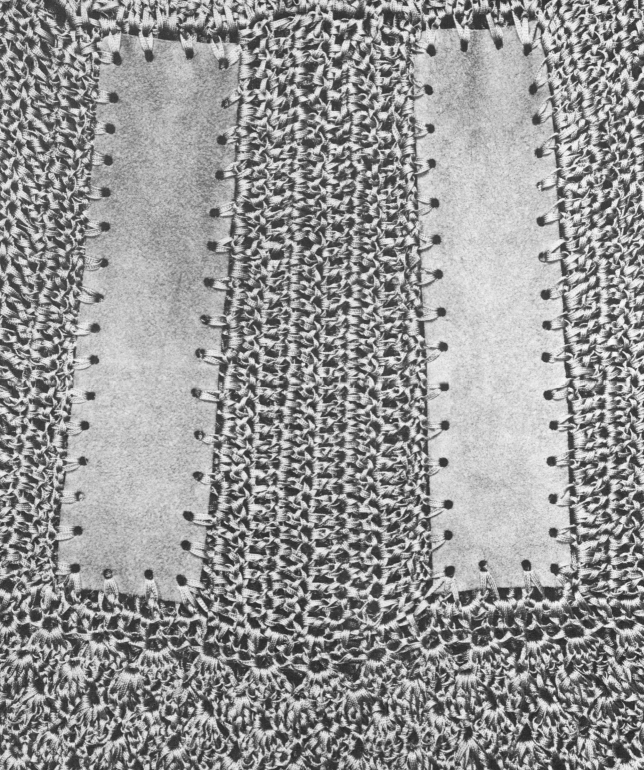

corporated in a piece of crochet to add dimensions and tactile interest. 'Holes' can thus be scattered over the area to give surface relief.

### Finishing

Frames and borders of stitches may be used to finish a piece of work and to extend it in any direction to correct the balance. Extra rows added can change a squat shape into a rectangular one.

Fringes and suspension tabs are more subtle ways of giving balance and they make attractive finishes to the edges of panels and some garments. Tabs are made by folding back the crochet and securing it with sewing. A rod may be inserted through the tab to suspend the piece.

Fringes may be simply tufts of yarn pulled through and knotted. They may be knotted in rows, beaded or decorated with chain loops. Strings of woolly pompons or bunches of feathers could form a fringe.

Curly fringes are made by working lengths of chains off the main edge. These are attached at regular intervals with a slip stitch. Twisted fringes are made from these by working a return row along the foundation chain, increasing the stitches and twisting the column as you work. Looped chain fringes of as many stitches as are needed for the loop, are attached with a slip stitch all along the edge of the piece. Another return row of loops is then made, attaching these in the spaces between those of the first row. Chain lengths can be simply threaded through edges.

Strings of beads, threaded and suspended, or single beads on the ends of chain stitch ropes, may be used to finish a piece and to give it weight (as in illus. 114). Springs, rings and washers, covered or uncovered, may be suspended on chains to weight a hanging. Plaits or bulky crochet chains decorated with shells would be appropriate for some designs.

Wrapped lengths of cord or yarn make a more rigid decorative finish.

### Crochet clothes

When working out the shape and size of crochet garments, a commercial paper pattern can be used. The seam allowance is ignored. When choosing designs and yarns allow for stretch. Some cotton threads have no stretch qualities, nylon and chenille threads do not stretch. Some yarns stretch as much as 2 in 20cm (1 in 8in). If close fit is required subtract a little from the actual measurements. For a looser fit keep exactly to the measurements or even add to them if the style is very loose fitting. When the garments are blocked, it is usually possible to adjust the size and shape a little. This should not be relied on to rescue a bad fit. A bad piece of crochet cannot be made good by blocking or pressing.

To make a garment taper at the waistline or wrist, use a hook a size smaller than the rest of the crochet or use fewer stitches for these areas. A combination of both methods may be used.

To make a section wider or fuller, either use a larger hook or increase the number of stitches. Rapid increases form gathers and frills.

A low, close stitch gives a firm texture and an appearance resembling fabric. The lowest of the stitches, slip stitch (known as 'fabric stitch'), creates a very close surface. A looser more stretchy fabric is made with a longer stitch or larger hook.

Allow for the garment to be pulled over the head, or provide an opening. Waistlines must either be of the drawstring or stretchy type, or they will need to have provision for the insertion of a zip-fastener or other opening.

Pants and trousers may be made from a dressmaking pattern, or worked in the round. The main part is worked from the waist to the crutch, then the tube of crochet is halved and each half is worked as a separate (tubular) leg. When dividing the stitches for the legs, add a few stitches as a chain to join the middle stitches of the back and front. Work over each side of this foundation chain when making the legs. The legs may be straight or flared. Flares may be introduced at any position by using gradual increases.

Skirts and dresses may be made as 'tubes'. Skirts may be started from the hem or the waist. It is probably easier to work from the waist down, as there are less stitches to begin with and the work seems to grow faster. Make a foundation chain to fit comfortably around the waist. Add more stitches for a gathered waist. Should an opening be needed, leave the joining of the foundation chain, working to-and-fro for 10 to 12cm (4 to 5in) before joining with a slip stitch. An A-line skirt needs gradual increases starting from hip level. Rapid increases can be made near the hem to make a flounce.

A bodice could be added to the skirt by crocheting into the stitches of the waistline and working upwards towards the armholes. If the bodice is being made as a tube, it will be necessary to divide at the under arms and work the back and front separately up to the neckline. Shape the neckline and shoulders. Sleeves may be added by crocheting into the armhole edge, adding a few extra stitches near to the top (shoulder) part of the sleeves. Sweaters may be made in this way also.

Flat shapes for sweaters or jackets can be started from the lower edge of the back or front and worked straight up to the neckline (see illus. 117). Shape the neckline, but do not cast-off for the shoulders, continue working over the shoulders and down the other side. Before joining the side seams crochet the sleeves into the side edges over the depth of the (straight) armholes, taking in the same amount back and front. Join along the underarm seam of the sleeves and along the side edges. It is also possible to start from the edge of the first sleeve, crochet to the underarm, then increase for the back and front, work over these stitches, allowing for the neck shape, to the side edge and underarm of second sleeve. Decrease back to the same number of stitches as were used for the first sleeve and work second sleeve. Sew up side and underarm seams.

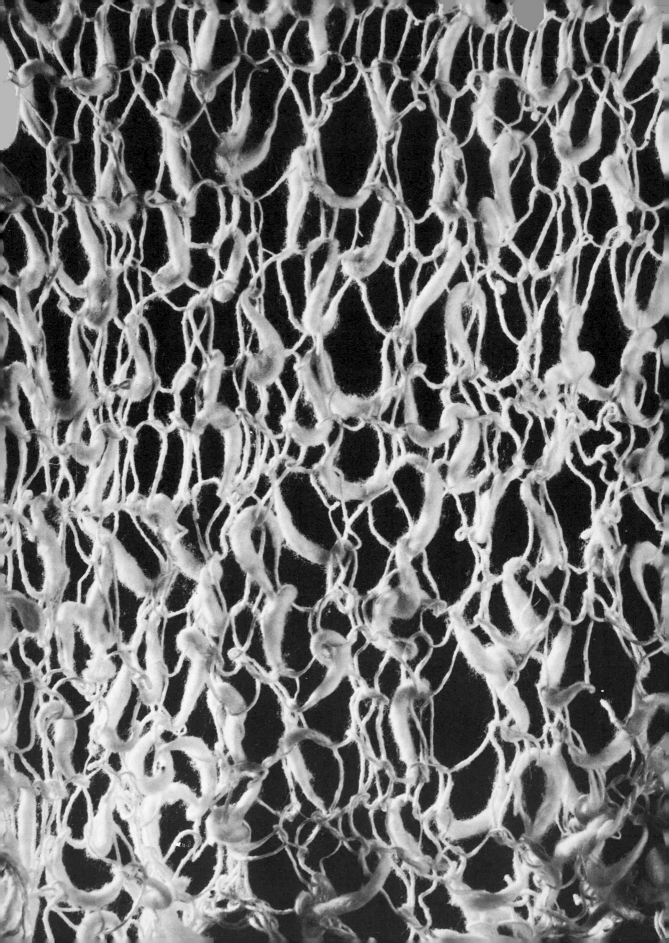

# Knitting
## Eve de Negri

Knitting has a new form. Once used mainly for sweaters and babies' clothes, the 'new knitting' is made into more adventurous body-coverings and environmental forms. Some are even dimensional in effect.

The classic, basic stitches by which the fabric is made, are knit (plain) stitch, and reverse knit (purl). There are many combinations of these two stitches. Used in varying sequences, and distortions of these, they form limitless patterning. In the past most knitting was made on very fine-gauge knitting needles, usually with fine yarns to produce luxurious fabrics. Now, in the interest of fast completion of the project, large needles and thicker yarns have taken over. The effects created are often surprising and amazingly varied.

Once, stitch patterns changed only after the completion of a row or round, now it is amusing and rewarding to vary the stitches by changing them within the row itself.

Textural stitches are used with more freedom and imagination. New-looking effects are created with this unconventional approach.

Directional effects may be made using only simple basic stitches, to give another kind of interest to the knitting. Starting a piece of work in such a way that the knitting is made from the side edge across to the other side edge, instead of from the bottom upwards, gives a new appearance to an ordinary stitch like garter stitch, in which every row is worked in knit (plain) stitch. (Garter stitch normally emphasizes the horizontal direction.)

Stocking stitch which is one row knit and one row purl, has always been a favourite fabric stitch, used since antiquity. Now that it can be produced easily on a knitting machine, there is a fashion for using the reverse side of the fabric, or replacing stocking stitch with garter stitch. Fashion influences the style of knitting, as it does everything else.

An understanding of the basic techniques is necessary before the creative possibilities of knitting can be exploited fully. Experiment and get to know what can be done with the equipment and with various threads. Understand the different knitting actions involved in making the stitches. Experimentation will lead to visual understanding and creative ability. Practice is invaluable, it develops an easy action, confidence and speed. The gradual development of these skills gives the creative knitter the freedom to invent new and sometimes sophisticated ways of using simple basic methods, rather than being content to copy from pattern books. In this way knitting becomes an adventure, and the results stimulating and modern.

**97** Multiple throws or yarn overs (an elongated stitch is formed by allowing the extra wrap or wraps to slip off the needle without being worked) making a very open and light texture. By varying the number of throws between stitches across one row an undulating pattern is made. The slub yarn creates a fascinating texture almost like a freely interpreted lace.
Photo: John Hunnex

**98** [1 and 2] Making a slip loop.
[3 to 6] The four stages of the thumb method of casting on: this produces an elastic edge ideal for any garment which has to be pulled over the head.
[7 to 9] Needle method of casting on: this produces a firm but looser edge. It is also used as an intermediate stage in increasing.
[10] Casting on to four needles: this produces a circular fabric without seams.
Artist: Mollie Picken

## Needles and threads

Needles and threads have to be carefully selected because of their close relationship with each other; the choice affects the overall appearance of the knitting made. Large needles used with limp threads produce a limp floppy fabric. The same needles used with a firm inelastic thread produce a firm open mesh. Stringy threads, linen, hemp, cotton, etc. are firm. Large needles used with thick bulky yarn give a thick dense fabric.

Outsize, jumbo needles may be as large as 2 or 3cm (1in) in diameter; these need thick rug wool or several strands of yarn used as one for a close fabric. Used with thinner threads, these giant needles produce a very open fabric. Thick needles are available in plastic and wood. It is easy to make the wooden ones from dowelling: file the ends to points and sand to smoothness; for extra smoothness lacquer the wood. In the past broomsticks were used and lovely lacy effects were made on them. Now, lengths of thick plastic tubing with a pointed dowel-stick inserted at one end may be used to work ropes and thicker strings.

When choosing needles and threads the stretch quality of knitting should be considered; it may also be exploited. Lateral (widthways) stretch and vertical (lengthways) stretch both have their uses. Some yarns have no stretch at all while others are very elastic. Some stitch patterns create the element of stretch, even stretch in both directions. Very openwork knitting is stretchy and may 'drop' several centimetres. Artificial stretch can be introduced by holding out the knitted fabric by means of rings, wires or suspension strings or weights. Ribbing has 'controlled stretch' inasmuch as it returns back to its original shape.

Carefully consider whether stretch is desirable for the project in hand, and plan for its inclusion or elimination.

## Basic techniques

The most complex knitting involves only the four basic steps of casting on, knitting, purling and casting off. Once these have been mastered and the knitter is familiar with the appearance of and possibilities of the basic stitches, there is then sufficient knowledge to create 'free knitting'.

### Casting on
The thumb method of casting on (illus. 98[3 to 6]) produces an elastic edge to the knitting. Make a slip loop in the yarn about 1 metre from the end; put it on the needle (held in the right hand) and, working with the short end of yarn in the left hand, make a loop round the left thumb. Slip the needle through the loop and wrap the yarn round the point, from the front to back, and draw the yarn through leaving the newly formed stitch on the needle.

The two-needle method produces a looser edging. Make a slip loop in

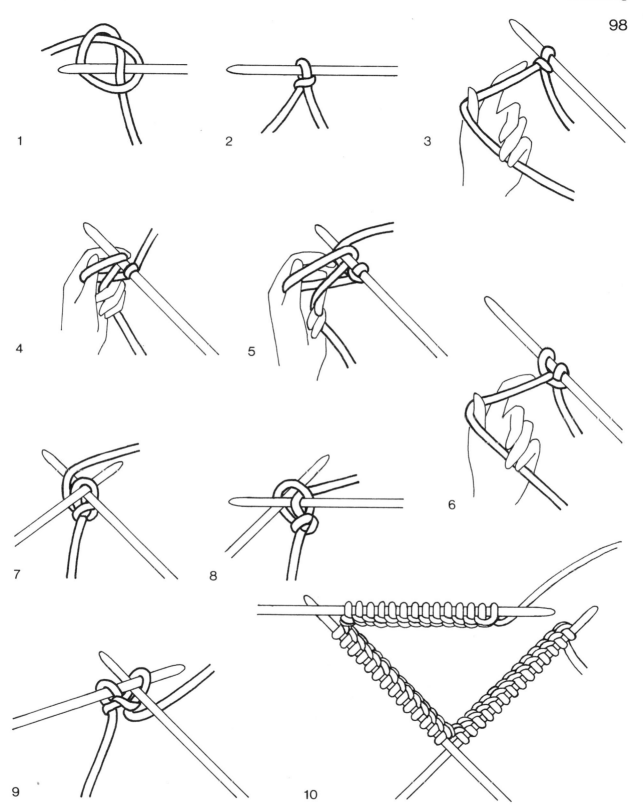

1

2

3

4

5

6

7

8

9

10

**99** Basic stitches:
[1] Knit (k).
[2] Purl (p).
Alternate rows of knit and purl make stocking stitch.
[3] Knitting into the back loops gives a twisted effect because the threads are crossed instead of lying side by side.
[4] Purling into the back loops gives a more openwork effect. Together, knitting and purling into the back loops in alternate rows also makes stocking stitch.
[5 and 6] Casting off.
[7] Decreasing on a knit row by knitting two stitches together (k2tog): this stitch will slant to the right.
[8] Decreasing by slipping a stitch over (sl1,k1,psso); this stitch slants to the left. This method is useful where decreases are paired, one slanting to the left and one to the right.
Artist: Mollie Picken

the yarn and place it on the left-hand needle. Holding the yarn in the right hand, insert the right-hand needle into the loop. Wind the yarn under and over the needle and draw a new loop through the first loop. Transfer this stitch to the left-hand needle (illus. 98[7 to 9]).

The between stitch method of casting on produces a twisted, springy edge. Follow the instructions above for the two-needle method but for subsequent stitches place the right-hand needle between the two loops on the left-hand needle instead of through the loop.

## Basic stitches

The basic stitches of knit and purl (illus. 99[1 and 2]) are used for all pattern permutations. Originality is brought to a design by the manner in which the stitches are used. An old form of the basic stitches was 'crossed eastern stitch', originally made by inserting the needle into the front of the stitch but throwing the yarn over the needle instead of under it. Crossed knitting in its modern form is sometimes called continental knitting. The stitches are worked by inserting the needle through the back of the loops (the side away from the knitter). The appearance of knitting is thus changed (illus. 99[3 and 4]).

## Casting off

Knit the first two stitches from the left-hand needle on to the right-hand needle. With the point of the left-hand needle, draw the first stitch knitted over the second and let it drop, knit the next stitch and repeat the process.

To cast off on a purl row, purl each stitch instead of knitting it before casting off.

## Circular or tubular knitting

While a great deal of knitting is made on two needles, working one section at a time and seaming the pieces afterwards, there is the alternative method of working in a circular or tubular form. This kind of knitting was once used for socks and hats but now its usage has increased: skirts, sweaters, dresses, hangings and many other knitted things are made this way. Circular knitting is not always in tubular form. Flat motifs or shapes are made which start from the centre and are worked outwards.

For circular knitting, sets of double-pointed needles are used. There may be from four to six or more needles used at the same time, depending on the size of the piece being knitted. Alternatively, a circular needle may be used, its length or circumference depending on the number of stitches being worked. (For very small items sets of needles are more suitable.) All rounds are normally worked on the right side of the fabric. Casting on to sets of needles is effected either by dividing the number of stitches between three needles as they are cast on, or by casting the whole number on to one needle and then distributing them equally between the other needles, so that each of the three needles carries the same number of stitches, the fourth needle being used to work off the stitches.

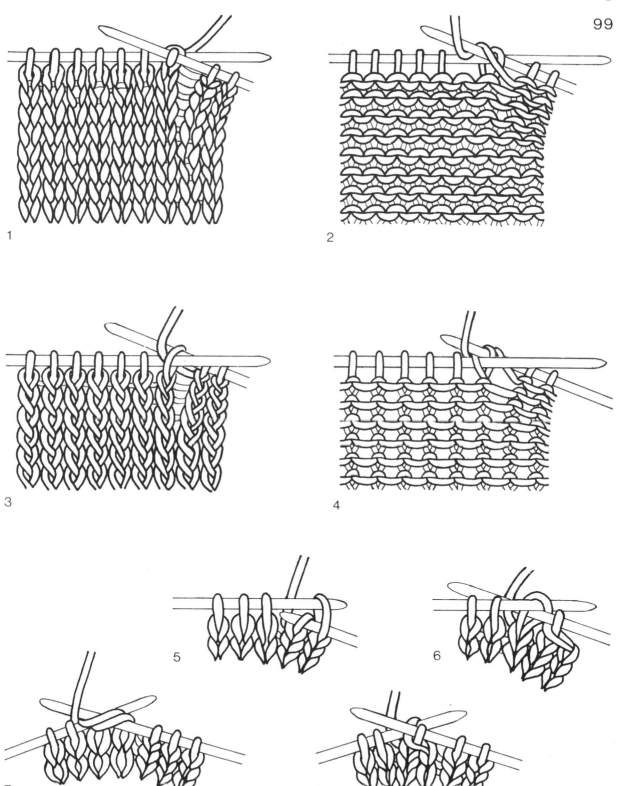

**100** Eight double-pointed needles used to work a flat shape. A ninth needle is needed to work the knitting.
Photo: John Hunnex

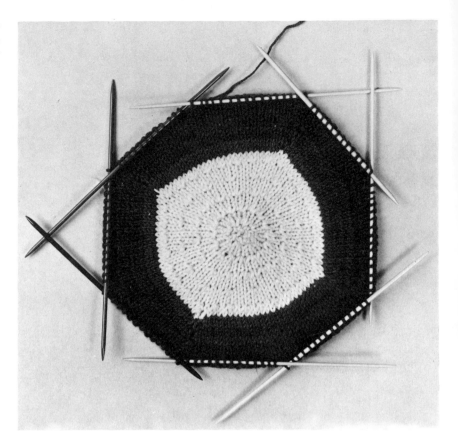

Work round and round, using the free needle to knit off the stitches. Pull up the thread to tighten any gap between the needles. Stocking stitch is worked with every row knitted. Garter stitch is made with one row purl one row knit, thus reversing the usual procedure of two needle (to-and-fro) knitting. Jacquard knitting done with coloured yarns worked as design motifs (see page 207) is always knitted from the right side, as plain knitting.

Amusing effects are made by changing the size of some of the needles here and there, making some parts have tighter knitting while others have more open knitting, giving an undulating effect. Narrow neck-like areas may be made over a small number of stitches which increase rapidly to a larger number, giving bulbous areas, and then return to the original number by decreasing rapidly (see pages 200 to 203). These areas might be stuffed, or a long snaky form made with lots of contrasting colours and stripes. When this is stuffed firmly it would make a draught excluder, a child's toy, or a sculptural form, depending on its colour and form.

**Experiments with basic techniques**
An excellent way to start free knitting is to take some threads which appeal, and are not too thin, a pair of medium-sized needles and, with little preconceived idea, just cast on and start knitting. Change the

yarn to a different texture and notice the different effect created with the same stitch. Change the stitch from knit to purl; try crossed knitting. Experiment with colour changes. Change the size of the needles.

To gain further experience and understanding of the effect of different stitches, yarns and methods on the structure of knitting, try some of the following exercises:

1 Work some knitting on needles of one size, then change to needles which are two sizes larger or smaller.
2 Instead of a pair of needles of the same size, use one of one size and the other of a different size.
3 Try experiments 1 and 2 using different yarns and a further variety of needle sizes for other contrasted effects.
4 Work a few rows in ribbing of knit one, purl one (k1, p1), then in the following row increase the number of stitches to double, by knitting first into the back, then into the front of every stitch. A ruched or puffed effect will result.
5 Reduce the stitches of exercise 4 to their original number by working two together all across the row. Knit a few rows. Observe the differences.
6 Try exercises 4 and 5 alternating shiny yarns and woolly or fluffy ones. Try colour contrasts, tonal contrasts and pale shades.
7 In the same row knit some stitches with large needles and others with small needles, changing here and there at random. Make the return row with one size only. (Note: the return row is the row knitted on the reverse or wrong side of the work.)

Widen the experience gained from working these exercises by making as many samples of different stitches and experiments as possible. Analyse and try to understand why and how the stitches are different from each other. Attempt new stitches, such as the textural stitches described on pages 207 to 213, or refer to a dictionary of stitches. Try to invent stitches of your own. Go over new stitches again, studying the method. Make a note of these in a book kept for the purpose. When noting down instructions for a design you have invented, write them so that they read from the bottom upwards as this is a more convenient way of reading them than the conventional top to bottom.

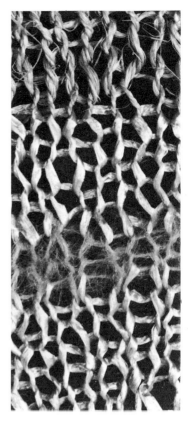

**101** An experiment with different needles and yarns: here sisal and plastic raffia are used in direct contrast to fine angora wool.
Photo: John Hunnex

### The stitch sampler and tension swatch
The stitch sampler is necessary when practising a new stitch. Keep all those made in a file for reference, with all relevant information.

The tension sample swatch is necessary when working out the design to a specific size. In this way a dressmaking pattern or a block pattern may be adapted to knitting.

With the yarn intended for the project, and the stitch and needles to be used, knit a tension sample not less than 10cm (4in) square. Press the sample. Measure the number of stitches and rows over a 5cm or 2in area. Calculate the number of stitches and rows that will be needed to carry out the design. When working from a commercial pattern, use a tension swatch to make sure that your own knitting corresponds to the tension given in the instructions. Adjust the knitting needles in order to correct any difference in tension. By filing all the samples you will have a dimensional dictionary of stitches ready for reference.

## Stitch patterns

Stitch patterns indicate the number of stitches and repeats of patterns to a row and how many rows and changes of stitches to each complete pattern set.

The groups of stitches forming the repeats have to be carefully calculated in relation to the number of stitches to be worked over, so that the groups are evenly placed, usually at either side of the centre of the piece with no odd groups or awkward spacing. For example, the width of the pattern group of stitches should multiply to fit the width of the row. Complicated stitch patterns are worked out first on graph paper, each stitch being represented by a square on the graph. By starting to work the graph from the centre there is less possibility of an incorrect arrangement across the row. Edge stitches should be allowed for at both edges, one or two are usually left unpatterned at either side. These help to keep the pattern correct.

Some stitch patterns involve a different knitting procedure in every row. A large number of stitches may be involved, making the pattern very complicated. These patterns are difficult to work, except by an experienced knitter. However, some pretty patterns make use of only two to six rows for the complete pattern.

### Abbreviations

| | | | |
|------|----------------------|-------|----------------------|
| dec  | decrease             | st(s) | stitch(es)           |
| inc  | increase             | tbl   | through back of      |
| k    | knit                 |       | loop                 |
| psso | pass slipped         | tog   | together             |
|      | stitch over          | yb    | yarn back            |
| p    | purl                 | yfwd  | yarn forward         |
| rep  | repeat               | yo    | yarn over            |
| sl   | slip                 | yoB   | yarn over back       |
| sl st | slip stitch         | yoF   | yarn over forward    |

## Directional effects

Emphasis may be given to the surface texture of knitting by directional effects created with the stitch patterns. The following exercises with basic stitches create horizontal and vertical effects:
1 Row 1: k. Row 2: p. Rows 3 to 8: k. Rep rows 1 to 8.
2 Rows 1, 3 and 5: k (right side). Rows 2 and 4: p. Row 6: k. Rep rows 1 to 6. Horizontal ridges are formed by the purl rows. Pick up and knit stitches from one of the edges and start working in a different direction.

**102** Large needles and bulky yarn (here two strands used as one) produce a dense bulky fabric, given directional emphasis with the horizontal ridges of the purl rows and the rows of holes formed by knitting two stitches together.

**103** (below) Stripes of colour introduce directional interest to stocking stitch. The design may be plotted on graph paper, each square representing one stitch.
Photos: John Hunnex

## Striped patterns

Stripes of colour, using two or more contrasting shades, are one of the simplest ways of introducing directional interest. Horizontal stripes are achieved by changing colour at the beginning of a row, and in every subsequent second or third row as required. The colour not in use is carried up the side of the work. When it is ready to come into use again it is twisted round the previous colour.

Narrow vertical and diagonal stripes are worked by twisting each yarn as it is brought into use with the last colour used, carrying the colour not in use across the back of the work. For wider stripes, divide each colour into small balls and use a separate ball for each stripe, twisting the colour together when a change is made.

A chevron or zig-zag striped effect can be made by the clever use of stitches combined with colour changes. The chevron shaping is formed by the vertical lines of increased and decreased stitches. Cast on a number of stitches divisible by fourteen, plus two. Row 1: k1, * inc 1 (by knitting into the loop below the next stitch on the left-hand needle and then knitting the stitch immediately above, see illus. 108[4]), k4, sl1, k1, psso, k4. Rep from * to end, k last st. Row 2: p. Rows 3 and 4: rep rows 1 and 2. Continue working four rows in this way, changing colours as necessary to make the striped effect.

## Ribbing

Ribbing is a simple stitch pattern using knit and purl stitches in different numbers for different effects. A vertical direction is given to the knitting. Several variations of ribbing patterns are possible, some with an even number of stitches, others with an odd number. In all forms of ribbing the knit stitches stand out from the background of

**104** Twisted ribbing made by working into the back of the stitches. An isolated line of ribbing gives linear interest.
Photo: John Hunnex

purled stitches as vertical ribs, the purled stitches forming horizontal bars between the ribs.

Ribbing causes a distinct 'pulling together' of the stitches which gives a spring or return quality to the knitted rib after it has been stretched out. If it is tight, ribbing needs compensating stitches added for the width. These should be included in calculations for the number of stitches to be cast on. When combined with stocking stitch, or garter stitch, two distinct areas of knitting are seen, the ribbed areas pulling inward, the others expanding outwards, creating another design possibility.

BASIC RIBBING This is made over an even number of stitches. Multiples of rib worked over an even number of stitches: *k1, p1, repeat from * to end of the row. Four-stitch rib is worked in multiples of four stitches: *k2, p2, repeat from * to end of the row.

BROKEN RIB All evenly ribbed patterns can be broken: the knit and purl stitches do not fall over each other and therefore do not form ribs but alternate instead. (When made on fine needles this looks like a woven fabric.) The last stitch should always be a knit stitch. For broken rib: *k1, p1, repeat from * to last stitch, k1, every row. Other broken rib stitch patterns include sand stitch, rice stitch and moss stitch. Sand-stitch: Rows 1 and 3: k. Row 2: *k1, p1. Row 4: *p1, k1. Rice stitch: Row 1: k. Row 2: p1, *k1, p1. Moss stitch: Each row: k1, *p1, k1.

Double broken rib is a stitch used to build up chequered patterns. It is worked over a multiple of four stitches and four rows. Rows 1 and 2: *p2, k2, to the end. Rows 3 and 4: *k2, p2, to the end. These four rows are repeated throughout. Chequered patterns always use the same number of stitches as rows to each block or 'check'. The width and height then correspond.

Broken rib patterns make a firm, non-curly fabric. Checks form when the width of the stitches equals the height of the row. No ribs will form if the number of stitches is uneven. Create fabrics from the use of this stitch pattern, using a variety of yarns and colour combinations in tweedy effects. One-colour chequered effects are interesting made with shiny threads. The fabric made is reversible.

TWISTED RIBBING Work into the backs of the stitches. This is useful ribbing to use when extra 'grip' is needed.

FRENCH RIBBING This is made by working into the stitch below every purl stitch, instead of into the stitch as normal (see illus.108[4]). The unworked stitch drops off.

**105** The various methods of decreasing: double decreasing, slanting double decreasing.
Photo: John Hunnex

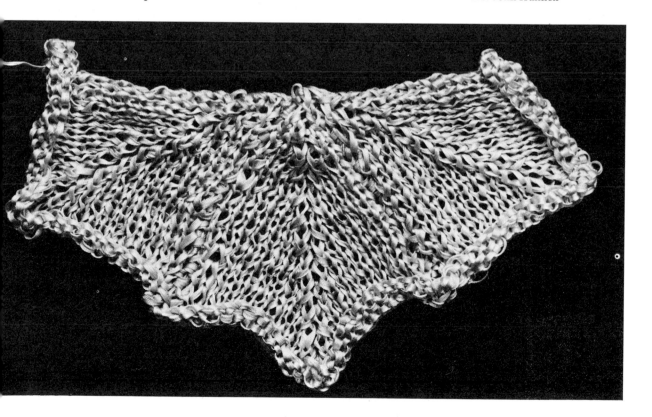

**106** Strips of material may be used to create exciting knitted textiles and textures. Here, knitted fabrics are cut into strips and re-knitted into interesting samples with the ends left to give raggy fringing wherever required. The plain knitting may be used on whichever side is preferred, smooth or rough and ragged.
Photo: John Hunnex

## Increasing and decreasing

Adding and subtracting stitches is an intriguing way to invent new knitting designs. Many stitch patterns are built around the principle of increase and decrease. Once the basic principle is learned there are possibilities to make the stitches 'move' or take on geometric outlines. Large and small apertures or slits can be made, to become an important part of the design or as functional features such as buttonholes. Increasing and decreasing allows for shape and spatial effects to be incorporated. Shaping in the form of darts, vertical or horizontal, is particularly interesting on panels as well as being useful for shaping garments. Combine different increases and decreases and study the effect of such combinations. Use them as the origins of new designs.

### Decreases

The simplest way to decrease is to knit two or more stitches together as one stitch. Another method is to drop a yarn over (see page 203) made in a previous row, instead of knitting it as a stitch. Passing a slipped stitch (or unworked stitch) over a stitch just knitted is another method of decreasing. Two stitches may be decreased by passing the slipped stitch over two stitches (this method is noted as psso2 or p2sso). Rapid decreases are made by any of these methods used several times or continuously along the row.

Slanting decreases are made either as single (simple) decreases or as double decreases. An axis stitch is knitted between each double decrease.

A single decrease to the right is made by knitting or purling two stitches together. A single decrease to the left is made thus: sl1, k1, psso to decrease one.

A double decrease to the right is made by knitting three together. A double decrease to the left is made by knitting three together, through the back of the stitches, as one stitch. Two stitches are decreased.

A mitred decrease to the right is made by sl1, knit 2tog, psso from R to L over the two-together stitch. Two stitches are decreased. A mitred decrease to the left is made by k2tog, sl1, psso from L to R over the two-together stitch.

Different decreases are used for different purposes. Sometimes it is necessary for decreases to fall exactly opposite each other and to match. For this, a double decrease slanting to the left and one slanting to the right are used, usually with an axis stitch placed between the double decreases. When using a yarn over, the over may be placed either before or after the decrease. It forms a temporary stitch which is dropped on the return row. A decrease is made when the over is dropped.

Diagonal slants may be made by working the decreases on one side only to form the required slant. Decrease by working two stitches together through the back loops (k2tog-tbl or p2tog-tbl).

Decorative decreases, used for decoration rather than for shaping, are slanted so as to underline or form part of the overall pattern of stitches and the design as a whole. Sometimes decorative increases are

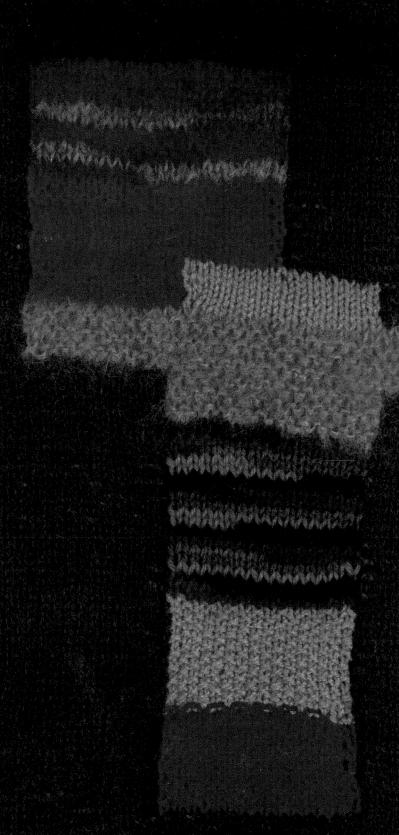

needed for compensation. For decorative decreases which slant away from each other: k2tog, paired with sl1, k1, psso. Decreases slanting towards each other are made in the reverse order: sl1, k1, psso. Decreases for scalloped edges are worked by placing the decreases so that they fall directly over each other in subsequent rows. Decreases keeping the edges straight are made by moving the decreases towards the centre each time.

Chevron effects are made with a combination of increases and decreases (see page 197). Single chevrons may have the point at the top or bottom. Zig-zags are a number of chevrons following each other. Multistriped zig-zags are a very decorative addition to a design.

## Increases

Increasing to make one or more stitches is done by different methods. The simplest way is to work into the back of the stitch and then into the front of the same stitch to increase one extra stitch. If this procedure is followed and the stitch knitted once more into the back, two increases are made. Ribbed increases are worked like this, but the increase stitches must be kept to pattern, as a knit stitch or a purl stitch.

Increases between stitches are worked by knitting the connecting bar between the stitches (illus. 108[1 to 3]). This bar (strand) is lifted with the right-hand needle and placed on to the left-hand needle. It is then knitted through the back loop. This method may be used for a purl increase.

Invisible increases make extra stitches which do not show on the right side of the fabric (illus. 108[4]). Instead of inserting the right-hand needle into the stitch, insert it into the front loop of the stitch below (under) it. Knit and drop off the loop. The loop may be picked up and placed on the left-hand needle and then knitted off.

Multiple increases are made on edges when several extra stitches are needed. Alternatively they are sometimes needed to cover (close over) an aperture or slit. A 'cast on' method is used. Stitches are cast on to the left-hand needle before working over them and the remainder of the row in the usual way. Any number of stitches may be added in this way.

Rapid increases are made by continually increasing. The effect is that of frilling on edges and of insertions between rows of 'non-changed stitches', giving the effect of puffs.

Yarn over increases are the basis of lace knitting (illus. 97). The throw, wrap or yarn over (yo) is an essential part of the technique. The method is simple: the yarn is wrapped or thrown over the right-hand needle before starting to knit the next stitch. This gives an extra loop; when knitted in the return row it compensates for the decreased stitch used to make the characteristic 'hole' of the lace pattern. Yarn overs are usually placed between two knit stitches. The yarn is brought from its position at the back of the knitting (away from the knitter), under the right-hand needle and over the top of it, ready for the next stitch.

Yarn over placed between a knit and a purl stitch is made by passing the yarn under the right-hand needle, towards the front, then over

**107** Areas of carefully chosen bright colour in stocking stitch, moss and garter stitch, against a dark background, show how dramatic interest can be created with basic stitches.
Photo: John Hunnex

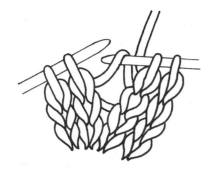

## 108

1

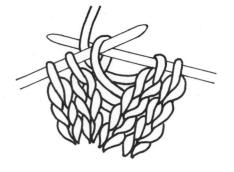

2

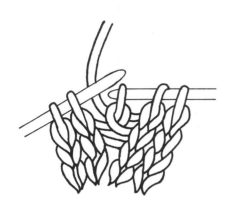

3

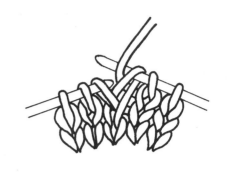

4

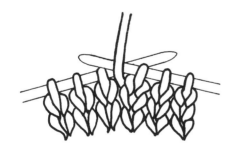

5

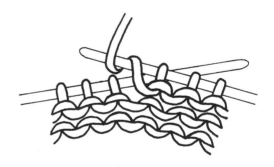

6

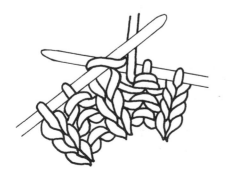

7

8

the needle and back again to the front, ready for the next purl stitch.

These methods are described as yarn over purl and yarn over knit, or as yarn over forward, and yarn over back (yoF and yoB). Yarn over is also known as yfwd or ybk or pass yarn over or wool round needle. In some patterns for lace knitting a large zero is the symbol for yo, with a numeral indicating the number of times the yarn is to be wrapped over: O = yo, OO = yo2, OOO = yo3 and so on, or by YO-2, etc.

## Corners and angles

These are made with increases or decreases. An acute angle, such as would be used on a V-shaped neckline band, is made with decreases, thus: at the marked point, work a decrease as sl1, k1, psso, the knit stitch being the central axis stitch, k2tog, sl1, k1, psso k2tog. Alternatively, work a double decrease (k3tog) at the marked point.

## Shapes and motifs

Shapes and motifs may be made with increases and/or decreases. They may be made as separate shapes and used as components for a larger piece of work, or as decorations for edges, or appliqué motifs. They are useful for practice in making simple forms of increase and decrease. Such motifs can be started from the tip or base, or from one corner of a side edge. Solid colours may be used or striped effects made.

1 Triangle which increases from a corner: cast on two stitches. Increase one stitch at the beginning of the second and each alternate row until there are twelve stitches (or as required for size). Start increasing more rapidly. Increase once, then twice, on each alternate row until the stitches are doubled (twenty-four). Start decreases on the same edge alternating, two stitches and one stitch, on every alternate row, until there are twelve stitches (stitches halved). Decrease one stitch at the beginning of each alternate row, until two stitches remain. Cast off.

2 Triangle worked with decreases from both sides: start with forty-eight stitches for the base (any number of stitches may be used according to width required). Decrease one stitch at both ends of each alternate row until there are twenty-six stitches. Now decrease more rapidly, with alternating decreases of two decreases and one decrease, at both ends of each alternate row, until two stitches remain. Cast off.

3 Triangle worked in two colours. Start from the base, cast on forty-eight stitches. Decrease one stitch at the beginning of every alternate row, for twenty-two rows. Work in second colour in the next row, thus: work twelve stitches in main colour. Knit remaining stitches in new colour. Twist the yarns around each other when changing colour. Continue in two colours while decreasing two stitches at the beginning of the next row, and one stitch at the beginning of the following alternate row. Repeat these four rows until twelve stitches remain. Knit these stitches in the main colour. Continue decreasing in this way until two stitches remain. Cast off.

**108** Increasing between stitches:
[1] Picking up the loop between stitches.
[2] Knitting into the back of the loop.
[3] The increased stitch put on the right-hand needle.

Invisible increasing:
[4] Picking up the loop. Insert the right-hand needle into the front of the stitch on the row below the next stitch on the left-hand needle and knit a new stitch.

Decorative increases may be used for shaping but they also form the basis for lace patterns:
[5] Increase between two knit stitches.
[6] Increase between two purl stitches.
[7] Increase between one purl and one knit.
[8] Increase between one knit and one purl.
Artist: Mollie Picken

# Textile Crafts

**109** [1] Working right to left cable twist of 6 stitches against a background of purl stitches. Cast on 24 stitches.

First row: p9, k6, p9.

Second row: k9, p6, k9.

Repeat these two rows twice.

Seventh row: p9, slip 3 st on to cable needle and hold them at the front of the work, with the right-hand needle knit the next 3 st from the left-hand needle, then knit the 3 st from the cable needle, p9.

Eighth row: as second row.

Repeat these 8 rows 3 times.

Jacquard knitting:

[2] To strand yarn across the back of the fabric.

[3] To weave yarn across the back of the fabric.

Artist: Mollie Picken

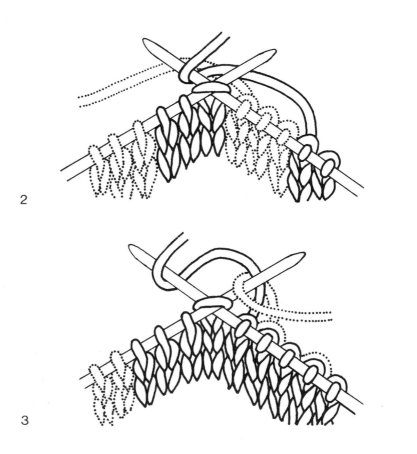

1

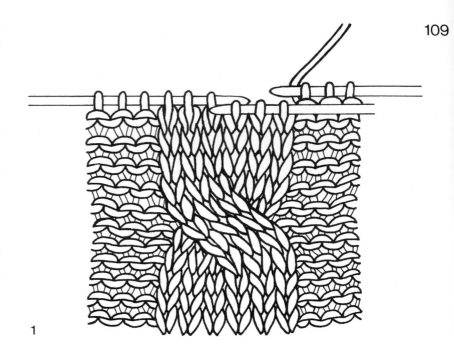

2

3

## Jacquard knitting

Jacquard knitting is the name given to patterned fabrics where more than one colour is used and where the pattern is knitted in at the same time as the background. The technique is simple provided the yarns are 'floated' or woven carefully behind the knitting. Stocking stitch is used to give a smooth fabric.

Graphs or tracings of the picture or motif are first prepared. These are easily done by tracing the design and laying the tracing paper over graph paper and filling in the squares with the colours chosen for the yarns. Alternatively the design may be charted directly on to the graph paper, filling in the squares with coloured pencils or felt-tip pens, and leaving the background squares blank. Number the rows, working from the lower right corner.

When working from the chart, start the knitting from the right-hand lower corner. Read the graph from right to left and back again with a return row on to-and-fro knitting. On circular (tubular) knitting where no return row is needed, just work in pattern round-and-round, reading every round from right to left.

Single motifs may be knitted into the background, or several motifs may be combined to form a patterned band or all-over pattern.

Separate motifs are best worked with separate balls or bobbins wound with each colour. To float or strand the yarns, twist them around each other when changing colours to prevent holes or 'gaps' forming between the groups of stitches and to prevent the floated threads from catching when in wear. When knitting several motifs, pass or float the yarns along behind the knitting, twisting them together after every fourth stitch. Allow for the stretch of the knitted fabric and avoid pulling the floated yarns too tightly. If the floats are tight the motifs will appear distorted in shape and spoil the work.

The weaving method of carrying the colour not in use avoids having long strands across the back of the work. Using two colours, say blue and red, knit the first stitch with blue, insert the right-hand needle into the next stitch and pick up the red and carry it across the point of the right-hand needle from right to left and knit the stitches with blue in the usual way.

## Textural stitches

Textural stitches have an intrinsic beauty and do not necessarily require the addition of colour. Some of the best examples of textural stitches are those used in Aran-type knitting which is carried out mainly in natural shades.

Simple textural stitches may be made by different entries into the stitch. Entry into the stitch(es) below forms 'dip' stitches. These are made like french ribbing (see page 199) by inserting the right-hand needle into the stitch below. The effect is heightened when dip stitches are made by pulling up the stitches. The dip stitch is formed by insert-

**110** Textural stitches are often most beautiful knitted in natural shades. Here, the Aran patterns include bobbles and clusters, mock cable stitch, twisted cable stitch and zig-zag stitch.
Photo: John Hunnex

ing the needle into a loop any number of rows beneath the stitch being worked. The stitch is pulled up and worked off with the next stitch. In this way a textured effect is given by the strands falling over the surface.

Crossed or moving stitches (not to be confused with crossed knitting) are made to cross in either direction, to right or to left. To do this they are knitted 'out-of-order'. The crossing may be to the back or to the front. Cross back is made by inserting the right-hand needle into the back of the second stitch on the left-hand needle, yarn under the needle and draw a stitch through. Leave stitch on needle. Insert right-hand needle into first stitch on left-hand needle, yarn round and draw a stitch through this first stitch. Slip first and second stitches off the needle. They will appear crossed.

Cross front is made by inserting the right-hand needle into the front of the second stitch, yarn round needle and draw a stitch through the second stitch. Leave the stitch on needle. Insert needle into the back of the first stitch, yarn round needle and draw a stitch through the first stitch. Slip off both stitches. Second stitch is seen to cross over the first stitch.

Crossed stitches may be made over a four-stitch group, working the fourth stitch first, then the third, then second and first.

Use crossed stitches on a background of another stitch pattern or reverse stocking stitch with colour contrasts or texture contrasts.

## Bobbles and clusters

These may be small or very large, isolated, or placed regularly in rows, or used to emphasize another shape. Bobbles and clusters may be knitted in at random or planned by charting the design on graph paper, the background of purl stitches being indicated as blank squares and the clusters of knit stitches being blacked-in. Work out the positions of the bobbles by first calculating the number of stitches involved across the row, finding the central stitch and planning each side from there. Some cluster groups are completed in one row, while others take two rows to complete.

The bobbles are formed by working back and forth over the few stitches allocated to each bobble, making a separate piece of knitting which is then drawn together. Three rows are usually made for the depth of the bobble. Any number of stitches are increased out of one stitch, from three to five for a large bobble. The bobble is closed by passing all the stitches increased over the first stitch. Other bobbles and clusters are not closed over, or are closed in the following row.

Bobbles may be placed singly, as all-over pattern, in stripes, or made to form geometric patterns. They may accent openwork effects and lace knitting. Make some samples in which the bobbles are (a) clustered together, (b) varied in size, (c) planned as geometric repeats.

Tyrolean designs use bobbles in geometric formation such as diamond shapes, with a flower embroidered in the centre of the diamond.

Novelty bobbles are afterwards threaded with a contrasting yarn. Cast on a multiple of ten stitches plus two. Row 1: (wrong side) p. Row 2: k. Row 3: p. Row 4: k1 *(k5, turn, p5, turn) 3 times, k10, rep to the end, k1. Rows 5, 6 and 7: as rows 1, 2 and 3. Row 8: k6, *(k5, turn, p5, turn) 3 times, k10, rep ending the last repeat group with k6 instead of k10. Repeat throughout. Thread with ribbon or contrasting yarn.

## Embossed stitches

Embossed stitches are those which stand out from the background, usually in the form of knit stitches against purl, or purl against knit. The embossed motifs are worked by the method of increasing several times into a stitch (the same way as a bobble is started). The method necessitates working an odd number of stitches out of a single stitch on the surface of purl (reverse) knitting. The extra stitches are worked in stocking stitch. Decreases are worked on each side of the motif, in subsequent rows, in order to bring the number of stitches back to its original. (Short rows are not used.) Eventually just the single stitch is all that remains.

There are many traditional embossed motifs, such as those used in Aran patterns, but new ones could be designed. By learning the basic principle there should be little difficulty in evolving individual ideas for embossed effects. Motifs can be combined and repeated in many decorative ways. The motifs may be of any size and it will be found to be

111 Hanging incorporating rapid increases to create a draped effect. Based on a square of plain knitting made on the diagonal (start with two stitches and increase each side until half the square is complete, then decrease back to two stitches), this hanging uses the simplest stitches. At the top two sizes of knitting needles give different effects to rib stitch. The hanging is completed with two rows of single crochet, the second with picots. Chains and tassels add decoration and weight.
Photo: John Hunnex

a fascinating deviation. Try a very large central shape which dominates a whole area or a free form panel. Sometimes stitches are increased on the sides of one central (axis) stitch. In this instance yarn over is the method of increase used.

Large motifs are formed by increasing more stitches and thus using more rows to decrease them off again. Embossed motifs could be worked in contrasting colours against a background of a different colour. Use a yarn which will hold the shape of the stitches. Experiment with cotton and linen threads to make areas of bobbles and embossed motifs and any other texture stitches that are learnt. Use thick yarn for a completely different effect.

Embossed triangular motifs within a repeat pattern, or as a single motif are worked by first planning the size of the motif. The width of the base of the triangle is introduced by making several yarn overs into one of the stitches in the place marked for the motif, along the row. Stocking stitch motifs could be worked on a reverse stitch background, or vice-versa. The outline shape of the motif is made by knitting decreases in each alternate row, along one side of the motif. This decreases the stitches back to the original one, gradually, and draws the stitches into a slanting line up to the final k2tog at the tip.

Certain embossed shapes and motifs, for example a diamond, worked in stocking stitch, on a reverse knit background, will need increases and decreases to form the shape. The shaping is done by increasing up to several stitches out of one stitch in a row, and working them off again as decreases, in subsequent rows. Sometimes the decreases are along only one edge, at other times equally disposed on either side of a central 'rib' stitch.

Leaves are made in the same way, charted first on graph paper as stitch repeats over the width and depth of a given area. Ribs or openwork stitches could be alternated or otherwise combined with the enbossed motifs.

## Cable knitting

Cable knitting is very effective and not as difficult as it is often thought to be. Again there is a basic technique to learn, afterwards the cables can be adapted to one's own designs.

Cables are often used singly, being inset between other stitches. In this way they form rope-like stripes or panels. They usually travel vertically, but the knitting can be turned around so that some sections appear as horizontal ropes. There are some patterns which give a horizontal effect.

Difficulties arise in cable knitting when shaping is required. Cables draw in the stitches so that extra stitches are usually needed to constitute the width of a row. Cable knitting uses a third needle, double pointed and shorter than usual. A size smaller is sometimes used for this. Cables can be knitted by working into the backs of all the stitches (twisted).

The basic method of knitting cables does not vary, only the number of stitches used. Cables are worked by taking half the stitches allotted

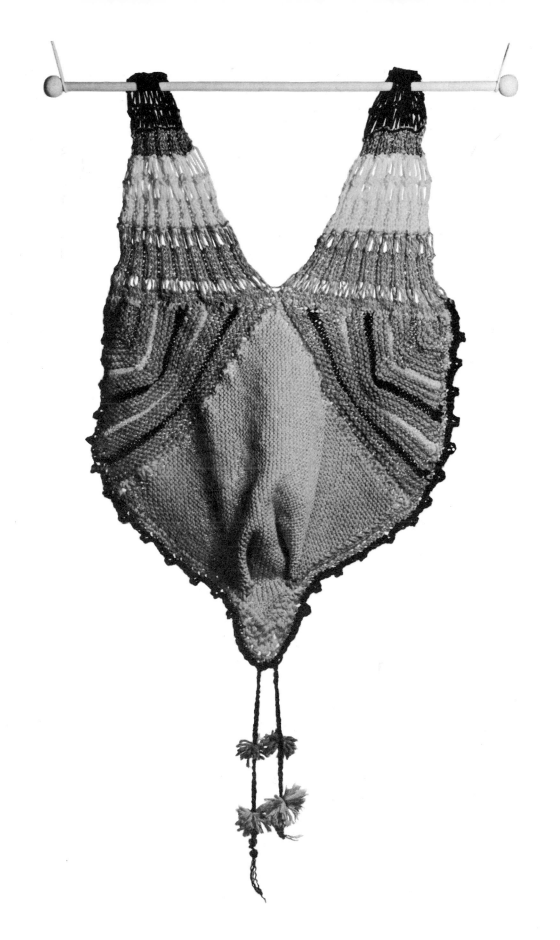

**112** *(above)* Simple cable stitch (twist from left to right) on a background of stocking stitch with one purl stitch either side of the cable. A third needle holds the cable stitches temporarily so they can move across the surface.
Photo: John Hunnex

**113** *(right)* Converging cables, an elaborate form of cable stitch, worked in panels of seventeen stitches.
Photo: John Hunnex

to the size of the cable, and holding them temporarily on the spare needle. This may be done by holding them to the front or the back of the knitting while the next half are knitted. Finally the stitches are knitted from the spare needle.

Cables are made to twist to the left or to the right depending on the way the stitches are temporarily held. Cables to the left are made by holding the stitches on the spare needle to the front of the knitting (towards the knitter). This is known as front cross. Cables which twist to the right are made by holding the stitches on the spare needle to the back of the knitting. This is called back cross.

Cables are composed of an even number of stitches, upwards of four. (Two stitches can be crossed but the effect is different.) The number of rows between the twists affect the tension of the cable and the appearance of the rope. Usually the number of rows between the twists equals the number of stitches used in the cable. However, a looser twist is made by adding two extra rows between the twists.

Variations may be made through different combinations and groupings, by interlacing, waving, doubling, etc.

Cable with four stitches and four rows. This is an easy cable to start with. Start by casting on eight stitches (four for the cable and two each side for the border). First row: wrong side: k2, p4, k2. Second row: p2, k4, p2. Third row: as row 1. Fourth row: p2, slip two stitches on to the cable needle. Hold these stitches either to the front or to the back, k2, knit the two stitches from the cable needle. Repeat these four rows throughout. Vary this cable by working two extra rows between the twists. Experiment with wider cables (more stitches).

Double cables, alternating the front and back crosses, should be tried next. Eight stitches plus two edge or border stitches each side of the cable, or any number of stitches divisible by four, may be used for the double cable. First row: wrong side: k2, p8, k2. Second row: p2, slip two stitches on to spare needle and hold to back, knit two stitches, then knit two from cable needle. Slip next two stitches on to spare needle and hold to front, knit two, then knit the stitches from the spare needle, purl two. Continue working all odd rows as first row, and all even rows (4, 6 and 8) as p2, k8, p2. Repeat these eight rows.

Reverse the order by starting with a front cross followed by a back cross. This changes the appearance.

Converging cables are worked as a panel of seventeen stitches. Start with a right side row: p2, k13, p2. Next row: k2, p13, k1. Next row: p2, s13 to spare needle, hold to back, k3, knit the three from the spare needle, k1, slip 3 to spare needle, hold to front, k3, knit the three from spare needle, p2. Next row: k2, p13, k2. Repeat these rows for each pattern. The direction of this converging pattern may be reversed, by changing the rotation of the crosses.

Another form of cabling is worked over a thirteen-stitch panel. Rows 1 and 3: k2, p9, k2 (wrong side). Row 2: p2, sl1 stitch to spare needle, hold to front, k2, k1 from spare needle, k1, s13 to spare needle, hold to back, k1, k3 from spare needle, p2. Row 4: p2, k9, p2. Repeat these four rows as required.

A variation of cabling uses slip stitches. Ten stitches are used for a panel. Row 1: k2, p6, k2 (wrong side). Row 2: p2, sl2 with yarn to back, k2, p2. Row 3: k2, p2, sl2 with yarn to front, p2, k2. Row 4: p2, sl2 to spare needle and hold in back, k1, k2 from spare needle, slip next stitch on to spare needle, hold to front, k2, k1 from spare needle, p2. (Note that the slipped stitches in rows 2 and 3 are not slipped on to the spare needle.) Repeat these four rows.

After making samples of different cable stitch patterns, try combining them to make a variety of panels with some other basic stitches included.


## Openwork stitches (lace knitting)

Meshes, faggoting, ladders and dropped stitches give beautiful light-giving texture. They are the simple forms of lace knitting involving yarn overs. They may be used as panels or as all-over repeating patterns.

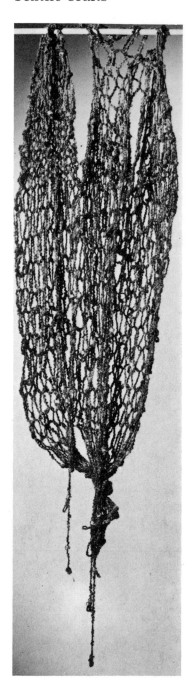

**114** Thin yarn knitted on giant needles produces a netted effect. The addition of coloured and transparent beads enhances the lacy effect.
Photo: John Hunnex

### Dropped or elongated stitches

These are the easiest openwork stitches to make. The light airy appearance of the elongated stitches is attractive. This may be combined with texture and colour. Such stitches may be used in body coverings and wall-hangings. Much depends on the kind of thread used, for there is a great deal of stretch quality in such knitting and this should be allowed for in the design, either exploiting it or counteracting it with rows of controlling knitting in another stitch or yarn. This is the element of compensation, in which open areas which are stretchy are held by others which are less stretchy.

Try this example of dropped stitches interspersed with stripes of knit and purl. Row 1: k2, (p1, k1) 3 times *k3 (p1, k1) 4 times, rep from * to end of row. This row is repeated until the fabric is the required length. Next row drop the stitches and allow them to 'run' right down to the lower edge, in the following way: k2, (p1, k1) 3 times * let 3 sts drop off the needle (p1, k1) 4 times. Repeat to end.

Dropped or elongated stitches may be made with yarn overs. Wind the yarn over twice, three times or more, allowing the yos to drop in the following row. The result is to make very long or not so long stitches depending on the number of yos used. An interesting variation is made by working yos from two to six or more and then down again to one. This gives little patches of dropped stitches in lozenge shapes. Intersperse this dropped stitch row with three rows of garter stitch. Work in two colours for further interest. The yarn over loop when dropped runs down like a ladder.

To make drop stitch clusters, cast on in multiples of six stitches plus two. Row 1: k. Row 2: k. Row 3, k1 *(yo)3, k1, rep to end. Row 4: k1 *drop the 3 yos of previous row, k1, rep to end. Row 5: k1, *sl3, k2tog, p3sso (k1, p1, k1, p1, k1) all into the same stitch, end k1. Rows 6 to 8; k. Row 9: as 3rd row. Row 10: as 4th row. Row 11: k1, *(k1, p1, k1, p1, k1) into same st. sl3, k2tog, p3sso, rep to last, k1. Row 12: k.

### Decorative holes

These are made with the yo principle combined with a suitable decrease. Rows of holes are sometimes used for decoration and sometimes for a casing for ribbons or elastic. Work the holes thus. Row 1: *k1, yo to the end of the row. Row 2: *purl the yos, p2tog, to end of row. A saw-toothed or picot-edged hem or fold is made by turning the knitting under along the row of holes. A corresponding number of rows is knitted for the depth of the fold. The edge of the folded piece is either sewn lightly to the main part or two sets of stitches are knitted together.

Decorative effects could be made with rows of holes threaded with contrasts all-over, or with folded edges made over the whole piece like layers.

The direction in which the yarn over slants is controlled by the position of the yarn over, that is, whether a yo is placed before or after the decrease. For a slant to the right (even stitches): Row 1: k1 (yo, k2tog) k1. Row 2: p. Repeat both rows in turn as needed. Here the yo is placed before the decrease; now try placing it after the decrease and compare the effects.

## Faggoting and ladders

The essential methods used for lace knitting are increase and decrease. Faggoting is a basic lace stitch which makes use of both. Vertical insertions are introduced through faggoting. It is a stitch pattern which combines well with others. There are several variations of the stitch, depending on the type of decrease used with the yarn over increases (compensation). Try these different decreases and compare the effects:

1 Using an even number of stitches, k1, *yo, sl1, psso, repeat to last, ending k1. Repeat as needed.
2 kl, *yo, k2tog, repeat to the last, ending k1. Repeat as needed.
3 As 2, but p2tog. Repeat as needed.

Other variations could be made by placing one or more stitches at each side of the faggoting. Calculate the stitch repeats before starting, so that they fit into the number of stitches in use.

A ribbed effect with faggoting is made with a three-stitch repeat: *k1, yo, k2tog, repeat along the row. Return row, purl.

There is only one row to each of these patterns so they are easy to do. Variations could be introduced at different points across a row. Faggoting can be used to lead the knitting into other areas of either closer or more open stitch patterns.

Another variation of faggoting is made by making the return row in knit: *k1, yo, k2tog, repeat to end of row. Return row, knit. Because the decreases are not balanced (being made on one side only of each yarn over), a slightly slanting effect is given to the knitting.

Balanced decreases are used to produce straight ladders. Work thus:

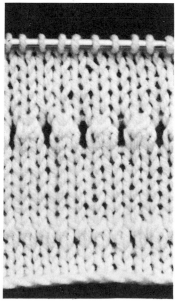

**115** *(left)* The effect of several yarn overs which have been allowed to drop and run down the work for several rows.
Photo: John Hunnex

**116** *(below)* Decorative holes made by the yarn over principle.
Photo: John Hunnex

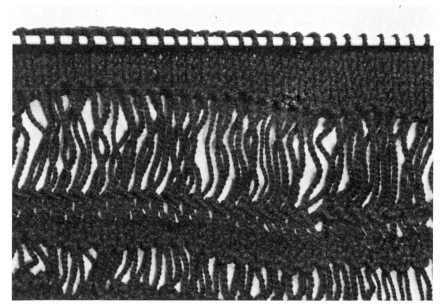

**117** Ideas for simple tops based on a rectangle:
[1] The basic shape.
[2] Rectangles form the back, front and sleeves of this top. Welts at the cuffs may be added afterwards.
[3] Two rectangles joined with simple shoulder straps.
[4] Start at the sleeve, work enough rows to form a sleeve, then cast on to make back and front. Use decreases to form a V neck.
[5] Jacket with front opening.
[6] Blouse using increasing on a flat shape for full sleeves and basque.
Artist: Mollie Picken

Row 1 (four stitch patterns): *sl1, k1, psso, yo twice, k2tog, repeat. Return row: *p1, p1-k1 into the double yo, p1, repeat to end of row. Work as an insertion or all-over pattern. Repeat both rows. Notice that a decrease is placed on either side of the double yarn over. This balances and straightens the pattern.

Faggoting slanting to the left is worked thus: k1*sl1, k1, psso, yo, repeat ending k1. Return row: purl. Repeat both these rows.

Faggoting slanting to the right is worked thus: k1, *yo, k2tog, repeat to end of row, k1. Return row: purl. Repeat these two rows.

After working the samples, notice how the direction of the ribs is changed. Zig-zags are made by combining both. Each direction is allocated a certain number of rows, depending on the size of the zig-zag, and then reversed. All return rows are purled.

Balanced openwork ribbing is made by using a multiple of ten stitches. Start with a wrong side row: purl. Next row: k1, *yo, k3, sl1, k2tog, psso, k3, yo, k1, repeat to the end of the row. Repeat both rows. Notice how the pattern is balanced. There is a central rib which is formed by the decreases. Any number of even stitches can be used, from four upwards. Try variations. This type of stitch looks good with a silky texture.

Holes and ribs are made by combining yarn overs with decreases. Some of the stitch patterns are simple, with only a few rows of repeat, while others may take up to sixteen or over twenty rows to complete one pattern block. Start practising with some simple ones, and try to understand the basic principle. After some practice try making up stitch patterns. Beautiful wall-panels can be made from this type of knitting. The areas may be broken up, apportioning some areas to very open effects and others to very close texture. Keep an account of the number of rows and stitches which have been worked, as these patterns must be absolutely accurate. Any mistake will show. Experiment with the same patterns but using thick yarns, and thin one-plys.

A vertical pattern worked over four rows. Cast on a multiple of twelve stitches, plus one: *k1, (k2tog) twice, (yo, k1) 3 times, yo (sl1, k1, psso) twice, repeat to the last stitch k1. Next row: purl. Next two: knit. The double decreases make quite large holes. Insertions of this pattern are good when set between other stitch patterns.

A horizontal pattern over a three row build up. Cast on a multiple of eighteen stitches: *(k2tog) 3 times (yo, k1) 6 times (k2tog) 3 times, repeat to end of the row. Return row: purl. Next row: knit. Return row: purl. Next row: knit. Return row: knit. Repeat throughout. It will be seen that there is only one row with changes of stitches within it. This stitch pattern makes a gently undulating effect with a horizontal direction (given by the reverse knit row).

For a panel of vertical faggoting: cast on a multiple of ten stitches plus two. First knit four rows. Next row: k2, *yo, k2, k2tog, (k2tog) through back of loops, k2, yo, k2. Repeat to the end of the row. Return row: k1, p to last stitch, k1. Repeat the last two rows three times to complete the pattern.

Having mastered this type of knitting, the next step is to draft your

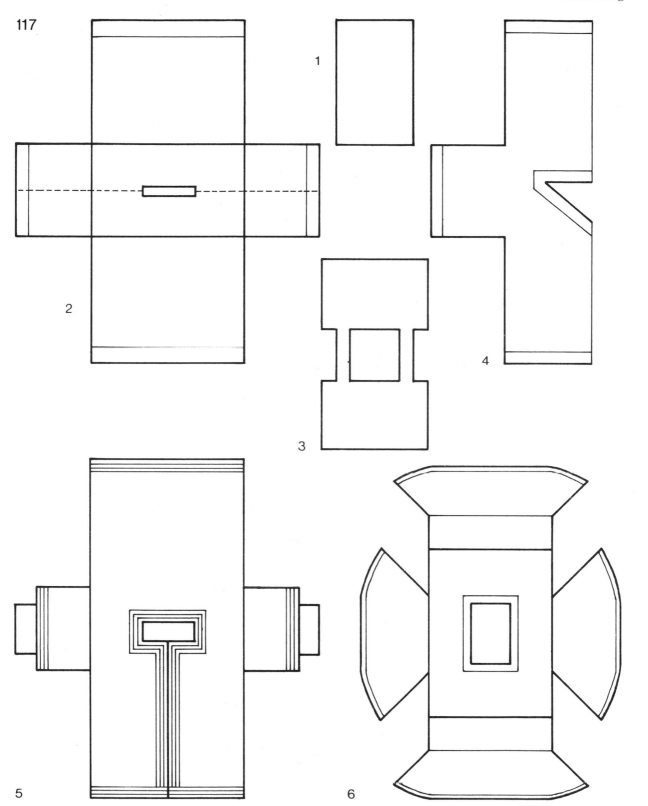

117

1

2

3

4

5

6

**118** (on page 219) *Moonscape* (detail) by Dorothea Nield, 56 × 30cm (22 × 12in). Illustration 120, on page 222, is of the pricking for this panel of half stitch variations. Photo: John Hunnex

own designs which you build up from yarn overs and decreases. Do this by finding a shape which you wish to interpret with knitting stitches, against a background, then work out the stitch patterns and repeats needed. Use a blacked in or 'x-marked' square for decreases, and a symbol such as a bracket lying on its side for the yarn overs. Chart both rows and stitches.

### Beads, shells and feathers

Surface interest may be created simply by slipping beads or other decorations on to the stitches while they are being knitted. The stitch loop is pulled through the hole in the bead either before or after making the stitch at the position where the bead is required. The beads are slipped into place so that they fall on the side away from the knitter.

Alternatively, beads may all be strung on to a thread before starting to knit. Colours may be arranged to form a specific design or left at random. The bead is then passed along with the working thread and slipped into place beside the stitch to be worked. Beads may be 'spotted' all over or in pattern effects. Shells, stones, pieces of wood and other found objects may need a 'cage' in which to suspend them if they have no hole or are heavy. To make an enclosing cage, knit to the position for the cage, then *k1, sl1* until there are sufficient stitches on the needle for the size of the cage. Continue working this group of stitches until the length is right. Now slip each alternate stitch on to a cable needle, insert the object into the cage, return the stitches to the main needle, and close-over the cage by working a complete row. This may be worked at any place where an object is to be enclosed.

Feathers may be added, by forming a loop at the end of one or a bunch of feathers and using this to suspend the feathers into the knitting. Work the loop in with the knitted stitches wherever they are needed.

### Finishing

The finishing of a knitted item, whether a hanging, cushion cover or garment, can make all the difference to the final effect.

Where pressing is appropriate to the yarn used, first pin out each section to the correct size and shape (right side down) on an ironing pad – a thick soft pad which prevents the texture of the fabric being flattened. Make sure the stitches run in straight lines. Place a clean piece of cloth over the knitting and press the whole area of the iron down on it. Do not move the iron to and fro over the surface.

To seam up a knitted garment, choose the method best suited to the item: an invisible seam avoids hard edges; ribbed sections are neater with a flat seam. Use a blunt-ended sewing needle which will not split the stitches.

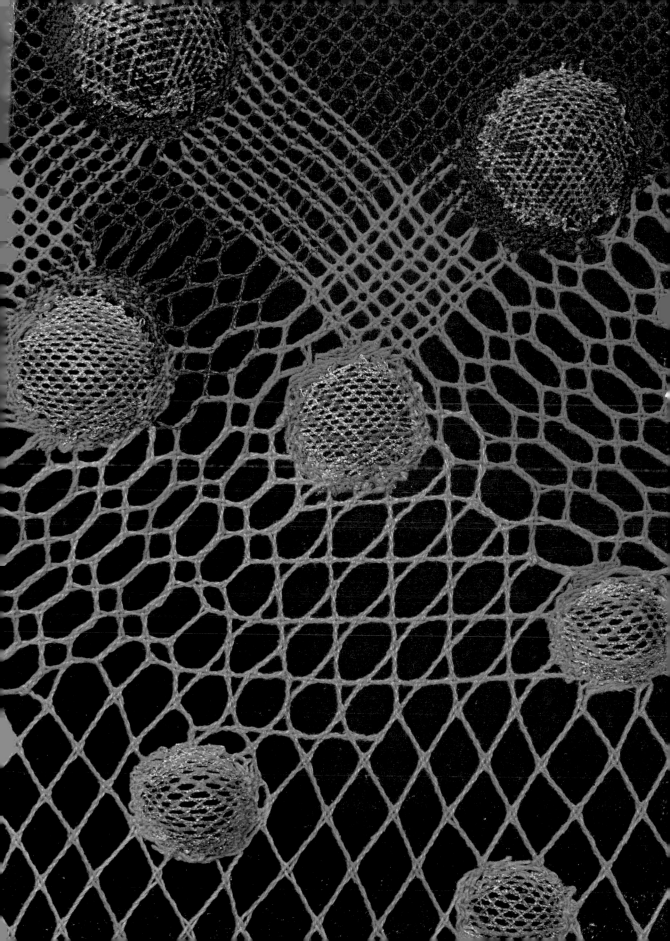

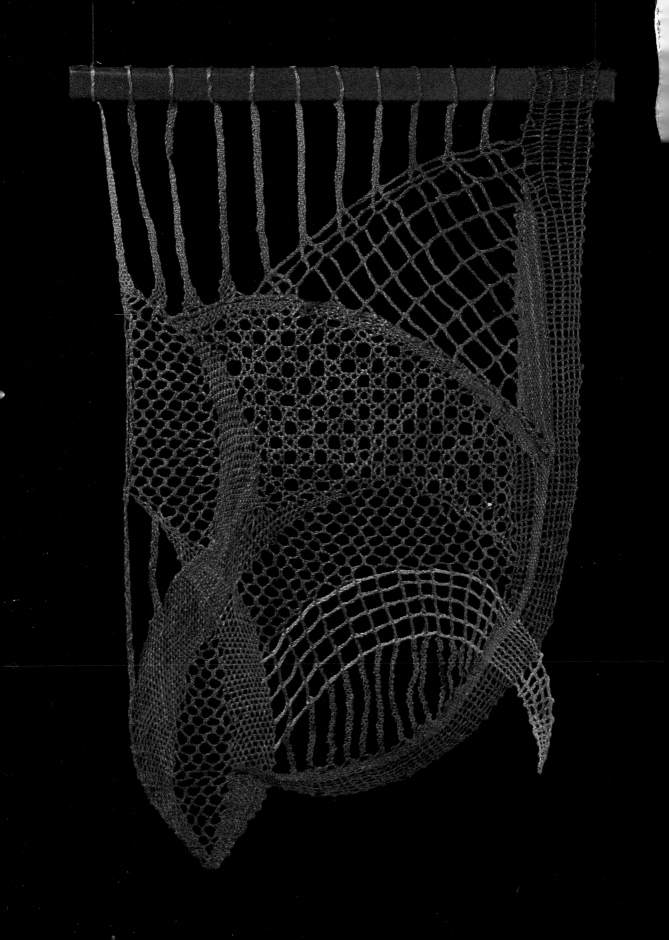

# Bobbin Lace
## Dorothea Nield

Bobbin or pillow lace is so called because the thread is wound on to bobbins and, with the aid of a pattern pinned in position on a pillow, the threads are plaited or twisted to form lace. The technique is simple, the most complicated patterns being based on two basic stitches, yet the fineness of period laces tends to put them in a category outside present-day interpretation or use. Today, however, there is no need to be limited to fine threads and to very delicate work. Lace techniques can be used on a much larger scale, using thick knitting and crochet cottons, handspun wools and even thick cords and strings. The use of such yarns and a freer approach to techniques enable the lace-maker to reconsider traditional methods and effects and to interpret them in new and exciting ways.

## History

The origins of pillow lace can be traced to fragments of sprang found in Egyptian tombs. These pieces of twisted and plaited threads were made on a square frame with the warp twisted with the fingers forming a symmetrical mesh (see page 89). Threads were held in place by a rod pushing the pattern to the top and the bottom and, when complete, the piece was cut in the centre and the ends knotted into a fringe. By using shorter lengths of thread and supporting them at one end, working on a pillow, they could be manipulated with greater freedom. At first the threads were held in place by pear-shaped weights tied to the ends. Bobbins on to which extra thread could be wound were a natural development. Pins to keep the lace in shape came into use, though tradition says that fish bones were used when pins were too costly and hence the technique has been known as 'bone lace'.

Europe became the centre of a flourishing lace industry by the seventeenth century. One Belgian writer claimed that lace caps were worn as early as the fourteenth century. The designs of bobbin lace followed those of needlepoint, interpreting the bars or brides, as they were called, into meshes or nets. Several centres such as Brussels, Mechlin, and Valenciennes became known for the perfection of their laces. Refugees from Flanders in the sixteenth century took their skills to England settling in Bedfordshire and Buckinghamshire. It is recorded that Queen Katherine of Aragon with her ladies encouraged the stitches in the villages around Ampthill. A net still made today is known as Kat stitch and the lace-makers annual festival was St Cattern's day. Honiton in Devonshire became the centre of sprig lace

119 Red panel by Dorothea Nield, 54 × 33cm (21½ × 12½in). Worked in shades of red linen thread on a freehand design, the panel was planned to include areas of open textured ground, including rose ground, contrasted with cloth stitch. One hundred pairs of bobbins were used but by the end of the work all the threads had been invisibly finished off: either by carefully darning in the cut ends or by resting bobbins towards the top of the board when no longer needed in the design, later trimming off the threads near the lace as other stitches held them in place.

A bevelled wooden rod, 36 × 2 × 0.5cm (14½ × ¾ × ¼in), was covered with red cloth. The pricking was set 30cm (12in) from the top of the board. This was turned and the bobbins, each pair having been wound from one length of thread, were pinned at the top of the pricking. The plaits were worked for 2cm (¾in) and the covered rod was pinned over them, the board turned round and the plaits continued over the rod. They were sewn to make beginning loops to hold the rod in position. The bobbins were then in place to work the panel.
Photo: John Hunnex

**120** The used pricking for the *Moonscape* panel (illus. 118, page 219) shows the development of the ground shapes and the position of the isometric paper introduced for the open ground. The top area was worked in Torchon ground (h st, pin h st) in diagonal lines at an angle of 45°. As the mesh became larger, a thinner thread and a change of colour emphasized the variation, also altering the mesh within the character of half stitch. For the open ground at the lower part of the panel, a sheet of isometric paper was fixed over the squared paper to make a simple change of angle without lengthy calculations and drafting.

The circles were worked entirely in half stitch. Pins were used to support the threads. Direction lines of the ground were added as work progressed. Sections cut from polystyrene balls were used as raised padding. A lurex thread was introduced for the circles and, when complete, this was stiffened by painting on two coats of clear varnish which were allowed to dry before removing the lace from the pricking and padding.

To finish the panel, the lace was stretched between two window mounts of heavy card covered with felt. These were then glued together. The threads at the edge of the lace were stitched to a length of cotton tape before removing the pins and taking the lace off the board.

Photo: John Hunnex

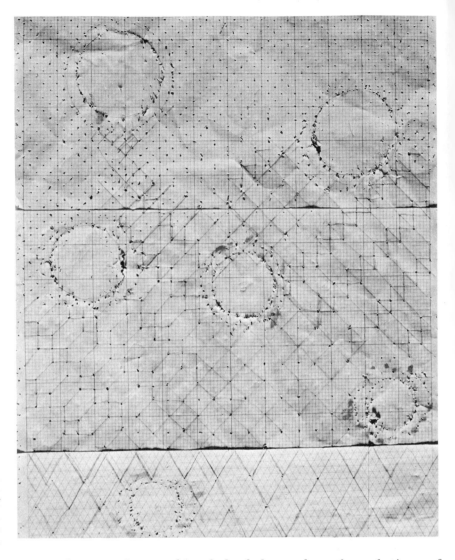

mounted on net. Lace-making helped the workers through times of poverty, but such wealth was spent by the upper classes in personal adornment with lace that governments found it necessary to tax lace imports. This led to local production of lace, such as at Tonder in Denmark, instead of importing lace from Dresden.

The invention of lace-making machines in the nineteenth century led to a complete decline in hand made lace. With the increased interest in handwork this century the skills have been revived and reinterpreted.

## Equipment and materials

The working of bobbin lace requires a minimum of equipment: a pillow or board to support the work, bobbins to weight and store the thread, pins to hold the bobbins in order and to work the pattern and a pricker for making and transferring patterns.

Lace pillows of various shapes have been handed down through generations and copied faithfully by lace-makers but, as with threads, equipment can be modified to suit modern needs. Instead of a pillow use a board made from a sheet of polystyrene or ceiling board 60 × 40 × 2.5cm (25 × 16 × 1in). Any board into which a pin can be inserted easily yet firmly is suitable. If the polystyrene tends to break away at the corners glue a piece of firm cardboard to the back. Some workers prefer to fold a plastic sheet tightly over the board to prevent the edges flaking. Cover the board with cotton fabric such as sheeting through which a pin will pass without extra pressure. Choose a plain pastel colour, pale blue, for example, to prevent any visual confusion while working. A second or even a third board may be required for large-scale work.

Fine antique bobbins are not practical as they do not hold sufficient length of the type of thread used by present-day lace-makers. Simple yet practical bobbins can be made using dowling rod cut into equal lengths, the size and weight depending on the thread to be used. For most work use 0.6cm ($\frac{1}{4}$in) dowling rod cut into 13cm (5in) lengths. Use thicker dowling rods to make larger bobbins in proportion to heavier threads. To smooth the ends trim but do not sharpen in a pencil sharpener.

With most threads ordinary dressmaking 2.5cm (1in) pins are suitable. A pin cushion facilitates the picking up of the pins and the most comfortable to use is one of 10cm (4in) diameter with a flat base padded to a dome shape. Pins not in use should not be pinned into the board as constant pricking in the same area will wear it out.

The pricker is a pin vice available from a tool shop; a needle, the size of the pins to be used in making the lace, is screwed into this vice. It is possible to use a needle in a cork but it is not so comforatable to hold.

Two pieces of cotton fabric about 40cm (16in) square are required as covers: one to place between the pattern and the bobbins and the other to be laid over the work when not in use to keep the lace and thread clean.

For patterns squared or angled paper, lace card, or lampshade 'vellum' will be needed. The lace card can be bought from suppliers of lace making equipment.

Threads of all types can be used for lace except those which do not maintain their twist when tested with a right-over-left roll between the finger and thumb. Threads should be chosen according to the final effect required. If a draped style is intended, for example, soft threads will enhance the effect. If texture is important to the piece threads can be varied in thickness but it would be better to limit them to one colour or a slight variation in shades. When colour is used for impact it is sufficient to work in one type of thread only, but two thicknesses may be introduced. For a large pattern it is not always necessary to choose a thicker thread – a firmer, more heavily twisted thread, for example, might be suitable. To see how the size of thread relates to the pattern,

# Textile Crafts

**121** *The Tree* by Isabel Elliott, 31 × 29cm (12¼ × 11½in). The two simple stitches of cloth and cloth and twist are used to interpret an individual idea. Using a dark brown rayon thread, fifty pairs of bobbins were hung along the top of the design and two rows of cloth and twist were worked to form a square ground; then cloth stitch was introduced to begin the shape of the tree. Where the design needed more solid cloth stitch for the branches, the threads were drawn closer together. Variations were made to indicate the rough knots of the main trunk. Throughout, the lace was worked in rows right across the panel, left to right then right to left.
Photo: John Hunnex

wind a few bobbins and work a small section. This sample working is particularly valuable when using twisted knitting yarns as they tend to take up so much room when worked in lace stitches.

The following list of threads, all of which are available from craft suppliers, is given as a guide to choosing a suitable thread for a project:

1 Thick knitting cotton in neutral shades and many colours is economical and suitable for practising stitches, braids, fringes and large-scale panels.

2 Finer knitting cotton in neutral shades has softer colours than the thick knitting cotton. This can be used for narrower braids and is also very versatile with other threads giving a matt finish which supports fancy yarns without altering the finished effect.

3 Crochet cotton of all sizes is a reliable thread and easily obtainable.

4 Linen lace thread in various sizes is obtainable from suppliers of lace-making equipment. It is usually in white and sometimes ecru, thus limiting its use. Some makes tend to fluff while working.

5 Cotton lace thread is available in various sizes, usually white.

6 Mercerized cotton machine twist though rather fine works well and is made in a good range of colours and shades.

7 Polyester sewing thread is fine but pleasant to use.

8 Metallic lurex knitting yarns come in various colours, also with a tinsel finish.

9 Embroidery threads of all types can be used to make the whole area

of lace, or combined with other yarns; a fancy knitting wool, for example, works in more easily if the workers are embroidery thread. A metallic thread might stretch during working so one bobbin of the pair wound with embroidery thread and the other bobbin with the metallic thread will help to keep an even tension. The shade should match as near as possible the metallic thread using medium yellow with gold and light grey with silver.

10  Mohair knitting wool gives a very interesting surface but does not move into position easily when working. Cloth stitch is the most suitable stitch to use because more elaborate stitches are lost in the fluff of the mohair.

11  Hand spun wool is usable but difficult to handle; because the threads cling together, each stitch must be arranged in position before moving to the next. The varied natural shades of the wool give a special quality to the lace.

12  Courtelle or other man-made yarns are easier to use than wool.

13  Ribbons, cords and plastic raffia are some of the unusual threads which can be worked into lace patterns.

## Pattern making

In traditional lace every detail of the design of the finished piece is established on the pattern or pricking. This shows its full size with pinholes already pricked and direction indicated. The pricking is pinned in position on the pillow and the lace worked directly on it. This traditional system is invaluable for learning to make lace, for practising and experimenting with the basic stitches and grounds and it is indispensable for recording and describing. Once experience has been gained, however, and the lace-maker requires more creative freedom, patterns can include less detail, giving only general outlines of worked areas and notations of stitch type.

Patterns are first worked out on squared or angled paper so they can be enlarged or reduced. When a more permanent pattern is needed, take a pricking from the squared paper through to the card or lampshade 'vellum'; if a pricking is going to be subjected to heavy use, lace card should be used.

When making the pattern on squared paper, the relative number of squares must be the same throughout: the pin holes are either $1\frac{1}{2}$, 3 or 6 squares apart. Any variation and the whole design will go askew.

## Setting up the work

Pin the pattern or pricking, smooth side up, in position towards the top of the board. Lay one cloth over the lower part of the pricking leaving about 13cm (5in) showing. If you are right handed place the pin cushion near the top right-hand corner of the board. Secure it with a large pin to prevent it slipping down the board.

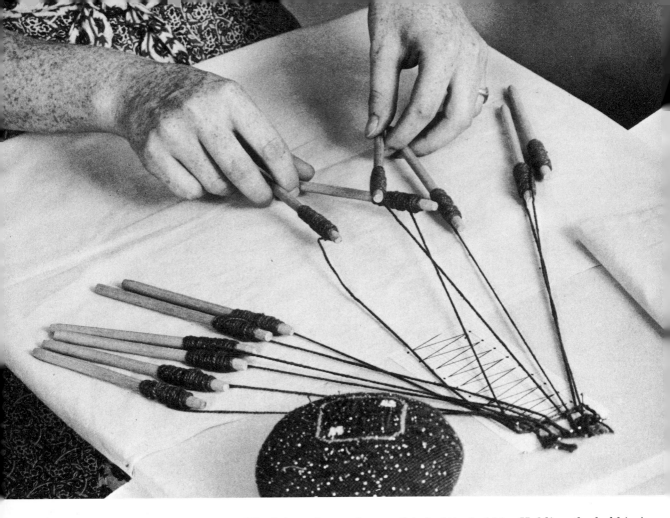

**122** The pricking and bobbins in position on a cloth-covered board. The workers have woven through the passives in cloth stitch from left to right and a pin holds them at the first pinhole. The hands now show how to work movement (a) (2 over 3) for cloth stitch.
Photo: John Hunnex

Wind thread over the top third of the bobbin. Holding the bobbin in the left hand start by laying the thread along the bobbin towards the top and, winding with the right hand, place the threads side by side over the laid end winding to and fro until there is sufficient thread on the bobbin (illus. 124[1]). Cut the thread about 15cm (6in) away from the bobbin and loop over as shown in illustration 124[2]. This holds the bobbin in position but by gently twisting the bobbin more thread can be released as needed without undoing the loop.

If a bobbin slips down longer than the others it may be wound too loosely and sometimes it is necessary to hitch knot twice. To lengthen for working it will have to be loosened with a pin.

If braid or ribbon is being worked into the lace wind it on to a bobbin and, instead of a hitch knot, carefully twist a rubber band over to prevent it slipping undone. Alternatively, braid or ribbon can be wound on a length of card but the bobbin is easier to pick up because it hangs in the same position as the other bobbins.

Bobbins are usually worked in pairs and a neat way to start the lace is to have the two wound from each end of a long length of thread. They will then loop over the pin at the top of the pricking; alternatively the two ends from a pair of bobbins can be knotted on to a pin. Each pattern requires a different number of bobbins and in each case they are hung in different positions. All bobbins should hang parallel across the board.

The board should be set at an angle supported at the top by a box, books or even a cushion. Alternatively rest the top of the board on a small table a little higher than one's lap. Sit in a comfortable position.

## Basic stitches

There are two basic lace stitches: cloth stitch (sometimes called whole stitch) and half stitch. These involve two basic actions, cross and twist, from which all lace stitches develop. Once these and the basic stitches have been mastered, the lace-maker is free to experiment.

Set up the board as a practice exercise. Prepare a pricking on squared paper arranging two vertical rows of dots 4cm (1½in) apart. Space the left row of dots 1.3cm (½in) apart and the right row half way between the spaces. Using ink (pencil will make the lace dirty) draw zig-zag lines across the paper from one side to the other, not quite touching the dots because it makes it more difficult to see them when making the lace.

Wind six pairs of bobbins with a heavy knitting cotton and hang them on to pins across the top of the pricking (as shown in illus. 122). In all lace stitches there are threads known as 'workers' which weave under and over across the board, and threads which do not alter their positions in the pattern of the lace but hang straight down, being held in place by the workers weaving across. These threads are called 'passives'.

## Cloth stitch

The first pair of bobbins, numbered 1 and 2 in illustration 124[5], are the workers. Start at the left-hand top corner and make the first stitch by using the first two pairs numbered 1, 2, 3 and 4 (see also illus. 123).

(a) Hold bobbin 2 between the first finger and thumb of the left hand and lay it over bobbin 3 so that the threads are crossed.

(b) Pick up the thread that has become bobbin 2 with the left hand and bobbin 4 with the right hand and lift them together to cross 2 over 1 and 4 over 3, so that the threads are twisted.

(c) Repeat (a), 2 over 3.

(d) Move on to the 2nd and 3rd pairs, and repeat (a), (b) and (c).

(e) Continue working with the 3rd and 4th pairs and finally the 4th and 5th pairs.

(f) The first pair have now woven under and over across to the right-hand side. Lift this pair, the workers, and hold them in position with a pin in the first dot on the right.

(g) The next stage is to weave the workers back to the left-hand side. Taking the workers and the 5th pair, work a cloth stitch in exactly the same way as before. Although the work is in the opposite direction it is not necessary to reverse the movement, just repeat the cloth stitch working to the left side putting a pin into the 2nd dot.

**123** Cloth stitch *(top)*: one pair of bobbins weaves from left to right through five pairs (which hang as passives) then weave back right to left; these workers are held in place by a pin in the pricking hole. Half stitch *(middle)*: the last movement of cloth stitch is omitted before leaving the pairs of bobbins twisted; this gives a honeycomb effect.
Cloth and twist stitch *(bottom)*: after each cloth stitch the right-hand bobbins are crossed over the left of each pair before the next cloth stitch is made.
Photo: John Hunnex

**124**

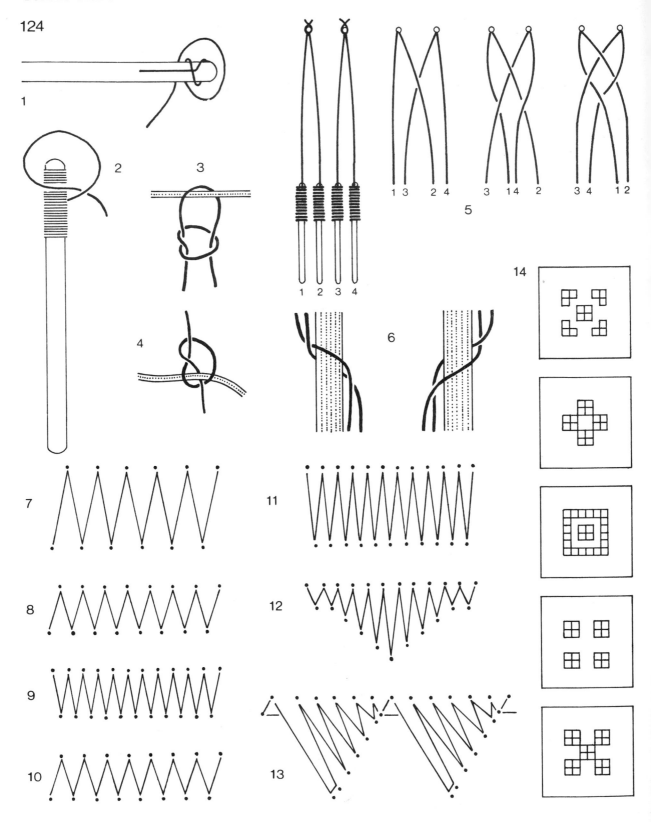

Practise working to and fro until it becomes a natural movement, watching the lace and not the bobbins.

## Half stitch

Working with two pairs, bobbins numbered 1, 2, 3 and 4 start as for cloth stitch, movements (a) and (b). Then (c) move to the next pair, bobbins 5, 6, 7 and 8 and repeat movements (a) and (b): 6 over 7, 6 and 8 over 5 and 7. The bobbins of each pair are thus twisted (crossed) right over left (illus. 123).

Using two pairs, work continuous half stitch to make a plait or braid. To join two plaits, take 4 pairs, hold each pair as one bobbin, half stitch, pin, half stitch, then continue as two plaits.

## Cloth and twist stitch

Working with two pairs start as for cloth stitch, movements (a) and (b) (2 over 3, 2 and 4 over 1 and 3). (c) repeat (a) and (b) with the same pair of bobbins, so that an extra twist is formed (illus. 123). This is not strictly a basic stitch but it is worth working as a length to get the feel of the extra twist and to understand the square effect it produces.

## Working methods

To join a new thread use a lace knot (weaver's knot). Take the end from a full bobbin and cross the thread to make a circle; then with the finger pull through a loop to about the same size as the circle. Slide the old thread through the loop. Gradually tighten keeping an even tension on both threads so in the last movement the old thread clicks through in the centre of the knot forming a complete interlock (illus. 124[3 and 4]). Trim the ends and wind up excess thread on to the bobbin and continue working.

As the lace grows and the bobbins are uncomfortably near the bottom of the board move the work up the board in the following way. Take the lower edge of the cloth under the bobbins and fold it upwards to form a pouch with the bobbins inside. Pin the cloth in position and lift it slightly to release the weight of the bobbins on the thread. Pin it into position on the board and remove all the pins from the lace; then release the cloth and gently lift it towards the top of the board and repin the lace at approximately 4cm (1½in) or until the weight of the bobbins will not distort the lace. Unfold the cloth and continue.

At the end of a piece of lace always cut off the bobbins leaving a few centimetres or inches of thread before removing the pins; otherwise the weight of the bobbins will pull the lace out of shape.

Passives can be knotted at the completion of the lace to form a fringe. A development of this would be to allow for extra threads of passives before starting the lace, working an oblong shape and knotting a fringe at each end. To prevent the excess thread from tangling at the beginning, wind it on to a strip of card before winding it on to the bobbins.

**124** [1 and 2] Winding a bobbin.
[3 and 4] The lace knot.
[5] Cloth stitch.
[6] Working in a gimp.

Prickings for the braids and fringes illustrated on page 232:
[7] braid 1
[8] braid 2
[9] braid 3
[10] braid 4
[11] fringe 1
[12] fringe 2
[13] fringe 3

[14] Prickings for the five variations in cloth stitch and cloth and twist stitch (illus. 125).
Artist: Mollie Picken

## Abbreviations

Lace patterns are best understood in abbreviated form:

| | |
|---|---|
| prs | pairs |
| t | twist – right bobbin of a pair over the left bobbin |
| c | cloth stitch |
| h | half stitch |
| ct | cloth and twist stitch |
| L-R | left to right |
| st | stitch |
| wk | workers |
| encl | enclose – with 2 pairs work a stitch, pin, repeat the stitch to enclose the pin. |
| L1 or L2 | left-hand pair of bobbins from pin 1 or 2 |
| R1 or R2 | right-hand pair of bobbins from pin 1 or 2 |
| c2 | cloth stitch through 2 pairs |
| 2t or 3t | 2 or 3 extra twists |

## Experiments with basic stitches

Practise making the basic stitches until the actions become automatic, always looking at the lace rather than at the bobbins.

To experiment with the stitches, consider the textures of each and try combining them. Cloth stitch and cloth and twist stitch can be used to complement each other, giving a solid texture in contrast to the holes formed by the twisted threads. Try using different stitches across a 15cm (6in) square. The thread could be varied in thickness. Support the threads with pins where necessary.

Simple arrangements of the holes can be planned on graph paper before starting the lace. Choose a thread which shows the contrast of solid texture and holes clearly. The squares in illustrations 124[14] and 125 were planned to form a necklace, but the idea could be used on a larger scale to make a belt using crochet cotton to match a day outfit, or metallic finish for evening wear. Worked in unusual threads a wall runner would show to advantage. On a much larger scale, using a knitting cotton, the idea could be worked as a border for a bedspread, working the ends into a fringe.

Try working a more elaborate fringe than the simple knotted one described on page 229. Using the six pairs of bobbins set up on the practice board, proceed as follows:

(a)   Twist the first two pairs (2 over 1, 4 over 3).

(b)   Work cloth and twist stitch (2 over 3, 2 and 4 over 1 and 3, repeat).

(c)   Repeat (a) and (b) with the 3rd and 4th pairs, then work the 5th and 6th pairs across to the right-hand side.

(d)   On the next row, twist the first pair (2 over 1) and continue across in cloth and twist stitch. Twist the last pair (6 over 5).

In abbreviated form, these instructions are as follows: 2pr t, ct, repeat with subsequent prs to right-hand side. 1pr t, next 2prs ct, repeat to right-hand side, t last pr.

## Exercise 1: flower made in cloth stitch

This exercise making a simple flower shape shows the lace-maker how to vary the width of cloth stitch and how to use 'sewing' to join strips of lace (illus. 126).

Choose a crochet cotton in the size best suited to the scale of the flower. Use seven pairs of bobbins, each pair wound from one length of thread. Then proceed as follows: Hang 4prs over pins at base of petal near centre of flower. Working left side of petal, c to 5th pin on outer line. Bring in 1 new pr by hanging on pin. c to vein, back to outer line. Repeat until there are 7prs in use. c until workers meet the worked half of petal on centre pin.

Join by sewing: remove the pin and, using a fine crochet hook, draw the thread from one of the workers through the loops of the lace already worked, pass the second worker through the thread loop and tighten into position. Replace the pin in the original pinhole. c rest of petal making 8 sewings down the centre. At the same time to narrow petal leave out 3prs matching those taken in on first side. To leave out: work through the pr, pin, work back leaving the outside pr unworked on next row. Twist the 3prs to make firm bars ready to be taken in on next petal, the number of twists depending on length of bar and size of thread. At centre, turn threads neatly ready for next petal. Finish off

125 *(opposite)* Five variations of cloth stitch and cloth and twist stitch worked in gold lurex knitting yarn by Isabel Elliott. The cloth stitch gives a solid texture in contrast to the holes formed by the twisted threads. The pattern was planned on squared paper (see illus. 124 [14]) using twelve pairs of bobbins. The squares of lace are mounted on thin card covered with soft leather with the turnings glued on the other side. A second piece of card forms the back of each medallion to make a neat finish. The medallions could be set on a cord or crochet chain to make a necklace. On a larger scale they could be used to make a belt. Photo: John Hunnex

126 Cloth stitch flower. Each petal pricking was drafted to be 10.5cm (4¼in) from the tip to the centre of the flower and 5.5cm (2¼in) at the widest point. Sewings were made where the petals touch. Photo: John Hunnex

the threads by sewing or by darning them back into the lace with a sewing needle.

Try making cloth stitch flowers in a variety of sizes, using different threads. Make flowers consisting of petals of different sizes bringing in more bobbins for larger petals. Make linking bars round three petals to form a triangular shape. A small flower could be stitched in the centre of a big one.

**Exercise 2: braids** (illus. 124 and 127)

Braids or simple narrow laces have many uses, for example for trimming soft furnishings. They are also an ideal way of making a record of different effects which later can be incorporated into larger laces (as in illus. 128). Many variations of these ideas can be made by altering the size of the pricking, the thickness of the threads and the colour arrangement.

BRAID 1 Position the bobbins: 1pr wks, 2prs, 1cm space, 2prs. Then work the braid as follows: c2, 4 t wks, c2, pin. Repeat.

Ribbon could be threaded through this braid to make a dress trimming or mounted on a contrasting colour for soft furnishings.

BRAID 2 1pr wks, 2prs, 1pr thick thread, 2prs. c5, pin. Repeat.

BRAID 3 1pr wks, 2prs, 1 bobbin threaded with beads, 1 bobbin, 2prs. c5, pin. Repeat.

A bead is pushed up into position as required.

BRAID 4 1pr wks, 4prs wound with a stiff plastic thread. H4, pin. Repeat.

Due to the character of the thread the honeycomb shape of half stitch makes a decorative texture.

During the Victorian era strips of narrow lace with a straight edge on both sides were joined together by hand sewing to make larger pieces of lace which could be used for dress or for one of the many mats or runners for the decoration of the home. This is an idea which the lace-maker of today might reconsider. A matching edging lace can easily be made, but if yards are needed to complete a project then fresh ideas for styles of lace are needed. Experiment using piping cord and knitting cotton, which is sold in large balls and works out as one of the cheapest ways of buying thread. Having decided on piping cord the design must be adjusted to the particular curve that the cord will follow. If speedy work is needed then the fewer the pin holes the quicker the lace may be made. Crossing the cords in the centre gives emphasis thus making the pattern more interesting than having just straight lines of cord.

An unusual use of this type of lace can be made in the style of log cabin patchwork. Plan a square, the size depending on the scale of the lace, arranging the lace across the diagonal then a length of ribbon each side and alternating with the lace to the short corners. The edges of lace can be neatly oversewn to the ribbon edges. When a number of squares have been prepared join them by a continuous line of wider ribbon, which if doubled will go back and front of the raw edges of the lace and narrow ribbon. Try adding one of the fringes described below to finish the lace off and weigh it down to hold it in shape.

**Exercise 3: fringes** (illus. 124 and 127)

As well as having many uses as trimmings, fringes are also a convenient and attractive way to finish off a lace piece. The fringes described below can be made in a variety of threads and colours to discover the effect of each.

FRINGE 1 (STRAIGHT) 1pr wks. 2prs to left side pricking. c2, pin at right edge to hold workers the full width of pricking. c1, t passives, c1 pin. Repeat.

The twist of the 1pr passives is to hold the c in position, preventing it from slipping to the middle and so reducing the width of the fringe.

FRINGE 2 (SHAPED) 1pr wks, 2prs. Worked as fringe 1, varying the shape by altering the position of the right-hand edge pins.

FRINGE 3 (SLANTING) This fringe is worked on isometric paper. 1pr wks, 2prs, 1pr contrasting colour.c3, pin c1, t passives, c1, t passives, c1, pin. Repeat keeping contrasting pr on right-hand edge. At point of triangle

**127** *(opposite)* Braids and fringes (see also illus. 124 [7 to 13]):
*Braid 1* arranging twists in the middle of the cloth stitch through which ribbon may be threaded.
*Braid 2* worked in cloth stitch.
*Braid 3* worked in close cloth stitch with beads threaded on one of the centre passive threads and pushed into position as required.
*Braid 4* worked in half stitch.
*Fringe 1* worked in cloth stitch.
*Fringe 2* worked in cloth stitch with the looped edge shaped into triangles on the pricking.
*Fringe 3* worked in two colours.
Photo: John Hunnex

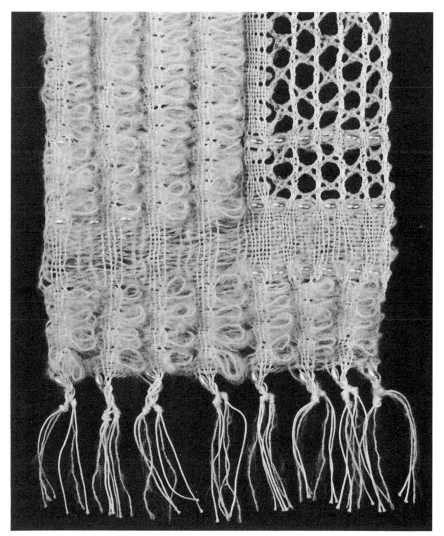

**128** Fringed lace by Dorothea Nield, 32 × 19cm (12¾ × 7½in). A simple fringe can be arranged in strips held together by workers taken right across between the loops of the fringe. The first time this idea was worked, a twisted rayon thread was used as the main supporting thread. When the lace was complete and the pins removed it sagged and lost its shape as the thread had the wrong twist and each time a pair of bobbins twisted right over left the thread untwisted. Those finally chosen were crochet cotton, mohair and courtelle knitting yarn. The method of weaving a pearl into position is shown in illustration 134 [3].
Photo: John Hunnex

**129**

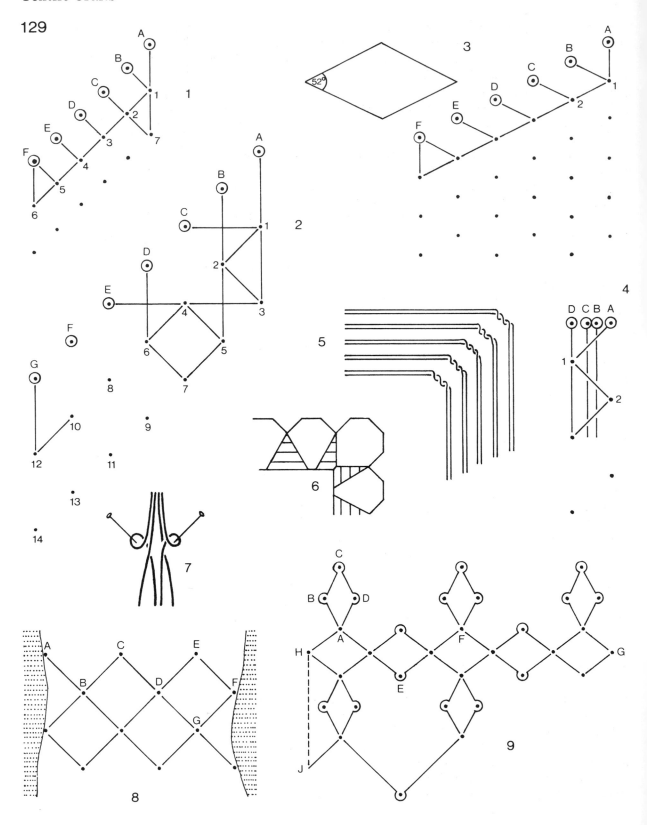

plait (h without pins until required length) wks and contrast pr. Contrast pr take over as wks and others are right-hand edge pr.

FRINGE VARIATIONS The simple fringe pattern based on diamond shapes is adjustable to any size. The workers form the fringe and weave a solid part in cloth or cloth and twist on the other half leaving out at least 3 pairs of passives as the diamond shape narrows; then these passives are twisted as pairs making a cord long enough to be brought in on the next diamond.

By omitting the long lines which form the fringe a matching braid can be worked.

Further elaboration can be included by working in a flat narrow ribbon at the edge of the solid part before the fringe threads. This could be in a contrasting colour or a variation in shade or texture. Even the easily obtainable ricrac braid might be used to add interest.

To insert a braid, cord or thick thread known as a 'gimp': t wks, pass gimp under R wk, and over L wk, t wks. This can be taken either to the left or the right (illus. 124[6]).

Most fringes are worked across the narrow width but if a long fringe is desired it may be worked the other way. Hang the bobbins which are to form the heading and the fringe and use the workers to hold them in place. The one problem with this method is that the length of lace is determined by the width of the board; otherwise joins would be necessary. In most of the patterns described above the fringes are looped but this method gives a cut fringe.

## Developed techniques

The contemporary approach to lace making is based on traditional stitches used in a different way. Variations of the basic stitches are technically limited and over the centuries lace workers have already found all the possible positions of the threads. By working traditional patterns and analysing them, however, a fresh approach can be explored and personal modifications can be made and deliberate distortions can be introduced.

An area of one stitch pattern is called a 'ground'. There are many traditional grounds, most of which indicate the particular district in the world where the lace has been made. Try working them in different thicknesses of thread and in different colour combinations.

### Torchon ground (illus. 129[1])
Repeat in diagonal rows always working from top right to left edge. When worked in one colour this simple ground, which is a continuous repetition of half stitch, makes an open mesh. Pairs which vary in colour can give a very different effect, forming large diamonds or a zigzag pattern. Pricking is made with pin holes angled at 45°. 7prs, 1pr at each pin A to E, 2 prs at F. Take prs from A and B h pin at 1 encl. Take prs from C and L1 h pin at 2 encl. Take prs from D and L2 h pin at 3 encl. Repeat to pin 6. Take prs from 1 and 2 h pin at 7 encl.

129 [1] Torchon ground.
[2] Rose ground.
[3] Bucks point ground.
[4] Edge method.

Designing a corner from a straight pattern:
[5] Twist pairs of threads across the diagonal and hold them in place with pins.
[6] Adjust the pattern to fill the corner shape.

[7] Single picot.
[8] Russian ground 1.
[9] Russian ground 2.
Artist: Mollie Picken

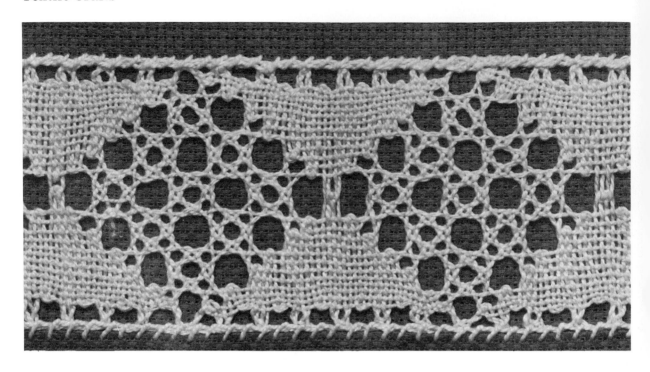

**130** A simple insertion pattern of rose ground contrasted with cloth stitch and mounted on linen. Photo: John Hunnex

**Rose ground** (illus. 129[2])

This ground forms a series of staggered honeycombs. Pricking is made with pin holes angled at 45°. 8prs, 1pr at each pin A to F, 2prs at G. h B and C without pin. h A and C pin at 1 encl. h L1 and b pin at 2 encl. h R2 and 1 pin at 3 encl. *h E and D without pin. h 2 and 3 without pin. h e and 3 pin at 4 encl. h R4 and 2 pin at 5 encl. h L4 and d pin at 6 encl. h R6 and L5 pin at 7 encl.

Repeat from * using prs from G and F with those from 6 and 7. To keep the edges straight, h G and L 11 pin at 12 encl. Continue in diagonal lines always working from top right to left edge.

To examine the journey that each pair of threads makes across an area of the ground, wind bobbins with black thread to come in on one side and with white on the other side of the rectangular pricking. Try using a very thick dishcloth yarn in one direction and a fine crochet cotton the other way. By working one direction in one colour and the other in another colour and using one black thread on each pair of bobbins, an entirely different effect from the basic rose ground can be built up. Vary the effect by filling alternate squares with cloth stitch and working rose ground on the other squares. Sequins sewn into the detached half stitch can add richness.

**Bucks point ground** (illus. 129[3])

This ground makes a honeycomb shaped net. It is effective worked on a large scale; the thread must be thick or firm enough to support the shape of the net. In period laces the pinholes were placed so close together that there were twelve to the inch.

Pricking based on a diamond which is angled at 52°. (Note: the pins

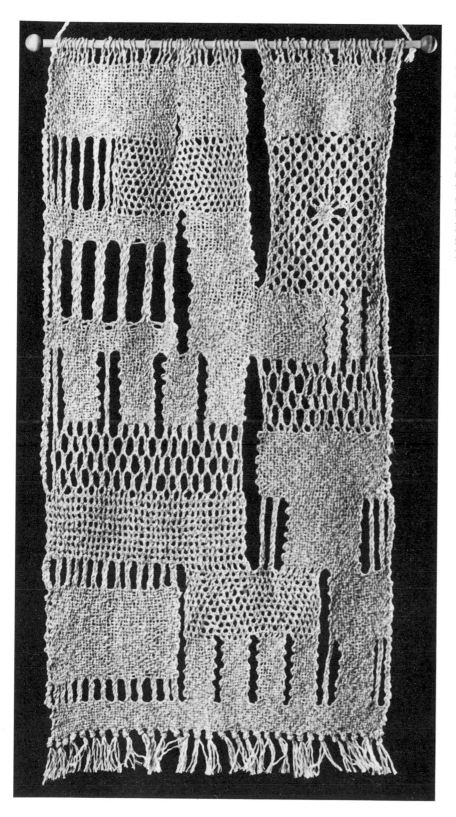

**131** Hanging worked in cloth stitch and Torchon ground by Janet Gross, 80 × 40cm (32 × 16in). The design was developed from the basic divisions of 8cm (3¼in) squares. The area of Torchon ground did not need the same number of bobbins as the cloth stitch at the top; therefore, some of the threads were darned back and reintroduced as required. A simple dowel rod was threaded through the loops formed at the top by winding each pair of bobbins from one length of thread and leaving sufficient loop before working the lace.
Photo: John Hunnex

are not enclosed.) 7prs, 1pr at A to E, 2prs at F. h A and B 2 t on each pr pin at 1. h L1 and C2 t on each pr pin at 2. Repeat to end of line.

Continue in diagonal lines always working from top right to left edge.

### Spider stitch (illus. 134[1])

Spider stitch features in many traditional lace pieces. Once learned, the stitch can be used to create original designs. Spiders are made on a pricking based on a square with the points North and South, East and West. There are pin holes at each point with 3 equidistant on each side and 1 in the centre of the square. 10prs, 1pr at A B C D E on the left of the pricking and F G H J K on the right. h A and F pin at 1 encl. h B and L1 pin at 2 encl. Repeat to pin 5. h R1 and G pin at 6 encl. Repeat to pin 9. 2 t for each pr from pins 2 3 4 6 7 and 8. c 2 through 6 7 and 8. c 3 through the same prs. Repeat with 4. Pin in centre between the six prs. c 8

**132** A development of the traditional spider pattern using four spiders arranged as one large square, framed by triangles of half stitch closely worked to vary the texture from the usual honeycomb effect.
Photo: John Hunnex

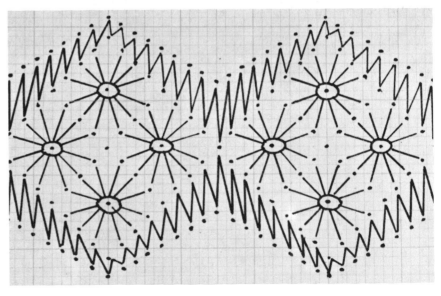

through 4 3 and 2. Repeat with 7 and 6. 3t for each of the six prs. h 4 and 5 pin at 10 encl. Repeat to complete the two sides of the square.

Spiders can be worked larger with 8prs. They can be used as a single square within a complete design incorporating other methods, or to break an area of plain texture, for example within a cloth stitch rectangle. Four spiders arranged as a large square framed by triangles of half stitch make an interesting border suitable for applying to a fabric. Pricking drafted from the illustrated pattern (illus. 133). 22prs, 10prs to left of centre pin at top of spider, 2 prs wks, 10 to right side. h 2 wks pin at centre hole encl. *h L wk through 10prs to L edge pin. h through 10prs pin. h through 10prs to edge pin. h through 9prs pin. Repeat leaving out 1pr on the inside pins to work the spiders until there are 2prs and 1pr wks at the narrowest point. Repeat from * on the right side. Work the top spider then the left and right and finally the fourth. Return to the half stitch wks, continue working the triangle bringing in 1pr before each of the inside pins to match the top half of the pattern.

In this pattern the half stitch is very close so the honeycomb effect of braid 4 is lost and instead an interesting woven texture is worked. This pattern can be worked on a larger scale using, for example, a tightly twisted viscose rayon crochet yarn.

## Working circles and ovals

By working lace spirally from the centre outwards many simple ideas can be developed. With the board in a flat position, pin the pricking in the centre. Start by hanging two or three pairs of bobbins in the middle of the pattern and work round and round, adding extra pairs when needed as the curves get larger. Turn the board to keep the bobbins hanging vertically. The ends of the threads are finished by darning, so the fewer the bobbins the neater the finish.

## Linking shaped lace

Having worked shaped lace motifs consideration must be given to the method of linking them. The Russian lace workers devised a simple way in which to fill varied shapes of background (illus. 129[8 and 9]).

RUSSIAN GROUND 1 Pricking: as for torchon ground the pin-holes are angled at 45°, drafted to fill the space between the worked lace motifs which are pinned in position on the pricking. 2prs. Sew the 2prs at A through the edge of the lace. Plait to B pin. Continue plait to C, D, E and F, sewing into the lace at F. Repeat across the pattern to the left sewing into the previous plait at D and B. Continue this zig-zag pattern until the background is filled. To neaten, the four ends of thread can be darned into the lace.

RUSSIAN GROUND 2 A more elaborate ground pattern can be made using the same principle with the addition of picots. A single picot is a decorative loop made by twisting the outside thread of a plait and holding it in place with a pin. Hold the thread in the left hand and with the right hand place the pin under the thread then over the thread

**133** Spider stitch by Prudence Steel, 17.5 × 5.5cm (7 × 2¼in). Thirty-four pairs of bobbins were used with mercerized cotton machine twist. Here the spider stitch looks delicate as the hard outline has been omitted, the threads for the spider coming direct from the ground, which is worked on a square foundation rather than the more usual Torchon ground based on the diagonal at an angle of 45°. Photo: John Hunnex

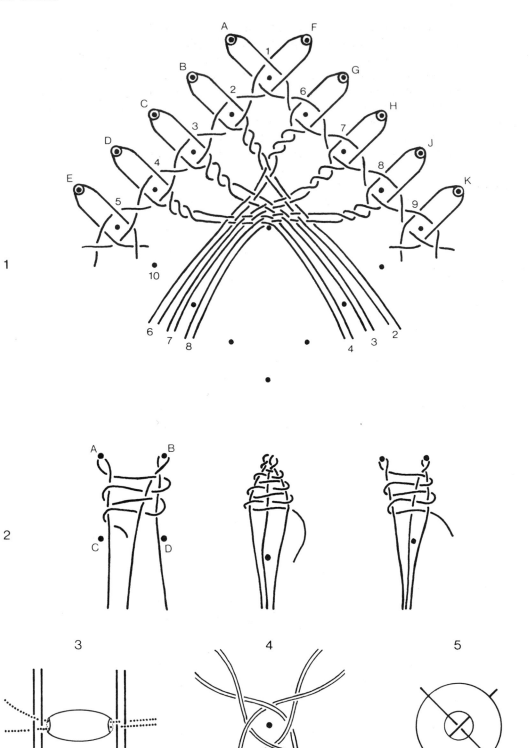

towards the worker; put the pin in the hole. Tighten the thread round the pin and, so the bobbins are in the correct position for the plaiting, pass bobbin *under* the next thread of the plait when the picot is on the left edge of the plait, and *over* it if on the right edge (see illus. 129[7]). On a pricking a curved line round a pin hole indicates a picot. Picots can also be worked on the edges of lace.

Pricking (illus. 129[9]): 2prs. Sew into lace at H, plait to A pin. *Plait to B picot pin. Plait to C pin. Plait to D picot pin. Plait to A sew. Plait to E picot pin. Plait to F and repeat from *. After sewing into lace at G zig-zag back to H sewing where the plaits cross. From H to J the threads can be plaited or sewn into the worked lace. Continue this zig-zag pattern until the background is filled, neatening off the threads by darning them into the lace.

LEADING Also called tally, cutwork or leadwork, this makes woven shapes, usually worked as an extra interest in an area of ground or in flower groups as in Cluny or Maltese laces. The leadings can be square, oval (petal shape) or triangular (illus. 134[2]).

For a square shape, a pin hole is needed at each corner. 2prs, 1pr at A and 1pr at B. t each pr. With 2nd bobbin from the left weave over and under B pr. Continue weaving over and under the 3 bobbins until a neat firm square is made. The weaving bobbin joins L passive with bobbins from the ground on pin C. R passives join ground bobbins on pin D.

To make oval shapes, 2 pin holes with the weaving widening in the middle of the shape. For triangular shapes 2 pin holes are needed at the top and both pairs join on a centre pin hole at the base.

FILLINGS Weaving and lace have much in common in the manipulation of threads but the equipment is so different that consideration is rarely given to incorporating the two processes in one item of work. In the technique described below, lace is combined with woven fabric (the method also invites comparison with counted thread work in embroidery, see page 72).

Select a fabric such as linen scrim from which the threads can be drawn easily yet is firm enough to support the technical requirements of reworking the threads. Withdraw a panel of warp threads to within a few centimetres of one edge. Cut away the weft threads. Make a neat edge with a line of zig-zag machine stitch or darn the threads into the side fabric. Stretch the material on a lace board and with squared paper underneath work a lace pattern using the drawn threads. Obviously the final size will be smaller as the pattern uses up the threads.

**Edge method**
To make lace with a straight edge suitable for sewing to a fabric, make the pricking with a vertical line of pin holes alternating angled to match the lace pattern. 4prs – 1pr wks at A, 1pr at B C D. c A with B and C. t wks pin at 1. ct with C. L1 2 t. R1 c C and B at 2 which would be the linking point with the rest of the lace pattern. Repeat.

**134** [1] Spider stitch.
[2] Leading: woven shapes forming a square, an oval and a triangle.
[3] Weaving a pearl into position.
[4] Joining plaits.
[5] Attaching a sequin.
Artist: Mollie Picken

This can be worked on the right or the left edges. Worked on both sides the method can be used to make strips of insertion lace.

### Shaped patterns

To draft a straight pattern to fit a curve, to decorate a neckline for example, first mark the shape of the neckline on squared paper. Draw the outlines of the lace. A centre construction line between the outlines will help to angle the workers accurately.

There are two methods of designing a corner from a straight pattern:
1 Cut the straight pattern on the diagonal. Then, allowing a small clear channel of about $\frac{1}{2}$cm ($\frac{1}{4}$in), place an exact repeat of the pattern in the direction for the next straight side. Each pair of threads is twisted across the diagonal and held in place by pins (illus. 129[5]). In this way the threads start off at the correct angle for the second side. If joining the lace round four sides begin and finish off on the diagonal line.
2 Design a corner adjusting part of the main pattern to fill the triangular space between the two straight sides (illus. 129[6]). By holding a small mirror diagonally across various parts of the pattern, a suitable shape will be seen more easily.

### Working with pearls, beads and sequins

These can be sewn on top of the lace after it is finished but it is more satisfactory to work them into the lace. Take a double thread of sewing cotton and thread on all the pearls. Wind them carefully on to a bobbin. When a pearl is needed in the design open the cotton threads and weave a pair of passives under and over the single threads of the cotton, then push the pearl into position and weave the next pair of passives through the cotton which will blend with the other threads until required again (illus. 134[3]).

To attach a sequin during the lace making, one bobbin passes behind the sequin; with a fine crochet hook or pin draw a loop of the bobbin thread up through the hole, pass a second thread through the loop, tightening the sequin in position (illus. 134[5]).

## Planning and further developments

Interpreting new ideas in lace requires much careful preparation, particularly if the piece is a panel. To decide the size first experiment with the lace board to find out the distance that can be reached comfortably to put in pins and, even more important, how far can be seen – the manipulated bobbins may make the stitch but unless it is within range, its appearance cannot be seen. For comfort the board can be propped on an almost upright stand to bring the top into focus. Or a second and even a third board of identical thickness can be added as the bobbins require more support. In the early stages the complete pricking will be too long for the first board so the excess can be rolled round a cardboard roller and fixed to the lower edge of the board, rolling out more as the next board is added. Small practice samplers

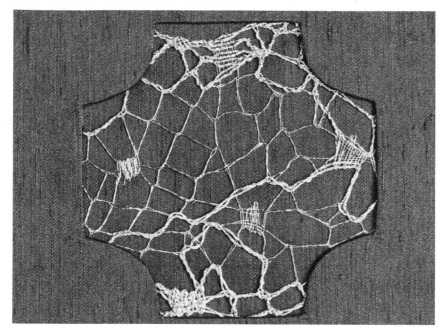

**135** Gold and silver freehand lace by Margaret Taylor, 20cm sq. (8in). Three different textures of fine lurex threads were wound on to bobbins and, instead of a lace board, the background fabric of green dupion was mounted on an embroidery slate frame and stretched taut. Working direct on the background ensures that the angles of the threads are accurate and not pulled out of shape when making up the article. The area of lace to be worked was outlined with tacking stitches and the beginning threads from the bobbins were stitched along the top of the shape. A polystyrene board placed under the frame supported the pins. Without a preplanned design the bobbins were woven freely over the area using a few pins to help hold the stitches in place. When the lace was complete the threads from the bobbins were stitched through the background material and finished off. The shaped fabric mount frames the lace and covers the edges.
Photo: John Hunnex

are necessary to work out the size of the design in relation to the stitches and the thread, also the angles the bobbins will come from one area of stitches to the next. Sometimes a gimp or narrow band of cloth stitch will make a neat change over.

Each lace worker will find her own way to plan a design; one of the following methods will lead to an individual approach:

1 Geometric layout on squared paper considering areas of pattern and the proportion in relation to solid stitches.
2 One stitch or ground pattern dictating the style of design.
3 Freehand simple line drawing which can be adjusted as the lace progresses and a line needs to be moved to fit a particular stitch.

The individual approach to bobbin lace has freed the technique from its traditional confines. Its future style is not easy to predict as each lace-maker has preferences. Some enjoy using heavy threads to make chunky wall hangings while others search for new ideas within the range of the delicate lacy character of the technique. New methods can be explored by combining stitches, inventing grounds and, once the basic movements have been mastered, by abandoning the restrictions imposed by detailed pattern making. Freehand lace is best worked over a simple sketch or outline or direct on to a fabric background. Shapes can be built up freely by adding or deleting threads, multi-layered lace and three-dimensional forms can be made by working new threads on the top of a background piece. The gold and silver freehand lace (illus. 135) is the work of a lace-maker experienced in traditional methods who uses them as a vocabulary to interpret fresh ideas expressed with lines, solids and spaces in relation to each other. This approach produces a style of lace worthy of our period and a continuation of the skills passed down to us through the centuries.

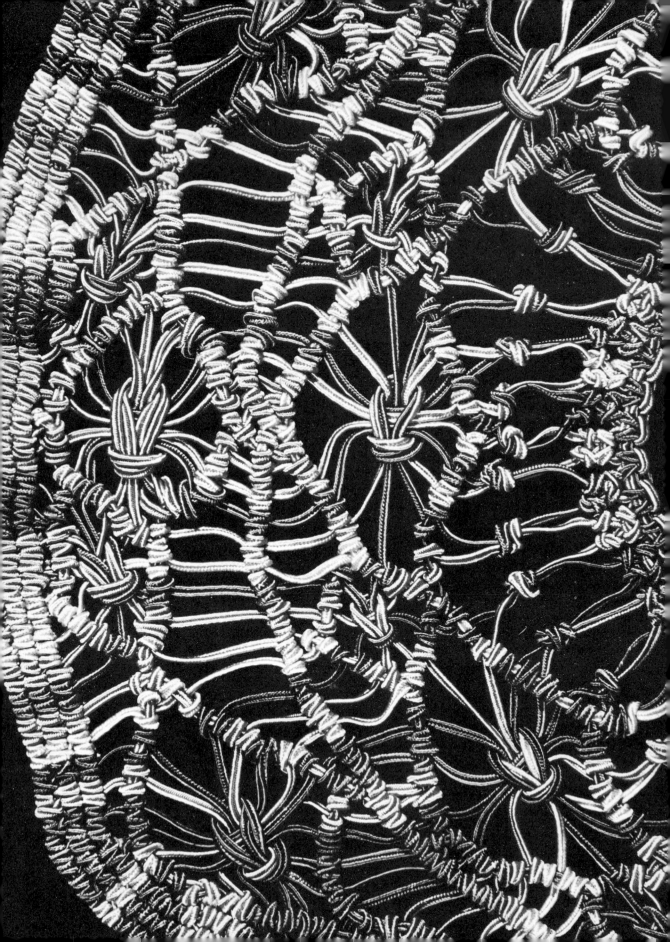

# Macramé
## Zoë de Negri

Macramé is a very old craft – the ancient Egyptians were acquainted with this art of knotting and constructed decorative fringes and other articles with threads and papyrus fibres. It was practised by the Assyrians and examples may be found in the stone carved friezes of the ninth century BC, where the costumes of many of the figures are decorated with thick, knotted fringes and heavy tassels. The craft reached Europe via Spain, through the Moorish invasions and in Italy was brought back by those returning from the crusades. It reached England at the end of the seventeenth century and became a particularly popular occupation in the nineteenth century. In the Mediterranean area macramé was made and exported to the Americas, while some of the Canadian Indians learnt the art from the sailors who helped to spread it to many countries.

The art of macramé knotting is now combined with other techniques such as weaving, twining and wrapping to produce exciting wall hangings and free form structures. It has also a use for fanciful garments and accessories as well as for household articles. Today macramé is much freer – many more varieties of thread are available than the light lacy threads used by the Victorians. Any thread, from heavy twine or hemp or woollen yarns of various weights to fine metallic threads, may be used.

Invariably a person who is not familiar with macramé believes it to be an extremely complicated craft. The designs may appear to have no beginning and no end, and to fashion an article from a mass of loose ends without a needle and thread seems an impossibility. The procedure is quite simple in fact: one needs to know only a few basic knots and techniques with which to start. By using imagination and inventiveness, exciting macramé pieces can be made with a knowledge of only a few knots. With further knowledge more varieties of texture and pattern can be achieved.

## Equipment

The most important piece of equipment is the knotting board on which the cords are held. The board should be of a rigid material but soft enough to stick 'T' pins into. To begin with the board should be 45cm (18in) square; with more ambitious pieces a larger one will be required. Cork or fibreboard make excellent knotting boards. When making a garment work directly on a dress stand if one is available. 'T' pins, long straight pins with bead heads, or millinery pins, are used for anchoring

**136** A geometric diamond pattern with square knots, curved to make a large collar (detail), in Russian braid. A neckpiece as complicated as this is best worked directly on the dress stand. The working threads are set on to the square knot sinnet neckband closely together to avoid adding in extra threads immediately. The upper half of the first set of diamonds is worked using only the threads originally set on. Extra threads are added in equal distribution on the lower half of the diamonds and again in the curved cording rows by hitching them over the lead cords in rows of double half hitches. The three rows of closely worked horizontal double half hitches at the outer edge provide both firmness and definition to the piece and also provide a 'screen' behind which the loose ends can be woven.
Photo: John Hunnex

the work. A pair of scissors and a tape measure, will be needed; a crochet hook (medium size), a darning needle and fabric glue (millinery solution) are useful for dealing with ends.

## Setting up the work

Every piece of flat work is started from a holding cord, on to which the working threads are anchored. This can be achieved in several ways:

1 Cut a length of thread about 15cm (6in) longer than the desired width of the piece of work that is planned. Form an overhand knot at each end of the thread. Put the thread in position on the knotting board and stick a pin through one knot, tightening the knot securely around the pin; stretch the holding cord taut and pin the other end.

2 Make a crochet chain and pin it in shape on the board. This is a useful method when making a piece of macramé that does not have straight edges because the working threads attached through the crochet chain loops remain where they are inserted. On a cord with a curved edge they would slip out of position. This method is useful for knotting garments.

3 Make a line of strong blanket stitching and attach the working threads over the stitch loops. This method is used when making a fringe directly on to fabric.

4 Use a wooden dowel as a holding cord when making a wall hanging. On each of these foundations the method of attaching the working threads is the same. They are set in place by using a double half hitch knot. Double the thread and put the loop under the holding cord (or crochet or blanket stitch), fold it over and thread the two loose ends back through the loop and pull them to tighten the knot over the holding cord. Threads should be closely packed together across the width.

## Planning the work

It is helpful to plan preliminary designs on squared paper; if a piece of work with geometric patterns is being made, it will be necessary to know exactly how many threads are required. For the diamond pattern (see illus. 139) ten threads are required for each diamond plus two lead cords. Thus for four diamonds twenty-four threads must be cut which when doubled over the holding cord produce the required forty-eight.

Judging the lengths of the threads required for the complete piece is not easy. As it is not always satisfactory, or even possible, to join in extra lengths of threads midway through the piece, it is better to overestimate the lengths. As a general rule the thread before doubling should be eight times as long as the finished piece (or when doubled, four times as long). Some knots, flat knots or sinnets, for example, take up even more thread length and so allowance should be made for this if it is planned to use many sinnets or much close knotting. An open knotted pattern piece will use less thread.

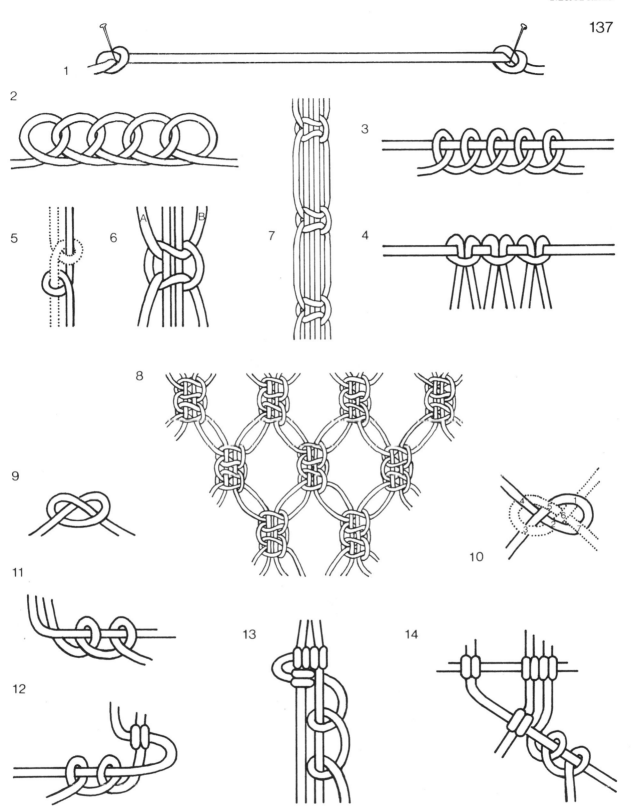

To join in an extra length of cord, the simplest way is to set an extra cord on the holding cord to replace the one that has become too short. This will give two extra cords, so if only one is needed cut the other fairly short and weave the loose end in (see 'finishing', page 255). If a thread is becoming too short it is best to set in a new one at the most convenient moment rather than waiting for it to finish completely.

If working on a square knot pattern when new cords need to be added, pin the new cord to the board anywhere, as this pinning is simply to keep it anchored, and work the square knot as usual using this new cord instead of the short one that is being replaced. Work a few more knots so that the new cord becomes securely involved in the work, then cut the beginning of the new cord short between the first knot and the pin and tie this loose end together with the now replaced short cord, at the back of the work.

Sometimes when making a piece of macramé with many sinnets the working threads become short while the centre core threads remain long. It is usually possible for them to switch places without disrupting the pattern, in other words the core threads become the working threads and vice versa.

Should the lead cord run out when cording or working double half hitches, lay a new length of cord parallel to the lead cord and work knots over both for a while until the new lead cord is secured and work can continue as usual.

## Macramé knots

The basic macramé knots can be used in an amazing number of combinations and variations and form the basis of all other knots. Practise these knots on samples, or small pieces of work. This will also serve later as a frame of reference and you can record any innovations or patterns of your own.

### The square knot

This knot requires four threads; the two centre threads which form a core or knot bearer are held taut while the outer two are knotted around them. It is actually formed with two half knots – one worked left to right and one right to left.

Facing the work take the left hand cord (A) *under* the knot bearer – to the right; bring the right hand cord (B) down *under* (A), up *over* the knot bearer and *through* the loop formed by (A) on the left side; pull knot firm. Cord B is now on the left side and A on the right – Bring B *over* the knot bearer, bring A down *over* B, *under* the knot bearer and through B's loop on the right hand side, pull knot firmly. The two knots form a complete square knot and when several are worked in succession form a bar – known as a sinnet, which will be flat. When learning this knot if still unsure which thread goes exactly where, the following gives exact directions: 'under, under, over, through; over, over, under, through'.

CORKSCREW SINNET A corkscrew effect is achieved by working a series of half knots all right to left for an anticlockwise twist, and all left to right for a clockwise twist. A corkscrew sinnet can be made to change directions at intervals of at least 5 to 8cm (2 or 3in) by varying the direction of the knot.

PICOT SQUARE KNOT SINNET This is made by leaving a space between two completed square knots as the work progresses and at the end pushing the knots up close together.

ALTERNATING SQUARE KNOTS This gives a pretty, lacy effect and can be worked in groups of one, two, three knots, etc. Form two sinnets of square knots; the outer adjacent cords from each sinnet form the core of the new sinnet and the one cord from each sinnet is worked around these.

## The half hitch

Again, this knot can be tied from left to right or right to left. Only two threads are necessary: the knot bearer is held tautly and the other is taken up across it and then underneath and then back over itself. An interesting textured effect can be achieved by working one left and one right half hitch. For a bulkier effect four or six threads can be used – two as the knot bearer and four as the knotting cord or vice versa. This also applies to the square knot.

**138** Fringe knotted with the unravelled warp threads of a woven shawl. The macramé pattern is a simple repetition of crossing rows of diagonal double half hitches. Tassels finish the fringe.
Photo: John Hunnex

### The double half hitch knot or cording

This is an extremely useful knot. It can be worked horizontally, vertically or diagonally or with a curve (over a paper pattern). With this knot shapes can be created within the piece of work; also two or three rows worked horizontally and closely together can help to give strength. It is also useful for creating a break between one pattern and another. It is formed by working two half hitches together. The direction of the 'cord' that is formed depends on the angle at which the knot bearing cord is held – horizontally, vertically or diagonally, etc. It is with this basic knot that diamond patterns and leaf patterns are made.

### The Josephine knot

This knot requires some mastering. It is best made with heavier threads or braids, or with several strands of a thinner yarn. Practise this knot with single heavy threads until quite familiar with it; then try with two or three strands. Take the left-hand thread and bring it up and over itself in a big loop and pin in position. Take the right-hand thread under the loop at (1) and (2), over at (3), under at (4), over at (5), under itself in the centre of the loop (6), and over at (7). Now pull the knot gently until the desired size is made.

## Samplers

Samplers provide a record of knots, patterns and ideas (illus. 142[1]). Also, they are the most useful means of practising, perfecting and experimenting with knot designs, textures and colours. The more adept one becomes with the technical aspects of macramé, the more understanding one has of the possibilities of the craft, the more successful should be designs for macramé. Samplers can be assembled or joined together for hangings; by selecting appropriate pieces, a patchwork cushion can be made or even a patchwork macramé bedspread (4 ply knitting wool used double, in a fairly closely knotted pattern would be suitable; the finished patchwork would need to be mounted on felt or on a blanket, to give sufficient body to the knotting).

Instead of making a sampler, practise the knots by making a belt. Sinnets make excellent belts.

As well as samplers a notebook is useful in which to jot down, or to make rough drawings or plans, of ideas. Make a written record of finished macramé pieces, as a permanent record of innovated designs or knots.

## Experiments with knots in geometric patterns

With twelve threads on the holding cord, work the following exercises in geometric patterns to gain knowledge of the effects that can be achieved with different knots. Diamond patterns are used in many macramé pieces and are particularly useful in making garments.

1 Form a basic diamond shape with diagonal rows of double half hitch knots (illus. 139[1]). Work two rows for each diamond to emphasize the pattern. This pattern and its variations can be used to make narrow vertical strips such as would be used in a belt. To cross the diagonal double half hitch, follow illus. 139[3]: when the left- and right-hand lead cords meet in the centre, a double half hitch knot is worked over the right-hand lead cord with the left-hand one and work continues as before.

2 Try working basically in the same way as in (1) but with a square knot in the centre of the diamond (illus. 139[4]). This is made by using the two outer threads from the double half stitches on either side of the upper half of the diamond as knotting cords and all the remaining threads as the core. These four knotting cords become the first and second-threads on each side of the lower half of the diamond. Take the next thread which was above them in the upper half of the diamond (now part of the core) for the next thread to be double half hitched below them in the lower half of the diamond. Continue until the two threads from the top of the diamond become the two threads at the base of the diamond.

3 Use a 'basket weave' to fill in the diamond shape. This is especially effective if working with flat ribbon-like threads; it works well with round threads also. Try using woollen yarns of different colours to produce a tweedy effect (illus. 150). The weave is formed by working the two top sides of the diamonds and one of the lower sides as described above. Before working the fourth side interweave those threads still free through those already joined from the upper to the lower side.

4 Fill in the diamond with rows of diagonal half hitches – either in a chevron pattern or in diamonds.

5 Work two or three rows of double half hitches and fill in the centre with square knots.

The diamonds can be made with any number of threads depending upon the size of the diamond that is needed. For example, a small diamond will need eight threads and two lead cords; a larger diamond, sixteen threads and two lead cords. The diamond patterns can be used successfully when a large area is to be covered in such a way that 'fabric' is formed (as opposed to the linear openness of sinnets). A square knot pattern and cording can also be used to make a 'fabric' but these knots can produce too great a firmness and solidity which is not always desirable or necessary.

## Working circular macramé

When working a circular shape, the working threads are set on or over a metal, plastic or wooden ring or over cord or yarn tied as a circle, or over a crocheted chain, according to scale. Alternatively, all the working threads can be tied together in the middle with a piece of cord or with an overhand knot. The first three methods result in a small

round space in the centre of the work, the size of which depends upon the size of the holding ring. The last method results in a wheel-spoke pattern at the centre as, after tying, the working threads are spread out evenly and a lead cord is introduced about 2.5cm (1in) or more as decided, from the centre and the working threads are double half hitched over it. Working in a circle requires careful pinning to keep the design even. Concentric circles can be drawn on paper and pinned to the knotting board to help to keep the shapes circular and the threads evenly spaced.

With each row of circular knotting the circumference becomes greater and it will be necessary to add in new working threads. Therefore set as many working threads up as is possible, by placing them closely together when the work is begun, to avoid having to add in new threads almost immediately. The best way to add in new threads is to set them on in a row of cording. It is also possible to add in during an alternate square knot pattern by looping a new thread over that immediately above the square knot to the left of the position where it is to be added and similarly to the right. Then work another square knot with these, now four new threads.

Because it is necessary to add in so many new threads while working a circular piece of macramé interesting colour effects may be achieved. For instance the circle may be lighter in colour at the centre than it is at the edges, or vice versa, or different colours can be set in in segments, or in staggers. This eventually will produce a swirl-like or catherine wheel effect.

## Cavandoli macramé

This type of macramé is worked entirely with horizontal and vertical double half hitches using two colours. Cavandoli macramé was in use in the early twentieth century in Italy, the overall effect giving a solid 'fabric', similar to canvas work or tapestry. Figures, geometric designs such as squares and triangles, stripes and blocks of colour can all be worked using this method and it is, therefore an ideal way to experiment with yarns and colours, the different directions in which the knots are worked producing variations in texture and colour.

The design is first plotted out on squared paper, each square representing one knot. Set up the board with cords in the main colour about six times as long, when doubled, as the finished piece. The lead cord is used to make the colour contrast; it therefore needs to be extremely long and can be rolled into a ball which is secured with a rubber band so that it stays untangled and is easier to work.

Practise this method by working four rows of horizontal cording in one colour, the main colour, to form a border. The cat (illus. 140) is worked in the colour of the lead cord and is formed by working a vertical double half hitch using the green as a lead cord and the grey as a knotting cord, wherever these are marked on the squared paper. Continue in this manner and finish off as explained on page 255. The

139 Diamond patterns:
[1] Basic diamond shape formed with diagonal rows of double half hitch knots.
[2] Double diamond pattern: extra effect is achieved by working two rows of double half hitch knots for each diamond.
[3] Crossing the diagonal double half hitch: when the left- and right-hand lead cords meet in the centre, a double half hitch knot is worked over the right-hand one.
[4] Diamond pattern with square knot centre.

Cavandoli macramé:
[5] Double half hitches making a solid 'fabric'.
[6] The design of the cat (illus. 140) plotted on squared paper.
Artist: Mollie Picken

**140** A distinct pictorial pattern can be achieved with Cavandoli macramé. The design is first plotted on graph paper, each square representing a knot (illus. 139 [6]).

Two colours of cord (rattail) are used. The colour for the design, in this case a cat, is used as the lead cord for the horizontal double half hitches of the background. It is then used as the knotting cord in the area of the design which is worked in vertical double half hitches, thus making a contrast both in texture and colour.
Photo: John Hunnex

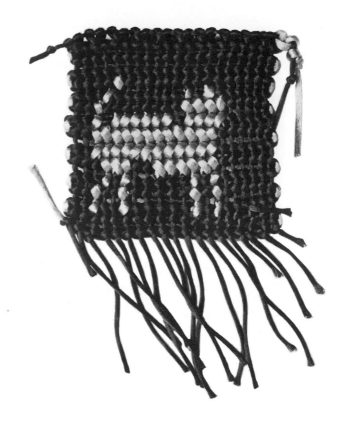

reverse side of the work looks a little different from the front, the knots being flatter (illus. 141). It may be preferred to use this side for the face of the work, so before finishing off the loose ends decide which effect is required, textured on the front or smooth as on the reverse. (By turning the work to the reverse side and making a few rows of cording so that the back of these knots appear on the face of the work often gives an interesting effect.)

A checkerboard pattern can be made using the Cavandoli method. Instead of plotting a design on squared paper, plan out squares each alternate square being worked in vertical double half hitch knots with the lead cord. As an alternative to the solid checkerboard pattern some squares can be filled with diamonds which in turn are filled with one's own designs such as square knots, basket weaving or any other knot patterns. This square is achieved by working a row of vertical double half hitches to form two of its sides, the third side is already worked and the fourth is worked later, so remember to make other knot patterns to the inside measurements of the squares allowing space for four rows of cording around each.

Striking areas of colour can be achieved also by using the double half hitch knot in the angling technique, which also changes the position of the cords. It is worked using a combination of horizontal and vertical double half hitch knots and produces diagonal bands of knotting which can be taken in almost any direction that is wished. More than two colours can be used with this technique.

141 A chevron pattern worked in Cavandoli macramé, showing the smoother texture on the reverse side. The striped chevron is produced by working rows of diagonal double half hitches with different coloured rattail. The outer cords in each row are used as lead cords, crossing in the middle of the piece. Photo: John Hunnex

Two or more colours can be used to make an exciting and very definite chevron pattern with diagonal cording. Set the different colours of thread on to the holding cord in stripes as they are to be seen on the chevron. Although the chevron stripes will appear as a series of inverted V shapes the diagonal knotting is actually done forming upright V shapes. Take the centre two threads on the holding cords and cross one over the other with a double half hitch in the usual crossing technique, take the thread to the left and that to the right of these, and work in a V shape, crossing them when they meet. Continue in this manner across the width of the set-on threads. Take the two outside cords and using them as lead cords work towards the centre, crossing where they meet. Continue in this manner until the work is the desired length. For a variation in texture the piece can be turned to its wrong side and the pattern continued for a few rows; the underside of the knots will then appear on the face of the work, providing a different knotting effect.

## Finishing off the work

Knowing how to finish off work successfully is important. There are several ways.

Loose ends can be made into fringes and tassles but often it is undesirable to retain them. Work at least two, three if possible, rows of horizontal cording; trim the ends to about 8cm (3in); with the wrong side of the work face upwards, pull the loose ends one by one up through the reverse side loops of the horizontal cording, diagonally with a crochet hook. Secure each end with fabric glue and trim neatly with sharp scissors. Should there be any loose ends left anywhere on your piece, tuck these in behind suitable knots, glue in place and trim.

If the macramé ends in sinnets, the horizontal cording method is unsuitable, so either trim the ends to about 8cm (3in) and pull them back up the sinnet through the third, fourth, fifth, etc. knots from the end of the sinnet, or tie adjacent overhand knots as before. If the sinnets are in groups or are wide, they can be made into a simple tassel by binding the ends tightly with cord or by tying an overhand knot.

**Fringes**

Loose ends can be made into a fringe, elaborate or simple. A simple fringe is made by tying adjacent threads with an overhand knot, working a second alternate row of overhand knots if desired. The first row of overhand knots secures the whole piece of work so that the knots do not work loose. Single loose ends of the fringe can be left plain, or each one may have an overhand knot tied near the end, trimming off the thread below this last knot; or a bead can be slipped on to each thread and then an overhand knot is tied to secure the bead and the thread is trimmed as before. As well as being decorative, beads act as weights if the threads do not 'hang' well. For extra effect several beads can be slipped at intervals on to the loose ends of thread, each being secured in place by an overhand knot.

More elaborate macramé fringes can be added to many articles – a crochet shawl, a poncho, cushions, the ends of a stole or scarf, etc. Set the threads for the fringing on to the holding cord, crochet chain or the stitching bordering the fabric and secure the setting with an overhand knot on each set of threads. This makes both a firmer and a more attractive edge. When making a long fringe which could require lengths of knotting, it is easier to work it in sections, which are completely finished, knotting about 22 to 30cm (9 to 12in) at a time.

A fringe can be made in more than one colour to produce a striped or checkered effect. Set on alternating colours for each V pattern: for example, blue, green, blue, etc. (illus. 150). Work the Vs with three rows of diagonal cording, tying a square knot at the base of each. The diamond shapes may be filled with 'basket weaving' to give a tweedy effect. Square knots may be worked on the centre threads for effect, the thread from the upper right-hand side of the diamond being worked in a diagonal row of half hitches to form the lower right-hand side of the diamond. Work a row of overhand knots around the entire perimeter of the fringe to secure it and to form a neat edge. A second and third row of alternating overhand knots can be worked for extra decoration if desired. Press the fringe, including the loose ends, and then trim. It is better to trim after pressing to ensure all the threads are hanging straight before cutting so that a neat edge can be made. Macramé tassels could be added to the points of the fringe.

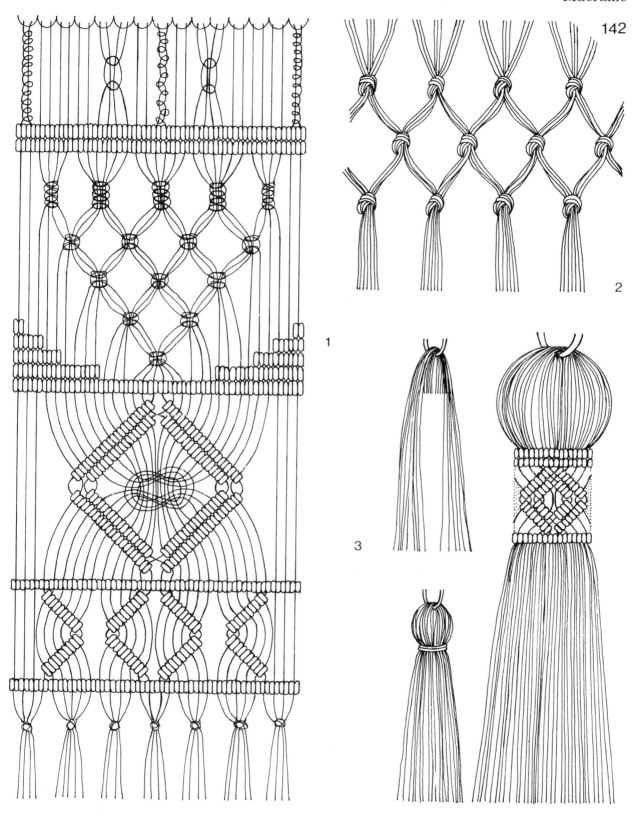

1

2

3

Another elaborate fringe is made by using the left patterns in diagonal cording. Curve the lines of diagonal half hitch knots so as to form a leaf shape. Work the lower curve using the first cord which was double half hitched over the lead cord of the upper curving row of knots, as the lead cord. The two lead cords are crossed using the same method as for diamonds. A square knot is worked at the base of two leaves using the four lead cords. The pattern can be made geometric by working one row of leaves across the width of the piece. Then, instead of using the lead cords from these leaves as the lead cords for the next row of leaves, take the middle two cords from the lower side of the leaves in the row worked, using them as lead cords to form leaves at right angles to the previous row.

### Tassels

Beautiful tassels can be made quite simply (illus. 142[3]). A fat tassel is made by cutting twelve short strands which act as fillers, for the 'head' of a tassel. The strands for the tassel are cut at least eight times (when doubled) the length of the finished tassel. Thirty-two strands when doubled make a plump tassel. Mount these as above the filler cords. Wind a cord three or four times very tightly around the tassel immediately below the filler cords, about 2cm ($\frac{3}{4}$in) from top and secure firmly. The macramé decoration on the tassel can be worked in a diamond pattern, diagonal cording or square knots. Divide the 'top layer' of strands into the required numbers for the pattern and work in the usual manner; 2 to 5cm (1 to 2in) of pattern is usually sufficient. Finish off with a row of tightly worked horizontal double half hitches to secure the pattern. Trim all the cords evenly.

### Mounting wall hangings

Wall hangings should be mounted on fabric. Before mounting the work, press it lightly on the wrong side under a damp cloth on a thickly padded surface. Do not apply too much pressure or the knots will be flattened. If any straight lines have become crooked or squares or diamonds have become irregular while working them it is possible during pressing to ease them gently into position. Stretch the backing fabric and pin it over a frame. Attach the macramé with long, light but secure stitches.

## Design

Design, with pattern, colour and texture are as important in macramé as they are in any art or craft. Having decided upon the idea for a piece of work, consider both the colours and the textures which would be most appropriate to complement it; if the piece is to be put to a particular use, choose yarns which are also the most practical.

### Texture

It is well worth searching for interesting yarns with which to work, beyond those which are generally offered for macramé. There are many different yarns, fibres and threads to be found, not always in the most obvious places. Foreign import shops and millinery supply houses often have materials that are interesting to use. A supply house for packaging materials will usually carry a wide variety of colours, weights and textures of string. Suppliers of yarns to weavers often have a more interesting selection than those who supply the knitters and crocheters. If it is planned to make several macramé pieces in the course of time it is a good idea to 'collect' threads, buying those which have interesting colour and texture when they are found. Illustration 5 (page 15) shows handspuns worked in macramé.

The lizard wall hanging (illus. 149) shows threads of the same weight but of different texture used successfully together. The hemp gives the piece a feeling of strength and also of earthiness, while the vivid colours of the soutache give an overall colour effect yet blend in with the brown, as a lizard skin is in monotone yet subtle in colour.

## Colour

Try to use colours which are of the same tones. For example a warm red and a clear, strong orange, rather than just any red and orange. A dark bluish red with a light orange would not look so well as it would be spotty. The number of colours under a heading, such as red or blue, are infinite and experimental samples using different colour combinations are a help in making final choices before starting a large piece of work. By possessing a collection of different colours of thread, it is a matter of selecting the right ones, to enhance one another, or to provide a dramatic contrast.

Shades of one colour can be used effectively. The colours become intertwined and the ultimate effect is of depth, light and shade. This effect is possible with varied tones of any colour. It is surprising to discover the number of different blacks and whites available, which intermingled produce a variety of greys.

Another subtle and exciting yet more obvious effect can be obtained by using adjacent colours, for example by taking green through to blue to purple. This is best done when working on a linear design, one using many sinnets or cording. Attach colours to the holding cord as follows: green, a more bluish green, a greeny blue, a blue, a purple blue and so on. This arrangement generally requires quite a stock of colours. It can be done successfully with any colour scheme, by taking orange through to pink to red; or yellow to orange to red to crimson.

## Pattern

It is possible to design a piece of work through the patterns made with the knots as well as through its colour, texture and shape. The diamond patterns of the lizard (illus. 149), which is controlled, rich and formal, would be inappropriate for the waterfall hanging (illus. 143) as the water is uncontrolled and informal. The richness of the water is achieved with the texture of the yarns; and the richness of the lizard through colour, knotting patterns and form.

## Macramé projects

Macramé can be made into both decorative and functional items and can be used in conjunction with other fabric making techniques such as knitting and crochet. The projects described below may be used as starting points from which to develop individual ideas. They demonstrate the use of knots, different yarns and colours. They show how macramé can be shaped to make functional items and garments. While practising knotting skills, use your imagination and, discover the many variations on the basic techniques described here.

### Wall hangings

Because of their size and the scope they allow for experiment, wall hangings are probably the most exciting articles to make. The artist may be free of the limitations imposed by function but the overall effect of a hanging should be one of harmony and balance.

Nature is an ideal source of inspiration for macramé hangings. The textures, colours, tones and movement in a waterfall are fascinating. In illustration 143, the top section is worked in tranquil blue through green. These colours are finished off at the top of the waterfall by working three rows of horizontal double half hitch knots, behind which the ends can be threaded with a darning needle or crochet hook, then glued with fabric glue. Using the lead cord of the last row of the horizontal double half hitch knots as a holding cord, new whitish threads for the water and rough textured brown/grey threads for the rocks are set on in between the existing knots. Thicker and more textured yarns are used for the water. Roughly spun wool or even unspun wool is good for this, as are heavy weight blonde coloured hemps or strings, the texture of which all add depth. Silky metallic threads or yarns, or knitting wool which has a silver stripe running through it, gives the effect here of the glint of sunlight on the water. Such yarns are best used as a single strand incorporated with a heavier yarn, being too fragile to stand alone. Large sinnets of varying textures and thicknesses – corkscrews, square knots, half hitches, etc. – are suitable ways of working this area giving vertical direction plus texture. The rock area can be worked separately as can the section to the right of the fall. A hanging of this type is best mounted, when finished, on fabric. Hessian (burlap) would be an appropriate background in this instance, being compatible with the idea of rocks behind the waterfall. The sinnets can be made long enough to be bent upwards and sewn in place on the fabric later, thus forming the splashes and spray at the base of the fall. Except for the longer sinnets to be sewn in place later, the ends are finished off as at the end of the first section. The lower section of the river is worked with deeper colours from a holding cord attached parallel to the fall, so that the river is worked at right angles to the rest of the piece giving the idea of it flowing in a different direction. Curving lines of double half hitches were used here, and the ends finished as before. To ensure the curving lines are exactly as wanted, it is a good idea to draw the curves on a piece of

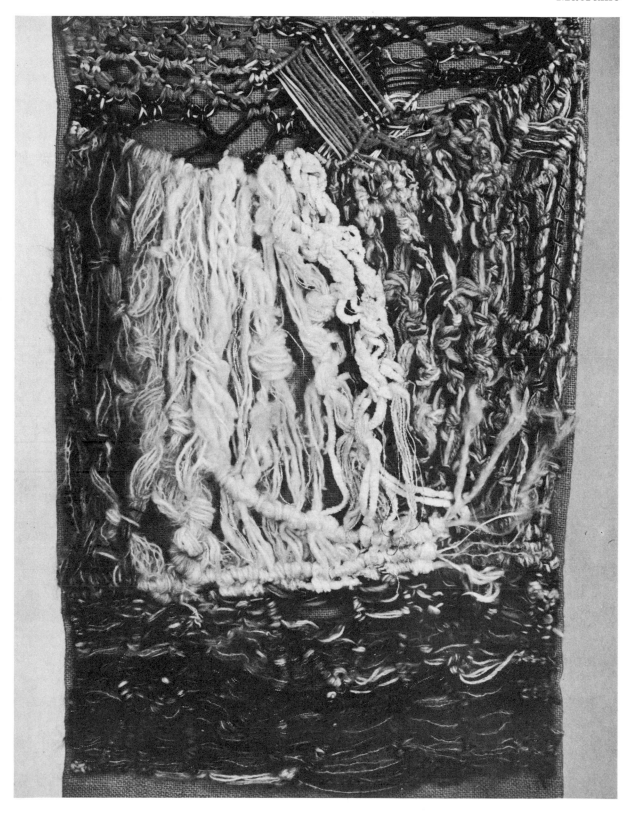

paper. Pin it to the board as a pattern. The horizontal section is attached to the vertical section by threading the lead cords of each row of this section between the double half hitches and over the lead cord at the finishing of the middle section. If the board is too small to carry the whole work it can be done in sections, unpinning and repinning as it progresses.

### Functional items

Besides being decorative, macramé can be made into functional items.

MITTENS A pair of mittens can be made very simply from several strands of 4 ply knitting wool. The size is obtained by placing the hand palm downwards on a piece of paper, drawing around it, and including the wrist. Make a right hand and a left hand pattern. Pin the paper to the knotting board. A fairly tight crochet chain is made and pinned securely in place along the outline of the drawing patterns and a little outside the line for the wrists, to allow entry for the hand. Use the top arcs around the finger tips and the thumbs as the holding cord areas. Attach the threads as described before. Work from the fingertips in the desired knots.

It is not absolutely necessary to make a crochet chain outline – the work can be started by holding cords in the usual way – but it gives extra strength and also gives a neater and stronger edge for joining to the front of the mittens.

The front of the mitten could be cut from a piece of soft leather, holes being punched around the perimeter and joined to the pressed macramé back with single crochet stitches or blanket stitching.

SLIPPERS These are made in basically the same way as the mittens – but use a soft shoe or sneaker around which to draw the outline, as a foot takes up more space inside a slipper than a hand does inside a mitten. Start knotting from the toe end of the slipper. After pressing, the slipper top can be joined to either a piece of leather cut to fit the foot or to a ready-made soft leather sole.

Sandals can be made by nailing, or tacking strips of macramé to wooden soles, such as can be obtained from shoe suppliers. Hemp or strong heavy yarns would be needed for this project. The uppers for clogs can also be made by the methods described above. The sandals and the clogs would be best lined as the heavy threads could rub the foot.

HANDBAGS The two handbags (illus 144 and 145) demonstrate clearly that the types of threads used can totally affect the appearance and thus the ultimate purpose of the work. Both are worked using variations on the diamond pattern as their main theme, yet each is quite different. The white bag is made with heavy textured and shaggy yarns in white and off-white shades as it is for winter use. These yarns have been obtained from a weaver's supply store, and include heavy cotton chenille, unspun goats hair for a 'hairy' effect, unspun wool with a fine strong thread running around it which holds it together and gives it a 'bubbly' effect, and a very tough, coarse 4-ply wool in two shades which, used double, gives strength to the whole bag.

The holding cord is a heavy piece of rope cut long enough also to form the handle, the join being covered with a piece of suede. The overall tweedy look of this bag has been achieved through the basket weave centre for the diamond pattern. The use of this particular pattern also results in a 'solid piece' of fabric which can stand up to the wear a handbag will have to take. The two sides of the bag are made separately. The gusset is a series of horizontal half hitches which gives both neatness and strength. Ends are finished off in the usual way with double horizontal half hitches, behind which the ends are tucked. After pressing, the knots on the holding cord are pushed very closely together forming the curved top of the bag. The outer knots are then securely stitched to the holding cord to keep them in place. The three pieces are then sewn or may be crocheted together. The bag is lined with a woollen fabric and the holding cords joined to make the handles.

The evening bag (illus. 144) is made with a tubular rayon yarn, rattail, which is silky in appearance, and is lined with velvet. It is made in one piece starting at the front with the straight edge and ending in the flap. The V shape is easily achieved by eliminating one diamond in each row. Four rows of diagonal cording give the flap strength and under this the loose ends are tucked.

To make the toggle for fastening, pin the work to the board. Using the centre x of the diamond pattern as a holding 'cord', or rather 'point', loop two threads double over it (making four working threads). Work a sinnet or six square knots, more if a larger toggle is required. Push the knots up closely together; pull the loose ends through to the wrong side of the work, immediately under the beginning of this sinnet and securely fasten at the back. This is known as a bead knot. To keep the toggle firm, secure with a few stitches. The other half of the fastening is formed by looping four threads through the centre of the third row of cording on the V of the flap; make an overhand knot; make a second overhand knot about 2cm ($\frac{3}{4}$in) lower so that the space in between these two knots will fit securely around the toggle.

The sides of the bag are sewn, but may be crocheted, together after a lining has been sewn in place. The handle of the bag is composed of a square knot sinnet using eight threads, four for the core and four for the knotting. To finish such a sinnet, pull the loose ends back up the centre of the sinnet for about four knots and glue in place; the loose ends of the holding cord at the other end of the sinnet are finished likewise. The handle is then sewn in position.

A bead knot such as that made for the toggle can be used anywhere on a piece of work to give added texture. A smaller bead knot is made by working one square knot, then with the two centre cords work a sinnet of about six alternate half hitches and bring this sinnet up through its own two cords directly under the square knot to the back of the work; secure it in place by working another square knot directly underneath it, using the original four cords.

144 Evening bag made with tubular rayon yarn, rattail, and lined with velvet. Simple knots were used, the only decoration being the square knot sinnets. Several rows of closely worked double half hitches along the edge of the flap give strength and weight.
Photo: John Hunnex

Beads can be used effectively in many macramé projects. A bead can be introduced into the knotting itself quite simply by threading this at the desired place and working the knot below it. An interesting effect is obtained by threading a bead on to the core thread of a square knot sinnet; the next square knot is worked in the usual way but below the bead, the knotting cords having been brought down around the bead. This is a useful way of dealing with loose ends as once the ends are weighted with the beads they hang better.

NECKLACES AND CHOKERS These do not take long to make and are ideal exercises for the beginner.

Chokers can be made simply from sinnets or they can become quite complicated. The Josephine knot makes a superb centre-piece for a choker, with various patterns worked on either side. Working the knot in the centre gives a slight variation to the knot. Cut the threads to the desired length; double them and pin the centres together on the board; work a Josephine knot with the threads on either side of the centre pin; pull the knot into position close to the pinned loops marking the middle of these threads; remove the pins. This makes a Josephine knot with an extra curving edge or scallop (three instead of two), which appears as an interesting and complex centrepiece. Continue to work the choker from each side of the Josephine knot.

The neatest way of making the holding cord for the necklace strands is to work a square knot sinnet with or without beads according to the design, of the desired length, usually about 35cm (14in). The knotting threads and the holding cord should be cut extra long so they can be used for ties. Tuck the core threads back up the sinnet and glue in position to finish off the sinnet; tie an overhand knot with the knotting threads at one end and with the holding cord at the other. These two sets of threads can then be used as ties with which to secure the necklace when worn.

A large curved neckpiece is best worked directly on a dress stand. Alternatively, use a dressmaker's paper pattern of a top with a high round neck, and place it on the knotting board as a guide. In the detail of the neckpiece (illus. 136) the precise geometric diamond pattern is used to lend an air of formality to the piece. The working threads are set on to the square knot sinnet neckband very closely together to avoid having to add in extra threads immediately, as being semi-circular the distance from the left-hand edge to the right-hand edge increases quite considerably and rapidly after about the first few centimetres of work. The upper half of the first set of diamonds is worked using only the threads originally set on. Extra threads are set on in the usual manner, that is with half hitch knots on the lead cords in between knots, on the lower half of the diamonds and again in the curved cording rows. The collar is deeper at the front than at the sides; this is achieved by working the centre second diamond with the greatest number of threads, those on each side of it with less, and each successive half diamond with less. When working it will be discovered soon where to add in extra threads; always remembering to add the

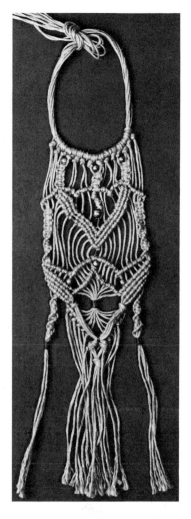

146 Simple necklace with beads threaded on to the cords and held in place by knots. The overhand knots and the wrapping at the edges of the knotting pattern give the necklace a well defined look. Photo: John Hunnex

145 (opposite) Woollen handbag made with thick and fibrous yarns. The more decorative knotting is confined to the top area of the bag while a close pattern is used elsewhere. The basket weaving helps to protect the unspun yarns used. Photo: John Hunnex

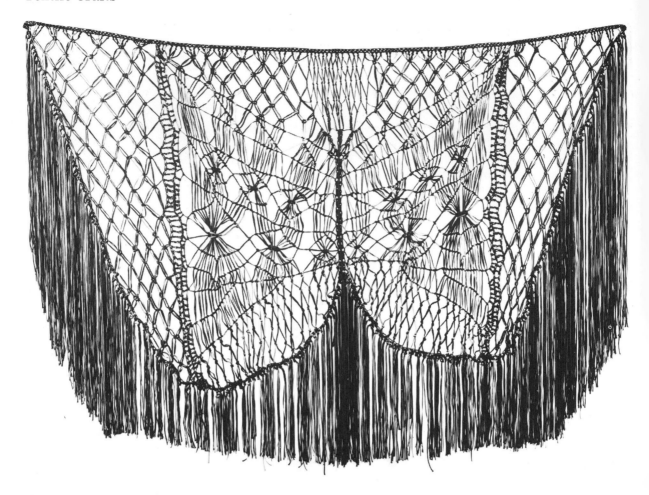

**147** Butterfly shawl, worked from the centre outwards. An alternating overhand knot section suggests the antennae, followed by a heavy square knot sinnet representing the insect's body. The wings are worked outwards from the sinnet. The areas to the right and left are worked downwards with very widely spaced alternating square knots. Because the shawl is knotted in such an openwork pattern, a row of cording is worked around the perimeter to give extra strength. Extra cords are added to make the fringe thicker.

Photo: John Hunnex

same number on each side of the collar. The final rows of cording give firmness to the piece. If it is not wished to have a fringe on the collar the loose ends can be trimmed and finished off behind the cording as described on page 256.

SHAWLS AND STOLES Fascinating shawls and stoles can be made with macramé, quite simply, by using alternating square knot patterns or diamond patterns; or the more complicated can be made to one's own ideas, such as the butterfly shawl (illus. 147).

A suitable size for a triangular shawl is 150cm (60in) for the longest side and 75cm (30in) from the centre of that side to the apex. When cutting working threads for a shawl the central ones need to be much longer than the side ones. A rough guide is to cut each set of threads 15cm (6in) longer than the previous ones, starting from the outside edge and working towards the centre. If it is planned to use these same threads to make a fringe on the shawl be sure to allow extra for this when calculating the lengths for the threads.

A macramé shawl need not, however, be a conventional semi-circular or triangular shape. Once the top is made firm enough to support the weight of the threads – about 15cm (6in) at the sides, 38 or 46cm (15 or 18in) at centre back, the remainder of the threads could either be worked in an open-work fringed design or be heavily strung with beads.

## Clothes

Clothes are an exciting way in which to use macramé. Basically there are two ways of approaching the design and working of these garments. One is to treat the garment purely as a decoration to be worn over other clothes, which avoids all the intricacies of sizing and shaping, as usually the neckline and upper half of a bodice only are worked and the loose ends are left very long. The garment is attached to the body by tying it under the arms and/or at the neck.

The second approach to macramé clothing is to treat the design and working out as for a garment and to deal with the sizing and shaping problems in much the same way as in dress making. Such articles are best made on a dress stand. As one cannot make darts, allowances for bust and waist can be easily incorporated in the working. Alternatively a dressmaker's paper pattern in the desired basic style can be used, pinned on to the knotting board and the outline followed.

The back of a garment can be made quite separately from the front or can be joined into the working of the front under the arms if the knotting board is large enough. Garments made with two or more pieces can be joined together by single crochet or hand sewing.

When working a garment, rows of horizontal cording help to give strength and firmness. If there is too much openwork knotting, the piece will tend to drop becoming longer and narrower than anticipated. Rows of alternate overhand knots make an interesting effect

**148** Waistcoat showing the strong holding cords, the crochet chains around the armholes and the rows of horizontal cording forming a firm lower edge. The knots were chosen to produce an openwork garment that was strong enough to hold its shape. The rows of horizontal knots hold the piece in shape.
Photo: John Hunnex

but these would need to be supported by firm rows of knots; a diagonal row of cording is more supportive for these knots than a horizontal one. A very charming lacy effect is obtained by using alternate rows of loosely worked square knots.

THE BASIC WAISTCOAT The steps in making a basic waistcoat apply to all garments that are to be shaped to the body.

1  Stretch strong holding cords across the back and front of the dress stand or pattern, from outside shoulder edge to outside shoulder edge at the lowest point of the neckline.
2  Attach the required number of working threads.
3  Crochet chains for the armhole outlines and attach them to the extreme ends of the holding cords and pin into place over the pattern on the knotting board or on to the dress stand. These provide a neat and strong armhole edge as well as a working guideline. A square knot sinnet could also be used.
4  Work the desired pattern, remembering to increase as the armholes begin to curve. The neatest way to add threads is to work a row of horizontal cording and attach new threads in the usual way between knots. Also new threads can be looped on to the crochet chain outline.
5  When the underarm area is reached many threads are required. These are simply set on to the crochet chain and worked in the usual manner along with the back threads.
6  If it is decided to work the back and the front of the garment as one piece, the front must now be worked to the underarm point.
7  Decide upon the width of the shoulders of the garment and attach the appropriate number of threads to the back holding cord in between the set-on back threads. Crochet a front armhole chain and pin into place. Crochet also one chain for the front neckline if the garment is without openings, or two chains one for each side front if opening at the front. Pin the chain into place. Work the required design adding in new threads where necessary either on a vertical cording row or set on the crochet armhole or front chains.
8  When the underarm point is reached set on new threads as before and work the entire piece, back and front, as one piece. This method avoids an underarm seam.
9  Alternately the back and front can be worked separately and joined together with single crochet or sewing stitches.
10  To make a very firm lower edge on the garment if the loose ends are not fringed, work rows of horizontal cording and finish off as before.
11  One or even two rows of single crochet around the perimeter of the garment and the armholes makes a neat and secure edge.
12  Press work lightly on the wrong side with a slightly damp cloth and leave flat until dry.

These twelve steps can be applied to the making of other garments – a bodice, an overblouse, a halter top, for example. Any shape of neckline,

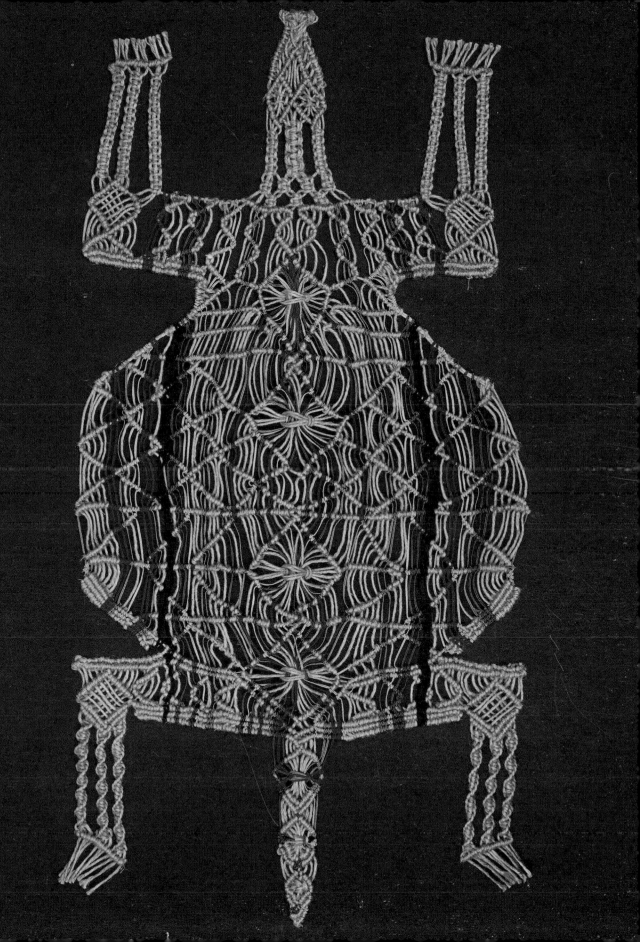

opening or armhole can be adapted from the basic waistcoat by pinning the crochet chain or square knot sinnet into the required position on the paper pattern on the knotting board, or on to the dress stand. The chains or sinnets give the outline of the garment and then it is a matter of filling in the 'space' with your chosen pattern.

Attach enough threads to the holding cord so that they lie closely but neatly, not bunched together, along the holding cord. Draw in a centre line on each piece of the pattern, especially centre front and centre back. This line helps you to check that each side of the garment has the same number of threads; remember when adding extra cords, at underarm or along the armhole, for example, to add the same number on each side.

A sleeve is best worked on a knotting board over a paper pattern, always remembering the elbow area would need to be worked fairly closely to prevent its protrusion – alternate overhand knots, for example, would be unsuitable here.

A flared skirt can be made in either two or four pieces by working over a paper pattern on the knotting board.

Where it is necessary to decrease for shaping, such as at a waistline on a semi-fitted top this can often be accomplished by working the knots very tightly and closely together in that area. This is especially useful if the width of the garment increases again later, saving the job of removing and finishing off cords, and of joining in new cords.

Tops which lace at the sides are an alternative to the front opening jacket. Zip-fasteners are best used only when there is a firm foundation upon which to sew them, such as a cording or closely worked square knotting. It is a good idea to sew a strip of straight binding over the macramé to which the zipper will be attached. Buttonholes pose little problem if the required number of small holes are incorporated into the macramé.

## Macramé as sculpture

Once one has become used to handling the various types of cords and knots, it is possible to translate ideas into three-dimensional 'sculptures'. Heavy ropes, twines and cords, such as are used for clothes lines and furnishings are best for this type of macramé as they are bulky and make firm shapes.

Such macramé is best worked suspended in a doorway or from a hook in the ceiling, its three dimensions making working on a knotting board unsuitable. The work can be started in the same way as a giant tassel is made, or the cords can be attached to a wooden or plastic ring. Heavy sinnets of different textures intertwined, and braided and bulky overhand knots are interesting to use for this project. Wire can be worked along with the threads or else inserted later to allow for the formation of unusual shapes. In a free form sculpture threads can be added or subtracted whenever necessary and it is usually possible to make any loose ends a part of the design. A hollow tubular form can be stuffed to give it more shape and solidity. Sometimes the design in mind could be better worked within a circular shape (see page 251).

150 Woollen shawl fringe in 4-ply yarn chosen to relate to the weave of the shawl. The threads for the fringe were set on to the fabric in alternating colours. The basket weave diamonds in the macramé continue the feeling of warmth and thickness in the shawl, while the square knot areas add interest and texture.
Photo: John Hunnex

# Coiled Basketry
## Helen Richards

A coiled basket was so labelled by those making the first reports on this technique because the basic element in building the structure is a continuous coil similar to the coils of a clay pot. The coil is stitched together in a circle, layer on layer with no beginning or ending of a row. There are many sources which suggest that the discovery of pottery was based on the fact that baskets were covered with mud prior to being placed on the coals for cooking. After repeated usage the basket would burn away and the clay structure would remain.

Students of stitchery will find wrapping the coil and stitching this row to the immediate row below relates to the long and short stitch of embroidery; weavers will feel that the figure eight or Navajo stitch is a lashing with its over one under one, the basis of weaving. So not only does the technique provide one with the joy of making a functional container, but also it can be a structural aspect of contemporary sculpture. The techniques of basketry are simple – a wrapping of one coil and lashing it to the row below. The stitching fibre does not interlace or loop on itself as is done in knitting, crochet or macramé.

The basket-maker of yore spent many hours creating the container that served two purposes – function plus beauty. Previous civilizations created their particular needs in sensitive designs without using any preliminary diagramming or laid out patterning. The act of creating the surface interest of the wrapping on the basket, the carving on the handle of a knife or the markings on a clay pot were a form of personal writing. When the written word came into common usage, the art of intuitive design was lost to most people. We now have to teach how to write with symbols and signs that create a design.

This is the crux of the return to basket-making: it can be done and done well by thinking about it, doing it; there is no particular skill required in drawing it out on paper. It is envisioned, many times as the work progresses, the materials and the basket-maker become one. The wrapping of a coil and stitching it together is a technique so basically simple, that it can soon be learned – and then the basket-maker is free to explore.

Creating with basic techniques soon opens the door to more complex methods of binding coils into a form. The form in itself becomes the important idea. How will it be developed; what will be the colours and textures of the patterns; will there be open and closed areas, surface embellishments? Will it be a sculpture, a space hanging, something to be worn? The answers to these questions are found in the past from the basket-makers scattered over the surface of the earth. They have given us our manual, visual and oral vocabulary that is a universal

151 Shaped container by Helen Richards. The long runs of colour in the space-dyed acrylic rug yarn contribute to the effect of colour patterning at random. Vinyl leather (brown on one side, black on the other) was stripped to be used in the wrapping and stitching of the paper rope coil. It automatically turned itself, creating a brown-black colour pattern. As the basket was stitched, using a combination of lazy and figure eight stitches, the shape was created by pushing successive rows down into the basket. The feathers were wrapped into the structure as work progressed. At the top of the basket a ridge was formed for the lid to rest upon.
Photo: Douglas Watson

language. Civilizations have advanced, but the language of basketry remains constant.

## History

The techniques of coiling a container, many sources agree, pre-date all other methods of creating a fabric. There are remnants of basketry that have been gathered from the Swiss Lake Dwellings; there are rough pictures of containers made with fibres appearing on the walls of caves in Spain that date back many centuries; baskets were carried into Rome by Julius Caesar's successors. In fact, coiled basketry techniques have been dated back to 9000 BC, the methods with minor variations being carried down from generation to generation.

The making of the basket was a part of the life of primitive man; the harvesting, the preparation of the material, and finally the shaping of the materials into a form for the particular need of the hunter, fisherman, farmer or religious or ritual man. Undoubtedly, the time spent in creating the coiled basket must have been one of the more pleasant tasks that the woman had to perform.

Baskets differed from area to area, not because of techniques, but because of the materials available in any particular region. Primitive woman had an instinctive knowledge of which materials should be gathered for basket-making. She would often travel distances to harvest, at exactly the right time, the grasses, reeds, barks, stems, roots, leaves, vines and corn husks. Often various materials would go into the making of one basket.

The gathering was done with deliberate care. The basket-maker chose her materials for strength, pliability and colour. She, undoubtedly, had her favourite locations, as do many basket-makers of today. It took a certain permanency of living for her to obtain the materials with which she worked, as she had to think ahead to the final step of creating a container.

After the gathering of the materials began the days and weeks of drying, sorting and stripping. If the green of the grasses was to be retained, they were dried for a time in the shade and then sun-dried to remove moisture, but not for too long or they would have become brittle. The basket-maker knew that certain grasses would turn various colours in the process of drying; that the inside of the stem was a different colour than the outside; also that one side could be shiny, the other dull. Most of the colour that is seen in very old baskets is the natural colour of the plant, undyed. Later vegetal dyes were used and today many natural baskets made of grasses and raffia are over-dyed with synthetic dyes into more brilliant colours before coiling.

During the drying time the materials had to be turned constantly, handled with great care to be sure that they dried evenly and did not mould. The turning was done with a rhythmic motion, creating a permanent length of dry material that would not split and crack in the coiling process. Short lengths were laid out, parallel to one another, so that many could be picked up at once to create the coil element.

Barks and roots might be buried in the ground to 'season' them. This would not only darken the materials but it would keep them soft and pliable until the basket-maker was ready to begin. Stems and barks had to be split to make the required size splint for the coil element. A sharp stone would be used for shredding, the teeth could also start a splint, after the bark had received a thorough pounding. The drying, turning, splitting, stripping or soaking transformed the original vegetal forms from stiff, brittle, heavy materials into soft, pliable fibres that could be coiled into circles or used as the wrapping and stitching materials. Basket-making involved rhythmic movements of the whole body and it is this involvement of motion that imparts the sensitive quality to the finished object.

Finally, the materials were ready and the basket-maker began to stitch the needs of her family into a container form. One source lists some hundred uses for all basket techniques used by primitive people. A woman not only carried a burden basket on her back with a sling around her forehead to help balance it, but she made a beautiful cap or headband to wear perched forward to ease the chafing of the burden sling. Head rings were coiled to make the basket, and later the pot, sit level while being carried on the top of the head.

Baskets were used for storage of grains, tobacco, cosmetics, jewelry, tools and hunting equipment. In many countries they were made in certain sizes to use as measures for grains and coffee. There were sieves, graters, winnows, cooking pots and mush bowls. The cooking pots when used in the fire, would be shored up with sand or smeared with mud. Sometimes hot stones would be dropped into the basket for heating the liquids. The North American Indian would make a basket watertight by daubing the container with pitch or asphaltum. Certain tribes of Africa would stitch so tightly that milk or millet beer could be drunk from them.

In some parts of the world, homes were roofed in basketry techniques. Mats, bedding and cradles for babies were created for everyday

**152** *(left)* Papago basket stitched over a bundle of many grasses held as one to form the coil element (see page 283). The long stitch bites into the top of the stitch in the row below, rather than encircling the coil below, thus not disturbing the colour pattern. The rising of the coil from the bottom to shape the sides and the tapering of the coil element to a point to finish are a part of the design proportions of the finished basket.
Collection: Linda Watson
Photo: Douglas Watson

**153** Papago basket: using bear grass for the coil and yucca for the stitching element, the Papago Indian of Arizona splits the lazy stitch to make a decorative vertical line. Note the beginnings of new vertical lines where necessary for the strength of the basket.
Collection: Helen Richards
Photo: Douglas Watson

use. Finally, at death, many tribes had the custom of interring the body and all of the owner's possessions into a basket for burial. Personal clothing and treasures were included to ensure comfort in the next world.

Baskets were developed for every occupation and for trading with other tribes in exchange for the everyday needs of the tribe. Boats complete with sails were constructed; quivers for arrows and traps for the hunter, as well as the sling to bring game back to the encampment.

Ritualistic and leisure time activities had their own particular basket form. There were gambling trays and musical instruments created simply by stitching several reeds together, inserting pebbles inside the reeds to make a shaker. Bells and shells could be hung from these to make additional music or the noise would help clear the atmosphere of evil spirits. The fetishes, the masks and the costumes worn while performing the dances and rituals often came from the techniques and materials of basketry. All of the accoutrements that were necessary for the performance of the various rites were kept safe in a covered container.

As life styles changed from nomadic to agricultural many new materials and uses were added to the long list of articles that could be created with the basketry techniques.

Basketry is usually identified and classified as belonging to a certain people by the materials used, the techniques, the shapes, the dyes, and the various symbols. However, as captives were taken by marauding tribes or inter-marriages between tribes occurred, designs and symbols were added to and subtracted from the originals. Each wife would carry with her designs that she had used and unconsciously symbols from her husband's people would be absorbed into her own original designs. Meanings of the symbols were usually known only to the maker of the basket and were not necessarily tribal. The descendants of these people, in most instances, are at a loss to explain any meanings of the patterns. However, the basket-maker was certainly influenced by her environment and the rituals with which she had grown to womanhood, so certain regularities of designs and shapes are formed between given peoples.

The classical shapes of the basket changed in regions with the coming of various nations seeking new lands and products. A part of this influence was the addition of handles and hinged lids. A handle on a basket in some countries designated that a man would be carrying it, while a woman had no need for a handle on her basket as it sat on her head. However, a new meaning was given to the handle with the coming of the white man to Central America. Natives, both men and women, who have accepted the white man's way of life, only carry baskets with handles to distinguish themselves from their 'country cousins' who still carry baskets on their heads.

Other features tell something about the creator of the basket or the individual for whom it was intended. A sun visor on a cradle that extended like a collapsible canopy meant that it was intended for a girl, whereas a boy's cradle had the sun visor fitted very snugly to the structure. Many of the cradles had flat indentations for the head, so that the backs of the babies' heads also became flat. This practice was considered necessary to the proper care of the child.

A blunt ending on a coiled basket meant the work was completed by an unmarried woman, a tapered ending on the coil was constructed by a married woman. Few blunt ends are found on baskets, evidently denoting that unmarried girls were not involved in basket-making. Also the user of the basket could have a choice as to how the basket would be carried; two slings might be added, one for shoulder carrying, one for hand carrying. A scalloped edge on the rim of the basket meant that a leaf or some other covering could be lashed to the basket to protect the contents.

As well as baskets constructed for personal use or for trading, small intricate baskets were found among some peoples that were used to store precious possessions or also may suggest the need to create something beautiful rather than functional. Production basket-making was not a part of the basket-maker's thinking until the invasion of white man and the further intrusion of tourists with their needs for souvenirs. Today, the basket is still created and shaped by an individual, but the human process in many instances is duplicating the machine, per se, because where labour and materials are cheap, baskets are turned out with machine-like precision, day in and day out. Children and adults stand or sit by the road side, deft fingers manipulating plastic strands, in many instances, to create the souvenir for the tourist to take home.

But the true creativity of basket-making is now being recognized by the contemporary artist, taking it out of the functional anthropological atmosphere and looking at it as an aesthetic experience. Contemporary basket-makers are working with present day materials and the natural ones of their environment, with the old techniques, to make statements relative to their time and mode of living. By so doing, the world has been made aware of the beauty and creativity produced by the basket-maker of the past. Once again it has been proven that there has been but little change in the techniques of clothmaking, only fresh, exciting approaches using the old techniques. We are now looking with new attitudes, to aesthetics and design, with an appreciation of the relationship between form and function, and of the qualities inherent in natural materials, and creating a harmonious unity. We are relating to the deliberateness, the orderliness of a by-gone people to create a well-crafted structure. We are once again using our 'intuitive' sense of symbol writing.


## Tools and materials

Complicated equipment for creating a coiled basket was not necessary hundreds of years ago, nor is it needed today. A needle, a coiling element, some stitching material and the basket-maker is equipped to start constructing a container.

Primitive people used an awl or a bird bone to punch a hole in the bundle of the coil and then push the stitching element through this hole. The artist of today will find that a needle to suit the fibre with which the stitching is worked is sufficient. If the stitching cord is too heavy for a needle, a crochet hook can be used.

### Coiling elements

In the past the coiling element consisted of grasses, roots, vines and other materials that were strong and yet could be formed into a circle, dampened if necessary. These were gathered from the nearby country-side. The contemporary artist rarely has access to wild materials or even a plot of ground where those natural materials could be cultivated. The gathering spots are local yarn shops, cordage centres, hardware stores, etc.

Seagrasses make a very firm, stiff structure. If dampened before using the rigidity increases making it very difficult to work in free

**154** Coiling elements (from the top): braided coconut fibre from the Philippines; two-ply paper cordage; jute; seagrass from Hong Kong; cotton clothes' line; unspun sisal; handspun sisal.
Photo: Douglas Watson

forms. Paper cordage can create a medium firmness and it readily adapts to sculptural techniques, as it is much easier to bend back on itself than seagrass. Jutes come in various plies, some tightly spun; others are like a roving that is waiting to be spun. The stitching, when using jute, would need to be pulled very firmly for a rigid structure, but for soft sculptures it is ideal. Jute and unspun sisal can create a hairy textural quality as the short ends tend to creep through the stitching material. Plied sisal in different diameters is very stiff and rigid. Such materials as braided coconut fibres, handspuns, horse and goat hairs are exciting when used as the coiling element and not completely wrapped with the stitching materials.

## Stitching fibres

Today's basket-maker has a great choice of stitching fibres, chosen according to the surface textural quality. Softly-spun handspuns and chenilles will create furry surfaces; plied jutes and sisals stiff, harsh-

**155** Stitching and wrapping fibres (from the top): plied Irish sisal; shiny rayon cord; Thailand jute; rug wool; knitting worsted; cotton chenille; Mexican handspun sisal; unspun sisal; handspun nylon fluff. Photo: Douglas Watson

to-the-hand surfaces, unspun fibres create a hairy texture and rug yarns, knitting fibres and novelty yarns each have their own soft, pliable qualities (illus. 155). There is also now a swing back to locating and using the natural materials with which some of the historical baskets were constructed. Some natural materials that are at first rejected by the artist, as too brittle are later discovered to be usable when the drying and handling processes are done properly. It is important to season the stems instead of picking and using all in the same day.

## Basic designs and working methods

The contemporary artist chooses the coil element as part of the design statement, sometimes using a single element, and at other times using several. Heavy coil elements make bulky structures, lighter weight coils create a more compact structure. The design of the basket is dictated by the size of the coil element and the fineness of the stitching element in relation to the largeness or the smallness of the finished basket.

There is never a counting of the stitches by the maker, but rather the eye picks up the evenness of the number of stitches which may vary from area to area, as the creator adjusts the stitches to keep a regular flow by the closeness of the lay. There may be very few more stitches at the flare portions of the basket than at the narrow area, the stitches have been adapted to the area by the eye and the hand working together to keep a flat surface on the sides of the basket to give a symmetrical appearance to the shape. Because the basket is rising in a coil – the row starts lower than it ends – the basket is never truly symmetrical.

In binding the coil elements together with the various stitches, some basket-makers work clockwise and others counter-clockwise. Some find it easier to wrap the coil towards themselves and others reverse the process. The design of the basket often dictates the direction of the path of the coil and the direction of the wrapping and stitching. Start one way or the other, towards or away from yourself in wrapping, moving the arm and hand in what seems to be the most natural direction. Enjoyment of the process of basket-making will hinge on finding a rhythmical way of working.

The techniques of starting the basket, adding new yarns and the shaping of the structure are done in exactly the same manner, but the stitch employed and the materials used provide variety. For example, exciting structures can be created by using a heavy coil such as rope or sisal and heavy stitching materials. If heavy materials are used for wrapping the coil, wraps must be spaced to create openings so that these materials can be pulled through. The end of a fibre that will not fit the eye of a needle can be wrapped with masking tape to keep it from fraying, the masked end serving as a needle. A crochet hook can also be helpful to pull the fibre through the space.

## Making the base

The base of the coiled basket is flat. The centre coil is started by laying the end of the stitching cord from left to right on the coil element. Wrapping is then started back towards the end of the coil, finishing about 1cm ($\frac{1}{2}$in) from the end. The coil is being wrapped towards the body. The wraps can be spaced so that the coil is not completely covered or the wrapping may be laid so that each wrap is touching the previous wrap.

When the wrap is completed to the end, covering the beginning of the stitching cord, then the wrapping is reversed going from right to left back over the area that was the beginning. After sufficient coil has been wrapped to make a circle, pinch it into as tight a circle as possible. This is the most difficult part of stitching a basket. If the core is very stiff, trim the end of the coil at an angle before starting the wrapping.

The stitches are now going to encircle the first coil and the new row of coiling, stitching into the centre of the starting circle (illus. 157). As the work progresses, the basket would become very heavy if all the stitches continued to cover the running coil and the row below. Illustration 161[3] shows the lazy stitch, so called because of the wraps spaced between the stitches. Any number of wraps may be taken prior to making the long lazy stitch in the row below. The spacing of the wraps and the long stitches can become a part of the design of the basket. There could be several long stitches taken and then a certain number of wraps. This would create a textural interest on the surface of the basket.

It is much easier to work with short lengths of stitching cords to avoid entanglements and twisting of long cords. To add a new cord lay

**156** Basket by Helen Richards started from the random coilings in the top of the form. Pearl cottons, chenilles and fine wools (using many strands as one) wrapped the coil from the top down.
Photo: Douglas Watson

**157** Detail of constructing the bottom of a basket, with the hole enlarged to show the cord being stitched into the centre. As the circle enlarges there are more wraps between the long stitches. If this continued, it would weaken the structure, so eventually areas should be set up with new long stitches.

**158** Shaping a basket: when the bottom of the basket has reached sufficient size, by laying the coil on top of the last row of coiling instead of parallel, a straight side can be created. Shaping is controlled by the lay of the coil, angled away from your body or towards you. Shaping progresses slowly in successive rows to keep the structure firm.

**159** To add a new cord lay the new cord on the coil and take a few wraps with the old cord. Then lay the old cord on the coil and do the wrapping and stitching with the new cord. If the coil runs out, taper the ends of the old coil and the new; lay one on top of the other and continue over the double layer.
Photos: Douglas Watson

**160** Detail of figure eight stitch with wraps between each stitch, showing the corrugated appearance of the coil structure.
Photo: Douglas Watson

it on the coil and make a few wraps over it with the old cord (illus. 159); then reverse the process, lay the old cord on the coil and continue stitching with the new cord. Tag ends can be clipped when the basket is finished. All tag ends are left on the basket by African basket-makers, even today, and then they are scraped off with a sharp rock.

### Shaping the sides
After the bottom of the basket is of sufficient size (the word sufficient is a very important descriptive word in basket-making meaning what seems right to the basket-maker), the sides are considered. The shaping is controlled by the lay of the fingers on the rim of the basket. If the coil is held directly on top of the row below, straight sides will occur (illus. 158), if it is angled inward or outward that shape will develop. A good basket-maker can feel the shape of the basket, varying it ever so slightly, by the pitch of the coil against the finger. Shaping must be done slowly, row by row, or the basket will be truly out of shape. Shaping is best controlled if the outside of the basket is facing the maker. Most primitive baskets are constructed with the outside facing the basket-maker except when making enormous storage baskets. At a certain height the man would stand inside the basket and literally construct it around himself.

### Variation: using more than one coil element
In creating the Papago basket illustrated on page 275, many grasses were held as one to form the coiled element. When there is more than one segment to the coil, it is known as a bundle. Primitive baskets were often constructed over a bundle because grasses were plentiful, as were pine needles. By using the bundle, the stitching bites only into the top of the bundle rather than encircling the coil below, thus saving precious stitching materials. In most instances this produces a flat surfaced basket.

As the basket was stitched, additional grasses were added to the

**161** [1] To start coiling, hold the coil in the left hand and lay the stitching fibre on it. Wrapping towards yourself, wrap the fibre over the tail; continue wrapping until the coil can be turned in a tight circle.

[2] Holding the circle as tightly pinched as possible, now take the needle down through the centre, wrapping over the previous row (see also [6] below). You may want to wrap the coil once, go into the centre and repeat this process. When you arrive back at the starting point, subsequent rows are stitched to the row below and not into the centre.

[3] Three wraps and one long stitch; all over the world this basic stitch is called the 'lazy' stitch for the obvious reason that the basket-maker could speed up the process.

[4] Figure eight stitch: the stitching fibre comes from behind coil 1, to the front between 1 and 2, over the front and behind coil 2, up between 2 and 1, over the front and behind coil 1. Repeat this process, making as many wraps between each figure eight stitch as desired.

[5] The lace or knotted stitch with wraps between each lazy stitch, showing the path the stitching cord travels in wrapping the long stitch.

[6] To finish coiling: the coil element is tapered and firm lazy stitches are taken one after another over the tapered end and beyond. The end can then be stitched in and out of the lazy stitches and cut close.

[7] The double thread lazy stitch pierced by the stitch from the row above. The needle pierces the strands and continues spacing the wraps on the coil.

[8] The imbricating material laid back to the left and tied down with the lazy stitch. After the stitch is taken lay the imbricating material to the right and then fold it back to the left.

Artist: Mollie Picken

bundle to keep it uniform as the work progressed. Sometimes it was necessary to keep both the coil element and the stitching thread damp while working so that they would not crack or break. The grasses or pine needles would be wrapped in a cloth to keep them in a dampened state after having been wet in the stream prior to the commencing of the work. To keep the stitching thread pliable, it was moistened by running it through the basket-maker's mouth. Various effects can be achieved by using the bundle, the elements can be held flat, rolled into a round coil, or separated and wrapped in parts, and all of them can be brought back to function as one.

### Variation: starting from the top

Not all baskets were started from the bottom, but that was the most common method. The green and yellow basket in illustration 156 started with a playful attitude at the top, letting the coil meander; at times the coil and stitching fibres were cut and new wrappings started. These pieces were eventually stitched together and brought into a circular shape which then progressed towards the bottom of the basket. To complete the bottom of the structure, a separate coiling was started and stitched to fill the open space. Before stitching this piece to the sides of the basket, a mirror was inserted. As the viewer looks downward into the basket the reflection of the top coil meanderings is reflected in the mirror.

## Basketry stitches

As well as the lazy stitch described on page 281 which creates a rather flat surfaced basket, because the long stitch is obvious, encircling the coil or coils below, there are many other stitches available to the basket-maker.

### Figure eight stitch

This stitch, sometimes known as the Navajo stitch, changes the appearance of the surface. By using this stitch, the structural appearance of the basket takes on the characteristics of corrugation (illus. 160). The stitching element starts behind the travelling coil, the needle comes up between the two coils; the cord is carried around the coil of the previous row and the needle once again comes up between the two coils, thus completing the figure eight (see illus. 161[4]). This process is repeated, each time wrapping a coil with the needle coming up between the two coils. The density of the structure of the basket can be varied by wrapping the travelling coil only, between the figure eight stitch the desired number of times.

The figure eight stitch seems to disappear, the corrugation of the coil and the texture of the stitching material dominate the structure. The only time there is an awareness of the stitch is when a colour change has occurred, then the stitch biting into the row below is obvious. The figure eight stitch is used by a great many contemporary artists. It

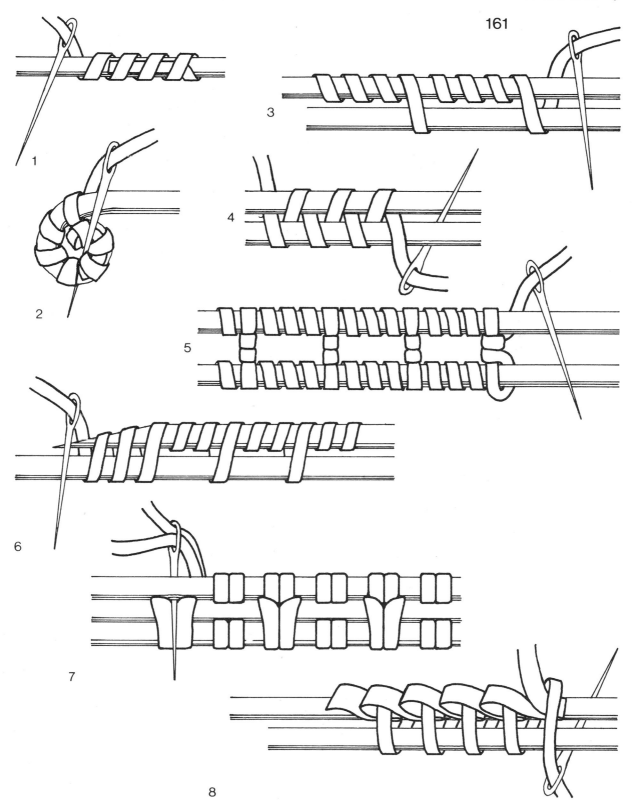

1

2

3

4

5

6

7

8

**162** Sculpture by Mieke Solari. Camel hair yarn, roughly spun, from Pakistan was used as the coil and the stitches were widely spaced so that the camel hair would make the dominant statement. Rusty nails and other found objects were included in the sculpture.
Photo: Douglas Watson

creates a firmer structure and most basket-makers find it much easier to shape the structure than when using the lazy stitch.

The hairiness, the sheen and the dullness of fibres creating visual impacts are enhanced by the use of the figure eight stitch. Shadows are created by the corrugated look of the coil and there is a movement of light and a rhythm across the surface of the basket that is not obtained with the flatness of the lazy stitch.

### Lace stitch

The lazy stitch and the figure eight stitch create a dense structure, varied only by the number of wraps between each binding stitch. One coil lies directly on top of the coil below with little or no negative areas. The baskets thus stitched are firm and functional because of the density of the surface.

In the Latin American countries and many of the South Sea Islands as well as other countries in the world, negative patterns are created by spacing the coils layer-wise using a wrapping technique around the lazy or figure eight stitch. This stitch is commonly known as the lace stitch, but other names such as Mariposa or the knot stitch have also been used. It is not a true knot, as it is wrapped around the long stitch and does not interlace upon itself. If the long stitch is wrapped more than once, it becomes what is known as the Samoan stitch.

If the basket-maker is wrapping the coil towards the body, after the long stitch has been completed the stitching cord is brought up between the two coils to the right of the long stitch, over the front of the stitch to the left and behind the stitch to the right coming up behind the travelling coil to start wrapping the coil again (see illus. 161[5]). For a firm structure, the long stitch must be covered full length with wraps or the wrapping will be very loose. The stitch may also be wrapped by bringing the needle up or down between the coils to the left of the long stitch. The stitch would be wrapped to the right.

The materials used for the wrappings either give a rounded or flat appearance to the stitch. If a stiff material is used that is also flat such as pandamus leaf or grasses then the wrapping is folded around the long stitch as a true wrapping would not hold. The small, flat triangle caused by this folding creates a rhythmic pattern accentuated by the negative spaces. These negative and positive areas created realistic designs such as flowers and stars for many people.

In the Mexican baskets the lace wrap over the figure eight stitch has been used (see colour illustration page 288). Designs are an intuitive laying in of colour while the fingers are manipulating the palm fibres. Colours not in use are carried along the coil and brought out at the proper time to create the figure that is building. The figures and designs have the appearance of graph paper or paper doll designs. This is caused by the blocks of wrapping between each lace stitch. Small children are taught the techniques and the designs from their elders, so there is not a need for any pre-planning. Designs have slight variations as the basket-maker adapts the spaces to personal visual pleasure as the coils are wrapped.

## Combining stitches

The toas weave is a combination of the figure eight and the lace or knot stitch. Usually the area of the basket is visually divided into sections and the two weaves alternate to create geometric patterns by the surface texture of the stitch. If the lazy stitch was used instead of the figure eight stitch, there would be flat planes in those areas instead of corrugated surfaces. Colour can be used to create a stronger contrast between the areas of lace stitch and figure eight stitch (see illus. 165). If one colour of the soft rug yarn had been used for the stitching, the design would not have been as apparent, whereas, if a hard surface material were used, both the wrapped and the figure eight techniques would be a dominant surface interest.

## Papago stitch

Until this point the surface of the basket through the stitching materials has been stressed, but in many of the historical baskets the material used for the core also made a strong visual statement. Sweet grasses and pine needles were used by many of the tribes to make small trinket baskets. The soft browns of the needles and the pastel greens of the grasses as they dried added to the over-all visual and smelling pleasures of the user.

The Papago basket-maker of Arizona discovered that by leaving a great deal of the coil exposed the length of time necessary to finish the basket was greatly reduced. The basket could then be sold to the tourist for less money than if the entire coil was wrapped, but also a new statement of beauty was created by the contrast of the coil and the stitching materials. Using either a wide, flat stitching material or a double thread in the needle, the long stitch was spaced on the coil by one wrap jumping across the coil to the desired spot. In place of the wide stitching element, a double thread may be used, then the needle comes between the two threads as it wraps the row below. The exposed coil, if using an exciting material such as rope, horsehair, nylon or velvet tubing, vinyl tapes or grape vines dampened, adds a great deal of beauty and surface interest to the basket.

The coil element if of soft materials creates a new concept (see colour illustration page 287). Stitches must bind tightly, creating a tension between the coiled layers, or the whole structure will sag and collapse. The tension of the stitch can cause the structure to shape in different directions at the artist's will.

## Decoration and the use of colour

Large storage baskets were usually made from one material from top to bottom but, obviously, this process was monotonous and tedious. Primitive man loved colour and also used it as a means to creating symbols and designs. The natural colours of dried plants gave the basket-maker soft, earthy tones. Later, it was discovered that certain berries would stain or dye the plant materials. With the coming of the

**163** Basket of palm fibre from the Toluca market in Mexico. The knot stitch technique was used on the entire basket; the handles were made by stitching two lengths of coil together with the knot stitch, then stitching the handles firmly to the basket. The stitching material was dyed, carrying several colours on the coil at once; the colour needed was brought forward to create the design.
Photo: Douglas Watson

white man to the Southwest, aniline dyes were introduced to the Indians. Vivid coloured fabrics were also torn into strips or completely unravelled. These, too, found their way into the baskets.

### Patterns

Colour patterns develop within the process of basket-making and are not predetermined by graphing on paper. From the time the coil is started, the development of the design of the basket is based on what has already been completed. Patterning gives the effect of counting or graphing, but the only diagrams made are by those who study the baskets, so the drawings on paper happen after the baskets have been completed. Many baskets are patterned, with the maker's own variations, from those that have previously been done, so it often becomes a difficult task identifying through the symbols and patterns. Meanings of symbols were known primarily to the basket-maker. Few basket-makers of today can explain the patterns of old baskets in terms of symbol-writing.

The patterns not only included all the geometric designs of triangles, trapezoids, squares and rectangles, but also figures of the natural world such as butterflies, rattlesnakes, flames and man. Line patterns were created by verticals, horizontals, diagonals, and swirls. Alternating bands of colour, either horizontal or vertical, could break the surface plane. Some of the designs of the Northwest Indians depicted intricate marine scenes telling the story of a whale hunt complete with boat and sea gulls.

The division of space for geometric patterns could be as simple as a marking with one coloured stitch in the lower portion of the basket, visually spaced around the circumference of the basket. From these markings, the patterning would move in all directions as needed. The colour not in use would be carried on the core unless it was a scarce material. Then it would be inserted as needed. The patterning of the entire basket was developed on successive rows based on what had already been accomplished (see illus. 163).

Several colours may be carried on the coil and, at the proper time, the colour in motion was returned to the coil and the desired colour did the wrapping (see illus. 164). To keep the colour from breaking into the coil below, use a slip stitch through the top of the lower stitch. Structural strength is forfeited when slip stitches are taken so an entire basket done in this manner would not be firm.

### False embroidery

Many basket-makers used a technique for surface decoration wherein the colour work did not show on the inside of the basket. This process of laying colour over previously wrapped areas is known as false embroidery (see illus. 166). One colour is laid back out of the way while the wrapping is done with the other colour. The first colour is then brought over the second to create the colour pattern. Various materials such as scraps of fur can be used in place of one fibre to give textural and pattern interest to the sculptural container.

**164** Carrying basket by Lou Ridder, combining rust Irish sisal with red Mexican yarns. The slip stitch was used in the vertical colour bands only, while the figure eight stitch was tightly pulled to create a solid construction which accents the coil. The handle is an extension of the coil from the basket. Bells and found objects were added for sound.
Photo: Douglas Watson

## Surface embellishment

Some decorative techniques were added after the basket was completed. The Northwest Indians of the United States and Canada painted designs on the surfaces of their structures. The design patterns so closely followed the stitching of the basket that often it was difficult to determine if it had been painted or stitched. Surface embellishment also occurs through the use of embroidery stitches. Long vertical stitches can be taken after the coiling is completed and small horizontal stitches can create diagonal patterns over the surface of the long stitches.

IMBRICATION This method of decoration was popular with the Northwest Indians of America and Canada. It is much like shingling a roof as one stitch overlaps another. The imbricating material is laid on the coil to the right, folded back to the left and a long stitch taken encircling the coil below with the stitching fibre. The imbrication material is again laid to the right, folded back to the left and another stitch taken (see illus. 161[8]).

In illustration 167 dyed cornhusks have been used as the imbricating

**165** Toas weave basket by Linda Watson. The wrapped long stitch creates small spaces between the coils, whereas the figure eight stitch makes a dense tight area. Sand box seed pods from Hawaii sewn in as the last coil was being stitched complete the classical shape.

**166** False embroidery technique: the second colour is laid over the first colour.
Photos: Douglas Watson

material. All plant material will receive the dye more plentifully if the material has been thoroughly dried. Sometimes it is necessary to keep dry material damp while imbricating with it so that it does not crack.

Variations in imbricating techniques can be obtained by using the figure eight stitch instead of the lazy stitch for the tie-down. If longer floats of imbrication are desired, several wraps or stitches can be taken, with the imbrication material laid over these stitches and tied down. If the imbricating material is the same width as the coil, the shingle effect is more obvious. Interesting imbrications can be created by using vinyl tapes, strips of leather and cloth; ribbons and braids, and various fibres.

BEADS, BONES, BELLS AND FEATHERS Primitive man's functional needs for containers for storage, cooking, clothing were executed on a circular flat-surfaced plane, but his religious and ritualistic beliefs were extended by adding noise, music, special gift offerings and movement to attract the attention of the spirits. Beads, bones, bells and feathers were either worked into the surface of the basket or dangled from the basket to give emphasis to his pleas.

The Pomo Indians are noted for their baskets completely covered with small tufts of feathers. Feathers in their natural colours were usually wrapped into the basket, but as some birds became rare or extinct it became common practice to dye feathers to simulate the proper bird feathers that should be used for the particular prayer. Beads, shells and bones were strung on a firm cord to hang free of the basket. Special baskets were beaded over the entire surface. The beads were usually strung on the stitching thread and wrapped over the core, pushing each bead into place, as the basket was constructed. A bead could also be part of the spacing created by the knot stitch. Occasionally, beads would be strung on another thread, which was car-

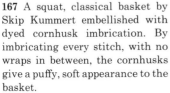

**167** A squat, classical basket by Skip Kummert embellished with dyed cornhusk imbrication. By imbricating every stitch, with no wraps in between, the cornhusks give a puffy, soft appearance to the basket.
Photo: Douglas Watson

ried along the coil and again the bead brought into the pattern. Beads, feathers, bones and trinkets could also be sewn into the basket when it was completed. Shells, such as abalone, would be broken into bits with edges painstakingly ground smooth on a rock, holes drilled by hand, the pieces then strung on a cord which would be tied into the basket. Shells usually swung freely, so that there was a rhythmic motion playing over the surface of the basket as the user moved about, performing his ritualistic tasks. It was hoped that the spirit would notice this motion and would be present to listen to his prayers. The contemporary artist receives these same sensual pleasures of selecting various beads, found objects and feathers to add to the beauty of the basket.

When using feathers for embellishment, rather it is the top rim or a coil within the basket, the feathers are laid away from the direction of work. The wrapping fibre can be pulled taut so that the feather will not slip. If the wrapping is being done with fibres such as handspuns, goat's hair or sisal use a fine strong thread to wrap the feathers to the coil and then wrap over it with the decorative fibre. On the next row, turn the basket so that work may progress from the inside. In this way the stitching fibre pulls away from the feathers and prevents them from pulling apart. On the third row, adjust the stitching so that once again the work is proceeding on the outside of the basket. Feathers may also be wrapped on cords and stitched into the basket after completion.

## Lids and coverings

Baskets that were used for storage purposes required some sort of a covering. Many primitive baskets were covered with leaves, dampened

**168** Fluff sculpture by Andrea Birch. The crest has a core of coiling added to it, that fits inside the lower portion. The ball of feathers, turtle vertebrae and beads sits securely on top of the structure because of this inner core.
Collection: Helen Richards
Photo: Douglas Watson

if necessary, to protect the contents. This type of covering was make-shift, however, as it would not only dry out, but also would break. Even in early times, it was found that man was constantly searching for permanent material objects. Baskets are found finished with loop edgings and flat mat-like lids created with this same loop edging, the two pieces lashed together, creating secure and permanent storage containers. Some lids were placed over the basket without being secured.

With the coming of the white man bringing boxes with hinged lid1s, came the appearance of the hinged lid on the basket (see colour illustration page 289). Some used the lashing technique of stitching the lid to the basket, others might use two loops that served as hinges. A yarn loop and a yarn button could be used as the lock.

The precious spices that were hoarded by primitive people required a basket with a snug-fitting lid, so some baskets had lids with inner cores that would extend into the necks of the baskets. The core can be several rows of coiling, made independently of the lid and then stitched to the lid. It also can be created by laying a new coil back one row from the inside of the lid and the first row of coiling and wrapping stitched through the lid. The first method is much easier and usually gives a snugger fit.

## Contemporary forms

The coiled baskets of by-gone days have communicated to us a way of life of these basket-makers. The beautiful designs have made us aware of their love of colour, their interest in repeat patterns and their magnificent craftsmanship. The simplicity of the technique allowed them to get on with the business of creating the basket once the materials had been prepared. The method of making the basket was easily transmitted from generation to generation. It faltered at times because of some of the later generations not wishing to be known as basket-makers or not wanting to take the long hours that are required to create the finished product. The collector of baskets today has had a good influence on basket-making, as ethnic groups are once again creating their baskets, sometimes in new ways, because the craft has become an art form which is now appreciated.

If the contemporary artist wishes for a basket to carry some product, to store yarn, or to beautify a corner in the home, baskets from every land are available in many shops around the world. The true artist would not wish to copy the ethnic baskets that have been done or are now being done, so seeks to make statements that are individual and original using the materials that are available, creating a design to make a meaningful structure that speaks of his contemporary environment. Each artist works with the materials that seem right for the thought, creating the sufficient form as it developed under the fingers. Such statements go beyond the functional container into the realms of sculpture and fine art.

**169** Sculpture by William Lockhart. Using three weights of rope, the artist created three pieces which stack one inside the other to create a floor sculpture. When the stitching of the coils was finished, he applied resin to the inside to give strength and weight.
Collection: Helen Richards
Photo: Douglas Watson

# Bibliography

## GENERAL

Albers, Joseph *The Interaction of Colour.* Yale University Press, London and Newhaven, Conn. 1975

*The Anchor Manual of Needlework.* Batsford, London 1968

Arnheim, Rudolf *Art and Visual Perception.* University of California Press, Berkeley 1965; Faber, London 1967

Birrell, Verla *Textile Arts: A Handbook of Weaving, Braiding, Printing and Other Textile Techniques.* Schocken, New York 1973

Birren, Faber *Colour, Form and Space.* Reinhold, New York 1961

Boas, Franz *Primitive Art.* Dover, New York 1955

Constantine, Mildred and Larsen, Jack Lenor *Beyond Craft: The Art Fabric.* Reinhold, London and New York 1973 (Good on weaving)

de Dillmont, Thérèse *Encyclopaedia of Needlework.* DMC Library, Mulhouse, France 1968; Running Press, Philadelphia, Pa. USA 1972

d'Harcourt, Raoul *Textiles of Ancient Peru and Their Techniques.* University of Washington Press, USA 1974

de Sausmarez, Maurice *Basic Design: The Dynamics of Visual Form.* Studio Vista, London and Reinhold, New York 1964

Emery, Irene *The Primary Structure of Fabrics.* Textile Museum, Washington DC, 1966

Hartung, Rolf *Creative Textile Craft.* Batsford, London and Reinhold, New York 1961

Itten, Johannes *The Art of Colour.* Reinhold, London and New York 1961

Itten, Johannes *The Elements of Colour.* Reinhold, London and New York 1971

Lubell, Cecil *Textile Collections of the World.* 2 vols: US and Canada, UK and Ireland. Reinhold, New York 1976. Other volumes to follow.

Paque, Joan Michaels *Design Principles and Fiber Techniques.* Published by the author, Shorewood, Wisconsin, USA 1973

Waller, Irene *Thread: An Art Form.* Studio Vista, London 1974

Ward, Michael *Art and Design in Textiles.* Reinhold, London and New York 1973

### PERIODICALS

*Crafts* The Crafts Advisory Committee, 12 Waterloo Place, London SW1Y 4AU

*Craft Horizons* Journal of the American Crafts Council, 44 West 53rd Street, New York

*Design* Journal of the Council of Industrial Design, Haymarket, London SW1Y 4AU

*Fiber Arts* 3717 4th Street NW, Albuquerque, New Mexico, USA

*Flying Needle* 3617 Oro Vista Avenue, Bakersfield, California, USA

*Shuttle, Spindle and Dyepot* 998 Farmington Avenue, West Hartford, Connecticut, USA

*Threads in Action* Box 468, Freeland, Washington, USA

*Weavers Journal* Quarterly Journal of the Association of the Guilds of Weavers, Spinners and Dyers, c/o Federation of British Craft Societies, 80a Southampton Row, London WC1B 4BA

*Webe Mit* D-7065 Manolzweiler, Post Winterbach, Germany

## SPINNING

Adrosko, R. J. *Natural Dyes and Home Dyeing.* Dover, New York 1971

Bemiss, Elijah *The Dyer's Companion.* Dover, New York 1973 and Evans, London 1975

Castino, Ruth *Spinning and Dyeing the Natural Way.* Reinhold, New York 1974 and Evans, London 1975

Crowfoot, Grace M. *Methods of Handspinning in Egypt and the Sudan.* Bankfield Museum, Halifax, UK

Cook, J. Gordon *A Handbook of Textile Fibres.* Marrow Publishing Co., Watford, UK 1968 and Technical Book Services, Plainfield, NJ, USA 1960

Davenport, Elsie *Your Handspinning.* Sylvan Press, London 1953 and Select Books, Pacific Grove, California USA 1964

Davenport, Elsie *Your Yarn Dyeing.* Sylvan Press, London 1955 and Select Books, Pacific Grove, California USA 1970

Duncan, Molly *Spin Your Own Wool and Dye It and Weave It.* A. H. & W. Reed, Wellington, NZ 1968 and Bell, London 1973

Gilmour, Pat *Dyes and Dyeing.* Society for Education through Art, London 1966

Hall, A. J. *A Standard Handbook of Textiles.* Newnes-Butterworths, Sevenoaks, UK 1976

Kluger, Marilyn *The Joy of Spinning*. Simon & Schuster, New York 1971

Mairet, Ethel *Vegetable Dyes*. Faber, London 1952

Matthews, J. Merrit *The Textile Fibres*. John Wiley & Sons, New York 1924

Robertson, Seonaid *Dyes from Plants*. Reinhold, New York 1973

Seagroatt, Margaret *A Basic Textile Book*. Herbert/Pitman, London and Reinhold, New York 1975

Thurstan, Violetta *The Use of Vegetable Dyes*. Dryad Press, Leicester, UK 1967

## EMBROIDERY

### STITCHES

Butler, Ann *Machine Stitches*. Batsford, London 1976

Enthoven, Jacqueline *The Stitches of Creative Embroidery*. Reinhold, London and New York 1972

Petersen, Grete and Svennas, Elsie *A Handbook of Stitches*. Reinhold, New York and London 1970

Snook, Barbara *Embroidery Stitches*. Batsford, London 1963

Thomas, Mary *A Dictionary of Embroidery Stitches*. Hodder, London 1934

Thomas, Mary *An Embroidery Book*. Hodder, London 1936

### DESIGN ETC.

Baker, Muriel *Needlepoint: Design Your Own*. Scribner, New York 1974

Colby, Averil *Patchwork*. Batsford, London and Branford, Newton Center, Mass. USA 1958

Colby, Averil *Quilting*. Batsford, London 1972

Dawson, Barbara *Metal Thread Embroidery*. Batsford, London 1976

Dean, Beryl *Creative Appliqué*. Studio Vista, London and Watson-Guptill, New York 1970

Geddes, Elizabeth and McNeil, Moira *Blackwork Embroidery*. Mills and Boon, London and Branford, Newton Center, Mass. USA 1965

Gray, Jennifer *Machine Embroidery: Technique and Design*. Batsford, London 1973

Green, Sylvia *Canvas Embroidery for Beginners*. Studio Vista, London and Watson-Guptill, New York 1970

Howard, Constance *Design for Embroidery*. Batsford, London 1956

Howard, Constance *Embroidery and Colour*. Batsford, London and Reinhold, New York 1976

Howard, Constance *Inspiration for Embroidery*. Batsford, London 1966; Branford, Newton Center, Mass. USA 1977

McNeil, Moira *Pulled Thread*. Mills and Boon, London 1971

Nield, Dorothea *Adventures in Patchwork*. Mills and Boon, London 1975

Risley, Christine *Machine Embroidery*. Studio Vista, London 1973

Russell, Pat *Lettering for Embroidery*. Batsford, London and Reinhold, New York 1971

Short, Eirian *Introducing Quilting*. Batsford, London 1974

Spence, Anne *Creative Embroidery: A Complete Guide*. Nelson, London and Viking, New York 1975

Swift, Gay *Machine Stitchery*. Batsford, London 1975

Whyte, Kathleen *Design in Embroidery*. Batsford London 1970

Willcox, Donald *New Designs in Stitchery*. Reinhold, New York 1970; London 1971

Williams, Elsa *Creative Canvas Work*. Reinhold, London and New York 1974

Wilson, Erica *Crewel Embroidery*. Scribner, New York 1962

Wilson, Erica *Needleplay*. Scribner, New York 1975

## SPRANG

Collingwood, Peter *The Techniques of Sprang*. Faber, London 1974
(Detailed description of all techniques and their history; large bibliography)

Kliot, Jules *Sprang, Language and Techniques*. Some Place, Berkeley, California, USA 1974
(Small pamphlet including many techniques and a suggested method of notation)

Skowronski, Hella and Reddy, Mary *Sprang: Thread Twisting, a Creative Textile Technique*. Reinhold, New York 1974
(Describes many varieties of interlinking, made by working at lower end of warp)

## WEAVING

Albers, Anni *On Designing*. Wesleyan University Press, Middleton, Conn. USA

Albers, Anni *On Weaving*. Wesleyan University Press, Middleton, Conn. USA 1965; Studio Vista, London 1966

Beutlich, Tadek *The Technique of Woven Tapestry*. Batsford, London 1967

Blumenau, Lili *The Art and Craft of Hand Weaving*. Crown, New York 1955

Blumenau, Lili *Creative Design in Wall Hangings*. Allen & Unwin, London 1968

Bress, Helene *Inkle Weaving*. Scribner, New York 1974

Chetwynd, Hilary *Simple Weaving*. Studio Vista, London and Watson-Guptill, New York 1969

Collingwood, Peter *The Techniques of Rug Weaving*. Faber, London and Watson-Guptill, New York 1967

Davenport, Elsie *Your Handweaving*. Sylvan Press, London; Select Books, Pacific Grove, California USA

Halsey, Mike and Youngmark, Lore *Foundations of Weaving*. David and Charles, Newton Abbot, UK 1975

Holland, Nina *Inkle-Loom Weaving*. Pitman, London 1975

Kirby, Mary *Designing on the Loom*. Select Books, Pacific Grove, California USA 1973

Lewes, Klaren and Hutton, Helen *Rug Weaving*. Batsford, London and Branford, Newton Center, Mass. USA 1962

Mairet, Ethel *Handweaving and Education*. Faber, London 1942

Mairet, Ethel *Handweaving Notes for Teachers*. Faber, London 1949

Mairet, Ethel *Handweaving Today*. Faber, London 1939

Morman, Theo *Weaving as an Art Form*. Reinhold, London and New York 1975

Rainey, Sarita *Weaving Without a Loom*. Davis Publications, Mass. USA 1973

Redman, Jane *Frame Loom Weaving*. Reinhold, New York 1976

Regensteiner, Else *The Art of Weaving*. Studio Vista, London and Reinhold, New York 1970

Seagroatt, Margaret *Rug Weaving for Beginners*. Studio Vista, London and Watson-Guptill, New York 1971

Specht, Sally and Rawlings, Sandra *Creating with Card Weaving*. Crown, New York 1973

Straub, Marianne *Hand Weaving and Cloth Design*. Pelham, London 1977

Tovey, John *The Technique of Weaving*. Batsford, London and Scribner, New York 1965

Tovey, John *Weaves and Pattern Drafting*. Batsford, London and Reinhold, New York 1969

Wilson, Jean *Weaving is for Anyone*. Studio Vista, London and Reinhold, New York 1967

Wilson, Jean *Weaving is Creative*. Reinhold, New York 1973

Worst, Edward F. *Weaving with Foot-Power Looms*. Dover, New York 1974

## KNITTING AND CROCHET

Aytes, B. *Knitting Made Easy*. Doubleday, New York 1970

Aytes, B. *Adventures in Knitting*. Doubleday, New York 1968

Blackwell, Liz *A Treasury of Crochet Patterns*. Pitman, London 1972

Broughton, Wynne *Crochet by Design*. Pitman, London 1976

Cone, Ferne *Knit Art*. Reinhold, London and New York 1975

*Crochet*. DMC Library, Mulhouse, France

Dawson, Pam *Knitting Fashion: A Step by Step Guide to Knitting and Crochet*. BBC Publications, London 1976

de Negri, Eve *Knitting and Crochet in Easy Steps*. Studio Vista, 1977

Edson, Niki Hitz and Stimmel, Arlene *Creative Crochet*. Pitman, London 1974

Kinmond, J. *Crochet Patterns*. Batsford, London 1969

*Knitting Dictionary: 900 Stitches, Patterns*. Crown, New York 1972

Koster, J. and Murray, M. *New Crochet and Hairpin Work*. Calder, London 1955

Mackenzie, Clinton *New Designs in Crochet*. Reinhold, London and New York 1972

Mayfield, A. (ed.) *Odhams Encyclopaedia of Knitting*. Hamlyn, London 1970

Norbury, James *Traditional Knitting Patterns*. Batsford, London 1962

Thomas, Mary *Mary Thomas's Book of Knitting Patterns*. Hodder, London 1973

Walker, Barbara G. *A Treasury of Knitting Patterns*. Pitman, London and Scribner, New York 1968

## BOBBIN LACE

Bath, Virginia Churchill *Lace*. Studio Vista, London 1974

Close, Eunice *Lace Making*. Gifford, London 1970 (Traditional lace techniques)

de Dillmont, Thérèse *Encyclopaedia of Needlework*. DMC Library, Mulhouse, France 1968; Running Press, Philadelphia, Pa. USA 1972 (A very clear chapter on bobbin lace)

Freeman, Charles *Pillow Lace in the East Midlands*. Luton Museum, UK 1958

Gubser, E. *Bobbin Lace*. Robbin and Russ, McMinnville, Oregon, USA 1975

Kliot, Kaethe and Jules *Bobbin Lace*. Crown, New York 1973

Maidment, Margaret *A Manual of Hand-made Bobbin Lace Work*. Reprinted Paul Minet, Chicheley, Bucks UK 1971

Nottingham, Pamela *The Technique of Bobbin Lace*. Batsford, London 1976; in US, *The Complete Book of English Bobbin Lace*. Reinhold, New York 1976

Pfannschmidt, Ernst-Erik *Twentieth Century Lace*. Mills and Boon, London 1975

Wright, Doreen *Bobbin Lace Making*. Branford, Newton Center, Mass. USA 1971

## MACRAMÉ

Andés, Eugene *Practical Macramé*. Studio Vista, London and Reinhold, New York 1971

Ashley, Clifford W. *The Ashley Book of Knots*. Faber, London and Doubleday, New York 1944

Harvey, Virginia *Colour and Design in Macramé*. Reinhold, London and New York 1972

Graumont, Raoul and Hensel, John *Encyclopaedia of Knots and Fancy Ropework*. Cornell Maritime Press, USA 1958

Meilach, Dona Z. *Macramé: Creative Designs in Knotting*. Crown, New York 1971

Pegg, Barbara *Macramé in Easy Steps*. Studio Vista, London 1977

Phillips, Mary Walker *Macramé*. Evans, London 1973

Phillips, Mary Walker *Step by Step Macramé*. Golden Press, New York 1970

Short, Eirian *Introducing Macramé*. Batsford, London and Watson-Guptill, New York 1970

Waller, Irene *Knots and Netting*. Studio Vista, London 1976

## COILED BASKETRY

De Jongh, Lilly *Indian Crafts of Guatemala and El Salvador*. University of Oklahoma Press, USA 1965

Harvey, Virginia *The Techniques of Basketry*. Reinhold, New York 1974; Batsford, London 1975

James, George W. *Indian Basketry and How to Make Baskets*. Dover, New York 1973

Kissell, Mary L. *Basketry of the Papago and Pima Indians*. Rio Grande Press, New Mexico 1916

Lamb, Frank W. *Indian Baskets of North America*. Riverside Museum Press, California 1972

Mason, Otis T. *Aboriginal Indian Basketry*. Rio Grande Press, New Mexico 1970

Meilach, Dona Z. *A Modern Approach to Basketry with Fibres and Grasses*. Crown, New York 1974; Allen and Unwin, London 1975

Navajo School of Indian Basketry *Indian Basket Weaving*. Dover, New York 1971; London 1972

Newman, Thelma R. *Contemporary African Arts and Crafts*. Crown, New York 1974; Allen and Unwin, London 1975

Rossbach, Ed *Baskets as Textile Art*. Reinhold, New York 1973

Stephenson, Sue *Basketry of the Appalachian Mountains*. Reinhold, New York 1977

Wright, Dorothy *Complete Book of Baskets and Basketry*. David and Charles, Newton Abbot, UK 1977; Scribner, New York 1978

# Index

Page numbers in **bold** type refer to colour plates; page numbers in *italics*, to black-and-white illustrations.

Textile Crafts

enriching warp and weft spacing 155, *156*; narrow loom weaving 119, 134–6; plain weaves *132*, 147; plain weave extensions 157–8, *159*, 160; planning 138–9; process 146–7; recording etc. *154*, 155, 157; setting up the loom 138–46; tapestry weave *see* Tapestry weave; twill weaves *132*, 148; twining thread *132*, 134; warp 7, 119, 140, 142, *143*, **149**, *159*; warping frame loom 126; weft 119; yarns for weaving 120–2, 124, 126, 134, 148
Welsh Mountain sheep 13, *13*, 26
Welsh woollen yarns 120
West of England tweeds 14
Whip stitch 70, 78
White work 76
Whole stitch 227

Wild silk 17
Wiltshire Horn sheep 13
Wool *2*, 7, 11, 12, 16, 120; carding 27, *29*; combing 28, 30; crimp or wave 15; dyes for 36, 37; fibre 15, *15*; handspun 221, 225, 260; properties of 15; rolags 28, *29*; spinning 28, 32; teasing 27; undyed wool 45
Wool threads 121; for embroidery 7, 44, 74, 76, 121; for knitting 121; for sprang 90; for weaving 120, 121, *121*, 124, 126, *131*, **150**, *153*
Woollen fabrics for embroidery 41, *49*, 79
Woollen spun yarns 11, 25, 28, 245, 251
Worsted spun yarn 14, 25, 28, 120–1, 279
Wrapping 73

Yarns *2*, 7, 11; carpet 13, 24, 25, 121; counts 121–2; fancy 35, 121; for knitting 190, *195*, *197*; for sprang 90; for crochet 164, 166; for macramé 258–9; for weaving 120–2, 124, 126, 134, 148; rug 11, 16, 120; S- and Z-twisted 26, *29*; snarling of 120; upholstery 16, 121; woollen spun 11, 25, 28, 245, 255; worsted spun 14, 25, 28, 120–1, *279*
Yorkshire Swaledale sheep 13
Yucca *275*

Zig-zag or Florentine embroidery 183
Zig-zag stitching 8, *38*, 40, *41*, 62, 66, *71*, 78, 85, *208*